D1596182

Shakespeare and the Hazards of Ambition

Shakespeare and the Hazards of Ambition

Robert N. Watson

Harvard University Press
Cambridge, Massachusetts, and London, England
1984

Publication of this book has been aided by a grant from the Andrew W. Mellon Foundation.

This book is printed on acid-free paper, and its binding materials have been chosen for strength and durability.

Library of Congress Cataloging in Publication Data

Watson, Robert N.
    Shakespeare and the hazards of ambition.

    Includes bibliographical references and index.
    1. Shakespeare, William, 1564–1616—Knowledge—
Psychology.   2. Ambition in literature.   3. Shakespeare,
William, 1564–1616—Characters.   4. Psychoanalysis and
literature.   I. Title.
PR3069.A42W37   1984   822.3'3   84-4590
ISBN 0-674-80390-6 (alk. paper)

To Barbara Bellow Watson

Acknowledgments

I AM PARTICULARLY grateful for the indispensable advice and encouragement I received from John Bender and David Riggs at Stanford University; from Robert Petersson, Richard Young, and William Oram at Smith College; and from Walter Kaiser, G. B. Evans, Gillian Kendall, and Claire Scovell at Harvard University. My thanks go also to Harvard University, the National Endowment for the Humanities, and the Huntington Library, for their generous contributions of funds and facilities; to my editors at Harvard University Press; and to the family, friends, and colleagues who gave me so much during the writing of this book.

❧Contents

Shakespeare and the Hazards of Ambition

All quotations and citations of Shakespeare's works are from *The Riverside Shakespeare*, ed. G. B. Evans et al. (Boston: Houghton Mifflin, 1974).

ಶಃIntroduction

T HE LEADEN CASKET containing Portia's picture tells her
suitors, "Who chooseth me must give and hazard all he
hath." A volume of Shakespeare's plays carries the same implicit
message to interpreters, both an invitation and a warning. A hazard
may be an act of faith or daring, requisite for blessedness or wealth,
or it may simply be a potential source of destruction. Shakespeare's
treatment of ambition suggests that he was keenly aware of the way
these overlapping meanings can generate a tragic dilemma. His world
exhorts its heroes onto an ambitious course that is as fraught with
perils as with glories, and his symbolism explains why the perils
and glories are inseparable.

These ethical paradoxes and symbolic patterns provoke hazardous
ambitions in the critic as well. Although this book must be limited
to selected aspects of ambition in a few selected works, the plays I
have chosen illustrate the evolution and boundaries of Shakespeare's
treatment of the subject, and the aspects of those plays I have emphasized unite them into a coherent pattern of moral symbolism.
There is a danger of procrustean thinking in any such project, but
my reading of Shakespeare's plays does not insist on their uniform-
ity; on the contrary, its interest lies in the way the symbolism varies
with the form and pressure of each play's time, yet is still itself.
The moral pattern becomes an index to the varying tolerance of
ambition in the various play-worlds, and perhaps also to the development of Shakespeare's own attitude toward ambition.

Montaigne concludes his "Apology for Raymond Sebond" by disputing one of Seneca's maxims:

Introduction

> "O what a vile and abject thing is man," he says, "if he does not raise himself above humanity."
>
> That is a good statement and a useful desire, but equally absurd. For to make the handful bigger than the hand, the armful bigger than the arm, and to hope to straddle more than the reach of our legs, is impossible and unnatural. Nor can man raise himself above himself and humanity; for he can see only with his own eyes, and seize only with his own grasp.[1]

This "absurd" desire, expressed by the great stoic ancestor of Elizabethan and Jacobean tragedy, is an essential constituent of Shakespeare's tragic heroes. Their struggles to surpass their own natural limits, or the normal limits of humanity, often founder on Montaigne's paradoxes of identity. Montaigne's examples of absurdity call to mind several instances where Shakespearean protagonists naively assert a dangerous self-transcendence: the "vain boast" of Othello's "good arm," the poses of Caesar and Antony astride the world like Colossi, even the alienation of Macbeth's hand from its owner. In striving for personal or political greatness, these characters give birth to new selves of greater though tentative dimensions. Countless figures in the plays assume borrowed costumes and roles; this book is concerned with the few who seek to assimilate those changes into durable new identities—in particular, Richard III, Henry IV, Macbeth, Coriolanus, and Leontes.[2]

The moral pattern that afflicts these characters and unites these plays is essentially a pattern of poetic justice, whereby characters who try to alter the limited identities bequeathed to them find themselves excluded from the regenerative system they have disdained. It is as if Shakespeare had a basic talionic myth of the ambitious person, a pattern of punishment reflecting the crime, which each of these characters lives out in a different way, according to the different imperatives of his play-world. As in so many fairy tales, the ambitious figures in Shakespeare suffer the logical but unforeseen consequences of having their wishes fulfilled—specifically, the wish to escape a flawed or subservient hereditary identity. The official Elizabethan "Homily Against Disobedience and Wilful Rebellion" defined ambition as "the unlawful and restless desire in men to be of higher estate than God hath given or appointed unto them";[3] for the purposes of this book, ambition may be similarly defined as the will to transcend the constricting self provided by one's birth. The danger in moving from a received position toward some preconceived ideal is that the ideal new self may never attain the integrity and stability of the original self. Montaigne writes that he chooses to "stay in the position where God put me. Otherwise I could not keep myself from rolling about incessantly."[4] Upward motion can lead to a dangerous roll downhill; ambition is a Sisyphean task in Shakespearian drama, a perpetual quest for elevation that is baffled by some moral equivalent of the law of gravity. Shakespeare portrays a doomed but necessary struggle between human identity and its lineal constraints, a struggle toward which the plays express a powerful ambivalence.

The self created by ambition is a poor substitute for the self provided by heredity. "A world of made," as E. E. Cummings says, "is not a world of born."[5] The original self, cut off from its roots, suffers a symbolic death in these plays, as it does in many other myths of heroic transformation;[6] identity must thereafter be sustained by what the medical profession aptly terms "heroic measures." Ficino traces back to Aristophanes the notion that men who become too proud will become divided against themselves.[7] Shakespeare's ambitious protagonists, having scorned their lineal identities, begin to resemble R. D. Laing's archetypal schizophrenic, who can no longer take his "realness, aliveness, autonomy, and identity . . . for granted" and must instead "become absorbed in contriving ways of trying to be real . . . to prevent himself losing himself."[8] Lacking a unifying core, the protagonists' identities become entangled with their changeable garments and their ever-changing names. Deprived of its original integrity, the ambitious figure's selfhood vacillates between nullity and self-conflicting multiplicity, between a terrifying void and a bewildering set of theatrical roles. His identity is either split or lost between the hereditary and adopted versions of himself, which are irreconcilable yet both ineradicable.

To escape both the constraints of their natural births and the artificiality of a manufactured self, Shakespeare's ambitious protagonists often attempt to enforce a symbolic rebirth, through which they can become the children of their own desires or ideals. Hegel has stressed the importance of birth and its determinism in creating the tragic conflict;[9] Shakespeare explores all the implications of his characters' struggle against that tragic limitation, understood in psychological and biological terms as well as philosophical ones. The ambitious figures apparently hope that a reborn self can be at once natural and perfect, but the process of rebirth is itself unnatural and degrading. Shakespeare associates the forcible re-creation of the self imagistically with rape and Caesarean section. He extrapolates from the symbolic rebirth a sexual metaphor about the way that rebirth was generated. In *Measure for Measure* Isabella accuses Claudio of attempting "a kind of incest" in seeking new life through his sister's sexuality (3.1.138); she implies that Claudio rather than Angelo will actually be her sexual partner, because the fornication will essentially comprise Claudio's attempt to conceive his own rebirth. More typically, Shakespeare extends this symbolic deduction by portraying the desire for a new self as a figuratively Oedipal desire, since it implies the incestuous re-use of the mother's womb to usurp the father's procreative authority. The widely noted Oedipal patterns in *2 Henry IV*, *Macbeth*, and *Coriolanus*, in other words, serve to anatomize the protagonists' struggle for self-overcoming, whether or not they can be read as prescient psychoanalysis. Shakespeare saw metaphorically what Freud saw scientifically, and Freud's system helps to enlighten Shakespeare's symbolic pattern. If, as Freud claims, the hero is the man "who always rebels against his father and kills him in some shape or other,"[10] that may be partly because the very acquisition of heroic stature entails at least a metaphorical overthrow of the father. The Oedipal situation is as suggestive a metaphor for the problems of self-definition as for the problems of infantile sexuality. Though the sexual interpretations of that myth have been more prominent, psychologists, anthropologists, and literary critics have also remarked on this other, meta-sexual aspect of the Oedipus story, which I prefer to emphasize.[11] Incestuous physical gratification, from this viewpoint, is not the ultimate goal of the Oedipal impulse, but rather the fantasized means toward an autogenous identity.

By the same token, this book is not a psychoanalysis of individual ambitious characters, but rather a study of how Shakespeare uses the realistic psychological mechanisms of the characters in service of a larger, metapsychological commentary on the implications and consequences of self-transformation. This is not finally an annotation of the homology between Freudian theory and Shakespearean characterization, but rather an exploitation of Freudian concepts to talk about an intricate correspondence Shakespeare discovered and developed, between the ramifications of ambition in the external world and the transactions of ambition within the individual psyche. Out of that correspondence Shakespeare builds the poetic justice and the symbolic patterns that give his portrayal of ambition's hazards two kinds of power: the power of seeming to derive from a universal moral congruence, and the power of arousing, penetrating, even implicating, the reader's individual psyche. If male ambition

4

is the quest for a rebirth that escapes patrimonial limitations, then it corresponds suggestively to the Oedipal impulse. The failure to repress illicit ambitions or desires, and to displace them onto safer objects than crowns or mothers, inevitably produces some sort of neurosis, an illness sketched in large for the audience while appearing in small in the ambitious character's psyche. Neurosis is a simulation of psychological normality that usually functions as well as normality itself; it is a house of cards built well enough to keep out the rain. Neurotic episodes are moments when the wind blows, revealing the difference between a normal psychological mechanism and one that had outwardly resembled it. My book focuses on the literary equivalents of these neurotic episodes, moments when the tragic pressures produce symbolic situations or verbal peculiarities that reveal the difference between an integral hereditary self and the brittle or ephemeral new self ambition has put in its place. The onset of insomnia, sexual dysfunction, and self-alienation in Shakespeare's ambitious protagonists, like the onset of similar symptoms in Freud's neurotic patients, betokens a failure properly to repress and displace what is essentially an Oedipal attitude toward the mother's womb and the father's authority.

Whether attempted rebirth is a crime against a specific sexual taboo, or against the hierarchies of the hereditary order, its consequences are fitting and grim. In denying the person his parents have made, the protagonist implicitly attacks his parents' reproductive authority, and Shakespeare hints at some crude physical analogues to that metaphorical attack. Oedipal rebellion and self-induced Caesarean birth suggest a patricide and a matricide directed specifically against the parents' generative aspects. To the extent that these parricides succeed, the protagonist eradicates the entire natural basis of his existence. He therefore finds himself trapped in a limbo where, to use a modern phrase Shakespeare anticipates, he is merely a shadow of his former self, like characters in the time-travel stories of science fiction who accidentally forfeit their ability to return to their original lives by changing the history that led to their births. To the extent that these parricides fail, however, the protagonist is left helpless as an infant at the hands of the vengeful paternal forces, whether they manifest themselves as actual parents or as agents of the natural order that stands behind those parents. Shakespeare's ambitious figures can be seen as failed versions of the archetypal figure who appears as Zeus, as Oedipus, as Moses, and as Jesus, all of whom elude the jealous patriarchal Slaughter of the Innocents and fulfill prophecy by overthrowing the tyrannical infanticides. Instead,

Introduction

Shakespeare's characters yield up their lives, and what they saw as their destinies, to some rough equivalent of Cronus and Laius and Herod, to a repressive paternal law. Shakespeare again aligns the rebellion based in sexuality with the rebellion based in identity. The child who threatens to overthrow his parents or their sexual rules runs the risk of retribution, even of murder or castration, designed to prevent his growing into a more dangerous strength.[12] Whether by psychosexual dynamics or poetic justice, the unruly son finds his reproductive powers and even his life endangered by his disobedience. Orderly procreation, and its cyclical analogues in sleep and seasonal change, desert him; eventually, by opposing, they end him. When characters seek to transcend the condition of their births, they face implacable and symbolically apt resistance from the forces of natural order. On this level the pattern is didactic, and its lesson resembles Augustine's warning: "Hands off yourself. Try to build up yourself, and you build a ruin."[13]

For most Elizabethan moralists, of course, the issue was at least that simple: ambition was the sentiment they most dearly loved to hate. On a spiritual level, it was the sin that caused Lucifer to fall from heaven and Adam and Eve to fall from Grace.[14] To aspire beyond one's given condition is to defy the will of the ultimate, heavenly Father. On a political level, the sin of ambition was again the most dangerous, since it led to the worst of social crimes: rebellion against the earthly king. These three levels—familial, religious, and political—on which ambition contended against filial obedience were suggestively connected to make the moral admonitions more forceful. Alexander Nowell's Elizabethan catechism insisted that the Fifth Commandment applied to all figures in authority, and that God the Father could only regard an attack on "the prince, the father of the country itself, and parent of the commonweal," as even more heinous than an attack on one's own parents.[15] Freud would later elaborate on these associations, portraying displaced Oedipal guilt, arising from a patricide in the Primal Horde, as the source of our obeisance to gods and to paternal political authorities.[16] For the Elizabethans, however, this morally synergistic conflation of the paternal figures served the very practical purpose of encouraging social order and unity. Sixteenth-century England therefore teemed with conservative homilies and cautionary tales, warning, in the most obvious ways, against ambition in its most obvious forms. The desire to rise above one's birth was the very essence of "villainy," as the word's history suggests.[17] High aspirations were a manifestation of sinful pride and a subversion against a benevolent order consisting of nature, nation, family, and God.

6

Shakespeare surely heard this warning, and may in part have believed it. But nothing in his works is finally so simple, finally reducible to so stark a moral. The conservative belief and the resulting political propaganda, like many other common beliefs and literary practices of his time, served Shakespeare merely as a skeleton onto which he bonded all the complications of humanity and of his symbolic imagination, until the subject took on a life of its own. The punishments in the plays arise unmistakably from the crime of ambition, but that crime does not always appear as a moral error in any conventional sense. In fact, virtuous aspirations encounter largely the same obstacles as evil ambitions, raising significant questions about Shakespeare's attitude toward the coercive natural order he so convincingly depicts. Is he insisting that ambition is more absolute an evil than even his tract-writing contemporaries asserted? Or is he—as seems more characteristic—merely extending the conventional morality to its logical absurdity, and thereby implying that the ordering force could easily be understood as a blind reflex or a defensive repression, rather than as a benevolent intelligence? What kind of a divine force is it that forbids and punishes Coriolanus' heroic quest for martial purity by the same mechanisms and with the same severity as it does Macbeth's villainous quest for the crown?

Some disclaimers are in order here. I am not claiming that this ethical problem is the true secret focus of these plays: they are neither so similar as a group nor individually so narrow. While Shakespeare's myth of the ambitious person is extremely important in shaping the action and the symbolism, it is far from being their only begetter. But the outlines and many of the specific elements of the myth do persist in the sharply differing contexts of these plays, and recognition of that myth illuminates one more component of Shakespeare's drama, and perhaps of his world view as well. In trying to make this pattern visible, I necessarily emphasize similarities rather than differences among the plays; the purpose is to delineate the points of persistence and Shakespeare's resourcefulness in adapting them to each of the works, rather than to deny that the differences are real and important.

Furthermore, since the pattern survives in subordination to other, more prominent themes, my interpretations will often rely on secondary meanings of words and lines rather than on their primary meanings. Phrases pertaining to birth, to family relations, and to nothingness often appear in contexts where their primary meaning does not speak directly to the moral symbolism this book describes.

Introduction

My resort to a secondary reading is not intended to imply that the usual reading is merely a veil over the truth; instead, my point is that Shakespeare composes the surface of his text, where ambition is concerned, in such a way that the words and concepts cluster into a coherent ethical pattern, a persistent theme by which the reader can appreciate and evaluate each character's moral variations. Notions of unnatural birth, Oedipal rebellion, and shadowy selfhood appear so regularly in conjunction with ambition that, even when they do occur on a secondary level, they seem to represent an association in Shakespeare's mind that we are bound to receive, if only subliminally. In many cases, in fact, the character of the symbolic pattern is such that it can exist only on such a secondary level. Such transactions as Oedipal rape and self-induced Caesarean rebirth are so bizarre, taboo, or horrifying, that they would render the plays laughable, grotesque, or unwatchable, were they presented explicitly. They are not the first meaning or the central focus, but rather echoes in the language, blurs at the edge of the picture, that combine to suggest a possible and powerful metaphor for what is taking place more plainly. The protagonists may not actually be killing their fathers, re-using their mothers' wombs, absorbing their garments, or becoming shadowy ciphers; but all of these secondarily suggested actions help to reveal and moralize the underlying implications of the ambitious actions on which Shakespeare chooses to focus, and about which he can afford to be more literal. The problem that generally faces the explicator—that if the author had wanted to say it that way, he would have done so himself—becomes more obvious than usual under these circumstances. To explain the shape and the appropriateness of the metaphors revealing the hazards of ambition in Shakespeare, I am obliged to make crudely explicit what I recognize is, and must be, only implicit and subliminal in the text.

The secondary patterning creates yet another problem. The references to the pattern must somehow be in the characters' voices without being of them; the author at those moments must speak through his characters, giving them words wiser in the ways of his symbolism than is plausible. They may seem at moments to be measuring their own safety and legitimacy by a symbolic system that we know to be the dramatist's later overlay on their stories. When I suggest that a character seems to accuse another of suffering from the ambitious syndrome, or tries to evade its symbolic markings in himself, the reader should understand that I am describing an effect of literary myth-making that makes no claim to verisimilitude. Characters cannot realistically react to a pattern the author superimposes on their words or deeds, but Shakespeare heightens his pattern's visibility by making them seem to do so.

I have chosen not to wrestle with the huge questions of social, intellectual, and theological history that my topic certainly raises. Cultural history, always complex and subjective, becomes more so in conjunction with specific literary criticism. The idea that Shakespeare lived in a transitional period between medieval stability of identity and modern individuality, social mobility, and self-consciousness—an orthodox notion, in one form or another, for the past century—might help to explain the pervasive theme of self-fashioning in his plays.[18] An ongoing shift from a rigid, hierarchical system of identity to the unstable, existential system proposed by Pico and elaborated by Descartes might explain the tragic entrapment of Shakespeare's ambitious protagonists. On the one hand, the newly emptied universe obliges them to fabricate an identity according to whatever ideal they can generate; on the other hand, the vestigial gods of the old order, though no longer potent enough to provide humanity with satisfactory roles, retain enough embittered power to punish men for creating their own. A world moving from what anthropologists call "attributed" identity to "achieved" identity provokes ambition, but does not necessarily reward or condone it. The human situation in such a world resembles the archetypal situation of the tragic hero, trapped between the conflicting imperatives imposed on him by two different sorts of godheads. In the history of the individual's psyche, rather than the culture's, this phenomenon can be understood as a version of the existential burden of "bad faith," in which a person is inherently unable to return to a primally authentic identity, yet is perpetually haunted by guilt for not returning; it is a classic double bind, tearing the person between what Sartre calls the "in-itself" and the "for-itself," the one irretrievable, the other inauthentic.[19]

Such speculation, as intriguing as it seems to me, cannot by itself sustain a literary interpretation; the readings of the plays must be capable of standing on their own. Extrapolating from social and intellectual history is particularly risky in this area, because the orthodox assumptions about the chain of being and Renaissance individualism have proved so vulnerable to attack in recent decades.[20] Extrapolating in the other direction, from the literature to the cultural history, entails its own problems. For example, did Italian Renaissance writers emphasize man's freedom because they felt liberated, or because their oppression shunted their appetite for freedom from life to literature, where it flourished as a fantasy?[21] Burckhardt assumes that self-fashioning is a free man's project; yet Shakespeare's most explicit self-fashioners—Richard III, Cassius, Iachimo, Edmund, even Rosalind—advocate such freedom largely because their present condition renders them impotent, subservient, excluded from the centers of power and the power of choice. Their dreams of autonomy, like those of Coriolanus, may be wish-fulfillment dreams, mechanisms of compensation.

This is not to deny that parallels between life and literature can be instructive and supportive for my theory, particularly when there is a mediating element, such as literature written with the specific purpose of warning against forms of ambition then common in society. Recent books on "aspiring minds" and Prodigal Sons among the Elizabethans distill from such didactic tracts a number of themes that parallel the warnings I see encoded in Shakespeare's representations of ambition: the universality of the sin of ambition, its lure to the individual and its punishment by all the structures around him, its strong implication of defiance of the father and disdain for his place, and its threat to replace any viable being with mere theatricalism and nothingness.[22] But, for the most part, social history must remain beyond the range of this book. In intellectual and theological history, the massive contentions of art against nature, free will against determinism, and works against election are all clearly germane to my study of the tension between the urge to fabricate an ideal new self and the warning that such a fabrication is dangerously unnatural or sinful. But these topics, too, are largely beyond my book's scope. Where social, intellectual, or theological history promises to be specifically helpful, I have tried to include it. For the most part, I have tried to permit and encourage the plays to speak for themselves. What this book offers is a new way of listening to the symbolic voice in which Shakespeare expresses his ethics.

My rapid tour of Shakespeare's major history plays is intended as a sort of medical grand round in the hospital of the ambitious, exploring the symptomatology of the starkest cases to establish the normal course of the disease and to permit some speculation about its literary etiology. Earlier cautionary treatments of English history suggested to Shakespeare a vast cautionary myth about heredity and identity. Violations of political hierarchy and betrayals of the hereditary self converge around disputes over royal lineage. Shakespeare presents the War of the Roses as an escalating series of crimes against the natural order in general and heredity in particular, instigated by political ambition and familial vengefulness. Richard III is both the culmination and the scourge of those crimes, both suffering and exacerbating their standard symptoms in a vicious cycle that only his death can end. That cycle began with Richard II abusing and jeopardizing, not only his political authority, but his identity as a whole, by misconceiving his own heritage and invading Henry Herford's. Henry, like Richard III, is obliged to punish an earlier violation of lineality in order to fill out his impaired selfhood, and is in turn punished for violating Richard II's hereditary rights in the necessary act of reclaiming his own. Hal is the Oedipal son who typically rises against the tyrannical father who was formerly a rebel himself; but in three confrontations that strikingly resemble the archetypal struggles of a young man's psyche, Hal arduously reconstructs a loyal filial identity, breaking the long, deadly chain-reaction of patricides. Shakespeare thus grounds his story of English usurpation in a study of the political history of all societies and in the psychological history of all young men. The second tetralogy makes Hal a model for the healthy assimilation of both the Oedipal impulse and its ambitious counterpart, and therefore a norm against which we can measure the disastrous simultaneous mismanagement of these two impulses in the tragedies.

Macbeth moves from history to tragedy by portraying the hazards of ambition in a purer and more haunting form, and with an undertone of profound moral ambivalence. The symbolic pattern suggested by the histories here creates its own sort of ethical drama. Macbeth and his wife share Richard III's symptomatology: their unnatural rebirths create only shadowy and divided selves that cyclical nature systematically excludes from its benefits. But the history plays have shown how arbitrary categories such as "natural" and "hereditary" can become. "Original" may connote purity and virtue, but a usurper can redefine origins to suit his own purposes, and the tyrants who claim sovereignty by such distortions may be gods as well as kings. A creator's authority may not deserve priority over human self-determination, if authority is so easily forged. It is facile to equate inheritance and nature with goodness without first asking what the human heritage truly is, and what is truly natural for human beings. Tragedy is often situated where virtue and evil are designated arbitrarily; in *Macbeth* and *Coriolanus*, tragedy occurs where hereditary nature is arbitrarily designated and virtue somewhat hollowly attributed to it. A jealous god (or a precarious social authority) would necessarily call ambition sinful, but rebellion against the creating father's authority is an essential part of a boy's psychological development. Shakespeare encodes in Macbeth's crime all our forbidden resentments against the limits imposed by our culture; Macbeth is everyman, except that his ambitious impulses are cursed with the efficacy of action. Even Macbeth's horrifying war on the natural order is revealed, by a fairy-tale motif, as the acting out of an impulse profoundly typical of human nature and essential to human survival.

Shakespeare's later treatments of ambition move further in this direction. The defiance of the father becomes at once more central and more distanced into a universal metaphor. The protagonist's aspiration appears less as standard political ambition—in Coriolanus it is virtually the opposite—and more as a symbol for human idealism in all its forms. Freed from the obligation to echo political propaganda, Shakespeare can now acknowledge some nobility in the denial of one's limiting human heritage, even while demonstrating how costly that denial may be. The didactic side of the pattern, whereby men violate an absolute order and are punished by it, becomes subverted and hence subversive: the ordering force appears less like a benevolent god and more like a jealous paternal tyrant. Since this book does not study works such as *King John*, *Julius Caesar*, and *Hamlet*, it cannot claim to be a comprehensive study of Shakespeare's transition from history to tragedy, from literal to figurative fathers, or from benevolent to ambivalent gods. But the variations presented by the omitted plays would not contradict these general lines of evolution.

Coriolanus aspires to an identity based on a classical model of manly virtue. Like the child in the "family romance" described by psychoanalysts, he fantasizes an ideal family that legitimizes his idea of himself as a hero. First, he turns his Oedipal defiance against the merely human father, who has been figuratively dispersed into the citizenry of Rome; and he does so on behalf of a posited father who is more responsive to his ambitions—the god Mars. Coriolanus' repressive politics, his unfeeling and unfeeding severity toward the body politic, are on this level a means of expressing an ambition to repress the compromisingly human aspects of his own body natural. Like any boy fleeing envelopment by his mother and disdaining his father's limitations, Coriolanus turns to a figure—Aufidius—he supposes can reflect and affirm his ego-ideal. But when Coriolanus attacks the wombs of Volumnia and Rome that bred him, to complete the sexualized Caesarean rebirth that began at Corioles' gates, the Oedipal implications of his ambition become intolerably explicit. The generational panorama at the gates of Rome, like Birnan wood at the walls of Dunsinane, enforces on the protagonist the limitations imposed by his natural context, by the regenerative system.

My book ends with a brief look at *The Winter's Tale*, in which Leontes forfeits procreation, sleep, and seasonal growth, by denying the great limiting father of Renaissance aspirations: the fallen Adam. By a hitherto unexplicated series of allusions to original sin, Shakespeare evolves his story of a new fall of man into a story of the Grace that is an alternative to the cruel gods and damning determinism of the tragedies. The historical and tragic subject of humanity's fatal ambitions gives way to the romantic subject of humanity's atonement to "great creating Nature." By imposing a Christian godhead on this pre-Christian world, Shakespeare sentimentalizes the Oedipal conflict out of existence: God and Christ conspire to eradicate the powerful ambiguities about the creating father's rights and the natural order's benevolence. That order returns, not as an avenger, but rather as a kindly guide showing Leontes a *via media* between his mortal depravity and his divine pretensions; he finds a humbler version of his immortal ideals within his familial context and his human nature. The protagonist's reconciliation with his family, so characteristic of Shakespeare's last plays, fittingly parallels the reconciliation of ambition with human limitations. When that which was lost in the false Edenic garden of Sicilia is found in the natural garden of Bohemia, ambitions that acknowledge heredity receive a theologically founded endorsement.

By showing the extent to which the symbolic pattern persists across different types of play (history, tragedy, and romance) and different modes of aspiration (political, martial, and moral), I hope to show that Shakespeare conceived of ambition as an independent dramatic and philosophical problem, with its own properties and its own weighty ambiguities. By showing his modulation and evolution of that pattern, I hope to illuminate the individual plays and reveal an aspect of Shakespeare's ethical thought.

❧1

Kinship and Kingship:
Ambition in Shakespeare's
Major Histories

SHAKESPEARE'S better-known history plays—*Richard III* and the second tetralogy—suggest a plausible source for the attitudes and symbolism developed in the later plays. Elizabethan admonitions against political rebellion, whether in chronicles, tracts, or plays, emphasized the importance of lineage, as opposed to manipulable names or garments, in determining rightful sovereignty. The warnings were moral, since they associated political ambition with Satanic ambition, suggesting a sinister unity to all crimes against benevolent paternal authority. The warnings were also pragmatic, since civil wars provoked by ambition shatter families, ruin agriculture, and exhaust the populace, inviting social chaos, widespread famine, and foreign invasion. Moreover, these writers noted, political realities as well as divine justice tend to make a usurper vulnerable to counterusurpation, a regicide vulnerable to regicide, and an unlineal king incapable of establishing a lineal succession.[1] The rebel who finds it impossible to gain a secure hold on the throne, furthermore, will also find it impossible to relinquish that throne and return safely to the humble pleasures of his former life.

Shakespeare takes these warnings about the moral and practical dynamics of a political situation, and aligns them with a cautionary myth about the hazards of ambition in general. New names and garments are a poor and evanescent substitute for a hereditary identity, whether or not the titles, robes, or lineage involved are specifically royal. The disobedience to the paternal figure on the throne and the "father who is in heaven" necessarily entails disobedience to the familial father, because it entails a disdain for the place, and

14

a denial of the self, that father provided. The destruction caused by civil wars that turn farmers into soldiers and fields of grain into fields of battle becomes in Shakespeare a logical extension of the ambitious man's defiance of his own nature and the regenerative system that created him; the proud rebellion against the Creator leads to a new loss of Eden's perfect fertility. The usurper's divided identity creates a conflict within him that deprives him of sleep, leaving him too exhausted to win the civil war analogously disturbing his nation's rest—a war that becomes the symbol, the method, and the punishment of his ambition. His susceptibility to other usurpers, and his inability to father acceptable heirs, become in Shakespeare a talionic pattern associated with the vicious Oedipal cycle, whereby the man who resists paternal dictates either loses his sexual powers entirely, or creates sons as defiant as he was. The impossibility of either stabilizing or safely resigning a stolen throne becomes a metaphor for the existential impossibility of either completing the adoption of a new self, or retreating to the primal innocence of the original one. What Shakespeare has done, essentially, is to discover within the shape of propagandistic versions of English history a highly complicated and evocative metaphor for the internal transactions that necessarily accompany ambition's outward deeds. He deepens his presentation of the political events by suggesting their correspondence to a set of psychological events, and by suggesting the way all these events combine into a coherent pattern of poetic justice.

Richard III

Richard III is virtually a textbook case of the ambitious disease. Several critics have ably demonstrated the ways Richard resorts to mirrors, shadows, and theatrical performances to conceal the void at the core of his disintegrating selfhood; some have also shown the ways this substitution develops from a stratagem into a curse.[2] Richard himself clearly suggests that his birth defects are both cause and symbol of his evil deeds, though we may to some extent mistrust his motive-hunting soliloquies. My emphasis therefore falls on the pattern uniting these various self-distortions, and on the figurations of rebirth Shakespeare uses to describe and moralize them. Shakespeare portrays Richard III's ambition as the culmination of a series of crimes against lineality, and as the procreation of a royal new self that becomes trapped in its own artificiality. In the history plays—and this principle is even more pervasive and subversive in the tragedies—lineality *is* identity. Disturbances in the one are both cause and result of disturbances in the other.

From the very start Shakespeare describes Richard's pursuit of the crown as compensation and revenge for his twisted and belated birth. Richard follows a course as deformed morally as he is physically, until that sinister unity of soul and body provides him with the perfect new identity of king. As 3 *Henry VI* ends, King Henry curses Richard as the killer of Edward's son, predicts that Richard will be the enemy of future families, and mocks Richard for the deformities of his birth. In case we have overlooked the pattern that connects the curse, the prediction, and the mockery, Richard clarifies it for us:

> Then since the heavens have shap'd my body so,
> Let hell make crook'd my mind to answer it.
> I have no brother, I am like no brother;
> And this word "love," which greybeards call divine,
> Be resident in men like one another,
> And not in me: I am myself alone. (5.6.78–83)

Such a declaration of autonomy verges on a claim to autogeny: it looks ahead to Coriolanus, who determines to "stand / As if a man were author of himself, / And knew no other kin" (5.3.35–37). Richard thus renders himself a suitable victim of the afflictions that Shakespeare usually visits on characters who disdain their common humanity. But this early version of the pattern seems distorted. A man whose ambitions result from his unnatural birth is the converse of the men in later plays whose unnatural rebirths result from their ambitions. The disordered self that is a psychological cause of ambition in Richard becomes a symbolic consequence of ambition in Macbeth, Coriolanus, and Leontes.

Yet the case of Richard III is not so twisted an example of the hazards of ambition as it might at first seem. Shakespeare's entire first tetralogy asks us to understand Richard as the culmination, and the scourge, of all the misdeeds involved in the War of the Roses. He is the lightning rod, or the scapegoat, in whom all the evils are gathered so they may be safely dissipated. René Girard argues that a society can quell the endless cycle of reciprocal violence that threatens to destroy it only by unanimously sacrificing a mock king or a totemic animal;[3] Richard the Boar plausibly embodies both sacrificial objects. The pattern of poetic justice attaching to ambition is not reversed here, but rather doubled. Prior ambitions had already damaged the nation's unity and lineal health, provoking God to create the fragmented and unlineal creature who will attack unity and the lineal order in an effort to compensate for his impairment. The vicious cycle of Richard's life, in which a chaotic self necessitates an ambition that only increases the self's chaos, turns our attention to the analogous transaction in the English body politic, and thus to the moral implications of the first tetralogy as a symmetrical whole.

Shakespeare invites such attention by presenting the War of the Roses as primarily an extended crime of ambition against inheritance. The central dispute concerns lineal rights to the throne, and in each of the Henry VI plays Shakespeare inserts at least one conflict that stresses this war's disruption of the normal process of patrimony. In *1 Henry VI* young Talbot finds that, in order to prove himself truly his father's son, he must die alongside him; his family's name—either its good name or the name of Talbot—will be exterminated whether he retreats or fights.[4] Jack Cade makes a ridiculous claim to a royal lineage in *2 Henry VI* (4.2.31–49) and is subsequently arrested by Alexander Iden, a man who declares that "The small inheritance my father left me / Contenteth me, and worth a monarchy" (4.10.18–19). At the beginning of *3 Henry VI* Henry refuses to surrender "my kingly throne, / Wherein my grandsire and my father sat," and Clifford vows to support him rather than "kneel to him that slew my father" (1.1.124–25, 162); but after a discussion of the unlineal means by which that grandsire, Henry IV, gained the throne, Henry elects to disinherit his son rather than be killed himself (1.1.132–50, 170–227). We subsequently encounter the emblematic figures of the "Son that hath kill'd his father" and the "Father that hath kill'd his son"—his "only son" (2.5.55–122). The natural order in which a father gives a son life, and the son in turn allows the father to survive beyond his death, has given way to mutual annihilation.

Richard of Gloucester is as much a symptom of this world as an inhabitant; he is the punishment as well as the culmination of the ambitions that have been afflicting England. He kills the sons of those who have killed sons, ends the lines of those who have ended lines, before being cut off himself by his barren political marriage and by Henry Richmond, the young man in whom the various lines supposedly reunite and revive. The great frequency with which the symbolic consequences of ambition attach themselves to Richard should therefore not surprise us, since they are what a psychiatrist might call "overdetermined": they may be derived from any one of dozens of overlapping crimes against the hereditary order.

Kinship and Kingship

From the moment he first introduces himself, in *3 Henry VI*, Richard embodies everything that opposes natural life and lineal identity. He curses King Edward, "That from his loins no hopeful branch may spring" to remove Richard further from the royal succession (3.2.126). In opposing the propagation of the royal line—a process here as later associated with vegetative growth (5.6.62; 5.7.21–32)—Richard asserts that his enmity toward procreative love preceded his birth:

> Why, love forswore me in my mother's womb;
> And for I should not deal in her soft laws,
> She did corrupt frail nature with some bribe,
> To shrink mine arm up like a wither'd shrub,
> . . . . .
> To disproportion me in every part,
> Like to a chaos, or an unlick'd bear-whelp
> That carries no impression like the dam.   (3.2.153–62)

Negatives dominate the wording—"*not* deal," "*dis*proportion," "*un*-lick'd," "*no* impression"—to the extent that Richard seems less misshaped than unshaped.[5] With the formative principle of heredity shattered, Richard must cast himself in some mode other than the parental one if he wants to acquire a stable and unified form. He therefore determines "t'account this world but hell, / Until my mis-shap'd trunk that bears this head / Be round impaled with a glorious crown" (3.2.169–71), as if he might experience as miraculous a physical reformation under that headpiece as Prince Hal did (by most reports) a moral reformation. Thus his desire to invade the royal line results from his lack of physical symmetry, which results in turn from a failure of lineal identity. The vicious cycle afflicting heredity in the War of the Roses has begun to move inside Richard, preparing him for his role as scapegoat.

The soliloquy hints at a chaos of the self that goes far beyond the physical deformity, though symbolically and psychologically related to it. As in *Macbeth*, a discontinuity among the senses and among the parts of the body becomes a symptom of the ambitious man's self-alienation, which is itself a symptom of his determination to invade the royal succession. Shakespeare capitalizes on the commonplace analogy between the human body and the body politic to expand on the moral themes of earlier history plays such as Sackville and Norton's *Gorboduc*. Most such plays imply that an individual's violations of humility, primogeniture, and other bonds of "kindness" threaten the nation's health and unity. *Gorboduc* converts

18

that causal pattern into a cycle by suggesting that a political division inspired the personal misconduct that worsened the political division; Shakespeare extends that pattern one step further, and inaugurates his study of the problems of ambitious identity, by showing political divisions fragmenting the men who created them. Richard compares his yearning for the crown to the experience of a man who "spies a far-off shore where he would tread, / Wishing his foot were equal with his eye," and concludes that "My eye's too quick, my heart o'erweens too much, / Unless my hand and strength could equal them" (3.2.134–45). His only means to resolve these disunities of selfhood is to gain the throne, and his only means to gain the throne is to aggravate these same disunities:

> I'll play the orator as well as Nestor,
> Deceive more slily than Ulysses could,
> And like a Sinon, take another Troy.
> I can add colors to the chameleon,
> Change shapes with Proteus for advantages,
> And set the murtherous Machevil to school.　　　(3.2.188–93)

He seeks a positive identity by doubling the negative.

If Richard is to establish a royal identity blessed with the stability and integrity of a self that is born and not made, he will have to create it by a figurative second birth. Symbolic rebirth, for several Shakespearean characters, is a trope against the belatedness of a particular aspiration, a particular idea of the self, enlisting in defense of that idea or aspiration the deterministic power of birth that formerly opposed it. Many cultures have initiation rites or myths that portray the emergence of the adult or the emergence of the hero as the birth of an entire new person, unfettered by any frailties of his childhood: the child symbolically dies and is buried, the adult rises up by his own force.[6] Shakespeare's chief elaboration on this mythic pattern is to portray the men enforcing their own rebirths by a sort of Caesarean section, carving out the opening through which the ambitious new identity appears. In *Henry VIII*, Norfolk remarks that Cardinal Wolsey, "being not propp'd by ancestry, whose grace / Chalks successors their way," has succeeded in advancing into power nonetheless: "The force of his own merit makes his way" (1.1.59–64). In *Macbeth* and *Coriolanus*, I will argue, the process by which the hero's own force "carv'd out his passage" (*Macbeth*, 1.2.19) becomes much more violent and imagistically suggestive. The idea of performing one's own Caesarean birth may sound far-fetched, but it has several precedents in myth and in classical and Renaissance literature, many of which describe a self-made man enforcing his greatness through his solitary sword, which cuts him free from an enclosure.[7]

The terms in which Shakespeare has Richard describe his pursuit of the crown in this soliloquy are therefore highly suggestive, particularly since Shakespeare reminds us elsewhere of the difficult labor involved in Richard's breech birth. Richard says that, in his quest for the power and the glory that his birth-order and his birth defects deny him,

> I—like one lost in a thorny wood,
> That rents the thorns, and is rent with the thorns,
> Seeking a way, and straying from the way,
> Not knowing how to find the open air,
> But toiling desperately to find it out—
> Torment myself to catch the English crown;
> And from that torment I will free myself,
> Or hew my way out with a bloody axe. (3.2.174–81)

The simile outweighs, and finally infiltrates, the ostensible subject. Tillyard, noting that this description was more vivid than the rest of *3 Henry VI*, concluded that Shakespeare must once have been lost in such a wood himself.[8] This impression that Shakespeare was here writing from intense personal experience supports my figurative reading as well as Tillyard's literal one, and the struggle for air seems more relevant to birth than to disorientation in a forest. Furthermore, the oddity of describing the passage to the throne as a route of escape rather than entry can best be explained, considering the speaker, as the result of Richard's unconscious association of this process with his birth trauma—that is to say, more precisely, a result of Shakespeare's simulation of such an unconscious association. But my purpose is not that of the many critics who have recently praised Shakespeare's psychological insight by demonstrating the similarities between his characterizations and modern formulations of developmental psychology.[9] Instead, my emphasis is on the way Shakespeare uses this psychological verisimilitude to give his symbolic patterns a compelling and satisfying inner logic. By suggesting that Richard subliminally perceives his ambitions as both a reflection of, and a corrective to, his original distorted birth, Shakespeare encourages us to recognize his own parallel perception that ambition is a violent and illicit quest for rebirth.

The only passable road to a legitimate kingship leads through rebirth; conversely, in the hall of mirrors that is Richard's dramatic life, the only passable road to a satisfactory rebirth leads through kingship. As Richard needs rebirth to establish himself as the royal heir, so he needs the throne to provide an ideal new identity to replace the deformed one. The perfect and immortal body politic, which resides in a monarch for the duration of his reign, would have been a tempting prize to a man so understandably unhappy with his body natural. According to Plowden's Elizabethan *Commentaries or Reports* on the law, "the Body Politic wipes away every Imperfection of the other Body": it "takes away the Imbecility of his Body natural, and draws the Body natural, which is lesser . . . to itself which is the greater, *quia magis dignum trahit ad se minus dignum.*"[10] Though there were other ways for a man to ascend into a new identity in the Renaissance, they were less suited to Richard's problem and temperament: "Instead of wishing to elevate one's personality in order to become as much as possible like Christ and so, in *Imitatio* theory, to become Christ—to reside in Him—one might attempt some purely apprehensible version of elevation. One might wish to become a king."[11]

The sharp moral distinction between these two modes of transcendence corresponds to the distinctions between Richard's rebirth and Clarence's death. Both politically and symbolically, that death is the necessary complement to Richard's rebirth. Richard intends to "find the open air" by winning the throne immorally; Clarence's struggle to reach "the vast and wandering air" in his premonitory death-dream (1.4.36–74) is what one critic calls a quest for "moral rebirth."[12] Richard rejects the burden of his mortal body, his crown of thorns, determined instead to kill as many royal figures as necessary (including Clarence) to gain possession of the body politic. The betrayed and martyred Clarence struggles, conversely, to repent his royal murder and thereby allow his soul to escape his sin-tainted body. Clarence recalls his brother's promise to "labor my delivery" from the Tower, a phrase suggesting midwifery as much as pleading (the ambivalent notion of "delivery" from the Tower appears also at lines 69, 75, and 115 of *Richard III*'s first scene); but as the First Murderer replies, the only "delivery" in which Richard will actually aid his brother is this strenuous rebirth of the soul out of the body (1.4.244–48). Even this spiritual liberation proceeds by a physical circumscription. The drowning in the butt of malmsey, a converse of Richard's forcible rebirth out of the wood, may represent a sort of enforced retreat into a degraded amniotic sac where the soul is detached from, not attached to, its body. Otto Rank identified the escape from a dark enclosure as a common symbol for birth; Freud saw the same symbolism in the emergence from an ocean.[13] Both those archetypal actions are inverted when Clarence's oceanic dream is realized in his strange murder. This is to birth what black mass is to Holy Communion: an undoing, a diabolical saying-backwards. Richard's sarcastic suggestion that Clarence has been arrested so that he may "be new-christ'ned in the Tower" (1.1.50) may be all too accurate: Richard's determination to seize Clarence's primogeniture causes him to retract Clarence's genesis. To effect his own rebirth, Richard has returned his older brother to the realm of the unborn.

Richard's mission, then, is the perversion of birth, a perversion he enforces because he already embodies it. All observers describe Richard's birth as a distortion of that natural process. He emerges out of shape (humpbacked), out of position (feet first), and out of the normal order of development (with teeth). His mother calls him "A cockatrice" that her "accursed womb" has "hatch'd to the world" (4.1.53–55); Queen Margaret later tells her that "From forth the kennel of thy womb hath crept / A hell-hound that doth hunt us all to death" (4.4.47–48). Both the process of birth and the creature it liberated, in other words, are far from human. As Henry VI exclaims moments before Richard kills him, this marks Richard as the enemy of the procreative order (3 Henry VI, 5.6.35–56). When Henry's successor, Edward IV, gathers the angry factions to insist that they swear amity, Richard's speech of conciliation has ominous undertones:

> I do not know that Englishman alive
> With whom my soul is any jot at odds
> More than the infant that is born to-night. (2.1.70–72)

Since we know that he remains murderously at odds with several Englishmen, we may infer that he is at odds with the world's new progeny as well. For Richard as for Macbeth, newborn babes are inherently his enemies, because his war for succession necessarily becomes a war on succession.

When he is not reshuffling the order of succession, as he does with Clarence, Richard is often engaged in obstructing, tangling, or eradicating the lines of hereditary connection. By locking the princes in the Tower, he isolates them from their closest relatives:

> *Queen Elizabeth*
>   Hath he set bounds between their love and me?
>   I am their mother, who shall bar me from them?
> *Duchess* I am their father's mother, I will see them.

Anne Their aunt I am in law, in love their mother;
  Then bring me to their sights.   (4.1.20–24)

While Richard is preventing any such resplicing of the hereditary
line, he is also busily tangling it at those loose ends: he sends out
Buckingham to rumor "the bastardy of Edward's children" as a way
of revoking their royal patrimony (3.5.75).

Richard's misdeeds convert the procreative powers of the royal
women into something unnatural. Having blasted their normal fertility, he uses their resulting sorrow to enlist them in the task of
giving him figurative rebirth as a royal heir. The language used to
lament the deaths of Clarence and King Edward in act two, scene
two, seems to imply such a rebirth. Richard, a prime cause of these
sorrows, becomes their embodiment; by a verbal substitution, he
becomes the figurative new occupant of the otherwise barren royal
wombs. The widowed Queen Elizabeth and the orphaned children
of Clarence cannot adopt each other as a consolatory family. Like
the wives of Richard II and Macbeth, Edward's queen can now become pregnant only with sorrows:

Girl Our fatherless distress was left unmoan'd,
  Your widow-dolor likewise be unwept!
Queen Elizabeth Give me no help in lamentation,
  I am not barren to bring forth complaints.
  All springs reduce their currents to mine eyes,
  That I being govern'd by the watery moon,
  May send forth plenteous tears to drown the world! (2.2.64–70)

This reference to her domination by lunar cycles, immediately jux-
taposed with the reference to her barrenness for all offspring except
grief, suggests that the tidal surge of tears has replaced the flow of
menstrual blood that the moon had formerly regulated. The salt sea
nurturing sorrow has replaced the blood that might have nurtured
a human offspring.

What is particularly intriguing about this substitution is its connection with the Duchess of York's figurative language in the same
scene, which identifies her son Richard as such a sorrow. The "sorrow" she claims to share with Elizabeth is plausibly as much her
living son Richard as her dead son Edward, particularly since the
preceding and following lines identify him as the offspring who
"grieves" his mother (2.2.47–54). Twenty-five lines later, the duchess tells Elizabeth, who is weeping for the family Richard has begun
to destroy, and Clarence's children, who are weeping for the father

Richard has killed, "Alas! I am the mother of these griefs," and "I am your sorrow's nurse, / And I will pamper it with lamentation." We may thus arrive, by substitution, at the peculiar image of the sorrow named Richard as the new fruit of Queen Elizabeth's formerly barren body—and, in fact, he soon becomes Edward's unnatural heir. He completes both his usurpation and the queen's sorrow by murdering the princes who could have exercised primogeniture over this highly belated birth.

The notion that Richard is the sorrow formed in the duchess's womb, and is then transferred, like a surrogate *in vivo* conception, into Queen Elizabeth's womb to be reborn, might be indefensibly strange and tenuous, were it not that the same implications recur later in the play. In an effort to solidify his hold on the royal identity, Richard asks Queen Elizabeth to woo her daughter for him, and he makes the request in oddly suggestive terms: "If I have kill'd the issue of your womb, / To quicken your increase, I will beget / Mine issue of your blood upon your daughter" (4.4.296–98). He is attempting to seduce the daughter through the mother, and one result is the suggestion that the mother herself will be newly "quickened" with "increase"—words heavily associated with parturition. The children, even the labor pains, will belong to the old queen, only somehow displaced into her daughter:

> They are as children but one step below,
> Even of your metal, of your very blood;
> Of all one pain, save for a night of groans
> Endur'd of her, for whom you bid like sorrow.   (4.4.301–04)

The wording seems deliberately designed to obscure the distinctions between grandmother and mother, and between mother-in-law and wife. Richard finally seduces and then scorns Queen Elizabeth much as he earlier seduced and then scorned the Lady Anne, and his arguments clearly recall those surrounding the similar entanglement of familial roles in act two, scene two; again the notion of tears being multiplied by a woman's "interest" in her offspring brings a usury metaphor to bear on the metaphorical use of a substitute womb (4.4.321–25).

By fathering children upon Elizabeth, Richard would relocate himself in the middle of the royal line; the marriage to his niece would make him the old king's son and the next king's father, thereby assisting him in the ultimate incestuous project of self-regeneration. Queen Elizabeth insists that Richard could never win young Elizabeth's love "Unless thou couldst put on some other shape / And not be Richard that hath done all this" (4.4.286–87). Richard may see the problem the other way around: he cannot put off the loathsome shape of the former Richard until Elizabeth's love confirms his new identity as king. He wins women's love so that he can love himself, and fathers children so that he can himself be refathered. Thus, when the queen again protests that "thou didst kill my children," Richard replies revealingly, "But in your daughter's womb I bury them; / Where in that nest of spicery they will breed / Selves of themselves, to your recomforture" (4.4.422–25). The involuted incest of her children breeding selves of themselves in her daughter's womb, reinforced by the phoenix-myth reference to the "nest of spicery,"[14] points back to Richard's own motives in this situation, particularly because very similar phrases have been applied to his ambitious self-alienation repeatedly in the preceding fifty lines.

Richard's effort to define a better self, then, entails defining a new family.[15] The task is implicitly Oedipal. His murders are intimately linked with his courtships; his role as a bloody and universal "sorrow," which Shakespeare uses as a verbal clue to the incestuous perversity of those courtships, Richard himself uses perversely as an emotional device in courting both Anne and Elizabeth. In Richard's overwhelming will to power, as Murray Krieger has remarked, the "sexual elements become curiously intermingled with political ones"; it is not simply a case of substituting the latter for the former, as Richard's self-introduction might seem to suggest (*3 Henry VI*, 3.2.124–95).[16] The murders and the marriages are linked both psychologically and pragmatically for Richard, and they are linked symbolically for Shakespeare. Richard's struggle to give birth to an acceptable new self requires both sorts of deeds, and thus resembles the archetypal rites of passage described earlier, in which a limiting self must be killed so that a heroic one, capable of hunting and marriage, can be born. Richard's plot, and Shakespeare's moral commentary on that plot, are thus perfectly integrated; the unnatural attributes of ambition seem to announce themselves inevitably whenever the ambitious impulse is indulged.

Richard's seduction of the Lady Anne supports the notion that these politic wooings express metaphorically a determination to breed a new identity. Though his tone is sardonic as he speaks of this seduction, he still seizes gleefully upon the new self it provides him, by mediated vision. Anne is merely a fun-house mirror to him, a distorting mirror that happens to make his distorted form look normal:[17]

> I do mistake my person all this while!
> Upon my life, she finds (although I cannot)
> Myself to be a marv'llous proper man. (1.2.252–63)

This use of the seduction throws light back onto the curse Anne
casts on Richard at the start of the scene:

> If ever he have child, abortive be it,
> Prodigious, and untimely brought to light,
> Whose ugly and unnatural aspect
> May fright the hopeful mother at the view,
> And that be heir to his unhappiness!
> If ever he have wife, let her be made
> More miserable by the life of him
> Than I am made by my young lord and thee! (1.2.21–28)

The second half of the curse comes true, like so many of the play's
curses, at the expense of the curser herself; and we are left to wonder
whether the first half of the curse is not equally reflexive. She herself
is the miserable wife; is he himself the abortive child whom that
wife bears? She bears him no other offspring, and by that very failure
she traps him outside the royal lineage he had hoped would cure his
original impairment. The wife who gives birth to her husband's
royally reconstructed self, here as in the Oedipus story and in *Macbeth*, fades away and dies in restless torment; the reborn self, as in
Macbeth and *Coriolanus*, proves to be an ambitious failure, virtually
a stillbirth, that can never escape the hereditary limitations it was
intended to overcome. The process of substituting self for self, as in
the seduction of Elizabeth, is tainted by overtones of violence and
incest. "What though I kill'd her husband and her father?" Richard
asks rhetorically:

> The readiest way to make the wench amends
> Is to become her husband and her father:
> The which will I, not all so much for love
> As for another secret close intent
> By marrying her which I must reach unto. (1.1.154–59)

He simply means his plan to gain the throne, but we have seen how
intimately the political project is linked with a rebellion against the
deformity of his original birth. In any case, his compulsion to renew
both the political and the psychological projects with Elizabeth suggests that this new self, like any other offspring he might have
conceived with Anne, proved abortive. This sort of reproduction is
too badly tainted with the hazards of ambition to be viable.

26

Buckingham's speeches claiming that Richard, rather than Edward or Edward's sons, should rightfully be king, protest far too much on the question of Richard's natural and lineal birth. He argues that Edward was a bastard, "not like the Duke," whereas Richard's "lineaments" make him "the right idea of your father, / Both in your form and nobleness of mind" (3.7.9–14). Richard's twisted form is obviously nothing like his father's normal one, but Buckingham proceeds blithely to urge the throne on the feignedly reluctant Richard in terms that everyone recognizes as a total inversion of the truth. He urges Richard not to yield

> your due of birth,
> The lineal glory of your royal house,
> To the corruption of a blemish'd stock;
> Whiles in the mildness of your sleepy thoughts,
> Which here we waken to our country's good,
> The noble isle doth want her proper limbs;
> Her face defac'd with scars of infamy,
> Her royal stock graft with ignoble plants,
> And almost should'red in the swallowing gulf
> Of dark forgetfulness and deep oblivion.   (3.7.117–29)

In urging Richard to obey the hereditary order which he will actually be disrupting, Buckingham hints at all the symbolic concomitants of that order which will be disrupted as well. His choice of metaphors to describe the costs of unlineal ambition is very close to Shakespeare's. Buckingham merely evades the fact that he is incurring, rather than precluding, those costs: the blemishing of progeny, the agitation of insomnia, the alienation from one's body, the eradication of the normal marks of identity, the corruption of the vegetative order, and the loss of the hereditary self into a terrifying void. Richard displays such a classic set of such symptoms that the play threatens to degenerate into a didactic scheme rather than a human case-history.

Richard, like the ambitious figures in later plays, succeeds only partly in eradicating his limiting original identity and in establishing his ideal new identity. The result, here as in those later plays, is that the aspiring protagonist falls into an abyss of nothingness between the two. He proves as "Deep" and "hollow" as Buckingham inadvertently wishes him (2.1.38). When he is told that Richmond is approaching "to claim the throne," Richard answers with a series of questions that are not so rhetorical as he intends them to be: "Is the chair empty? is the sword unsway'd? / Is the King dead?" (4.4.468–

70; cf. 2 *Henry IV*, 4.5.94). The play implies that the chair Richard occupies may indeed be empty, and that his life is a sort of death-in-life, as a result of his choosing to "not be Richard" (4.4.287) and instead to usurp an identity. Richard's nasty joke on Clarence, in which he speculates that Clarence is in the Tower to "be new christ'ned" rather than (as Richard confidently hopes) to be killed (1.1.50), returns to haunt him as much as Clarence himself does: Richard's rechristening of himself becomes a form of suicide. The author of *Locrine* contends that the man who usurps another man's sovereignty merely "glories at his owne decay" and "triumphs at his proper losse"; Sir Thomas Smith warns similarly that those who refuse to accept their domination by a rightful prince will "bring themselves to nothing."[18] This political moral is closely allied to the orthodox theological belief that evil constitutes a privation of being rather than an alternative sort of being, since the orthodox viewpoint was Augustinian rather than Manichaean. In the first scene of the play, Richard and Brakenbury exchange puns about the relationship between "naught," evil deeds, and "nought," nothing (1.1.97–100). This association afflicts everyone Richard touches, including the Lady Anne and the Scrivener (1.2.237; 3.6.10–13), both of whom dramatically disappear after they slip into Richard's web. By making the world either play his scenes or die, Richard seats himself in an empty chair, surrounded by hollow obedience and the ghosts of fallen enemies.

The battle at Bosworth field fittingly culminates this suicidal ambition. Civil war, as in Shakespeare's later plays of usurpation, is not merely the practical consequence of the fact that the usurper has divided his country against itself; it is also a metaphorical reflection of the fact that he has divided his identity against himself. For Richard, as for Brutus, Macbeth, Antony, and Coriolanus, the obligation to fight an interior civil war against one's former self— one's birth or conscience—incapacitates the naturally stronger creature for the actual civil war that is both causally related and symbolically parallel to the interior one. Richard determines, "If not to fight with foreign enemies, / Yet to beat down these rebels here at home" (4.4.529–30), much as Henry IV unhappily turns his attention repeatedly from conquests in the Holy Land to suppressing rebellions in England. We sense that this distinction between foreign and domestic enemies reflects a distinction between each king's outward and inward enemies, between his political rivals and his alienated hereditary conscience. Richard's mother describes in suggestive terms how the civil wars between families have degenerated into civil war within her family: her sons no sooner conquer the Lancastrians than they "Make war upon themselves, brother to brother, / Blood to blood, self against self" (2.4.60–63; cf. *1 Henry IV*, 3.2.122–23). It is not a long leap from recognizing that Richard thus "Preys on the issue of his mother's body," as Queen Margaret says (4.4.57), to recognizing that he is himself the issue of his mother's body, and is striving to eradicate precisely that bodily identity. By the time we arrive at Bosworth Field, even Buckingham, whom Richard describes as "My other self" (2.2.151), has turned against him.

Richard, then, becomes a creature at war with himself, most pronouncedly when he is preparing to battle others. He becomes the last best example of the many figures in the play whose curses, intended for their enemies, turn against themselves. In his soliloquy before the battle, Richard explicates his divided selfhood with a starkness that is almost embarrassing:

> What do I fear? Myself? There's none else by.
> Richard loves Richard, that is, I am I.
> Is there a murtherer here? No. Yes, I am.
> Then fly. What, from myself? Great reason why—
> Lest I revenge. What, myself upon myself?
> Alack, I love myself. Wherefore? For any good
> That I myself have done unto myself?
> O no! Alas, I rather hate myself
> For hateful deeds committed by myself.
> I am a villain; yet I lie, I am not.
> Fool, of thyself speak well; fool, do not flatter:
> My conscience hath a thousand several tongues . . . .
>
> (5.3.182–93)

This image of the thousand tongues, confirmed in its accuracy by the sharp disjunctions in the speaking voice of the soliloquy, prepares us to see the darker private side of Richard's subsequent public boast that "A thousand hearts are great within my bosom" (5.3.347). This is rather like a Freudian slip: we see through the boast because we know the inward psychic crisis that seems to have determined its verbal shape. Richmond's forces, in contrast, are strengthened rather than divided by such multiplicity: "Every man's conscience is a thousand men, / To fight against this guilty homicide" (5.2.17–18). A similar contrast appears in *Richard II*, between "the blood of twenty thousand men" that triumphed in Richard's face until the Welsh army dispersed, and the counterproductive effort to fight on afterward with merely the "twenty thousand names" inherent in his name of king (3.2.75–85).

In Richard III, these various components of identity—face, heart, tongue, and name—become alienated from each other, as well as multiple in themselves. The play rapidly demonstrates that Hastings is fatally misguided in supposing that "by [Richard's] face straight shall you know his heart"; Buckingham, for his part, disavows any ability to know Richard's heart by knowing his face (3.4.51–57, 10–11), and even the wavering Lady Anne senses that she is dealing with a villain so alienated from himself by ambition that his "tongue" and "heart" have only their falsity in common (1.2.192–94; cf. *Macbeth*, 1.7.82). Ambition creates a conflict among the various parts of the body, as if the new aspects of the self were transplanted organs under attack by the body's immune system; and as ambition destroys the alignments that keep people integral to themselves, so it destroys the boundaries that distinguish people from each other. Richard, for example, tries to confuse his name and his heart with those of Anne's dead husband (1.2.141–43).

Anthropologists have suggested that societies experiencing threats to their hierarchies become obsessed with "liminality," and that individuals who are liminal—who threaten to mix or shift categories of identity—are ostracized.[19] In Shakespeare's plays of usurpation, a sinister discontinuity of mind from body, and even of parts of the body from each other, becomes both the technique and the punishment of those who seek to gain a sovereignty already conferred on someone else. Personal and social liminality conjoin, even cause each other, in Shakespeare's analysis of this threat. While the villains are seizing someone else's place on a throne (and usually in a bed as well), the normal components of unitary identity become lost in a jumble. The resulting civil war within the usurpers, combined with the civil war their societies wage against them, obliterates the ambitious men and the liminal threat they represent simultaneously. Richard's nightmare before the battle of Bosworth Field is merely the fulfillment of a self-alienation he deliberately sought: Richard is finally ambushed, as Lady Anne and Hastings have been, by the radical divisions in his identity.

This unnatural fragmentation of Richard's person runs parallel to a fragmentation of the natural cycles that normally sustain and renew life. Richard disguises himself with mirrors, shadows, and theatrical roles to invade the royal succession; his punishment is to be trapped permanently in mirrors, shadows, and roles, but only temporarily invested as king. Similarly, Richard initiates a disruption of the cycles of day and night, of sleeping and waking, and of seasonal vegetative growth, as necessary corollaries to his assault on the normal cycle of royal succession. Again the punishment fits the crime: though the nation suffers briefly from these disruptions, Richard himself is the one who suffers most from his interference with the natural order. In the body politic it is only a temporary illness, as much an inoculation against the ambitious disease as it is the disease itself.

In the very first lines of the play, Richard offers a sarcastic salute to King Edward's succession to the throne, and the metaphor he chooses to convey his bitterness implies an enmity toward seasonal renewal: "Now is the winter of our discontent / Made glorious summer by this son of York" (1.1.1–2). Edward, as Elizabeth's arboreal metaphor at 2.2.40–42 makes explicit, is the root of an entire family tree, and Richard is determined to prevent that tree from propagating new scions to whom the crown would descend.[20] The man who describes his own arm as "a wither'd shrub" and "a blasted sapling, wither'd up" (*3 Henry VI*, 3.2.156; cf. 5.6.52, and *Richard III*, 3.4.69) must obstruct the branching of that tree, which will otherwise spread its fruit further and further from his reach, emphasizing rather than curing the humiliation of his birth that the deformed arm represents. Having claimed (for the sake of being contradicted) that "The royal tree hath left us royal fruit" in the form of the princes, (3.7.167), Richard drains "the purple sap" from their bodies before they mature enough to assume the throne (4.4.277). Buckingham's announcement, at Edward's death, that "though we have spent our harvest of this king, / We are to reap the harvest of his son" (2.2.115–16) has obliged Richard to blight that crop. Richard thus becomes precisely what the First Murderer said he was: as kind "as snow in harvest" (1.4.242). He also fulfills his own forecast, issued upon witnessing the precocity of young Prince Edward, that "a forward spring" often points to "Short summers" (3.1.94). The princes, described by themselves and by their mother as flowers (2.4.15, 4.4.10), have their lips like "four red roses on a stalk" smothered "in their summer beauty" (4.3.12–13). Having severed the royal line of the Red Rose of Lancaster, Richard has turned his murderous attentions to the White Rose of York. But, as in *Macbeth*, regenerative nature springs back up miraculously and vengefully against the man who sought to suppress it on behalf of his ambitions—ambitions that have made "Old barren plants" of those "whose children [Richard] hast butcher'd" (4.4.393–94). Richmond promises his army that, if they can destroy the "usurping boar, / That spoil'd your summer fields and fruitful vines," they will "reap the harvest of perpetual peace" (5.2.7–15). He will "unite the White Rose and the Red" in a fertile new royal line, a new family tree, that will "Enrich the time to come with smooth-fac'd peace, / With smiling plenty, and fair prosperous days!" (5.5.19, 33–34).

These triumphant lines promise a victory of fair days over darkness as well as of harvest over barrenness, and throughout the play the struggles of daylight and of vegetation against Richard's reign are intimately linked. As in Shakespeare's other plays of usurpation, the man who wages war on the hereditary cycle finds himself at war with nature's other regenerative cycles as well, impressing both him and us with the unity of the benevolent order he sought to overthrow. The first lines of *Richard III* imply resentment toward the new son- or sun-king as well as toward the summer fruits he brings with him to the royal family: this may be the light Richard experiments with shadowing later in the soliloquy (1.1.25–26). The Third Citizen makes the connection clearer in expressing his fears about Richard's intentions following Edward IV's death: "When great leaves fall, then winter is at hand; / When the sun sets, who doth not look for night?" (2.3.33–34). When Queen Elizabeth mourns that Richard has destroyed her "poor princes," her "unblown flow'rs," Queen Margaret secretly gloats that he has "dimm'd [the princes'] infant morn to aged night" (4.4.9–16). Before the final battle, Richard makes a threat of lineal extinction that he links to a figurative forestalling of the sunrise, obliging Lord Stanley to "bring his power / Before sunrising, lest his son George fall / Into the blind cave of eternal night" (5.3.60–62). In making himself the enemy of the new generation's rightful inheritance, Richard has thus made himself the enemy of the new day's dawning, and as the battle begins we discover he is actually deprived of natural sunlight:

Richard Who saw the sun to-day?
Ratcliffe   Not I, my lord.
Richard Then he disdains to shine, for by the book
  He should have brav'd the east an hour ago.
  A black day will it be to somebody.
  Ratcliffe!
Ratcliffe   My lord?
Richard   The sun will not be seen to-day,
  The sky doth frown and low'r upon our army.   (5.3.277–83)

It will be a black day to somebody, but not, implicitly, to somebody else on the same field. This is obviously not a case of cloudy weather:

32

it is Richard's own shadow that benights him and his army. The man who prematurely "the day o'ercast" of "The lords at Pomfret" now suffers the same fate at the hands of Richmond, who is assigned by the ghosts of Richard's enemies to "win the day" (3.2.83–86; 5.3.145).

The ghostly figures who help blacken Richard's final day compound their vengeance by ruining his sleep with nightmares; the extension of darkness into the daytime converts the fatal battle into an all-too-real re-enactment of his nightmare. Richard had earlier spoken daringly to Queen Elizabeth, "Myself myself confound! / ... / Day, yield me not thy light, nor, night, thy rest" if his desire to marry her daughter did not spring from "Immaculate devotion, holy thoughts" (4.4.399–405). In the self-confounding nightmare before the battle, Richard is granted his plea. The same enervating combination of extended darkness and sleeplessness within that darkness appears in the curses laid upon Richard by Lady Anne: "Ill rest betide the chamber where thou liest!" and "Black night o'ershade thy day, and death thy life!" (1.2.112, 131). Queen Margaret, too, contributes a curse against Richard's rest: "No sleep close up that deadly eye of thine, / Unless it be while some tormenting dream / Affrights thee with a hell of ugly devils" (1.3.224–26).

Insomnia normally signals guilt or insecurity, and in Shakespeare it attaches particularly to the guilt and insecurity of ambition, as if anyone raised to an unnatural height had to strive constantly to remain there or else plunge fatally back to his original level.[21] Hastings, in a speech that anticipates Henry IV's comparison of his royal wakefulness with the sleep of a boy on a masthead (2 *Henry IV*, 3.1.18–25), thus bemoans the costs of his own worldly ambitions:

> O momentary grace of mortal men,
> Which we more hunt for than the grace of God!
> Who builds his hope in air of your good looks
> Lives like a drunken sailor on a mast,
> Ready with every nod to tumble down
> Into the fatal bowels of the deep.   (3.4.96–101)

But Richard submits to such uneasiness by his own design more than by accident; his ambitions, like those of Macbeth, entail an active decision to murder sleep, and his subsequent restlessness evinces a vengeful reflex in the regenerative order he has consciously offended. His bloody ascent to the throne gives premonitory nightmares to his brother Clarence and Lord Stanley, and rouses both of them (as well as Hastings) from sleep to meet their deaths (1.4.1–

161; 3.2.1–33). When Richard sends the princes to the Tower, the younger brother complains that "I shall not sleep in quiet at the Tower" (3.1.142), and Richard soon arranges to have them smothered in their sleep with their pillows; he justifies the deed to the murderers by calling the princes "Foes to my rest and my sweet sleep's disturbers" (4.2.73). This is the same argument he makes to his troops before the battle of Bosworth Field for killing Richmond's soldiers: "You sleeping safe, they bring to you unrest" (5.3.320). This argument sounds remarkably hollow, since Richard has been the great enemy of sleep, yet we also know that for him it may be true. The nightmares populated by his enemies, by the ghosts he has made into ghosts, have drained his strength, while Richmond is refreshed by a blessed sleep (5.3.129–30, 150, 164–65). Shakespeare's warning, furthermore, seems as effectively self-generating as Richard's horror. No playwright *ex machina* descends to moralize on the hazards of ambition, and none is needed: Richard is destroyed by a nemesis that is practically indistinguishable from his ambition itself.

In his first tetralogy Shakespeare attempts to moralize the War of the Roses into an elaborate pattern of reciprocity—a reciprocity of curses and betrayals, not only between the two factions, but also between mankind and regenerative nature. To make Richard a suitable scapegoat for these evils, however, Shakespeare had to compress all the depredations of ambition into Richard's individual experience. The effort to sustain a moral symmetry by making Richard's inward evil a microcosm of the political evils committed by the Houses of York and Lancaster evidently led Shakespeare to seek psychological parallels to the retribution the two Houses inevitably brought on each other. The necessity of resolving his tetralogy through Edward Hall's "Tudor Myth" may therefore have been the mother of a Shakespearean invention: the symbolic pattern he attaches to ambition throughout his career, where schizophrenia and suicide and crimes against one's own lineage become the inward concomitants of the ambitious impulse.

Richard II

When he returns to this crisis in English history to explore its origins, in *Richard II*, Shakespeare has become a much less formulaic playwright, and he is less committed to building political propaganda out of obvious moral symmetries and the moral lessons they convey.[22] The skeleton of poetic justice, hanging starkly in a sort of anatomy classroom in the first tetralogy, retreats gracefully inside

34

the human form in the second tetralogy. The moral pattern seems to evolve from the human experience of those who arouse and suffer from it, rather than vice versa.

One aspect of this new subtlety and complexity is the absence of a pure villain of ambition, opposed to a pure hero of hereditary order, as Richard and Richmond are opposed in *Richard III*. In *Richard II*, neither side can enlist as its ally, wave as its banner, or wear as its armor the symbolic forces defending lineality; and therefore Shakespeare cannot demarcate either the moral pattern or his moral preference so directly. No one denies that Richard II has properly inherited the throne, but the royal eminence that is the ultimate goal of one sort of ambition is merely the springboard of another sort. His sort of ambitious rebellion, like that of Leontes in *The Winter's Tale*, resembles the fatal error J. M. R. Margeson sees represented

> in the figure of the ruler or king who had dominated the
> Pride of Life moralities. . . . By the very loftiness of his
> position and by the peculiar temptations of his birth-
> right—pride, self-assurance, and luxury—he is tempted
> to a glorification of his own will against any greater will
> or law that might be thought to exist. As A. P. Rossiter
> observes, the king-figure had a peculiar fascination for
> those who lived under the Tudors, since he possessed a
> freedom of thought and action unique in human exis-
> tence.[23]

Latent here is the material for Shakespeare's later exploration of ambition in much broader and morally more equivocal terms than propagandistic attacks on political ambitions would ever have allowed him. For Richard, pride, self-assurance, and luxury unite in the vanity his royal prerogatives nurture. His costly self-indulgences, including his indulgence of Bushy, Bagot, and Green, oblige Richard to distort the royal patrimony (by farming out his rents) and to usurp Henry Herford's patrimony at the death of John of Gaunt. To defend his hereditary rule over the Irish, Richard finds he must disrupt the process of heritage. Henry Herford, in turn, discovers that returning to England to assert his lineal rights leads him toward overthrowing the lineal succession to the throne. Richard's failings as a king have trapped Henry in a classic tragic dilemma, torn between the conflicting commands of two manifestations of his world's godhead—in this case, the hereditary order. Henry could aptly complain, with Hamlet, that it is cursed spite that he was born to set it right; his obligation to strike on his father's behalf puts him in conflict with the very rules that were supposed to defend his birthright and his father. In most of Shakespeare's usurpation plays, the usurper's ambitious disease temporarily afflicts the nation he rules; in *Richard II*, what the king transmits to his subject Herford is the impossible dilemma his rebellious will has created, a dilemma that makes Herford both mirror and scourge of his king's misconduct.

Richard II begins to undermine the traditional order when he forestalls the trial-by-joust of Norfolk and Herford. He justifies this act by insisting that the men are fighting, not out of loyalty as they claim, but rather as a form of civil war, and that their "ambitious thoughts" have "set on you / To wake our peace, which in our country's cradle / Draws the sweet infant breath of gentle sleep" (1.3.129–33). He condemns the enemies' ambition, in other words, as an assault on the combined figure of sleep and infancy that is often the victim of ambition in Shakespeare. It soon becomes clear, however, that Richard is the ungracious pastor who reaks not his own rede. He rouses war, neglects to father an heir, and starves away the hereditary health of John of Gaunt, who complains,

> For sleeping England long time have I watch'd,
> Watching breeds leanness, leanness is all gaunt.
> The pleasure that some fathers feed upon
> Is my strict fast—I mean, my children's looks;
> And therein fasting, hast thou made me gaunt.
> Gaunt am I for the grave, gaunt as a grave,
> Whose hollow womb inherits nought but bones.   (2.1.77–83)

Richard thus becomes responsible for the overthrow of generational blessings by wakefulness, hollowness, and stillbirth. Gaunt expands this personal complaint to the national level in his next speech, accusing Richard of forefeiting his rule by renting out his lands. These violations seem almost capable of disrupting the kingdom's succession retroactively:

> O had thy grandsire with a prophet's eye
> Seen how his son's son should destroy his sons,
> From forth thy reach he would have laid thy shame,
> Deposing thee before thou wert possess'd,
> Which art possess'd now to depose thyself.   (2.1.104–08)

By plucking himself from his own patrimony, Richard is figuratively "possess'd" by a new and alien identity.

Naturally enough, Richard bridles at these assertions, yet promptly proceeds to prove them accurate. York, a defender of traditional

36

values throughout the tetralogy, questions Richard indignantly about his confiscation of Gaunt's legacy to Herford:

> Did not the one deserve to have an heir?
> Is not his heir a well-deserving son?
> Take Herford's rights away, and take from Time
> His charters and his customary rights;
> Let not to-morrow then ensue to-day;
> Be not thyself, for how art thou a king
> But by fair sequence and succession? (2.1.191–99)

This is fair warning: the cycle of day and night is not more natural, and the very business of being oneself depends on sustaining an interwoven set of successions. The play fulfills Gaunt's prophecy when Richard's misconduct renders him as destitute of heirs, of name, and of substance, as the man who puns on his own "gauntness" to emphasize the connections among all three losses (2.1.79–99). No sooner has he seized Gaunt's property than Richard declares, in inadvertently ominous terms, that he has created York governor "in absence of ourself" (2.1.219)—one of many indications that this king has become a thing of nothing, to use Hamlet's phrase (4.2.28–30), by rebelling against the order that made him king. Northumberland blames Richard's deed on the fact that he is "led by flatterers," and that therefore "The King is not himself" (2.1.241–42), but we are invited to recognize that Richard's not being himself is an effect as well as a cause of such misconduct.[24] The royal army subsequently disperses because of rumors that "Richard their king is dead" (2.4.7, 17), rumors that are both symbolically apt and eventually self-fulfilling. Richard despairs of retaining what he now calls his "hollow crown" (3.2.160) when he learns that the army whose blood "Did triumph in my face . . . are fled" (3.2.76–77). This is a deadly emptying of his body politic and, wishing to join his friends "in the hollow ground" of his kingdom, Richard turns to the most gaunt of thoughts:

> Let's choose executors and talk of wills;
> And yet not so, for what can we bequeath
> Save our deposed bodies to the ground?
> Our lands, our lives, and all are Bullingbrook's,
> And nothing can we call our own but death,
> And that small model of the barren earth
> Which serves as paste and cover to our bones. (3.2.140, 148–54)

37

His destruction of Herford's hereditary name and substance has become a form of suicide as it rebounds on him, and his description of his loss recalls Gaunt's portrayal of his grave as a "hollow womb" that "inherits nought but bones." What Gaunt calls "this England, / This nurse, this teeming womb of royal kings," becomes a tomb to which those offspring are returned, and from which no more lineal royalty can be generated.

Richard, like others in Shakespeare whose inward insurrections have cost them their identities, attempts to give figurative birth to a new self to replace the one he foolishly betrayed; but, as in the other cases, this new birth is so alien to the regenerative order that it proves a stillbirth. His queen calls him "King Richard's tomb, / And not King Richard" (5.1.12–13), and out of this tomb he cannot resurrect himself. Instead, Richard fittingly dies from complications in giving birth to Henry as the royal heir. Having killed Gaunt's spirit, name, and heritage in making himself Gaunt's unlineal heir, Richard finds his own life, title, and patrimony forfeited to the man who should have inherited those of Gaunt. The usurpation of the throne entails a twisted form of inheritance—"Cousin, I am too young to be your father, / Though you are old enough to be my heir," Richard tells Henry at the deposition (3.3.204–05)—and a form twisted in a way that suggests poetic justice enforced by the order of paternity itself.

Richard's efforts to recreate his forfeited identity take several forms, but they all share an unnaturalness that makes them futile. If the self cannot be reborn, Shakespeare suggests, neither can it be reconstructed; Richard's body is shattered as irreparably as England's body politic by the sale of rightfully hereditary lands. The Aesculapian task of vivifying a reassembled body proves consistently beyond human powers in Shakespeare. Aumerle encourages Richard to retake England's throne with his scattered loyalists, urging him to "learn to make a body of a limb" (3.2.187), but successful cloning is beyond the abilities of a king who confuses heads with hands, and three men with one or nine, in condemning his former intimates (3.2.132–38). Eventually Richard's tomb-like body finds itself in a tomb-like cell in Pomfret Castle, a barren womb in which he can generate only dreams of a lineal heir: "My brain I'll prove the female to my soul, / My soul the father, and these two beget / A generation of still-breeding thoughts" (5.5.6–8). This self-referential sort of procreation, which Richard describes as a potential substitute for the world he has lost, takes place within a fatally confining womb; anyone seeking rebirth, Shakespeare repeatedly implies, must cut the new identity free from such a womb with what might aptly be called Caesarean fortitude. Richard's still-breeding contemplations compel their own stillbirth: his wording suggests a fetus urged toward freedom, but grown too large to achieve it in the normal way. His musings

> do set the word itself
> Against the word,
> As thus: "Come, little ones," and then again,
> "It is as hard to come as for a camel
> To thread the postern of a small needle's eye."
> Thoughts tending to ambition, they do plot
> Unlikely wonders: how these vain weak nails
> May tear a passage thorough the flinty ribs
> Of this hard world, my ragged prison walls;
> And for they cannot, die in their own pride. (5.5.13–22)

The fragmentary nature of his Biblical texts, excerpted by his gloomily breeding thoughts, is fittingly what prevents him from perceiving any saving unity in the texts. Fragmentation and inwardness forestall physical and spiritual regeneration alike.

The queen's conversation with Bushy and Green in act two, scene two, reinforces, through an extended birth-metaphor, the impression that ambition has distorted the reproductive process in general, and Richard's hope for a lineal heir in specific.[25] She speaks of her womb as populated first by Richard, who has departed, then by sorrow, then by shadows, then by a nameless nothingness, and finally by the royally reborn Bullingbrook. It is roughly the equivalent of a grotesque cinematic dissolve-shot, with the royal figure retreating from our focus into the womb, from which he re-emerges into focus with the face of Henry rather than Richard. Through a series of implied substitutions, much like the ones that made sorrow and Richard the unnatural offspring of barren noble wombs in *Richard III*, Shakespeare suggests the perversion of procreation involved in Richard's eclipse and Henry's emergence as England's ruler.

The queen first speculates that she entertains "such a guest as grief" because she has had to bid "farewell to so sweet a guest / As my sweet Richard." The plausible sexual metaphor of a husband as a temporary guest of the womb, dormant in the queen's parallelism, is awakened when she adds that "Some unborn sorrow, ripe in fortune's womb, / Is coming towards me, and my inward soul / With nothing trembles." Richard and grief, as parallel guests in the queen, and the queen and fortune, as parallel pregnancies, converge toward identity as the conversation continues. Bushy insists that "Each substance of a grief hath twenty shadows, / Which shows like grief itself, but is not so," and that her grief is therefore "nought but shadows." The lurking irony is that Richard's conversion into a shadowy nothing through his violation of the hereditary order, and his related inability to fill her womb with an heir, are themselves the griefs her stirring but empty womb foretells. When Bushy repeats that " 'Tis nothing but conceit, my gracious lady," the queen answers with a revealing analogy to intermitted procreation and inheritance:

> 'Tis nothing less: conceit is still deriv'd
> From some forefather grief; mine is not so,
> For nothing hath begot my something grief,
> Or something hath the nothing that I grieve—
> 'Tis in reversion that I do possess—
> But what it is that is not yet known what,
> I cannot name; 'tis nameless woe, I wot.   (2.2.34–40)

This is inelegant to the point of incoherence, but some of the rhetorical incoherence serves to suggest that all coherence is gone from the hereditary process. The genesis of this grief is ominous, because it lacks a father; it remains nameless for the same reason. When the cause of the premonitory grief finally appears, it turns out to be the damage Richard's violation of paternity has done to his own paternal role as king. As soon as these lines are spoken, Green arrives with the news that Richard has become a king of nothing, without substance or name. In begetting a void in his royal wife's womb, Richard is therefore paradoxically reproducing himself.[26]

As the usurping Richard III became the agent and the physical manifestation of the sorrow bred in Queen Elizabeth's barren womb, so the usurping Henry here becomes the only heir Queen Isabella's false pregnancy can deliver to the throne. Richard, having stolen Henry's name and birthright, is reborn to nothingness, while his name of king and the accompanying birthright revert to Henry. The queen concludes,

> So, Green, thou art the midwife to my woe,
> And Bullingbrook my sorrow's dismal heir.
> Now hath my soul brought forth her prodigy,
> And I, a gasping new-deliver'd mother,
> Have woe to woe, sorrow to sorrow join'd.   (2.2.62–66)

The Duchess of York, who "brought forth less than a mother's hope" (3 Henry VI, 5.6.50), can hardly have been more distressed and revolted by what she saw emerge from her womb. Before he actually dies, the royal Richard fades away, and is unnaturally reincarnated in Bullingbrook, who springs full-grown from England's troubled body politic. The figurative death of King Richard that precedes his physical death is matched by the figurative birth of King Henry that occurs long after his physical birth.

When Henry actually seizes this royal identity, the nothingness and namelessness of the deposed Richard explain and fulfill the queen's vague forebodings. Richard becomes an ever-shifting set of theatrical costumes barely concealing the void beneath. He hints that he will be able to exchange his forfeited "name of king" for the identity of a monk, with all its trappings, but that proves to be merely one of many new Richards who lie stillborn in "A little little grave" (3.3.144–54). When Henry invaded the body politic deeply enough to confront Richard's sovereignty directly, knees, hearts, and eyes became entangled (3.3.190–95), and Richard virtually deconstructs himself when Henry asks whether he is "contented to resign the crown?":

> Ay, no, no ay; for I must nothing be;
> Therefore no no, for I resign to thee.
> Now mark me how I will undo myself:
> I give this heavy weight from off my head,
> And this unwieldy sceptre from my hand,
> The pride of kingly sway from out my heart.　　(4.1.200–06)

These physical parts will be nothing without the royal quality that had interfused them. In a punning response to Bullingbrook's question, Richard demonstrates ironically how void of "content" he will be once he resigns the crown. He will have "no 'I,'" and can only plead with God to "Make me, that nothing have, with nothing griev'd" (4.1.216).

This coincidence of self-alienation, self-fragmentation, and inner nullity, as in *Richard III*, implies that identity is a more precious and elusive prize than the shallow thoughts of ambition recognize: to abandon the hereditary self is to erase all the lines of connection and divison that permit selfhood to exist. The fatal irony, for most of Shakespeare's ambitious protagonists, is that to try to be another person as well as oneself is to be no one at all. Richard's plea, that his griefs might become as trivial as his possessions have become, is granted, but only ironically: like his queen, who bore it in her womb, Richard is horribly "griev'd" by the "nothing" that constitutes his unnatural new self. The pun on the "content" that the king of "nothing" lacks recurs in Richard's dungeon soliloquy, where it is associated with the radically various roles among which this unmoored identity vacillates:

> Thus play I in one person many people,
> And none contented. Sometimes am I king;
> Then treasons make me wish myself a beggar,
> And so I am. Then crushing penury
> Persuades me I was better when a king;
> Then am I king'd again, and by and by
> Think that I am unking'd by Bullingbrook,
> And straight am nothing. But what e'er I be,
> Nor I, nor any man that but man is,
> With nothing shall be pleas'd, till he be eas'd
> With being nothing.   (5.5.31–41)

This is the dark counterpart of the Florentine notion that man was free to determine his own place and stature in the world through the transforming power of his mind. As Alvin Kernan writes, "If the theater is the prime expression of Renaissance humanism's hope about the possibility of changing character, society, and world from what they were formerly thought immutably to be, then it is at the same time an image of fear, of transiency, of insubstantiality and endless mutability."[27] The dream of a glorious new self becomes a nightmare of lost identity for Richard II as for that other great self-dramatizing figure, Richard III, whose last soliloquy, like the one quoted above, is actually a dialogue, a vacillation between polar identities that can end only in an exhausted despair. It is not surprising that both men are obsessed with the images of themselves provided by mirrors and shadows.[28] As Richard III recoils in fear "Lest I revenge. What, myself upon myself?" (5.3.186), a similarly self-alienated and self-betraying Richard II says that "if I turn mine eyes upon myself, / I find myself a traitor with the rest" (4.1.247–48). Ambition has deprived each king of the quality that gave his identity more authenticity, even more reality, than his reflection; each therefore remains divided against himself. Richard II's wish, "that I could forget what I have been! / Or not remember what I must be now!" (3.3.138–39), expresses a problem haunting many of Shakespeare's ambitious protagonists. He cannot even acquire a new name, but only a divided one: the rebels behead the title "King" from the name "Richard," now that he is unable to behead them for doing so, and Richard thereafter despairs of knowing "what name to call myself!" (3.3.6–14; 4.1.255–59).

Henry Bullingbrook's dilemma also expresses itself in a divided name, a name he too must unify to reclaim his full hereditary identity. The severance of Richard's lineal name of king is the natural consequence of a crime against Henry's lineal name:

> *Berkeley* My Lord of Herford, my message is to you.
> *Bullingbrook* My lord, my answer is to Lancaster,
>   And I am come to seek that name in England,
>   And I must find that title in your tongue,
>   Before I make reply to aught you say.   (2.3.69–73)

The bifurcation of self by which Henry evades his banishment is only a sophistic splitting of heirs: "As I was banish'd, I was banish'd Herford, / But as I come, I come for Lancaster." He claims a surrogate father in York, but only for the sake of reclaiming his natural father. All of this fits plausibly under a "claim / To my inheritance of free descent" (2.3.113–36). Even while preparing for the initial duel, Henry addresses his father in terms that keep the rebirth and multiplication of his aspiring spirit within the bounds of hereditary identity:

> O thou, the earthly author of my blood,
> Whose youthful spirit, in me regenerate,
> Doth with a twofold vigor lift me up
> To reach at victory above my head . . . .   (1.3.69–72)

This might be called, in Hal's phrase, "The quarrel of a true inheritor" (*2 Henry IV*, 4.5.168), but it soon leads to a quarrel with the throne's true heir that traps both Henry IV and Henry V in a lifelong struggle to retain the shreds of hereditary identity. *Richard II*, like *Richard III*, describes the standard ailments of the usurper; but by establishing similar symptoms in the rightful king, Shakespeare alerts us to the fact that the ambitious disease punishes all crimes against hereditary identity, all violations of patrimony. The warning against the hazards of rebellion thus becomes a parable about the hazards of ambition. In both the robber of the throne and the robber of the inheritance, the self threatens to disappear into role-playing, and the body threatens war against itself. King Henry's replacement of King Richard, as York's simile indicates (5.2.23–25), is merely a case of one actor replacing another—a better actor, but an actor nonetheless. Bullingbrook's speech sending greetings and demands to the beaten Richard at Barkloughly castle reveals, in its diction and its scrambled metaphors, how badly both men's bodies have been fragmented by their abuses of lineal rights:

> Go to the rude ribs of that ancient castle;
> Through brazen trumpet send the breath of parley
> Into his ruin'd ears, and thus deliver:
> Henry Bullingbrook
> On both his knees doth kiss King Richard's hand,
> And sends allegiance and true faith of heart
> To his most royal person; hither come
> Even at his feet to lay my arms . . .

He goes on to promise that even "while we here march" his "stooping duty tenderly shall show" that it is "far off from the mind of Bullingbrook" that "the wounds of slaughtered Englishmen . . . should bedrench / The fair green lap of fair King Richard's land" (3.3.32–50; see similarly 3.3.57, 72–83). The metaphor of the body politic collides with several other bodily metaphors here, and the result is a grotesque.

This use of the body politic metaphor also suggests ambition's characteristic oppression of the kingdom's vegetative health, and again both men are implicated in that oppression. Richard tells Bullingbrook that

> ere the crown he looks for live in peace,
> Ten thousand bloody crowns of mothers' sons
> Shall ill become the flower of England's face,
> Change the complexion of her maid-pale peace
> To scarlet indignation, and bedew
> Her pasters' grass with faithful English blood.   (3.3.95–100)

He goes on to warn that his tears and sighs "shall lodge the summer corn, / And make a dearth in this revolting land." But in the very next scene the Gardener moralizes heavy-handedly about Richard's own failures to tend the national garden. Richard's cropping of the "too long withered flower" John of Gaunt (2.1.134) without allowing him to transfer his life to a scion causes the "fair rose" Richard himself to "wither," despite his queen's effort to "dew" him with tears (5.1.8–10).

Richard's speech exemplifies Shakespeare's tendency to associate an agricultural blight with a disruption of the procreative order. In returning from banishment to claim his hereditary lands, Henry necessarily violates the king's hereditary rights over England as a whole, and becomes another ambitious figure whose multiple names and fragmented body result from an enforced rebirth of the self. He arrives in England promising to reward his supporters once "my

infant fortune comes to years" (2.3.66). York explains that he has
"labor'd all I could" to restore Bullingbrook's rightful patrimony,
but condemns him for seeking to "be his own carver and cut out
his way"; York fears that "the issue of these arms" may be the
overthrow of the king himself (2.3.142–52). The danger, in other
words, is that Henry's aspiration to a royal identity will replace the
natural progress of "labor" with the unnatural Caesarean means of
"issue." The loyalist Carlisle warns at the deposition that a violation
of the royal birthright will bring with it a devastation of the kingdom's agriculture (4.1.134–49, 322–23). One result is that, when
rebels arise against Henry's own kingship, he cannot "weed" them
out because they are "enrooted" with his friends, and his land is
therefore "like an offensive wife" that "holds his infant up" to prevent his blows (2 *Henry IV*, 4.1.203–12).

Ambition again makes it difficult to save the national garden
without destroying its human offspring in the Aumerle subplot. The
Duchess of York describes Henry's reign as a "new-come spring"
whose "green lap" is strewn with violets, but her husband reminds
their son to "bear you well in this new spring of time, / Lest you be
cropp'd before you come to prime" (5.2.46–51). However, by avoid-
ing the error the Gardener condemned in Richard, who allowed the
prodigal scions to destroy their parents' fertility, Henry risks destroying the continuity of family and of selfhood, in his subjects as
well as in himself. When his letter reveals his regicidal plot, Aumerle
can only plead, "read not my name there, / My heart is not confed-
erate with my hand" (5.2.58, 65–68, 5.3.52–53); he eradicates his
own name by dividing his body into opposed factions. Later in the
act, his father contracts a similar disease, his mouth (according to
his wife) clashing with his breast in his plea that their familial and
parental names be eradicated (5.3.90–102). The same problem soon
afflicts the Groom, whose "heart shall say" what his "tongue dares
not" (5.5.97), and Henry himself, who wishes against his own will
that someone would "divorce this terror from my heart" and then
blames the "fatal hand" that put the deed "upon my head," despite
the fact that the suggestion came "From your own mouth," as Exton
says (5.4.7–10; 5.6.34–40). Henry's disturbance of the hereditary
order has created a world where such bodily disharmony is all too
reflective of the divided body politic, and where the cry, "O loyal
father of a treacherous son!" is all too typical of the conflict now
possible between parent and child. In fact, the Duke of York is
trapped in very much the same dilemma that troubles Lord Talbot
in *1 Henry VI*: either his family name will be eradicated by his only

son's death, or it will be ruined by the disgrace that would live with that son. The world has become poisonous to lineal health. If his son is pardoned, York complains,

> he shall spend my honor with his shame,
> As thriftless sons their scraping fathers' gold.
> Mine honor lives when his dishonor dies,
> Or my sham'd life in his dishonor lies:
> Thou kill'st me in his life; giving him breath,
> The traitor lives, the true man's put to death. (5.3.68–73)

We have come full circle from Gaunt's plea that his son be pardoned so that Gaunt himself may live. York's loyalty to his merely adopted son Henry takes absolute precedence over his loyalty to his natural son Aumerle.[29]

Shakespeare chooses to fill the brief interval between the discovery of this treason at the Duke of York's palace, and the arrival of the principals to expose or excuse it to the king at Windsor Castle, with Henry's first complaint about his own "unthrifty son" (5.3.1). The wording of this complaint, and its placement between the two halves of the subplot, seem clearly intended to establish a parallel between the disorder Henry's usurpation has created in the noble families around him, and the disorder that arises in his own line of succession. York's "thriftless" son is all too similar to Henry's "unthrifty" one, at least on the surface. Aumerle's determination to kill Henry creates an essentially Oedipal conflict, since (according to York) either the father or the son must now kill the other. This life-and-death struggle, partly figurative in York's speech, threatens to become literal in the actions of Prince Hal, for whom the regicide would also be a patricide. Aumerle's two linked offenses condense into the figure of the rebellious Hal, whose faults are described for us in the midst of the Aumerle story. During the crown-stealing scene in 2 Henry IV, which is the starkest explication of Hal's apparent Oedipal destructiveness, Henry bemoans the bitter trap of paternity in much the same terms York uses, describing the son as a murderous wastrel of the father's hard-earned treasure:

> This part of his conjoins with my disease,
> And helps to end me. See, sons, what things you are!
> How quickly nature falls into revolt
> When gold becomes her object!
> For this the foolish over-careful fathers
> Have broke their sleep with thoughts, their brains with care,

Their bones with industry. . . .

. . . . .

We bring it to the hive, and like the bees,
Are murd'red for our pains. This bitter taste
Yields his engrossments to the ending father.   (4.5.63–79)

By describing the point of contention as "gold," instead of specifying the golden crown, Henry conveniently evades acknowledging the justice of his having to endure disobedience. But Hal is clearly the embodiment of his father's ambition: it is Hal who now breaks the father's sleep with a version of Henry's own deed, which Henry might have lain awake devising a few years earlier.

As Hal is here part of Henry's "disease," so in the *Richard II* passage is he the "plague" (5.3.3.) that hangs over his father. In both cases, the medical allusion instructs us to understand Hal as an internal insurrection in Henry, a revolt of his own flesh-and-blood, parallel to the ongoing national insurrection against his reign. The outward and inward problems of usurpation in Shakespeare are condensed into the figure of Hal, whose filial disobedience gives aid and comfort to the rebels, illness to the unlineal king. Two reciprocal metaphors were commonplace among the Elizabethans. One described illness as a microcosmic political rebellion within the human body; its counterpart described political rebellion as a macrocosmic illness within the body politic. In *Richard II* the two metaphors work in tandem, because Hal, the symbolic extension of the rebellion, both derives from and afflicts King Henry's body. The dual nature of Aumerle's murderous rebellion—against his father and against his king—forbids us to oversimplify the relationship between the two sorts of insurrection Henry faces. Neither the political version of the pattern, in which the usurper is usurped, nor the familial side of the pattern, in which the disobedient son is disobeyed, can be dismissed as merely a metaphor for the other. Instead, each contributes to a pattern of universal and ineluctable poetic justice; each is a necessary manifestation of a single deeper disturbance.

The *Henry IV* Plays

At the end of *Richard II*, Shakespeare's ambitious figures become versions of primal criminals such as Oedipus and Cronus, whose myths associate father/son rivalry with political rebellion. The Henry IV plays use this association to study the evolution of filial identity,

47

the individual's imperative and dangerous growth toward sovereignty. Here, even more elaborately than in *The Tempest*, Shakespeare offers a sort of morality play about an individual's moral and psychological development; but while it may be helpful to make that allegory explicit in a systematic, Freudian way, it is crucial to remember that the playwright uses it as a merely subliminal resonance to his analysis of ambition. Shakespeare exploits his deterministic power over his play-world to simulate a divinely determined world in which ambition is limited by the constitution of the individual as well as the universe. The psychoanalytic allegory which seems to arise naturally from the narrative events is one more way in which Shakespeare makes us feel that there are deep moral imperatives, not only in the universe but also in its human microcosm, for ambition's rise and fall. A coherent pattern attaches to ambition, which may be experienced in similar ways by an individual psyche at one phase in its development, and by English society at a crisis in its historical evolution. In the Henry IV plays, the private and public experiences of ambition are not only congruent, they are simultaneous, and mutually causal.

The rebels in the Henry IV plays suffer their own versions of the ambitious syndrome when they try to replace the reigning king. In *1 Henry IV*, Hotspur and Worcester discuss in suggestive terms the news that Northumberland will not appear for the battle. Hotspur argues that his father will therefore provide

> A rendezvous, a home to fly unto,
> If that the devil and mischance look big
> Upon the maidenhead of our affairs.
> *Worcester* But yet I would your father had been here.
> The quality and hair of our attempt
> Brooks no division.   (4.1.57–62)

Worcester's fear makes practical sense, but it also reminds us that Northumberland's absence constitutes the sort of bodily division that generally disables Shakespeare's rebels: It is "a very limb lopp'd off" (4.1.43), as Hotspur momentarily admits. When Hotspur subsequently boasts that "our joints are whole," and Douglas rejoins, "As heart can think," the statement is as self-contradictory as Douglas's restatement of the idea: "There is not such a word / Spoke of in Scotland as this term of fear" (4.1.83–85). The Scot has just spoken the word, and the notion of joints as whole as heart can think suggest an unhealthy jumbling of limbs, breast, and brains. The threat to this rebellion's birth is all the greater because Northumberland is figuratively the father of rebellion in these plays, and literally the father of Hotspur, who embodies the rebellious spirit. Without the father's presence at "the maidenhead," the insurrection seems doomed to a sinister, unnatural sort of birth.

In *2 Henry IV*, the implication that rebellion is born only through a dangerous distortion of the procreative process becomes more explicit. Lord Bardolph worries that unless Northumberland's forces arrive, the rebellion will resemble a man's "part-created" construction that must be left "A naked subject to the weeping clouds" of "churlish winter's tyranny." Though the analogy is to the building of an over-ambitious house, the lines immediately following encourage us to recognize the suggestion, on a secondary level, of an infant exposed to the winter by a paternal tyrant, as Oedipus was by Laius, or Perdita by Leontes. Hastings answers:

> Grant that our hopes (yet likely of fair birth)
> Should be still-born, and that we now possess'd
> The utmost man of expectation,
> I think we are so a body strong enough,
> Even as we are, to equal with the King.   (1.3.60–67)

In the same speech, Lord Bardolph also worries about the empty naming and the vegetative death that often accompany rebellion: an insurrection that uses "the names of men in stead of men," he argues,

> Lives so in hope, as in an early spring
> We see th' appearing buds, which to prove fruit
> Hope gives not so much warrant, as despair
> That frosts will bite them.   (1.3.57, 38–41)

The abnormal and premature birth of this uprising generates a nemesis consisting of stillbirth, paternal vengeance, diseased nature, disconnected names, and discordant bodies.

In *1 Henry IV* Glendower portrays his birth as another archetypal perversion of procreation. The archetype here is not a bodily rivalry with the father that must end in stillbirth or infant exposure, but rather the self-induced Caesarean birth by which the father may be overcome. Such a birth—though, significantly, it is merely a boast in Glendower's case—sometimes signals a classical or Renaissance hero's determination to conquer his natural limitations, to surpass his hereditary constraints. When Glendower claims that various disturbances of nature "mark'd me extraordinary" and above "the

49

common roll of men" at his birth, Hotspur replies with a sarcastic, degraded version of Glendower's personal myth:

> Diseased nature oftentimes breaks forth
> In strange eruptions; oft the teeming earth
> Is with a kind of colic pinch'd and vex'd
> By the imprisoning of unruly wind
> Within her womb, which, for enlargement striving,
> Shakes the old beldame earth, and topples down
> Steeples and moss-grown towers. At your birth
> Our grandam earth, having this distemp'rature,
> In passion shook. (3.1.26–34)

Hotspur has twisted Glendower's analogy between his mother's labor and the world's eruptions, which carries with it an implicit claim to autochthonic birth, into its least appealing form—a form which also allows Hotspur to dismiss Glendower's boast, by metaphor as well as tone, as merely hot air, of a particularly unattractive sort.

Figures in English Renaissance literature whose ambitions compel them to claim autogenous or autochthonic status often claim this sort of birth: they carve their own way out of mother-earth in an eruption of air, and in doing so they topple down the old towers or trees of paternal sexual authority. Such births, or rebirths, are in both senses Caesarean.[30] Tamburlaine makes a new self by martial assertion, disdaining his "parentage" in order to command a thunderous army who "make the mountains quake, / Even as when windy exhalations, / Fighting for passage, tilt within the earth."[31] Spenser's autochthonic giant Orgoglio, the embodiment of pride and partner of the sexually sinister Duessa, performs a figuratively Oedipal attack to permit his own Caesarean rebirth:

> The greatest Earth his uncouth mother was,
>   And blustring Aeolus his boasted sire,
>   Who with his breath, which through the world doth pas,
>   Her hollow womb did secretly inspire,
>   And fild her hidden caves with stormie yre,
>   That she conceiv'd.

This derivation makes it all the more suggestive that "all the earth for terrour seemd to shake, / And trees did tremble" when Orgoglio advances on Redcrosse. The giant tears "a snaggy Oke ... Out of his mothers bowelles," and swings its so hard that he could strike down "a stony towre"; the wind from that "thundring" swing, clearly analogous to the force that originally conceived him, strikes down

50

his rival for Duessa (I.vii.7–14).[32] When "his dreadfull club" reaches his mother-earth, he seems to be planting himself to reenact his birth by his own power:

> The idle stroke, enforcing furious way,
> . . . . .
> So deepely dinted in the driven clay,
> That three yardes deepe a furrow up did throw:
> The sad earth wounded with so sore assay,
> Did grone full grievous underneath the blow,
> And trembling with strange feare, did like an
> earthquake show. (I.viii.8)

The next stanza compares this blow to Jove's lightning—an impregnating force in myth—which "making way, / Both loftie towres and highest trees hath rent, / And all that might his angrie passage stay, / And shooting in the earth, casts up a mound of clay." But Orgoglio's club becomes stuck there, permitting Redcrosse to cut off the arm of the giant, whose resulting howls suggest sexual suffering, (I.viii.10–11). Toppled towers and severed arms are still towers and arms in the poem, of course, as cigars in dreams may represent cigars. But the close coincidence of these Oedipal and Caesarean motifs strikes me as significant, particularly because it occurs so consistently in the context of ambitious quests for heroic rebirth.

Milton's Satan is evidence that this archetype survives through Shakespeare's lifetime, and again the creature boasting of rebirth is a creature determined to claim that his own energies have conquered the derivativeness, and hence the fatedness, that limited his aspirations. By his incestuous conspiracy with the parthenogenetic Sin, and with their son Death who so resembles his father, Satan has made an open highway in the windy space beneath the earth, where he himself

> Toil'd out my uncouth passage, forc't to ride
> Th' untractable Abyss, plung'd in the womb
> Of unoriginal *Night* and *Chaos* wild,
> That jealous of thir secrets fiercely oppos'd
> My journey strange, with clamorous uproar
> Protesting Fate supreme. (Book X, 475–80)[33]

The birth of the rebel Glendower, which Shakespeare revises from Holinshed's account toward this archetype, associates him with a tradition of windy, ambitious, and self-induced rebirths; the efforts of Richard III, Henry IV, Macbeth, and Coriolanus to carve out their own passages to glory may be associated with, and moralized by, the same sexually fraught tradition.

Other symptoms of the ambitious ailment afflict these rebels. When he hears of his son's death in the failed insurrection, Northumberland himself becomes a furious rebel, calling for an end to natural order, individual identity, and family harmony, in a world that has become merely a stage (2 *Henry IV*, 1.1.153–59). His allies urge him to eradicate rather than exaggerate those characteristic ailments of their cause. If he will join forces with the Archbishop of York, the instinct against rebellion that rendered his son's troops divided creatures and lifeless shadows can be reversed:

> *Morton* My lord your son had only but the corpse,
> But shadows and the shows of men, to fight;
> For that same word, rebellion, did divide
> The action of their bodies from their souls.   (1.1.192–95)

The archbishop would prefer to blame the ambitious syndrome— the disruption of time's normal order and humanity's normal form— on Henry's bad fatherhood. In repressing his subjects' pleas, Henry has bred a multiheaded and sleepless son in their place:

> The time misord'red doth, in common sense,
> Crowd us and crush us to this monstrous form
> To hold our safety up. I sent your Grace
> The parcels and particulars of our grief,
> The which hath been with scorn shov'd from the court,
> Whereon his Hydra son of war is born,
> Whose dangerous eyes may well be charm'd asleep
> With grant of our most just and right desires.   (4.2.32–40)

Unless the bad son Henry becomes the good father Henry by such concessions, Hastings adds, this unnatural procreation of Hydras through death will permanently replace England's life-giving process of generational succession: "And so success of mischief shall be born, / And heir from heir shall hold his quarrel up / Whiles England shall have generation" (4.2.47–49). Inheritance thus becomes a blight on birth, a doubling and redoubling of miscarriages.

The rebels revealingly describe Henry's violation of his own heritage and Richard's as an archetypal parricide, with themselves in the role of abused parent rather than abusive child:

> *Worcester* ... being fed by us you us'd us so
> As that ungentle gull, the cuckoo's bird,

Useth the sparrow; did oppress our nest,
Grew by our feeding to so great a bulk
That even our love durst not come near your sight
For fear of swallowing.   (*1 Henry IV*, 5.1.59–64)

The simile uses Henry's warlike approach to confirm his identity as an unlineal child, and even implies that he acts this way precisely because he knows he is not a natural heir. Worcester concludes by telling Henry that he and his fellow-rebels "stand opposed by such means / As you yourself have forg'd against yourself," and when Henry compares himself to a father-bee murdered by the child (Prince Hal) he has fed to strength, we recognize that Worcester was speaking more wisely than he was aware of.

Henry answers by dismissing these accusations as merely "the garment of rebellion" and the "water-colors" that "impaint" their excuse for insurrection; he thus locates the rebellion in the realms of costuming and painting that so often characterize ambitious identity in Shakespeare. This accusation, too, rebounds on Henry, without losing its validity as an accusation, when the king becomes a thing of costumes and colors at Shrewsbury:

Hotspur A gallant knight he was, his name was Blunt,   .
    Semblably furnish'd like the King himself.
Douglas A fool go with thy soul, whither it goes!
    A borrowed title hast thou bought too dear.
    Why didst thou tell me that thou wert a king?
Hotspur The King hath many marching in his coats.
Douglas Now, by my sword, I will kill all his coats;
    I'll murder all his wardrop, piece by piece,
    Until I meet the King.   (5.3.20–28)

Douglas's remarks carry several unpleasant implications for Henry: first, that his own "borrowed title" of king may prove as costly an acquisition as it was for Blunt, and second, that the kingship may itself be only a wardrobe, clothes with no emperor, since his own act of usurpation has made the royal identity so easy to transfer and divide. When Douglas finally discovers King Henry beneath the colors that have become a disguise rather than a proclamation of identity, he finds him only by a process of elimination that is easily mistaken for a process of multiplication:

Douglas Another king? they grow like Hydra's heads.
    I am the Douglas, fatal to all those
    That wear those colors on them. What art thou
    That counterfeit'st the person of a king?

Kinship and Kingship

> *King* The King himself, who, Douglas, grieves at heart
> So many of his shadows thou hast met
> And not the very King.   (5.4.25–31)

Again Douglas raises troubling questions for King Henry. Is there actually any "very King" to be met, in the aftermath of a usurpation, or is there merely an assemblage of borrowed robes, painted colors, and two-dimensional shadows? Is "The King himself" yet one more ordinary mortal "That counterfeit'st the person of a king," as Henry's answer can be taken to imply?

Douglas alludes to Hydra merely to express his exasperation at the fact that each time he beheads a king, two new kings seem to appear. But this allusion may also serve to remind us that Henry has pitted himself against the same sort of unbeatable foe. By causing the assassination of the one rightful king, he has created two heads (as the factions are often called) that are vying for the throne; if the kingship has Hydra's heads, it is because Henry has initiated a splitting of identity that his counterfeits at Shrewsbury nicely symbolize. The myth of Hydra, at least in the Henry IV plays, seems to be a cautionary myth about inheritance: Hydra resembles a gruesome family tree, and the monster that must be quelled is the fraternal strife that would arise over the division of property each time a person died, were there no system of legacies. Civilization successfully represses this monster until Richard and Henry unleash it by violating that system, leaving each legacy open to deadly contention. Shakespeare reveals an England resembling the primal societies described in Freud's *Totem and Taboo* and Girard's *Violence and the Sacred*, societies whose rituals are essential to prevent an endless competition for patrimonies and an endless reciprocity of violence.[34] Some seventy lines before the archbishop blames Henry's misdeeds for generating "this Hydra son of war," Shakespeare prepares us to understand the allusion's larger implications by having the archbishop argue that Henry will not dare to execute the rebels after a negotiated peace, "For he hath found to end one doubt by death / Revives two greater in the heirs of life" (4.1.197–98). As Henry's "buried fear . . . Richard of Burdeaux" (*Richard II*, 5.6.31–33) produces the warring heads of Henry and Mortimer, and as Henry's death is expected to produce a war between Hal and some rival, so will the heirs of the archbishop's rebels second their fathers' rebellion, and their heirs will second the seconding, and so on through eternity (4.2.45–49). That is precisely what we see in Shakespeare's version of the War of the Roses, until Richmond cauterizes the

54

wound in God's order (as Hercules cauterized Hydra's severed neck), and thus turns the two heads—the two Houses—miraculously into one.

Henry V's succession provides an interim solution by setting legacies back on a lineal track. That may help explain why Shakespeare has Canterbury describe the miraculous transmigration of Henry IV's solemn virtue into his son, concurrent with the transfer of the royal body politic, as a glorious conquest of "Hydra-headed willfulness" (*Henry V*, 1.1.24–37). Until his glorious transformation, though, Hal is the unnatural "Hydra son" who threatens to become simultaneously the royal heir and the enemy of royal heritage at his father's death. Hal vacillates repeatedly between his disobedient Eastcheap identity and a noble filial identity. When Hal inherits the unlineal crown, he faces the Herculean task of uniting those conflicting identities, as good and bad son, and as subject and monarch, into a single natural successor. Two crucial scenes, in which Henry's conflict with Hal parallels Hal's conflict with himself, prepare us to recognize the ethical imperatives of that task.

Act three, scene two, of *1 Henry IV* begins with Henry's interpreting Hal's misbehavior as a divine punishment for his own misdeeds. Though Henry, as usual, pretends to be slightly uncertain what his own crime might have been, a son's rebellious refusal to rise to the level of his royal blood would be an entirely appropriate rebuke to his father's rebellious insistence on rising to claim that royal heritage. The psychoanalytic maxim that the bad son has bad sons, and the physical maxim that what goes up must come down, both work to subvert Henry's hopes for a royal heir:

> I know not whether God will have it so
> For some displeasing service I have done,
> That in his secret doom, out of my blood,
> He'll breed revengement and a scourge for me;
> But thou dost in thy passages of life
> Make me believe that thou art only mark'd
> For the hot vengeance, and the rod of heaven,
> To punish my mistreadings. Tell me else,
> Could such inordinate and low desires,
> Such poor, such bare, such lewd, such mean attempts,
> Such barren pleasures, rude society,
> As thou art match'd withal and grafted to,
> Accompany the greatness of thy blood,
> And hold their level with thy princely heart? (3.2.4–17)

55

This insistence on blood finding its own level may be Henry's effort to bluster away the fact that "his blood was poor" until he stepped "a little higher than his vow" and usurped Richard's throne (4.3.75–76). Hal's "affections" may indeed "hold a wing / Quite from the flight of all thy ancestors," making him "almost an alien to the hearts / Of all the court and princes of my blood" (3.2.29–35), but Henry is also on an errant flight from his hereditary place. The system rights itself from within: in the very act of being a punitively bad son to Henry, Hal is said to resemble Richard, to stand "in that very line" of the man whose right it was to place his likeness on the throne (3.2.85–94).[35]

As Henry becomes caught up in the excitement of scolding his son, his language reveals a recognition that this throne is actually founded on such externalities as costume rather than such internalities as blood. He boasts of clothing himself in the simulation of an inward virtue, and of maintaining his person as if it were a borrowed garment: he won the people's affection when he "dress'd myself in such humility / That I did pluck allegiance from men's hearts," yet retained their respect by keeping "my person fresh and new, / My presence like a robe pontifical . . ." (3.2.51–56).[36] Marvell's warning to Cromwell in the "Horation Ode" that "The same arts that did gain / A power must it maintain" (lines 119–20) seems applicable to Henry here: he discovers that the kingship gained by replacing a natural identity with an artificial one, replacing a person with a garment, can only be maintained by his remaining a polished costume rather than an authentic human being.

The redefinition of kingship implicit in Henry's usurpation is inextricably linked to a redefinition of identity, and one result is that not only Hal, but Sir Walter Blunt, and even Jack Falstaff, can play the role of King Henry IV with some success (2.4, 5.3). If Hal is what his father here calls him abusively, "the shadow of succession," there is good reason for it (3.2.99). Even Hal's promise that he "shall hereafter . . . / Be more myself" (3.2.93) has ironic overtones as a response to his father's criticisms, since Henry has just finished arguing that he won the throne by retaining an artificial self, or at least an artificial distance from himself. Whether it is Hal's irony or Shakespeare's, Henry's effort to define a true heir is trapped in a contradiction of his own making.

Finally the king manages to express his ultimate fear, the fear that uncivil disobedience (such as defying a banishment) will become outright murderous rebellion (such as killing a king). The way Henry expresses this fear suggests that he is projecting his own guilty

56

deeds onto Hal, and thus conflating the roles of bad son and bad subject:

> But wherefore do I tell these news to thee?
> Why, Harry, do I tell thee of my foes,
> Which art my nearest and dearest enemy?
> Thou that art like enough, through vassal fear,
> Base inclination, and the start of spleen,
> To fight against me under Percy's pay,
> To dog his heels and curtsy at his frowns,
> To show how much thou art degenerate. (3.2.121–28)

One of the psychoanalytic tenets about this play is that "Hotspur's rebellion represents also Prince Hal's unconscious parricidal impulses. Hotspur is the Prince's double."[37] If this is so, then Hal's denial of his father's accusation represents a classic Freudian compensation-mechanism: the son's avowed wish to protect the father is really a response to his forbidden desire to destroy that father.[38] But whether events at Shrewsbury simply demonstrate Hal's filial loyalty, or whether they allegorically anatomize the psychological struggle that precedes and permits such loyalty, the crucial fact is that Hal re-establishes his identity as a true son by defeating Hotspur. He does so, on the figurative level, by retreating with that patricidal alter ego to an earlier developmental phase. There they both struggle for Caesarean rebirth with their swords, both seeking glory, but seeking opposite sorts of glory. Separated from his father, rebelling, "this Hotspur, Mars in swathling clothes, / This infant warrior" (3.2.112–13), is doomed to stillbirth in his own blood with his noble name revoked. Hal, in contrast, reverses the usual dangerous pattern of Caesarean rebirth, since his rebirth entails reclaiming, not evading, his lineage:

> I will redeem all this on Percy's head,
> And in the closing of some glorious day
> Be bold to tell you that I am your son,
> When I will wear a garment all of blood,
> And stain my favors in a bloody mask,
> Which wash'd away shall scour my shame with it. (3.2.132–37)

The king is right to take this as a complete answer to the indictment at hand. Hal has discovered a way to prove his royal merit while reconciling blood with garments, and the hereditary self with the adopted self. By drawing the battle back to that quasi-infantile stage, Hal can undo his status as an inferior changeling for "this same child of honor and renown, / This gallant Hotspur" (3.2.139–40). Now it is Hotspur who is abandoned by his father, and Hal who has recovered a healthy lineal identity. The son who was, in several senses, "degenerate," is now, in the same senses, regenerate.

The same pair of intermingled confrontations—Henry against Hal, and Hal's loyalty against a representation of his rebelliousness—appears again in 2 Henry IV, during the crown-stealing sequence (4.5). Shakespeare's willingness to resurrect the doubts that were apparently put to rest by the end of Part One, and to retain so many elements of the first confrontation, suggests that he considered the psycho-symbolic situation very fruitful for exploring his theme. Again the Oedipal threat arises to punish Henry's usurpation, and again the suppression of that threat, by re-enlisting Hal in a healthy filial role, prepares for the martial victory that will affirm the new royal family's place on the throne.

Through most of Part Two, Hal's filial identity is badly in doubt. He is right, both on a personal and a symbolic level, to break Falstaff's head "for liking his father to a singing-man of Windsor" (2.1.89–90): the comparison implies that Henry is a eunuch,[39] his procreative powers ruined like those of Shakespeare's other usurpers, and that Hal therefore cannot be his authentic son or a legitimate successor. In the next scene Hal is reminded that the world still thinks his ambitions and rebelliousness preclude his mourning his father's illness (2.2.39–57). This observation grows out of banter about the ways "kindreds are mightily strengthen'd" by illegitimate births, and leads into two discussions about the ambitious ways people distort their kinship. First, Poins mocks people who seize every conceivable occasion to mention some distant consanguinity with the royal family (2.2.110–18); then Hal mocks Poins for his rumored plan to marry Hal to Poins's sister (2.2.127–41). These ambitious claims to royal kinship are recognizable versions, and hence recognizably symptoms, of Henry's unlineal usurpation and the national disease it caused. Hal, in Eastcheap, is trying to cure that disease by actions precisely opposite to the ambitious claims: he evades his close kinship with Henry, and avoids close contact with the seat of royal power. Naturally his father is unable to recognize the corrective character of this conduct, and the misunderstanding over this paradox sets the stage for the crown-stealing confrontation.

As the scene begins, Henry's visage reveals the ambitious man's emptiness and mutability: "His eye is hollow, and he changes much" (4.5.6). Hal is greeted with the information that "The King your father is dispos'd to sleep," but he soon reminds his father that sleep is forbidden to the ambitious, and reminds us why it is forbidden. Slumber in an unnaturally elevated position—whether literally, as a boy on a masthead (3.1.18–20; cf. *Richard III*, 3.4.99), or figuratively, as a man wrongfully on a throne—is both difficult and dangerous. As soon as Henry lets go, yields to that natural urge to relax, he also implicitly yields to his natural self, and the crown is taken from him. Hal describes the crown as "so troublesome a bedfellow" (4.5.22), as if it were a restless spouse in the king's bed, then steals that spouse from the king's pillow where it was supposed to remain until death did them part. Again the Oedipal overtones are clear, and again they serve a broader purpose than providing a fragmentary psychoanalysis of a character. The fact that Hal must steal his father's "bedfellow" in order to create his royal new self is the most incisive condemnation of his self-promoting impulse.[40]

Henry's response when he awakens sharpens our awareness of an Oedipal pattern, adding to the hint of mother-son incest a clear accusation of patricidal impulses (4.5.63–79) and the suggestion that these impulses have been abetted by a subconsciously chosen error of recognition: "Is he so hasty that he doth suppose / My sleep my death?" (4.5.60–61). The patricidal implications would doubtless have been strengthened for much of the audience by the precedent of *The Famous Victories of Henry V*, in which Hal comes to the brink of actually murdering his father for the crown. Henry's first words to his returning son verify that the mechanisms described in Freud's theories about errors and about the Oedipal impulse are both at work here:

> *Hal* I never thought to hear you speak again.
> *Henry* Thy wish was father, Harry, to that thought:
>   I stay too long by thee, I weary thee.
>   Dost thou so hunger for mine empty chair
>   That thou wilt needs invest thee with my honors
>   Before thy hour be ripe? O foolish youth,
>   Thou seek'st the greatness that will overwhelm thee.
>
> (4.5.91–97)

The wording of this reproach points to all the symptoms of overreaching in Shakespeare, and as Henry points out, Hal's overhasty seizure of the crown would indeed convert what could be a natural inheritance into another usurpation. Hal would, in taking the bedfellow-crown, be fathering his own wishes into substance; he would therefore, like his father, be a sort of ghost or void while seated in that royal place, as a secondary reading of line 94 suggests. He might eventually have to ask, as Richard III does after battling and seducing his way to the throne, "is the chair empty?" (4.4.469). Hal's acquisition of these honors under such circumstances would be, again like his father's, a mere investiture, an act of costuming; and it would preclude Hal's ever becoming fully "ripe" for the throne, since Shakespeare generally suggests that a life forcibly cut off from its source cannot be given vital growth again (see *Othello*, 5.2.13–15; *King Lear*, 4.2.34–36). Whether Shakespeare is merely using Henry's speech to remind us of these hazards, or whether he intends us to believe that Henry is at least subliminally aware and expressive of them, the cluster of suggestive wordings at such a crucial moment in the transfer of identities seems significant.

Hal, for his part, hastens to re-establish his position as a natural successor, combining his answer to the charge of ambition with an answer to the charge of patricidal intentions:

> Accusing it, I put it on my head,
> To try with it, as with an enemy
> That had before my face murdered my father,
> The quarrel of a true inheritor. (4.5.165–68)

Again, a Freudian might argue that the son who imagines avenging his father's murder derives his pleasure from the premise of the fantasy, and adds the vengeance as a compensatory cover. But Henry is well satisfied with this answer, and asserts that Hal, because he is "a true inheritor," will be spared the unrest and mere theatricality of his father's reign:

> All these bold fears
> Thou seest with peril I have answered;
> For all my reign hath been but as a scene
> Acting that argument. And now my death
> Changes the mood, for what in me was purchas'd
> Falls upon thee in a more fairer sort;
> So thou the garland wear'st successively. (4.5.195–201)

Even this formulation, of course, depicts kingship as a garment, rather than an immanence, to be inherited; and Hal enjoys only a partial immunity to the ambitious disease as a lineal heir to an unlineal throne. His very first lines as king indicate that, as in Macbeth (5.2.20–22), the giant robes of majesty hang incongruously on a successor of questionable legitimacy: "This new and gorgeous garment, majesty, / Sits not so easy on me as you think" (5.2.44–

45). Even his heart and its inmost filial sorrow are tainted by the theatrical world his father's role as player-king created:

> Yet be sad, good brothers,
> For by my faith it very well becomes you.
> Sorrow so royally in you appears
> That I will deeply put the fashion on
> And wear it in my heart. (5.2.49–53)

The difficulty in discerning what is sincere feeling here and what is acting alerts us to the fact that this world has only been partly redeemed from its artificialities, and that it will be virtually impossible to return it to a Golden Age. The nation's loss of innocence about identity, like the ambitious man's loss of self that often causes it in Shakespeare, is extremely difficult to reverse.

Perhaps the terrible difficulties that critics have in agreeing on who Hal really is provide a good measure of Shakespeare's success in portraying a world where moral distinctions and distinct identities have clouded simultaneously.[41] Is Hal entirely a cynical manipulator of his Eastcheap companions, or does he truly enjoy their kind of life and their version of friendship until the time comes when he must abandon them? Is he a ruthless king, or merely a king who must avoid thinking sentimentally about individuals so that he can be kind to his kingdom as a whole? Significantly, these questions about Hal's personality are intimately connected with questions about his legitimacy as a king (over France as well as England) and as a son (to Falstaff as well as Henry). The problems of kingship and kinship remain as deeply interwoven as they were in *Richard III*.

One index to the elusiveness of Hal's identity is the number of different names he is given; one indication of his peculiar genius is the way he converts this multiplicity, which shatters Richard II, Henry IV, and Macbeth, into a political advantage.[42] From his famous first soliloquy onward (*1 Henry IV*, 1.2.195–217), Hal seems conscious of an opportunity that his father grasps only sporadically. Henry makes use of theatrical identity in wooing the common people (3.2.39–59) and in sending counterfeits into the field at Shrewsbury, but nearly all of Hal's actions are based on the theory that, if identity must be merely role-playing, he should make the most of it. He wins a new set of adherents to his reign by befriending "a leash of drawers" who "take it already upon their salvation, that though I be but Prince of Wales, yet I am the king of courtesy, and tell me flatly I am no proud Jack like Falstaff, but a Corinthian, a

lad of mettle, a good boy (by the Lord, so they call me!)" (2.4.6–13).
By letting them choose his names, he becomes their master. In
France, he uses the name Harry le Roy for another strategic incursion
into the lower ranks of his subjects.

In his confrontation with Hotspur, Hal's quest for an ideal name
becomes deeply interwoven with his quest for a filial identity. Hal
fights Hotspur to regain his good name—we may think of Edgar
whose "name is lost" until he proves himself a loyal rather than a
patricidal son (*King Lear*, 5.3.121)—and wins "proud titles" by defeating him (5.4.79). But the process of winning back those noble
names involves not only a superficial act of loyalty to the father,
but also a deep, quasi-allegorical acceptance of the father's role in
forming Hal's selfhood. Hal's encounter with Hotspur—like the returning Henry's first encounter with Richard's lieutenants (*Richard
II*, 2.3.69–75)—begins with a dispute over names:

> *Hotspur* If I mistake not, thou art Harry Monmouth.
> *Hal* Thou speak'st as if I would deny my name.
> *Hotspur* My name is Harry Percy.
> *Hal*   Why then I see
>   A very valiant rebel of the name.
>   I am the Prince of Wales.   (5.4.59–63)

There is something archetypal in this combat, where "Harry to Harry
shall, hot horse to horse, / Meet and ne'er part till one drop down a
corse" (4.1.122–23): it recalls the symmetrical mythic combats, the
desperately serious shadow-boxing between the hero and his Doppelgänger, in which the hero's survival is rewarded with a name.[43]
England cannot "brook a double reign," as Hal here tells Hotspur,
and a name cannot brook a double occupant; only one of them can
be Harry the Fourth's royal heir. In seeking to win the "name in
arms" that Hotspur acknowledges is at stake (5.4.70), Hal is actually
trying to recapture the names Harry Monmouth and Prince of Wales—
in other words, the identities as his father's son and his king's rightful heir. Both were nearly forfeit to Hotspur, as King Henry warned:
Hal's relative dishonor left his political succession uncertain, and
made his father wish,

> that it could be prov'd
> That some night-tripping fairy had exchang'd
> In cradle-clothes our children where they lay,
> And call'd mine Percy, his Plantagenet!
> Then would I have his Harry and he mine.   (1.1.86–90)

Hal's roles as bad prince and bad son, by jeopardizing his name, have nearly dislodged him from his political and familial patrimonies; to retrieve them he must retrieve the name along with his royal father's love, and become the Harry who succeeds a Harry (2 *Henry IV*, 5.2.48–49).

Shakespeare emphasizes that Hal's victory over Hotspur is essentially an incorporation rather than an obliteration of the vanquished man's identity. Hal promised to "make this northren youth exchange / His glorious deeds for my indignities" (3.2.145–46), and that is what he has done; Hotspur, like Henry IV later, must have "gone wild into his grave" (2 *Henry IV*, 5.2.123), because all Hal's faults went with him, while his glories revert to Hal. Those glories consist of all the noble public virtues, all the things Hal knows his society and his father admire and expect him to embrace—in Freudian terms, they are the superego. The argument by analogy, especially an anachronistic analogy, is very risky, but in this case it suggests some intriguing possibilities, some deep resonances to Shakespeare's study of a conflict over filial identity. Freud argues that the superego is shaped in the renunciation of the Oedipal desires, and consists essentially of the father's censorious will within the son's psyche; the construction of the superego is at base the son's incorporation of the father.[44] Such a superego triumphs on several complementary levels at once when Hal promises to become the glorious Hotspur of the world and simultaneously vows not to rebel murderously against his father.

The standard psychoanalytic interpretation that makes Hotspur the embodiment of Hal's patricidal impulses therefore needs revision. Until Shrewsbury, only Shakespeare, and not Hal, could create such a displaced self; but the battle allows Hal to alienate his own rebellious spirit by both destroying and incorporating the opponent who is both rebel and noble son. When he retreats to a figuratively infantile level to compete with Hotspur for his filial identity, Hal may be retreating to a point prior to the Oedipal struggle and its shaping of the superego. In taking over Hotspur's glories while defending his father, what Hal really appropriates is a loyal filial posture. The fact that Hal can fully incorporate his father's nominal identity only by seizing Hotspur's glories corresponds strikingly to Freud's suggestion that the acquisition of a superego and the incorporation of the father are inseparable transactions.

In *1 Henry IV* Hal must defeat Hotspur for possession of his names and the accompanying hereditary roles; to reclaim his hereditary identity in 2 *Henry IV*, Hal must similarly overcome his base rebellious impulses in order to reject the names Falstaff offers him. Hal accepts the many playful epithets his Eastcheap companions apply to him in place of his actual name, but only in the way that he accepts their clouding of his royal light in general: temporarily, strategically. A king's name, to twist Richard II's phrase, must not be twenty thousand names, and when Falstaff renews the epithets after the coronation, Hal rejects them and him simultaneously (5.5.41–47).

Several critics have observed that the repudiation of Falstaff is the repudiation of an alternative father.[45] The names that Falstaff bestows on Hal compromise his transformation into Henry's heir. Rejecting them is a forceful and fitting way of rejecting Falstaff's claim to paternity, which was already rendered dubious by procreative powers so badly abused that Falstaff, not Henry, deserves to be slandered as a eunuch. He spends those powers on prostitutes and "begets" only "lies" (1 Henry IV, 2.4.225). Even the children that his pillow-stuffed whore claims to be carrying are mocked or willed to miscarriage from all sides (2 Henry IV, 5.4.7–15). He taints Hal with a degrading patrimony, claiming credit for making Hal somehow no longer consanguineous with his father or his brother, Prince John:

> Good faith, this same young sober-blooded boy doth not love me, nor a man cannot make him laugh, but that's no marvel, he drinks no wine ... Hereof comes it that Prince Henry is valiant, for the cold blood he did naturally inherit of his father, he hath, like lean, sterile, and bare land, manur'd, husbanded, and till'd with excellent endeavor of drinking good and good store of fertile sherris, that he is become very hot and valiant. If I had a thousand sons, the first humane principle I would teach them should be, to forswear thin potations and to addict themselves to sack.   (2 Henry IV, 4.3.87–125).

We are invited to recognize that Falstaff does indeed have thousands of such sons, all of whom have belatedly become consanguineous with him. They are what they drink. He is the father of the appetitive id, and those who give themselves over to that force incorporate him and become his more-than-adopted children. With the filial id as with the filial superego, the father is in the son as the son was in the father.

Of course, in claiming that Hotspur and Falstaff correspond suggestively to Freud's superego and id, I do not mean to imply that Shakespeare set out to write a psychoanalytic allegory in the Henry

IV plays. Several critics have become understandably testy about the tendency to read literature as if it were secretly a series of morality plays that have lain inert awaiting a Freudian key to the characters.[46] But the history these plays describe was made by complex human minds, and the plays themselves were made by and for such minds. Characters who exist as words on a page do not have a superego and an id, but the historical person they are designed to evoke presumably did, and the reader or listener presumably does too. What would be absurd to attribute to Shakespeare's characters may nonetheless be relevant to the responses of his audience. As we watch Hal struggle with his alter egos, "we are made to experience a kind of psychomachia or internal civil war."[47]

If Falstaff bears a strong resemblance to what we call the id, then we may legitimately ask what deep associations he might have aroused in Shakespeare's mind and might be capable, whether Shakespeare was conscious of it or not, of arousing in ours. Several of the play's eminent critics have flirted with this issue. Jonas Barish argues that "To banish plump Jack is to banish what is free and vital and pleasurable in life, as well as much that is selfish and unruly," and that there is therefore an "element of *self*-rejection in the new king's action."[48] Franz Alexander calls Falstaff a "pleasure-seeking principle" that "the prince must master in himself."[49] W. H. Auden makes it more explicit: "Once upon a time we were all Falstaffs: then we became social beings with superegos."[50] Most other readings of Falstaff's allegorical identity are compatible with the idea that he represents the id. E. M. W. Tillyard lists several such readings: Satan's assistant since the Fall, youthful vitality, incorrigibility, the fool, the adventurer, the Vice, the epitome of the Seven Deadly Sins, the lord of misrule, and "a perpetual and accepted human principle" resembling Orwell's "principle of man's perpetual revolt against both his moral self and the official forces of law and order" which we may love but must banish from within ourselves.[51] If we accept the contention of J. Dover Wilson and Bernard Spivack that Falstaff is a version of the medieval Vice, we may still inquire what the medieval Vice was supposed to represent, and how it was intended to engage and rebalance the audience's psychic forces.[52] The combination of universality and elusiveness in Falstaff's character invites us to anachronism: we may call him the id if that is the name by which we most effectively understand the force he represents. When some new system for explaining the human psyche emerges, critics will doubtless find another name for Falstaff within it, and another reading of the Henry IV plays arising from it.

Kinship and Kingship

The identification of Falstaff with the id provides its most valuable insights at the moment when Hal banishes him, just as the identification of Hotspur with the superego became most valuable at the moment when Hal defeated him. Hal's visible act of loyalty to his father in defeating the rebel Hotspur complements the psychological transaction implicit in that conquest, namely the incorporation of the paternal superego. In the same way, Hal's actual banishment of Falstaff is an act of obedience to, and imitation of, his father, as its precedent in the tavern suggested (*1 Henry IV*, 2.4.481); simultaneously, on the level of the psychological allegory, Hal is banishing his own id, which urges him to resist the demands of his father and of his social role. The outward and the inward transactions in Hal's moments of crisis are equally real; they are absolutely necessary concomitants to each other under the circumstances. Shakespeare has again shaped a situation where the political and the psycho-symbolic imperatives coincide, giving us the impression of a deep moral truth in a morally resonant universe.

This striking coincidence also encourages us to accept one of the stranger implications in Shakespeare's treatment of ambition: the notion that refashioning one's identity constitutes an Oedipal crime. The theft of Hotspur's honor and the banishment of Falstaff establish Hal as a loyal son and a rightful heir; they represent at the same time his incorporation of the paternal superego and his willingness to suppress his id in accepting the hereditary royal role. The establishment of the superego, according to Freud, is necessary to intercept the Oedipal desires put forward by the boy's id, which might lead to castration or death if they were obeyed.[53] The correspondence in Hal between granting the superego power to repress the id, and accepting the hereditary identity, may suggest that an Oedipal desire has been forestalled in both cases, whether it is the literal desire to kill the father and sleep with the mother, or its figurative counterpart in the desire to suppress the self the father made and to let one's deepest wishes conceive a replacement, perhaps in some version of the original womb.

What interests me especially about the banishment of Falstaff, in terms of the psychological allegory, is Hal's use of the Lord Chief Justice as the enforcer of that edict. The notion that this corresponds to the superego's assignment of suppressing the id has been suggested, but its implications have not been fully explored.[54] In *1 Henry IV* Hal faces the ego's usual problems in dealing with the id and the superego. He must conceal the criminal Falstaff from the sheriff in the tavern, worrying at the same time about the political rebellion taking place in the nation as a whole (2.4.500–45); this recalls Freud's description of the ego as "a poor creature owing service to three masters and consequently menaced by three dangers: from the external world, from the libido of the id, and from the severity of the super-ego."[55] When Hal stands between the dead Hotspur and the supposedly dead Falstaff at Shrewsbury, he has apparently solved that ego's problems. Unfortunately for him, fortunately for admirers of *2 Henry IV*, Falstaff simply rises back up from his latency, as the id tends to do, and the superego must be reinvigorated to deal with him. The Lord Chief Justice is essentially a reincarnation of the paternal conscience, and his confrontations with Falstaff early in *2 Henry IV* resemble the evasions and encounters of the psyche's mighty opposites. Falstaff declares himself blind and deaf to the Justice's existence, and the Justice replies that Falstaff is indeed insensible or uncomprehending of any moral consideration (1.2.55–69). In their next encounter, the Justice tells Falstaff that "You should have been well on your way to York," and that he should "Pay [Hostess Quickly] the debt you owe her, and unpay the villainy you have done with her" (2.1.67, 118–20). He tells Falstaff, in other words, to meet his unpleasant social obligations in war, money, and marriage—the standard message of the superego.

Falstaff expects to be fully indulged when Hal becomes king, and Henry IV fears that Hal's id will know no restraint once he acquires the power to indulge it:

> For when his headstrong riot hath no curb,
> When rage and hot blood are his counsellors,
> When means and lavish manners meet together,
> O, with what wings shall his affections fly
> Towards fronting peril and oppos'd decay! (4.4.62–66)

The metaphor portrays Hal as an unruly horse, which is a symbol of the id from Plato's *Phaedrus* up through Freud himself, and which here associates Hal with Phaethon, the Renaissance archetype of the disastrously disobedient son.[56] Falstaff's response, on hearing that Hal has gained such power, is "woe to my Lord Chief Justice" (5.3.138). But Hal refuses to accept either the name or the role of Falstaff's "sweet boy" (5.5.43); he turns instead to the father of the superego, or more accurately, the superego of his father, embodied in the Justice. We may not enjoy watching this choice, but no one says the suppression of instinctual desires is a pleasant, generous act, only that it becomes a necessary one at maturity. When Hal, feigning indignation, asks how the Lord Chief Justice earlier dared arrest and imprison "Th' immediate heir of England," the man replies that he dared as the one who gave the heritage:

> I then did use the person of your father,
> The image of his power lay then in me,
> . . . . .
> Your Highness pleased to forget my place,
> The majesty and power of law and justice,
> The image of the King whom I presented,
> And strook me in the very seat of judgment;
> Whereon (as an offender to your father)
> I gave bold way to my authority.   (5.2.70–82)

The emphasis on the Oedipal overtones of Hal's deed could hardly be stronger; but the surrogate father against whom he has done violence also offers himself as a surrogate father to whom Hal may submissively return. The Lord Chief Justice warns quite clearly what the consequences might be of not submitting. In this confrontation as in all of Hal's dealings with his actual father, Shakespeare's cautionary pattern looms ominously. The son who disdains his father, the subject who disdains his sovereign, invite similarly violent disobedience from their own sons or subjects:

> Be you contented, now you wear the garland,
> To have a son set your decrees at nought?
> . . . . .
> Nay more, to spurn at your most royal image,
> And mock your workings in a second body?
> Question your royal thoughts, make the case yours:
> Be now the father and propose a son,
> Hear your own dignity so much profan'd,
> See your most dreadful laws so loosely slighted,
> Behold yourself so by a son disdained;
> And then imagine me taking your part.   (5.2.84–96)

This exchange, it seems to me, looks all the way back to the birth of civilization. This decisive moment in the re-formation of English society involves the same forces and choices that, according to Freud's furthest-reaching speculations, led to the formation of the first human society: we are watching the superego evolve its authority from the compelling need to prevent endless strife. According to *Civilization and Its Discontents*, the sons in the Primal Horde suffered an ambivalence much like Hal's, and with like consequences. Their hatred yielded guiltily to love, whether or not they actually committed the patricide they fantasized, when they saw their wish fulfilled by their father's death. That love "set up the super-ego by identification with the father; it gave that agency the father's power, as though as a punishment for the deed of aggression they had carried out against him, and it created the restrictions which were intended to prevent a repetition of the deed."[57] The description of this transaction in *Totem and Taboo* bears an equally suggestive resemblance to Hal's submission to the Lord Chief Justice. As penance for a patricidal impulse, even one that was never acted on, the son bows in worship to the dead father's surrogate: "Totemic religion arose from the filial sense of guilt, in an attempt to allay that feeling and to appease the father by deferred obedience to him . . . They revoked their deed by forbidding the killing of the totem, the substitute for their father."[58] The superego originates from this totemic conversion, Freud argues, and always takes the form of a surrogate father,[59] as the Lord Chief Justice does here: Hal urges him to "be as a father to my youth," then calls him simply "father" (5.2.118, 140).

Freud adds that we re-enact such a transaction in each of our lives: we form the superego by incorporating idealized versions of the self that have been lost as external objects—a dead rival, or, especially, a dead father.[60] Hal announces:

> My father is gone wild into his grave;
> For in his tomb lie my affections,
> And with his spirits sadly I survive,
> To mock the expectation of the world.   (5.2.123–26)

This is an unnatural sort of succession, more the transmigration of a soul than the procreation of a body; but as at Hotspur's death, Hal becomes ideally filial by absorbing the ideal father in his superego. The opportunistic revival of the appetitive impulses embodied by Falstaff has, as I suggested, compelled a reincarnation of the conscience to cope with those impulses. The best part of Henry lives on in his repressive actions, which the Lord Chief Justice both symbolizes and performs; this new father becomes a part of the royal Hal, becomes the new king's censorious agent against Falstaff's pleas, the id's pleas, for special consideration. "The first requisite of civilization," Freud writes, "is that of justice—that is, the assurance that a law once made will not be broken in favour of an individual."[61] The laws of England are not at Falstaff's commandment, as he claims (5.3.136–37), because Hal has installed a new father within his own sovereignty. Such a substitution is possible, however, here as in Freud's analysis, only when the threatening real father is dead, and a surrogate, understood as protective rather than repressive, has taken his place by the son's own will. The Lord Chief Justice says he will now protect Hal (5.2.96), rather than restrain him on behalf of the previous royal father; the same shift occurs from the repressive father in the horde to the protective totem-animal that takes his place, a shift on which Freud comments extensively.

This intricate correspondence between Hal's psychological events and his nation's political events helps to justify the notion that both correspond to the events of human society as a whole. The psychomachia allows Hal's struggle to resemble the struggle of every human mind; its political counterpart may therefore allow us to generalize to the struggle of every human society. Freud argues repeatedly that the individual psyche relives metaphorically the experience of the sons in the Primal Horde, as if phylogeny were recapitulating ontogeny in psychological development, as it was once supposed to do in physical development.[62] Societies established throughout history, he also argues, have all experienced their own versions of the Primal Horde's formative trauma.[63] Nor is the notion wholly anachronistic. In medieval morality plays, the central figure in psychomachia of the sort Hal clearly undergoes was *Humanam Genus*; "Mankynde" is the name of an entire species. Shakespeare himself, in the Prologue to *Henry V*, asks us to "Into a thousand parts divide one man," and freely to jump

> o'er times,
> Turning th' accomplishment of many years
> Into an hour-glass: for the which supply,
> Admit me Chorus to this history.   (lines 24, 29–32)

At the end of *2 Henry IV*, Shakespeare has already tacitly requested admission as such a Chorus.

What the Lord Chief Justice offers to Hal is precisely what the institutionalization of the superego offered to the liberated sons in Freud's Primal Horde: prophylaxis against an eternal cycle of rebellion. Without a surrender of the id to the totemic father-surrogate, the result in virtually any society would be "an ever-recurring violent succession to the solitary paternal tyrant, by sons whose parricidal hands were so soon again clenched in fratricidal strife."[64] The only solution is a law, embodied in the totemic father-surrogate, that distributes rights fairly among the brothers and becomes internalized by each of them as the superego; both this creation of the surrogate, and its internalization, are clearly outlined in Hal's submission to the Justice who promises to end rebellion by even-handedness. Hal has learned the bitter lesson of his father's usurpation, which loosed "this Hydra son of war" not only by the violent precedent it set, but also by Henry's refusal to share the royal privileges among those who helped him overthrow the previous tyrant (2 *Henry IV*, 4.2.35–40). The Percies resemble the younger brothers in the Primal Horde, who, having assisted in killing the repressive father, find they have no choice (and no qualms) about attacking the repressive new father-figure as well. The dying Henry IV seems to recognize the problem, urging Hal's favorite brother Thomas to nurture their affection so that "noble offices thou mayst effect / Of mediation, after I am dead, / Between his greatness and thy other brethren," and thereby provide, as if he were an Anglo-Saxon ring-giver,

> A hoop of gold to bind thy brothers in,
> That the united vessel of their blood,
> Mingled with venom of suggestion
> (As, force perforce, the age will pour it in),
> Shall never leak. (4.4.19–47)

Three scenes later, when Hal actually succeeds his father, his first words to his brothers are a defense against this danger: he encourages them to continue in their communal mourning for the dead father, but assures them that "Not Amurath an Amurath succeeds," that he will not be like the man who murdered all his brothers when he took power (5.2.46–50). Instead, he has taken into himself the protective (and therefore protected) qualities of the totemic father whom the brothers now mourn and reverence unitedly. For England, as (Freud argues) for societies in all times and places, this is the only way to break the violent cycle. Shakespeare has again grounded his English history in the history of all human societies.

Hal thus becomes a sort of St. George, or perhaps a sort of Beowulf, defending England against the monster of fratricide that his predecessors have awakened, whether that primal dragon takes the name of Hydra or Amurath or Cain. Bullingbrook first appears before Richard II to avenge the spilt blood of the Duke of Gloucester, "Which blood, like sacrificing Abel's, cries, / Even from the tongueless caverns of the earth, / To me for justice and rough chastisement" (1.1.98–106). The lurking accusation, apparently well founded, is that Richard (through Mowbray) played the role of Cain against his kinsman; this accusation starts in motion the horrible fratricidal struggle that dominates both of Shakespeare's tetralogies. Perhaps the worst thing about this moral ailment is that it is contagious, and that it is paradoxically congenital to any *unlineal* inheritance of the throne. When Henry completes the promised vengeance by an indirect murder of his own, he desperately tries to displace his primal culpability onto his agent Exton, whom he sends to wander through the dark world "With Cain" (5.6.43). But the circle cannot so easily be broken. Henry must war with Northumberland, his son Hal with Northumberland's son Hotspur, and when the word of Hotspur's death arrives, Northumberland states the danger only too plainly in bitterly endorsing it:

> But let one spirit of the first-born Cain
> Reign in all bosoms, that each heart being set
> On bloody courses, the rude scene may end,
> And darkness be the burier of the dead! (*2 Henry IV*, 1.1.157–60)[65]

The crime that "hath the primal eldest curse upon't," in the Henry IV plays as in *Hamlet* (3.3.37), combines patricide, fratricide, and usurpation, in an invitation to endless bloodshed. The same sort of conflation appears in *Gorboduc*, and in the Elizabethan "Homily against Disobedience and wilful Rebellion," which warns that insurrection can only lead "the brother to seek and often to work the death of his brother, the son of the father."[66] Half a century after Shakespeare wrote the Henry IV plays, Thomas Hobbes expressed similar fears in terms that anticipate Freud's interpretation of the primal murder.[67] So the danger Freud perceived was at least partly visible to Shakespeare's contemporaries, and therefore a plausible subject for Shakespeare's stage.

In forbidding Falstaff (and therefore his own id) from using royal power to gratify his appetites at the expense of others, Hal is re-enacting society's first triumph over the force that threatened to destroy it, and renewing English society's will to resist that force. It is natural enough, given the respective occupations of Falstaff and the Lord Chief Justice and the relations between the two men, that accepting one as a surrogate father would entail excluding the other; but that natural situation carries a sharp allegorical import. On a realistic level, Hal's suppression of his own unruly impulses allows him to accept the Lord Chief Justice, and that acceptance leads to the rejection of Falstaff. On the level of the psychomachia, the rejection of Falstaff is merely the acting-out of the suppression of the id that we have seen moments earlier in the acceptance of the Justice. We are on shifting levels of allegory that disguise themselves as chronological sequence, as for example when the Redcrosse Knight's battle with Error is essentially an acting-out of a battle he has already fought in traveling through the Wood of Error with Una to reach that dragon, or when Christian and his companions fall into the net of Flatterer only after being coaxed out of the rightful path by flattery and led some distance, in *The Pilgrim's Progress*.[68] Hal's embrace of the Justice and his casting-out of Falstaff can be viewed as a single psychological moment. Time yields to allegory in that archetypal situation, even as that moment in the history of English society becomes suddenly synchronous with the formative moment of all human societies.

The psychomachia lends metaphorical richness to Hal's comparison of his experience of Falstaff to the experience of a wicked dream, in which the appetites of the id run rampant. The self-transformation Hal claims to have accomplished in the rejection speech becomes a slightly presumptuous exclusion of one side of his human heritage, one half of his divided father-figure. The speech shows clear traces of the self-alienation and the wakefulness that characterize the ambitious syndrome, but this is an alienation only from the id, and an awakening only from the dreams of the id:

> I have long dreamt of such a kind of man,
> So surfeit-swell'd, so old, and so profane;
> But, being awak'd, I do despise my dream.
> . . . . .
> Reply not to me with a fool-born jest,
> Presume not that I am the thing I was,
> For God doth know, so shall the world perceive,
> That I have turn'd away my former self;
> So will I those that kept me company.
> When thou dost hear I am as I have been,
> Approach me, and thou shalt be as thou wast,
> The tutor and the feeder of my riots.   (5.5.49–62)

The precedents of this announcement are not promising: other Shakespearean characters who use such phrases are unhealthily at war with their own natures and with nature itself. Richard III asks Queen Elizabeth to "Plead what I will be, not what I have been; / Not my deserts, but what I will deserve" (4.4.414–15); Richard II struggles to "forget what I have been! / Or not remember what I must be now!" (3.3.138–39). Hal's proclamation may even anticipate Iago's "I am not what I am" (1.1.65). From these moments through his last plays, Shakespeare persistently asks whether we can leave a degrading but natural part of ourselves behind, kill the heart of its father, without inviting a devastating nemesis. He refuses to adopt

73

the notion, offered by most of his sources, that Hal simply underwent a miraculous transformation at his coronation; the problems
of identity are too important and too complex for him to accept such
an evasion.[69] The psychomachia invites us to recognize Hal's self-
askesis, his amputation of the facets of his identity that do not fit
with his royal role. What I am raising again, from a different perspective, is the vexed question of whether Hal's humanity survives
the task of assuming a kingship that is only partly lineal, only partly
legitimate in its birth.

If *Richard II* ends with Henry being brought "Thy buried fear"
(5.6.41), *2 Henry IV* ends with Hal confronting his buried id; and
both cases invite our fear that the triumph may prove Pyrrhic, that
the king may have buried an essential part of himself in burying his
supposed enemy and assuming the crown. Hal's manipulation of his
former companions and his wording of grief for his father seem to
lack human grace, and may betoken a lack of human feeling. But
this apparent heartlessness, and his bloodless mode of inheritance,
unattractive and unhealthy as they may be, represent a plausible
way for Hal to fulfill his role as the nemesis generated by Henry's
violations, without incurring a similar nemesis of his own. Shakespeare and Hal virtually conspire to find an escape from the vicious
cycle of Oedipal justice. Hal's political strategy of imitating the sun
by hiding his glory temporarily in Eastcheap corresponds, in timing
and symbolic form, to the psychological strategy whereby he merely
imitates the rebellious son. He plays the disobedient and potentially
patricidal part long enough to punish his father and fulfill the general
expectation, meanwhile retaining an identity as a temporarily loyal
son to Falstaff, against whom he can later carry out the patricidal
violence that Shakespeare's pattern insists he must have inherited.
Falstaff, like Richard III, becomes a scapegoat in his dramatic creator's system of poetic justice. Like the Lords of Misrule to whom
he is often compared, Falstaff is placed in his exalted role only to
allow an outlet for hostilities that would be dangerous to express
against the actual sovereign. Then, at Henry's death, Hal reclaims
his lineal virtues metempsychotically, with the Lord Chief Justice
as the visible father of this immaculately conceived new royal self.
Hal proves himself his father's natural son by coming to the royal
identity as unnaturally as his father had, without committing his
father's crimes against lineage in the process.

But if Hal's genius is his ability to live constantly in the familial
and political roles his world demands of him, that is also his torment.
The unity of his character must always be its capacity for multi-

plicity, including an unappealing talent (like his brother John's) for duplicity. His innermost self may be so difficult for critics to locate and define because it is equally elusive for Hal himself. The difference between Hal and other victims of the ambitious pattern is not that he retains a vital inner self—it is not clear that he does—but rather that his theatrical self is hereditary, and that he has the *sprezzatura*, the art of disguising his artfulness, to make it viable. To inherit his father's role as king, as Henry had warned him (*1 Henry IV*, 3.2.46–59), he must inherit first his father's theatrical use of his "person," the arm's-length manipulation of the self. Hal learns this lesson and betters the instruction.

Henry V

Henry V is something of an afterthought in Shakespeare's historical treatment of the hazards of ambition—the symbolic pattern is less rich and central than it was in the Henry IV plays—and serves here as postscript to my analysis of the history plays. But if it is an afterthought, it is an intriguing one. Falstaff announces his intention in *2 Henry IV* to "turn diseases to commodity" (1.2.248); that is essentially what Shakespeare and the new king do with the disease of ambition in *Henry V*. This paradoxically hereditary role-player, this naturally unnatural successor, rebaptizes the English body politic in blood, starting it on a brief new life of unity and fertility.

Even the play's Prologue suggests a deliberate manipulation, rather than a passive suffering, of the standard symptomatology. The Prologue wishes for "A kingdom for a stage" on which we might see "the warlike Harry, like himself, / Assume the port of Mars" (3–6). One lurking implication is that Harry has a stage for a kingdom, and that even if the man himself were in the Globe theater, he would still be trying to live up to his public self by posing as a mythic warrior. The fact that "your thoughts . . . must now deck our kings" is as true of a nation where lineal annointment has been overthrown as it is of a play about historical royalty. The actors, like the Shakespearean characters whom ambition has nullified and fragmented, are merely "ciphers" in a "wooden O," each of whom our thoughts must divide "Into a thousand parts" (13–24). The ambitious ailments, in other words, are now abetting the overly ambitious dramatic project.

One part of Hal's political inheritance is the strategy of busying giddy minds with foreign quarrels (*2 Henry IV*, 4.5.212–15), which occupies the stage as the play proper begins. René Girard suggests

75

that the principle behind the use of communal sacrifice to avert endless strife is similar to "the principle behind all 'foreign' wars: aggressive tendencies that are potentially fatal to the cohesion of the group are redirected from within the community to outside it."[70] This interpretation points back toward Freud's own understanding of the mechanism preventing such strife in the Primal Horde: after the first patricidal usurpation, peace was established among the brothers by a ritual resubmission to the father, now converted into a benevolent paternal God. This use of religion as a sort of circuit breaker in the cycle of domestic violence combines neatly with the use of foreign wars for the same purpose: subservience to a higher King, and the communal action it encourages in the Holy Land or in France, might protect England's king from a new cycle of rebels.

None of this is lost on Henry V. He presents the expedition to France as something demanded by the nation's noble forefathers, approved by the nation's churchmen, and fought on behalf of "God for Harry, England, and Saint George!" (3.1.34). If this is to be a world of distorted inheritance and exploited piety, he will make the most of it. He sends the bishops scurrying to falsify the rules of succession so that the English king can claim hereditary rights over France, a topic that usefully diverts attention from this king's questionable rights over England. He sends, through Exeter, a "pedigree" that makes Henry a "native" to the French throne, and makes Charles VI's royal identity merely a costume defying lineality:

> He wills you, in the name of God Almighty,
> That you divest yourself, and lay apart
> The borrowed glories that by gift of heaven,
> By law of nature and of nations, 'longs
> To him and to his heirs, namely, the crown. (2.4.77–81)

Like Buckingham extolling the rights of Richard III, Exeter goes on to protest suspiciously much on the subject of hereditary rights. Richard II would have offered a rather different definition of Henry V's relation to heavenly, natural, and national law. In the honesty of soliloquy and prayer, in the midst of all these exhortations that the English prove "worth your breeding" (3.1.28), Henry concedes that the lineal order is rightly more enemy than friend to his royal claims: "Not to-day, O Lord, / O, not to-day, think not upon the fault / My father made in compassing the crown! / I Richard's body have interred new" (4.1.292–95). Henry IV's "buried fear" would not remain buried, and this plea is evidence that it still arises to haunt the Lancastrians' sovereign pretensions. Henry V uses his churchmen to exorcise that ghost, to dispel the ambitious curse by the traditional method of saying backwards the initial spell. Canterbury tells Henry that the French throne was "Usurp'd from you and your progenitors," and urges him to "Look back into your mighty ancestors; / Go, my dread lord, to your great-grandsire's tomb, / From whom you claim; invoke his warlike spirit." Ely and Exeter whistle the same notes in this graveyard, telling their king to show the "blood" that makes him heir to England's earlier monarchs and "brother" to the world's other monarchs (1.2.102–24).

It could be argued that no inferences can be drawn from this thematic focus, since any technical discussion of Henry's rights in France is bound to emphasize lineage. But the fact that Henry harps on the same themes in encouraging his troops cannot be so easily dismissed, and invites us to view the churchmen's remarks as signifying a deliberate strategic emphasis:

> On, on, you noblest English,
> Whose blood is fet from fathers of war-proof!
> Fathers that, like so many Alexanders,
> Have in these parts from morn till even fought,
> And sheath'd their swords for lack of argument.
> Dishonor not your mothers; now attest
> That those whom you call'd fathers did beget you.   (3.1.17–23)

Henry's goal in portraying himself as a true son is to become a true father: he tries to enlist the hereditary system as another fighter in his army. The paternal role, furthermore, is both a stratagem in his campaign and the object of that campaign, an inversion of Richard III's and Macbeth's tendency to make violations of natural order both method and goal of their ambitions. Henry reunites the English family under his sovereignty by making the triumph of his pretended lineal rights in France a necessary parallel to the lineal claims of his soldiers within their own families. Unless they win this right for him, he argues, they can make no claim to descent from the noble Englishmen who first conquered France. He gratefully accepts Fluellen's suggestion that he has an ancestral history of victory in France (4.7.92–96), and even offers to make a nobly consanguineous brother of any soldier, however basely born, who spills blood alongside him (4.3.60–63).

Any Frenchman who defies him, on the other hand, is threatened with a violent destruction of his familial order. Henry warns the defenders of Harfleur, much as Exeter had warned the French king (2.4.96–109), that if they do not submit to him as a benevolent father,

> in a moment look to see
> The blind and bloody soldier with foul hand
> Defile the locks on your shrill-shriking daughters;
> Your fathers taken by the silver beards,
> And their most reverend heads dash'd to the walls;
> Your naked infants spitted upon pikes,
> Whiles the mad mothers with their howls confus'd
> Do break the clouds, as did the wives of Jewry
> At Herod's bloody-hunting slaughter-men. (3.3.33–41)

The comparison with Herod is meaningful: if the French deny Henry's paternal authority, he will become another archetypal bad father who tries to slaughter every child for fear that one might someday overthrow him. What Henry understandably neglects to acknowledge is that bad royal fathers such as Herod or Cronus or Macbeth are inevitably overthrown by a son they overlook. But Harfleur's governor declares that the Dolphin has failed in the role of a paternal protector, asks Henry to treat the city's children gently, then offers him the role of its husband: "Enter our gates, dispose of us and ours" (3.3.45–49). The sexual metaphor may be latent, but it is fully appropriate to the situation, and "gate" was commonly both a metaphor and a medical term in the Renaissance for the vagina.[71] This sexual metaphor becomes all the more plausible when it is followed by Katherine's introduction to the English language, which prepares her to receive Henry and consists of a series of sexual *double entendres*. Sexual, linguistic, and political imperialism all converge in Henry's seizure of the paternal role over France.

Vegetative fertility again serves as an index to human fertility, which again depends on respect for hereditary identity. But in *Henry V* the conventional correspondence between the king's fruitfulness, human and agricultural, and his adherence to the lineal order, is exploited by Shakespeare and by Henry to bolster Henry's dubious claim. The Dolphin, whose "horse is my mistress" (3.7.44), can offer little hope of fathering a legitimate royal line, and his defeat is portrayed as a triumph of agriculture as much as of soldiership. When the Dolphin argues that Henry is a wastrel son whom France need not fear, the Constable replies that Henry has merely been "Covering discretion with a coat of folly, / As gardeners do with ordure hide those roots / That shall first spring and be most delicate" (2.4.38–40). King Charles adds that Hal is "a stem / Of that victorious stock" which conquered France in the past (2.4.62–63). Vegetative nature threatens to march on the supposed usurper's enclave, as Birnan wood does on Dunsinane, to restore the monarch who is more concordant with agriculture's regenerative character.

The Dolphin is shocked by this return, insisting that the invaders are of illegitimate descent, like Perdita's "bastard" gillyvors:

> shall a few sprays of us,
> The emptyings of our fathers' luxury,
> Our scions, put in wild and savage stock,
> Spurt up so suddenly into the clouds
> And overlook their grafters? (3.5.5–9)

But this paradoxical mixture of lineal and unlineal energy, of ambitions that both enforce and deny hereditary rights, conquers both the agricultural and procreative aspects of France. Eventually Burgundy urges on France the same combination of military and sexual surrender that preserved the fertility of Harfleur, asking

> Why that the naked, poor, and mangled Peace,
> Dear nurse of arts, plenties, and joyful births,
> Should not in this best garden of the world,
> Our fertile France, put up her lovely visage?
> Alas, she hath from France too long been chas'd,
> And all her husbandry doth lie on heaps,
> Corrupting in it own fertility. (5.2.34–40)

The world is solving the problem created at the start of *Richard II* (1.3.129–33), where the infant Peace was disturbed, leading to a collapse of lineality through a failure of gardening. Here the latent puns on "chas'd" and "husbandry," and on "issue" a few lines earlier, promise that Henry will restore the kingdom's healthy generation by marrying Katherine, who is clearly ready for sexual love, and whose hand he promptly demands.[72] King Charles finally assents, in the hope that their "issue" will "plant neighborhood . . . 'twixt England and fair France" (5.2.348–55).

Henry has taken on the role of son to one more father, and sun to one more land, legitimizing his succession by promising to function as a procreative and agricultural fisher-king. His very ability to bring unity out of division, and fecundity out of sterility, suggests through Shakespeare's symbolic system that Henry is the rightful king. Shakespeare concedes in the Epilogue that the natural order will soon overthrow his and Henry's theatrical impostures; but the playwright and his hero have created a momentary stay against the confusion that befalls the ambitious. Henry's task is exactly the one that Richard II failed to perform, "to make a body of a limb" by converting his small army of English loyalists into an invincible defender of his rights over the body politic (*Richard II*, 3.2.187). Exeter argues that Henry V need fear no Scottish insurrection while his army is in France, because "While that the armed hand doth fight abroad, / Th' advised head defends itself at home" (1.2.178–79). This may remind us of the fatal bodily divisions that afflicted overreachers in the other plays, but in this case the division is both efficient and entirely natural, with the hand fighting at a distance from the defended head to which it is still fully connected. This is harmony, as Exeter adds, rather than disunity (1.2.180–83), and it carries the useful implication that England and France constitute a single body politic, congruent to King Henry's. Such an expedition will actually restore rather than compromise the integrity of English bodies: according to Westmerland, Henry's subjects' "hearts have left their bodies here in England, / And lie pavilion'd in the fields of France." "O, let their bodies follow, my dear liege," responds Canterbury (1.2.128–30).

Like the troubled kings before and after him, Henry acquires an extra name, but this time the addition is not merely an index to an overextended man's fragmentation. Henry chooses to take on another identity so he can work more efficiently on his army's morale. The name he chooses, furthermore, is "Harry le Roy" (4.1.49), which does not signal a loss of the hereditary role (as "Richard," "Richard of Burdeaux," and "My Lord of Herford" do in *Richard II*), but points rather toward the completion of the supposedly hereditary self, the extension of the name of Harry the King over the French nation. Harry makes this pseudonymous midnight visit to the troops "not like yourself," as Williams later complains (4.8.50), a self-alienation indispensable for the testing and bolstering of his soldiers' will to win that greater identity for him. Even the provocation of Williams to a fight may be seen as a way of absorbing the potentially regicidal resentments, and making them finally grounds for greater loyalty. When the filial subject threatens to strike the unrecognized paternal king, he does not encounter a punitive Laius, but rather a kindly father who shares with him his gold (4.8.1–72); the Oedipal impulse is aroused for the purpose of disarming it. The very insomnia that permits this midnight walk, though Henry complains about it in much the same terms that his father employed to complain about the wakeful price of ambition, contributes to Henry's cause. The notion that the kingship is merely a garment that belongs to a man who is naturally no more exalted than others, a notion that threatened to topple Henry IV's reign, becomes a way for Henry V to elicit the courage and sympathy of his troops on the eve of battle: "His ceremonies laid by, in his nakedness he appears but a man," the disguised Henry tells the soldiers, apparently proving his assertion in the very way he finds to convey it (4.1.104–05). We may suspect that this concession is actually serving to cover a more frightening truth: that when this emperor has no clothes, he may be not naked, but virtually invisible, because his natural identity has been subsumed by his royal costume. But Henry's political identity has never actually stopped operating: the description of himself outside of his royal role is itself an essential part of his royal role. His skill and audacity convert the hazards of ambition into an extremely profitable wager. Even the threat that destroyed Richard III and Richard II—the loss of the royal self into a mirror—becomes a signal of triumph in Henry V: he is "the mirror of all Christian kings" (2.Pro.6).

The story of Prince Hal's development into Henry V, as this tetralogy tells it, is on one level an allegorical narrative of normal psychological development. It is the story of externalizing and repressing forbidden desires; of realistically subjugating the id to the paternal superego; of finding the proper objects onto which to transfer the murderous and sexual aggressiveness originally directed toward the father and the mother, and thereby preventing any renewal of the primal cycle of violence that formerly threatened human society as well as its individuals. But what does this grand psychoanalytic parable have to do with the play's ostensible historical subject? Perhaps Shakespeare chose to superimpose this psychological study onto this particular historical narrative to allow the problems of Oedipal repression and the problems of ambition to illuminate each other. The story of a healthy psychological development consistently corresponds to the story of an entire nation's healthy assimilation of its ambitious impulses. Hotspur embodies the latest phase of what appears to be an endless cycle of ambitious rebellion; at the same time, Shakespeare and Hal exploit him as an external embodiment of Hal's patricidal impulse, itself part of a destructive cycle. As Shakespeare uses Hotspur to portray dramatically Hal's crucial act of repression, which would otherwise be invisible, so Hal himself uses Hotspur to externalize and repress his own unhealthy desires, Oedipal and political. In turning Falstaff aside, in favor of the Lord Chief Justice, Hal not only performs an outward version of the essential inward Oedipal adjustment, but also allows a society ravaged by ambition to make an analogous adjustment.

Kinship and Kingship

The expedition to France, designed to prevent any renewal of the cycles of filial and fraternal violence, is an ideal strategy for safely assimilating both the Oedipal and the ambitious impulses. The desire for sexual conquest of the mother and violent conquest of the father become safely displaced into the conquest of this foreign country, described as a fertile woman and defended by men who cannot perform their threatened reprisals. The use of a foreign quarrel to busy the giddy minds itself corresponds to the mechanism of displacement. Hal's subsequent marriage to Katherine betokens and bolsters the viability of his ambitious identity, just as it betokens and bolsters the viability of his Oedipal adjustment. The multiple conquest strengthens England and Hal's authority over it; at the same time, it is a victory of healthy object-transference. France provides him with a manifestly exogamous woman toward whom he can productively express his sexual desire, as well as a foreign country toward which he can express the violence of political ambition. The tetralogy is far more than a psychoanalytic parable, but the parable is there. The homology between Hal's story and Freud's theory is not the entire play, and not my entire subject. What that homology reveals is the complexity and profundity of Shakespeare's treatment of the hazards of ambition.

◆❧II
"Thriftless Ambition,"
Foolish Wishes, and the
Tragedy of *Macbeth*

T HE CRUDE OUTLINES of *Macbeth* as a moral drama are visible in Elizabethan panegyrics to universal order:

> Now if nature should intermit her course, and leave altogether though it were but for a while the observation of her own laws. . . . if the prince of the lights of heaven, which now as a giant doth run his unwearied course, should as it were through a languishing faintness begin to stand and to rest himself; if . . . the times and seasons of the year [should] blend themselves by disordered and confused mixture . . . the fruits of the earth pine away as children at the withered breasts of their mother no longer able to yield them relief: what would become of man himself, whom these things now do all serve?[1]

A dozen years after Hooker's "Laws of Ecclesiastical Polity" asked these questions, Shakespeare's *Macbeth* provided some fairly conventional answers: man himself becomes a disordered mixture, with no regenerative cycles to rescue him from his mortality and no social system to deliver him from his evil impulses. The cosmic and bodily disorders that accompany Macbeth's rebellion distinctly resemble the ones predicted in the official "Exhortation Concerning Good Order, and Obedience to Rulers and Magistrates":

> The earth, trees, seeds, plants . . . keep themselves in their order: all the parts of the whole year, as winter, summer, months, nights, and days, continue in their order . . . and

83

man himself also hath all his parts both within and without, as soul, heart, mind, memory, understanding, reason,
speech, with all and singular corporal members of his
body, in a profitable, necessary, and pleasant order: every
degree of people . . . hath appointed to them their duty
and order: some are in high degree, some in low, some
kings and princes, some inferiors and subjects . . . and every
one hath need of other . . . Take away kings, princes . . . and
such estates of God's order, no man shall ride or go by
the highway unrobbed, no man shall sleep in his own
house or bed unkilled, no man shall keep his wife, children, and possessions in quietness . . . and there must needs
follow all mischief and utter destruction both of souls,
bodies, goods, and commonwealths.[2]

In *Macbeth* as in *Richard III*, this deadly loss of personal and natural
integrity does not result (as in Hooker) from some careless indolence
of the world's ordering forces, but rather (as in the "Exhortation")
from a human determination to disturb the political aspect of that
order. In murdering the princes who would exclude him from the
throne, Richard willingly "smothered / The most replenished sweet
work of Nature / That from the prime creation e'er she fram'd"
(4.3.17–19). In unseating Duncan, Macbeth willingly made "a breach
in nature" through which "the wine of life" was drained (2.3.113,
95). Both usurpers push back toward primal chaos a Creation that
thwarts their desires, hoping to reconstruct it in the image and
likeness of their aspiring minds. Ambition, in its inherent opposition
to heredity and the established order, thus becomes the enemy of
all life, especially that of the ambitious man himself.

But these passages, like most others cited by critics seeking to
define a unified "Elizabethan world view," are taken from works
expressly written in defense of England's political and theological
authorities. Those authorities had a tremendous stake in maintaining order and hierarchy, and in defining them as natural and divinely
ordained. If we can recognize in such passages the voice of self-
serving pragmatism rather than objective philosophy, we can infer
a contrary voice, the voice of the disempowered that the propaganda
is struggling to refute. To understand Shakespeare's play, as to understand English cultural history as a whole, requires this sort of
inference.[3] The play, like history, like the witches who are agents
of them both, "palter[s] with us in a double sense" (5.8.20). Where
the witches' prophecies seem to endorse ambition, but warn on a

more literal and less audible level against its futility, *Macbeth* contains a silent, figurative endorsement of ambition, even while loudly and eloquently restating the principles expressed by Hooker and the "Exhortation Concerning Good Order."

The spirit of tragedy itself cuts against such single-minded, heavy-handed moralizations, striving subversively on behalf of the individual human will. Shakespeare moves from history to tragedy by clarifying and universalizing the hazards of ambition: this cautionary pattern, which was shaped by the propagandistic aspect of *Richard III*, creates its own sort of moral drama in *Macbeth*. We may view Richard with horrified admiration, but we identify with Macbeth from within.[4] Shakespeare accomplishes this, makes Macbeth eligible for the fear and pity that permit catharsis, by encoding many of our repressed impulses, many of the rash wishes society has obliged us to abandon or conceal, within Macbeth's conventionally dramatic desire to replace the king. In his soliloquy before the regicide, Macbeth acknowledges that his deed will entail all the kinds of violence civilization has been struggling to suppress since it first began: violence between the guest and the host, violence by subjects against a monarch, and violence among kinspeople. When Shakespeare wants to show society's descent into utter depravity in *King Lear*, the moral holocaust consists of exactly these crimes: crimes against the host Gloucester, crimes against the royal father Lear, and crimes among siblings over legacies and lovers. In fact, Macbeth's misdeed resembles the one Freud says civilization was formed to suppress: the murder of the ruling father of the first human clan because he refused to share his reproductive privileges with his filial subjects.

In the history plays, Shakespeare established Oedipal desires as a metaphor for ambition; in *Macbeth*, he exploits the metaphor to implicate his audience in the ambitious crime, by tapping its guilt-ridden urges against authority and even against reality. On an individual as well as a racial scale, the Oedipal patterns psychoanalytic critics have noticed in this play, with Duncan as a father-figure and Lady Macbeth as the sinister temptress who is both mother and wife, may be a way of making the men in the audience intuitively identify with Macbeth's wish fulfillment. For most young men, that Oedipal guilt is a perfect focal point for more general resentments like the ones that turn Macbeth against Duncan: resentments against those who have power over us, those who have things we want, and those whom we want to become. The conflicts Shakespeare is addressing here are not merely the sexual ones. As he demonstrates the deeper meanings and broader ramifications of ambition, he necessarily implies that any desire to change the given order is a scion

85

of that sin; and such a moral inevitably collides with the basic imperatives of life. To live is to change the world, to shape the environment to meet one's needs; even before the Oedipal phase begins, every infant is profoundly involved in the struggle to learn how far that shaping can go, and how best to perform it. So what might at first have been merely analogies or resonances by which Shakespeare suggested the foundations of his cautionary political tales become, in *Macbeth*, the openings through which we enter the story and receive the tragic experience.

To make these openings more accessible, Shakespeare expands and details a motif implicit in the history plays' treatment of ambition: the "foolish wish" motif of folklore, in which a person's unenlightened way of desiring converts the power of gaining desires into a curse. Richard III and Henry IV pursue an unlineal, unnatural kingship, and that is precisely what they get, much to their distress. In *Macbeth* this motif acquires the imaginative breadth, and hence the universal applicability, that it has in fairy tales, where it usually involves a narrow-minded disruption of nature's complex balances. The stories achieve their cautionary effect by showing the logical but terrifying ramifications of having such wishes granted. King Midas, for example, acquires the golden touch only to discover that it isolates him from food, love, and family—all the joys of natural life.[5] Perhaps more strikingly relevant to *Macbeth* is the Grimm Brothers' story called "The Fisherman and His Wife." The humble man discovers a magic fish in his net and, at the insistence of his shrewish wife, obliges it to replace their hovel with a castle. The wife steadily increases her demands for splendor and power, the ocean becomes angrier with each new request, and the couple becomes more discontented after each wish is granted, until the fish finally returns them to their original humble state.

But once Macbeth has rashly "done the deed" of self-promotion at his wife's instigation, they both learn that "What's done cannot be undone" (2.2.14, 5.1.68). Bruno Bettelheim "cannot recall a single fairy tale in which a child's angry wishes have any [irreversible] consequence; only those of adults do. The implication is that adults are accountable for what they do."[6] As such tales fascinate children by providing them with metaphorically coded lessons about the conduct of their own, more basic problems, so *Macbeth* conveys its harsher lessons to us. We do not need magic fish or bloodthirsty witches to provoke us; nature doth teach us all to have aspiring minds, as Tamburlaine asserts, or at least fickle and envious minds. We desire this man's art and that man's scope, with what we most

86

enjoy contented least. Shakespeare alerts us to the fact that, to this extent, we participate in the murderous ambition we witness on stage, creating and suffering its poetically just consequences. While the official homilies claim that rebellion contains all other sins and provokes universal alterations,[7] *Macbeth* suggests reciprocally that all other sins—indeed, all impulses toward change—partake of rebellion.

Foolish-wish stories serve to develop in the child a mechanism and a rationale of repression, a necessary device for subordinating immediate urges to long-term goals and abstract rules—necessary, because infantile desires are no less selfish, violent, and murkily incestuous than the ones propelling Macbeth. Human beings seem to share a stock of foolish wishes, and society survives on its ability to discourage their fulfillment. That may be one reason why the play (as several of its directors have emphasized) suggests that this crisis is only one instance of an endless cycle of rebellion: the play is less the story of two evil people than it is a representation of impulses—ambitious, rebellious, Oedipal—that the hierarchical structures of family and society arouse in every human life. Normal behavior resembles Macbeth's successful curbing of insurrection's lavish spirit early in the play; but deeply human motives constantly impel each person toward a comparable rebellion, differing in scale but not necessarily in basic character from Macbeth's.

In opposing the lineal succession to Scotland's throne, Macbeth and his wife foolishly wish regenerative nature out of existence, then suffer the consequences of their wishes' fulfillment. An attack on the cycle of parents and children necessarily affronts the cycles of night and day, sleeping and waking, and planting and harvesting, as well. Perhaps Rosse's warning against "Thriftless ambition, that will ravin up / Thine own live's means" (2.4.28–29) seems all too obvious a moral, but it is worth remembering that Rosse here supposes that his observation refers simply to a patricide; the play obliges us to generalize it for him, into an axiom about our relationship to great creating nature as a whole. Even this grander lesson, that people should not rashly disrupt the web of nature for the sake of their individual desires, was as clearly deducible from the Elizabethan concept of a beneficent universe as from the modern concept of ecological networks. Some seventy-five years earlier, John Heywood's "Play of the Wether" ridiculed the idea of tampering with that natural system to satisfy the whims of individuals. There needs no ghost come on the stage to tell us this.

But evidently it was not obvious enough for Macbeth and Lady

Macbeth, and in a sense it is not obvious enough for anyone who has ever idly wished for more light in December, more flowers in February, or less rain in April. In a fairy tale such wishes would cost us dearly, and justly; yet we cannot really feel guilty for having them. In his susceptibility to conventional human desires, and his momentary willingness to forget the reasons they must be suppressed, Macbeth is one of us. He shows us the logical extension, and the logical costs, of our own frailties. Macbeth merely encounters those frailties in a situation that magnifies them into something momentous and horrible; and he encounters them in a dramatic context that blurs the borderline between nightmarish fantasy and reality. When the witches first appear, they take us into a region where the distinction becomes foggy; when they first appear to Macbeth, they do the same for him. Their status as partly a product of his mind and partly actual witches, and their talent for self-fulfilling prophecy, confirm that liminal function. They convey him, as they convey us, into a world where one might suddenly find one's destructive impulses magically fulfilled, where crimes are "thought and done" simultaneously (4.1.149). Place any person in such a world, and who should 'scape whipping, or even hanging for murder; though we are indifferent honest, we could accuse us of such things that it were better our mothers had not borne us.[8] If we can recognize Macbeth's crime as essentially an extension of our most casual recalcitrance at the ways of natural and social order, a symbolic performance of our resentful impulses against the aspects of the world that inconvenience us, we may find it hard to hold him accountable for his sin. The Porter and Macbeth have much to say against equivocators in this play (2.3.8–36, 5.5.42), but Shakespeare himself performs a Jesuitical equivocation in conveying the play's beliefs. Everything on the play's stated level follows the orthodox line against ambition; the heresy resides where the words trail off into unspoken thoughts, Shakespeare's and ours, a heresy that (to state the case most extremely) portrays Macbeth as a martyr who dies for our sins at the hands of an order so strictly repressive that it makes the very business of living a punishable crime.[9]

The Vengeance of Regenerative Nature

The foolish-wife motif, with its overtones of poetic justice, was extremely popular among Jacobean moralists, particularly those warning young men against defying their fathers' instructions and leaving their hereditary places. Samuel Gardiner's *Portraiture of the*

Prodigal Sonne declares that "There is nothing that hurteth so much as the having of our wils," and elsewhere that "a sinner may be killed with his owne poyson, even the poyson of his sinne"; several other prodigal-son tracts echo this idea.[10] Macbeth himself worries about teaching

> Bloody instructions, which, being taught, return
> To plague th' inventor. This even-handed justice
> Commends th' ingredience of our poison'd chalice
> To our own lips. (1.7.7–12)

We can see, even if Macbeth cannot, how this axiom about regicide applies to the violations of universal order implied in that regicide, just as we could see that Rosse's remark about "Thriftless ambition" could apply to any assault on sovereign nature as well as to a patricide. Henry IV's practical fear of counterusurpation thus expands into a tragic intuition about Pyrrhic victories over regenerative nature.

Macbeth and his Lady find their entire world sickened by the poisonous gall they fed to the Scottish body politic in place of its nurturant milk. Like Richard Brathwait's prodigal-son figure, Macbeth is "ill to others, worst unto himselfe."[11] He murders sleep and plunges the world into an uneasy darkness, but he and his wife suffer the worst insomnia of all, and the long night exhausts them before finding day in Malcolm's vengeful return. They attempt to steal life and patrimony from the new generation of babes, but die without a living heir. The kingdom's vegetation, like its sunlight, fades at Duncan's death, but while Macbeth's life falls "into the sear, the yellow leaf" (5.3.23), Malcolm echoes his father's metaphors of seeds and planting in reclaiming his father's throne. In a stratagem that resembles a Maying festival, Birnan wood comes like a sudden spring to the walls of Dunsinane castle. Sun, sons, and seedlings all return together to destroy the man whose ambition has made him their enemy.

The fisherman's wife in the Grimm Brothers' story crossed into the realm of the forbidden when she demanded control over the sun and the moon; Lady Macbeth provokes and performs a similar ambitious violation. When she exults that the regicide "shall to all our nights and days to come / Give solely sovereign sway and masterdom" (1.5.69–70), we may detect an aspiration to sovereignty *over* those nights and days, as well as during them. Bettelheim observes that "Many fairy tales depict the tragic outcome of . . . rash wishes, engaged in because one desires something too much or is unable to wait until things come about in their good time."[12] As long as Macbeth plans to let natural events gain him the throne, he thinks in terms of letting time run its diurnal course. His aside about letting chance "crown me without my stir" is immediately followed by his aside that "Come what come may, / Time and the hour run through the roughest day" (1.3.144–48). But when Duncan extends that cyclical inevitability to include the succession of son as well as sun, Macbeth attacks the balance of light and dark as well as the unity of his own identity in opposing Duncan's choice: "Stars, hide your fires, / Let not light see my black and deep desires; / The eye wink at the hand . . . " (1.4.50–52).

In the following scene, Lady Macbeth suggests a similar pair of assaults, against light and organic identity, to aid the assault on Duncan. Her first words are read from her husband's letter about the witches: "They met me in the day of success" (1.5.1). But the witches specialize in false encouragement and secondary meanings: daylight and succession are precisely what they induce this couple to sacrifice. Lady Macbeth quickly concludes that she must eradicate the vision daylight permits, along with the nursing succession demands, in order to fulfill the witches' promise:

> Come to my woman's breasts,
> And take my milk for gall, you murth'ring ministers,
> Wherever in your sightless substances
> You wait on nature's mischief! Come, thick night,
> And pall thee in the dunnest smoke of hell,
> That my keen knife see not the wound it makes,
> Nor heaven peep through the blanket of the dark
> To cry, "Hold, hold!" (1.5.47–54)

She will abandon her maternal role in the nursery in favor of a phallic role in the bedroom.[13] To engineer their rebirths as monarchs, she and her husband will perform a forbidden deed on the paternal Duncan, under a blanket that leaves us uncertain whether the deed is essentially sexual or essentially violent. Such a cover is useful, not only in preventing Macbeth from thinking conscientiously of his mother and Lady Macbeth of her father (1.5.16–18, 2.2.12–13), but also in making us think about Shakespeare's symbolic pattern, which blends incest with parricide, and insemination with Caesarean section, in the forbidden act of self-remaking.

These requests for a crime-facilitating darkness soon lead to inadvertent predictions that the crime will actually forestall the progress of night into day.[14] As they test each other's susceptibility to the idea of regicide, Lady Macbeth asks when Duncan will leave their castle. When Macbeth answers, "To-morrow, as he purposes," she exclaims, "O, never / Shall sun that morrow see!" (1.5.59–61). She means that Duncan will not live to go forth—*that* day will never come, we might say—but by saying it indirectly, she seems to imply that the murder will deprive future days of sunlight. Duncan, generally a solar figure,[15] is the light that will not see the morrow, and that the morrow will not see.

The archetypal crime against the healthy progress of night and day for the Renaissance was also the archetypal crime of filial ambition: Phaethon's disastrous usurpation of Phoebus' solar chariot.[16] Phaethon's premature seizure of his father's place neatly conflated two sorts of rebellion: the attempt to unseat the sun-king, and the Oedipal attempt to take the father's mount, against his strictest prohibition and before developing the abilities to manage or even survive the attempt. The story's moral is clear enough, and Shakespeare alludes to it to moralize his own cautionary tale: such ambitions, whether they are the seditious ones of a subject or the sexual ones of a son, threaten the universal order by which humanity survives, and the rebel must be sacrificed to preserve that order. After Duncan is murdered, Rosse reports that the royal horses "Turn'd wild in nature, broke their stalls, flung out, / Contending 'gainst obedience, as they would make / War with mankind" (2.4.16–18). Like Phoebus' horses, they mirror the unruliness of the son who has stolen their reins, and thereby threaten the entire human race. Lennox's report that "The night has been unruly" (2.3.54) may therefore suggest to us more than that disorderly events have occurred during the nighttime hours: since Macbeth—one of "Night's black agents" (3.2.53)—has usurped the sun's royal chariot, darkness refuses to yield to day as the natural order dictates. In the speech preceding his comment on the unruly horses, Rosse remarks,

> By th' clock 'tis day,
> And yet dark night strangles the travelling lamp.
> Is't night's predominance, or the day's shame,
> That darkness does the face of earth entomb,
> When living light should kiss it?
> *Old Man*   'Tis unnatural,
> Even like the deed that's done.   (2.4.6–11)

Their association of the sun's misconduct with a regicide (and, they are soon told, a patricide) invites us to adduce Phaethon's archetypal crime, which unites and moralizes Macbeth's various violations of nature.

Banquo's literal and figurative resistance to the onset of darkness parallels his resistance to the temptations of regicide. As Duncan falls asleep in Macbeth's castle, Banquo notes uneasily the very blackness Macbeth and his wife eagerly invoke: "There's husbandry in heaven, / Their candles are all out" (2.1.4–5). He seems to echo this observation shortly before he, too, is murdered. His offhand remark to Fleance that "It will be rain tonight" suggests that he sees a dark, blank sky. In the form of his torch, he tries to keep daylight alive against this darkness; he has, as he promised Macbeth, "become a borrower of the night / For a dark hour or twain" on his journey (3.1.26–27)—the opposite movement to Macbeth's rush to nightfall. Macbeth's murderous ambition, as Rosse's remark suggested, again "strangles the travelling lamp"—this time the travellers' torch rather than the travelling sun. Macbeth intends to snuff out the final light of the old order, and relatedly the final obstacle to his new identity as a royal patriarch, by killing Banquo and Fleance in another artificial darkness that hides the deadly hand from the conscientious eye:

> Come, seeling night,
> Scarf up the tender eye of pitiful day,
> And with thy bloody and invisible hand
> Cancel and tear to pieces that great bond
> Which keeps me pale! Light thickens, and the crow
> Makes wing to th' rooky wood;
> Good things of day begin to droop and drowse,
> Whiles night's black agents to their preys do rouse. (3.2.46–53)

Macbeth now seems to be working for night as much as night is working for him. Day will suffer in this assault precisely what the First Murderer reports that Banquo suffers: wounds that constitute "a death to nature" (3.4.27). Banquo and Fleance represent the final force of daylight, the last gleam of hope: as the murderers close in on them, one comments that "The west yet glimmers with some streaks of day" (3.3.5). As their knives come down on Banquo, they answer his prediction of rain with, "Let it come down!" (3.3.16), as if the rain blotting the starlight and the knives taking his life were the same "it." Like Othello, they put out the light, and then put out the light:

> *Third Murderer* Who did strike out the light?
> *First Murderer*   Was't not the way?   (3.3.19)

But it was not. Fleance, prophesied to be the source of a new royal succession, escapes because the murderers have followed Macbeth's self-benighting policy to its misguided extreme by striking out the torch. By completing the nightfall, Macbeth and his "black agents" invite the next day to begin. Macbeth had told those agents that Fleance, like his father, "must embrace the fate / Of that dark hour" (3.1.136–37). As so often in this play, the "double sense" of words returns to haunt Macbeth: the luminous father (3.3.14) and his son embrace the dark hour as dusk and dawn embrace midnight. In *Macbeth*, the generational cycle and the solar cycle are like two clock-faces with a single dial. The striking out of the final light, like the stroke of midnight, announces the start of a new cycle. Nature regenerates itself miraculously from this terrible moment of nullity, as when Macduff rises to life after the terrible pause between his mother's death and his own birth. From the dire stillness of no light or life at all, a new light and a new life emerge. Rosse tells Lady Macduff, "Things at the worst will cease, or else climb upward / To what they were before" (4.2.24–25); in *Macbeth*, the sun or son always rises up again—except within the Macbeth household, which made itself an enemy of such resurrection. Some time passes before the renewed forces make themselves felt, but from the moment of Fleance's escape, we sense that they own the future. Macduff can still ask rhetorically of his country, "When shalt thou see thy wholesome days again?"; but Scotland's new sun king provides a compelling if vague answer: "The night is long that never finds the day" (4.3.105, 240). This aptly echoes the lesson Macbeth forgot: "Time and the hour run through the roughest day" (1.3.148). Macbeth's has become a "distemper'd cause," and only at his death can it be declared that "The time is free" (5.2.15, 5.9.21).

As soon as Banquo's light has been put out, Macbeth and his wife become stagnant in time and benighted at noon. Macbeth calls Banquo's ghost a "horrible shadow" which has "overcome us like a summer's cloud"; trying to recover his temporal bearings that same night, he asks his wife, "What is the night?" and she replies, "Almost at odds with morning, which is which" (3.4.105–26). Her somnambulism is also a confused battle between a day-action and a night-action, and though "she has light by her continually, 'tis her command" (5.1.22–23), it cannot bring back the previous day's sun, nor give her a place under the new one. As Lady Macbeth wanders through the night in futile pursuit of a previous day, Macbeth wanders into a series of undefined tomorrows. But he, too, finds that his crime against the regenerative cycles has compelled him to exchange life for a "brief candle" (5.5.23); his figurative exchange resembles her literal one, and both represent the fool's bargain involved in the creation of their unnatural royal selves. That bargain may be moralized as Montaigne moralizes the resort to garments: "like those who by artificial light extinguish the light of day, we have extinguished our own means by borrowed means."[17]

When Birnan Wood springs up in Scotland's new dawn, a sort of heliotrope to the new generation's royal sun, Macbeth shrinks away from it: "I gin to be a-weary of the sun" (5.5.48). Daytime itself, as he inadvertently willed it, becomes his oppressor, joins the war against him. Young Siward, part of that new generation, assures Malcolm at the battle that "The day almost itself professes yours, / And little is to do" (5.7.27–28). Siward may simply mean that Malcolm's forces have nearly "won the day," to use a common phrase. But the active phrasing suggests that daytime itself seems almost to fight on Malcolm's behalf in an alliance with regenerative nature that leaves little to be done by the actual military force. In *Richard III* Richmond was urged by the ghosts of Richard's enemies to "win the day," and shortly thereafter we learned that the sun itself was refusing to shine on Richard's army, literally foreshadowing his defeat (5.3.145, 276–87). The same pattern underscores the character of Macbeth's defeat. He battles Malcolm's sunlight forces as an agent of the "black, and midnight hags" (4.1.48), and as surely as the sun rises, his brief dark kingship falls.

If Macbeth's suppression of daylight is a symbol, a tactic, and a punishment of his usurpation, then so is his attack on sleep. Having foolishly trapped himself in an endless night, he compounds the error by wishing away night's regenerative aspect. Insomnia, as I have said, is a fitting concomitant of ambition in Shakespeare: Henry IV must strive constantly to remain above his hereditary level, whereas Falstaff, who has sunk about as low as a human being can in the chain of being, as if it were a hammock, sleeps deeply at the very moment he is threatened with arrest. In *Macbeth* the correspondence between wakefulness and ambition takes on a greater importance and complexity.

Though Macbeth and Banquo are kept awake on the murder night by the same ambitious fantasy, the differences are crucial. Macbeth remains awake to overcome his political limitations, the same insomnia Henry IV suffers; Banquo remains awake to overcome his moral limitations, precisely the insomnia Falstaff spares himself. The distinction between these two responses to temptation resembles the distinction by which Milton's Adam consoles Eve for her own dreams of disobedient aspiration toward the Father's power:

> Evil into the mind of God or Man
> May come and go, so unapprov'd, and leave
> No spot or blame behind: Which gives me hope
> That what in sleep thou didst abhor to dream,
> Waking thou never wilt consent to do. *(Paradise Lost*, V, 117–21)

Banquo is such an innocent, telling Fleance:

> A heavy summons lies like lead upon me,
> And yet I would not sleep. Merciful powers,
> Restrain in me the cursed thoughts that nature
> Gives way to in repose!   (2.1.6–9)

Ten lines later we learn that he "dreamt last night of the three weïrd sisters." The bad dreams, here as in Hamlet's "bounded in a nutshell" speech (2.2.254–59), are the fantasies of patricide, regicide, and incest that seem to haunt the whole world. No sooner are Banquo's words out than a vast image out of *spiritus mundi* troubles his sight: his partner in the sinister prophecy, also walking late. Banquo, apparently returning from seeing Duncan safely to bed (2.1.12–15), with any regicidal fantasies newly repressed, encounters Macbeth as a Doppelgänger, a Second Coming of his evil impulses. Macbeth is the waking figure of the cursed dream Banquo would be having were he asleep; Banquo might remark, as Leontes does in *The Winter's Tale*, "Your actions are my dreams" (3.2.82).

The notion that Macbeth is like any of us, only doomed to live in a world where one's dreams and desires become reality, is clearly bolstered by this moment, where we see Banquo horrified by the appetitive dreams the witches have aroused in him, then see his alter ego, stirred by the same force, condemned to live those dreams. Macbeth is again a version of the rash wisher in fairy tales: dreams are generally wish-fulfillments that evade the judging and censoring faculties, faculties that remain alert in us and in Banquo, crying "Hold, hold!" while we watch Macbeth stalk his desires. Freud cites approvingly "the old saying of Plato that the good are those who content themselves with dreaming of what others, the wicked, actually do."[18] Our identification with Banquo cannot completely reassure us about our moral worth because we are forced to realize how fine and even fortuitous the distinction is between Banquo's

95

soul and Macbeth's. No one who has ever awakened with relief from a dream of evildoing should feel any easy superiority to Macbeth at this decisive moment in his fall.

Half-asleep from exhaustion, Banquo watches the beginning of his regicidal nightmares acted out by Macbeth, who is crossing the stage in the opposite direction. Macbeth then watches distantly his own predatory advance, as we often watch ourselves in dreams; he announces that "wicked dreams abuse / The curtain'd sleep" (2.1.50–51). Macbeth has somehow *become* Banquo's bad dream, and Duncan's sleep seems to be tortured at this same moment by that same nightmare, which is closing in on him as a reality. The three characters are fatally jumbled together, as are the waking and dreaming states of consciousness. One result is that, after the regicide, Macbeth becomes both its perpetrator and its victim in an endless half-waking nightmare. As in the tortured sleep of Henry IV, the memory of committing a regicide and the prospect of serving as king work together against one's peace of mind; indeed, as Richard III discovers before Bosworth Field, they combine into symbolically appropriate nightmares of self-slaughter, the internal civil war implicit in ambition. Richard, in fact, foreshadows Macbeth's problems in another, more intriguing way. His nightmares, too, become reality; his dreams of defeat in battle come true under a sky that has stubbornly refused to turn to day. In the waking hours, when actions have real consequences, he is trapped in a repetition of the previous night. Macbeth, having lived out Banquo's evil dreams and fulfilled Duncan's, finds the boundary disappearing for him as well, finds it impossible to escape his nightmare either by sleeping or by waking. Awake, he is visited by terrifying ghosts, moving forests, deceptive riddles, prophetic and symbolic visions—the sorts of things that most people encounter only in dreams. But his dreams seem to be only an extension of his waking deeds and his waking fears. He would rather disrupt the universe than have himself and his wife sleep

> In the affliction of these terrible dreams
> That shake us nightly. Better be with the dead,
> Whom we, to gain our peace, have sent to peace,
> Than on the torture of the mind to lie
> In restless ecstasy. Duncan is in his grave;
> After life's fitful fever he sleeps well.
> Treason has done his worst; nor steel, nor poison,
> Malice domestic, foreign levy, nothing,
> Can touch him further. (3.2.18–26)

For their purposes, in fact, Duncan sleeps too well. By breaking the cycle that would normally have awakened him, they have inherited and perpetuated the nightmares of regicide which Macbeth imagined were tormenting Duncan's final hour. The implication is that the fear of a traitor bearing steel or poison wrenches Macbeth from his own sleep these nights. When the now dangerous world comes pounding on Macbeth's door, he says, "Wake Duncan with thy knocking! I would thou couldst!" (2.2.71). He wants the solar sovereign to rise again, bringing the new day's sun with him, thereby rescuing Macbeth on two levels from his nightmarish situation by revealing that he merely dreamed his evil deed. But cyclical renewal is precisely what Macbeth unwittingly forfeited when he abused "the curtain'd sleep":

> The death of each day's life, sore labor's bath,
> Balm of hurt minds, great nature's second course,
> Chief nourisher in life's feast.
> *Lady Macbeth*   What do you mean?
> *Macbeth*   Still it cried, "Sleep no more!" to all the house;
> "Glamis hath murther'd sleep, and therefore Cawdor
> Shall sleep no more—Macbeth shall sleep no more."(2.2.35–40)

The voice consigns him to sleeplessness by the same set of names the witches used to assign him to ambition. When he asks them for reassurance against Macduff, so he may "sleep in spite of thunder," their answer is immediate and ominous: thunder, and the apparition of "a Child crowned, with a tree in his hand" (s.d. at 4.1.86). The forces of generational and seasonal rebirth unite against his craving for rest—"the season of all natures," as Lady Macbeth all too aptly defines it.[19]

Insomnia, like the other cyclical failures Macbeth and his wife cause, briefly afflicts all of Scotland. To restore "sleep to our nights," Macduff must leave his native body politic for England, "To wake Northumberland" (3.6.31–34); but no such cure is available for the nightmares and somnambulism that erode the bodies unnatural of the king and queen. The Doctor and the Waiting-Gentlewoman "have two nights watch'd" to observe Lady Macbeth's "slumb'ry agitation," but are then free to tell each other "Good night" and flee to their own restful worlds. The Doctor calls it "A great perturbation in nature, to receive at once the benefit of sleep, and do the effects of watching," but we may suspect that Lady Macbeth's perturbation of nature has entailed the opposite, an appearance of sleep with none of its regenerative qualities (5.1.1–79). She is propelled through an endless night by a driving nostalgia for the moment before the ambitious crime that rendered her both literally and symbolically ineligible for rest. Her sleep-walking thus complements her hand-washing: both represent a futile effort to erase the consequences of a deed that murdered sleep both in Duncan and in her.

Shakespeare portrays Macbeth's crimes, from first to last, as costly violations of the procreative cycle. Dr. Isadore Coriat, one of the play's first psychoanalytic critics, identifies the witches who insti-gate these offenses as "erotic symbols, representing, although sex-less, the emblems of the generative power in nature. In the 'hell broth' are condensed heterogeneous materials in which even on su-perficial analysis one can discern the sexual significance."[20] But su-perficial analysis dismisses too easily the discordant aspects of that emblem. These bearded women provoke Macbeth to mix the sexual elements ruinously, as they provoked him to mix the elements of the other natural cycles that must be polarized to be regenerative: night with day, dreaming with waking, and fall with spring. Under their influence he misuses his generative powers in such a way that he undermines the hereditary order, rendering his sexuality as barren and distorted as their own.

The Oedipal crimes constitute a man's ultimate offense against his hereditary nature, and the most insidious mixture of the gen-erational cycles, which must remain distinct to remain healthful. Since so much has been written about the Freudian implications of *Macbeth*, however, this chapter will examine only those aspects of the Oedipal situation that relate to ambitious revisions of identity. Macbeth conspires with the temptress to "do the deed" that will make him king, or remake him as king. Norman Holland outlines the standard psychoanalytic axioms about the play: "Macbeth acts the role of a son who replaces the authority of his father by force and substitutes himself. The motive for this father murder is Lady Macbeth, the 'demon woman' who creates the abyss between father and son."[21] Since Gertrude is the prize of Claudius' crime, Hamlet holds her partly responsible for that crime; Richard III entraps the Lady Anne by a trickier version of the same deduction. Freud argues that the woman's passive role gradually became misinterpreted in "the lying poetic fancies of prehistoric times" until the mother be-came an active instigator.[22] Lady Macbeth seems to offer herself as the sexual prize of Macbeth's regicide, and threatens to become the murderous mother rather than the seductive mother if he refuses the task (1.7.56–59).

But, from my point of view, the reading of the crime as essentially ambitious rather than essentially sexual squares better with the situations the psychoanalysts describe. What Lady Macbeth actually provokes in her husband is an ambitious deed; the analogy to the Oedipal situation may be a resonance rather than a primary but veiled meaning. In offering to become either the seductive mother or the murderous one, she is reminding him that it is in his own power to decide whether to create this new royal self or to destroy it in its infancy. His success in creating it will be a measure of his sexual capacity, but that sexual provocation remains at the distance of a metaphor, and is intimately linked to the goal of a new birth rather than to any goal of sensual gratification. Occam's Razor seems to cut against the traditional Freudian reading in this case. Sexuality is Lady Macbeth's means to an ambitious end in the play's superficial psychology, and it would be fitting for the same transaction to apply on the play's deep figurative level. If psychoanalytic critics argue that "Macbeth's killing of Duncan represents hatred and resentment of a fatherlike authority" and that "Lady Macbeth embodies or projects Macbeth's ambitious wish," as Holland summarizes it,[23] then the tensions seem more applicable to the hazards of ambition than to the "family romance" as such. Duncan is not Macbeth's actual father, but plays the paternal role in limiting the legitimate range of Macbeth's aspiration; the play makes it clear that Duncan is not a restrictive authority except in holding his preeminence and in promising it to another heir before Macbeth. Lady Macbeth is not Macbeth's actual mother, but plays the maternal role in offering to "embody" an ambitious new self for him.

Several critics have suggested that the murder of Duncan is figuratively a rape, or that the murder is only the offspring, or the projection onto Duncan, of a sexual crime between Macbeth and his Lady.[24] Rather than making either the violent or the sexual aspect of the "deed" merely a metaphor for the other, however, my thesis makes them mutually dependent: this is a rape with procreative purposes, and it entails ripping the hereditary body politic untimely from its haven in Duncan's body. (The revelation of Macduff's Caesarean origins is, in this sense, another example of Macbeth's crime functioning as a rash wish that unwittingly invites its own punishment.) But this sinister seduction turns out to be a dismal failure. One critic equates the spirits of drink that the Porter says inspire but hinder sexual activity with the spirits that appear to Macbeth as witches: for each man, "The spirits that seem to make him potent actually render him impotent."[25] The sexual situation is again not

merely parallel to the political situation, but intimately linked to
it: the attempt to conceive a new self becomes instead a loss of the
original birth, and the effort to seize sovereignty over the process of
procreation and lineage is steadily revealed as a forfeiting of all
procreative abilities and lineal aspirations. Macbeth is left with a
"barren sceptre" (3.1.61): the ambitious abuse of his sexual powers
has ruined those powers. His castration, like that of Oedipal sons,
is the final result of indulged Oedipal impulses; his impotence, like
that of fisher-kings in myth, leads necessarily to his expulsion from
rule.

The phallic character of Macbeth's crime is clear enough, however
one chooses to interpret it. Led by a dagger, he advances toward
Duncan's bed-chamber "With Tarquin's ravishing strides" (2.1.55).
Newly convinced by his wife to assert his sexual manhood by this
deed, to become the "serpent" striking up through the "innocent
flower" (1.5.64–65), Macbeth claims to "bend up / Each corporal
agent to this terrible feat" (1.7.79–80); and when conscientious fear
renders him impotent to act, she says, "You do unbend your noble
strength" (2.2.42). When she mocks him for lacking the "manhood"
to finish that task, she chooses to call him "Infirm of purpose"
(2.2.49). The murder is described by everyone, including the per-
petrators, as a "deed" or "act"; but these euphemisms for the horror
that "Tongue nor heart cannot conceive nor name" (2.3.64–65) refer
to sexual deeds or acts as often as murderous ones in Shakespeare.[26]
This convergence of the two acts suggests the mixed crime of Oedipus; since the direct result is the creation of an exalted but sinister
Macbeth, it may refer to the aspect of the Oedipus story that focuses
on pride and identity, rather than the aspect that focuses on sexual
psychology for its own sake.[27]

The regicide is not the first time Macbeth has violently "conceived" an exalted new self and hewed its Caesarean path to life
through another's body. Scotland is conventionally described as a
mother throughout *Macbeth*, and only a few lines into the play we
see Macbeth emerge as her heroic child. Using his "brandish'd steel"
to make himself "valor's minion," he "carv'd out his passage" to
Macdonwald and "unseam'd him from the nave to th' chops." A
"passage" was a standard term in Renaissance medicine for "the
necke of this wombe" at the base of the uterus.[28] Richard II uses the
same term when he strives to "tear a passage thorough the flinty
ribs / Of this hard world, my ragged prison walls" for his rebirth in
"A generation of still-breeding thoughts" (5.5.6–21), and Shakespeare will use it again to describe Coriolanus' determination to

chop "his passage" through "Rome gates," which (as I will argue)
become the symbol of his mother's womb through which any viable
rebirth must pass.

Macbeth's first rebirth, however, is a defense of Duncan's paternal
privileges rather than an assault on them. Disdaining the sinister
allure of the "rebel's whore" Fortune—a version of the Oedipal
temptress—Macbeth and Banquo confirm their identities as "children and servants" to Duncan's throne (1.4.25). But once the prospect
of creating heroic new identities with their swords has presented
itself, the loyal soldiers become susceptible to the lure of the sinister
witches, who offer them a rebirth that evades rather than affirms
their hereditary subordination. The witches are Jocasta-figures, ava-
tars not only of the temptress-figure Lady Macbeth with whom they
share a provocation and a sexual ambiguity, but also of that sinister
temptress Fortune, with whom they share a name: etymologically
as well as mythologically, "the three weïrd sisters" are the women
of fortune. Furthermore, witches and midwives were strongly identified with each other in sixteenth-century England, particularly in
accusations that midwives induced birth to give the child a soul,
then consecrated that soul to Satan by ritualistically killing the
infant before it could be baptized.[29] The parallels between this accusation and the witches' instigation of Macbeth's rebirth, death,
and damnation, are certainly speculative, but also intriguing. Once
it becomes clear that his first rebirth has not granted Macbeth a
place in the royal lineage, he determines to use the same figurative
technique that made him Duncan's loyal son to become Duncan's
rebellious son. As with Prince Hal, Shakespeare undoes the dream-
work of a boy's father-saving fantasy, revealing the latent father-
killing fantasy that was lurking symmetrically behind it. The witches
perform the same psychoanalytic function, for Macbeth and for us,
encouraging him to recognize the inevitable Oedipal conflict arising
from his role as Duncan's child and servant, and thereby to recognize
the perverse psychological mechanism connecting his loyal deeds
with his "horrible imaginings."

The witches' prophecy is what sets the play's tragic aspect in
motion, and it does so by luring Macbeth away from the normal
cycle of generation. The prophecy seems to announce an equitable
distribution of glory to the two triumphant soldiers: rule to Macbeth
and succession to Banquo. But, as Lucien Goldmann suggests, the
tragic hero generally finds that his gods "speak to him in deceitful
terms and from afar off, the oracles which he consults have two
meanings, one apparent but false, the other hidden but true, the

demands which the Gods make are contradictory, and the world is ambiguous and equivocal."[30] The hidden truth in the riddling prophecy, arising from the fog of the "foul and fair" day on the heath, is that the two promised forms of glory are mutually exclusive. A cause-and-effect relationship lurks unrecognized in the witches' division of the spoils: since Macbeth will seize a paternal identity that does not belong to him hereditarily, he will be forbidden to father a lineal successor. The prophecy that confronts Macbeth is therefore an Oedipal prophecy—specifically, a warning about filial rebellion and the castration that avenges it—as Lévi-Strauss argues all riddles are.[31] Such a riddle tempts man toward the fatal violation it describes, sends him in pursuit of self-destruction through a desperate and deluded attempt at self-preservation. The "paradoxical impression that Macbeth gives of being morally responsible for his own destruction even though he is so heavily fated to destroy himself that the lines of his destiny can be read by prophecy"[32] may be partly resolved by recognizing the unwitting act of choice that invites his fated barrenness. His fatal error, like that of Oedipus, is a failure to notice the cautionary aspect of the prophecies affixed to the gloriously inciting aspect; the contrastingly cautious Banquo avoids that Oedipal (and figuratively castrating) mistake. Banquo, the acknowledged enemy of Macbeth's "genius" or generative force (3.1.48–69), may safely partake of the crown by growing into it through generation rather than transforming himself forcibly into a figure of royal stature. As Edward Forset wrote in the same year that Shakespeare wrote *Macbeth*, "when wee be disposed to alter any thing, we must let it grow by degrees, and not hast it on too suddenly."[33] The flesh of Banquo's flesh eventually grows into the kingly robes that hang so loosely on Macbeth's artificial person.

Lady Macbeth is quicker than her husband to recognize that murdering Duncan will entail murdering the procreative order. The fisher-king Duncan basks in the natural fecundity that he half-perceives and half-creates in the couple's home. Banquo explains Duncan's enjoyment of this castle in suggestive terms:

> This guest of summer,
> The temple-haunting martlet, does approve,
> By his lov'd mansionry, that the heaven's breath
> Smells wooingly here; no jutty, frieze,
> Buttress, nor coign of vantage, but this bird
> Hath made his pendant bed and procreant cradle.
> Where they most breed and haunt, I have observ'd
> The air is delicate. (1.6.3–10)

Just as Lady Macbeth has already begun replacing this martlet with a raven, and the domesticated jutties with battlements (1.5.38–40), so has she begun to replace this nurturant sexuality with its antithesis. Her plea that the spirits "unsex me," according to a recent study, contains a specific request that her menstrual cycle be intermitted:[34]

> Make thick my blood,
> Stop up th' access and passage to remorse,
> That no compunctious visitings of nature
> Shake my fell purpose.   (1.5.43–46)

Even her request that the spirits "take my milk for gall" suggests that the reborn Macbeth (like the reborn Coriolanus) can be nurtured into life only by fluids opposite to "the milk of human kindness" by which he was originally formed and fed (1.5.48, 17).

Freud understood this couple's loss of progeny as essentially such a rash wish, a barren instruction returning to plague the inventors: "It would be a perfect example of poetic justice in the manner of the talion if the childlessness of Macbeth and the barrenness of his Lady were the punishment for their crimes against the sanctity of geniture."[35] The inconsistencies concerning Lady Macbeth's children, despite L. C. Knights's famous argument, actually makes Freud's point all the more convincing.[36] If the children were concretely presented to us, Shakespeare would be obliged to provide a literal cause for their parents' poetically just lack of an heir. That would likely both alter the polarity of our sympathies and conceal the important symbolic cause behind a crudely physical efficient cause. This is opportunism on Shakespeare's part of the sort Knights describes, where the play works as something other than a realistic story, but if (as Knights urges) we ignore the apparent disappearance of the children, if we refuse to think of Lady Macbeth as a procreative creature, then we lose the moral import of that disappearance. Macduff's reasons for abandoning his family to slaughter remain somewhat unclear, perhaps for same didactic purpose.[37] By including only the comment that this Caesarean figure "wants the natural touch" (4.2.9), Shakespeare suggests that the products of disordered procreation are deprived of heirs by a jealous natural order. Since it requires Duncan's death, Macbeth's royal rebirth thriftlessly ravins up his own life's means (2.4.28–29); since Caesarean operations were virtually always fatal to the mother in the Renaissance,[38] Macduff's birth entails the same unwitting offense. By refusing us a complete factual explanation for either man's loss of progeny, Shakespeare focuses our attention on the defect they share and the nemesis it provokes.

This shared unnaturalness and childlessness enables Macduff to cure the disease that threatens the nation's procreative health. Macbeth's crimes against Malcolm's "due of birth" and against "nature's germains" in general have blighted Scotland's fertility (3.6.25; 4.1.59). The threatened kingdom is, as Macduff says, truly a threatened "birthdom" (4.3.4). In reply, Malcolm portrays himself as merely another agent of that blight, a creature of indiscriminate lust in conceiving children, and hardly better than Lady Macbeth in nursing them thereafter: he will "Pour the sweet milk of concord into hell" (4.3.98). This causes Macduff to wonder whether there can be any hope for Scotland's regeneration,

> Since that the truest issue of thy throne
> By his own interdiction stands accus'd
> And does blaspheme his breed? Thy royal father
> Was a most sainted king; the queen that bore thee,
> Oft'ner upon her knees than on her feet,
> Died every day she liv'd. (4.3.106–11)

What this speech emphasizes is generational continuity: Malcolm's royal virtues should follow from his hereditary rights, almost as if orderly succession were virtue itself. The quality Macduff eulogizes in Malcolm's mother is her daily exchange of death and life, a pattern associable with the regenerative virtues of sleep, "The death of each day's life" as it is called at the time of Duncan's murder (2.2.37). This figuratively posthumous mother merges with Macduff's literal one into the notion of Scotland as such a mother:

> Alas, poor country,
> Almost afraid to know itself! It cannot
> Be call'd our mother, but our grave; where nothing,
> But who knows nothing, is once seen to smile. (4.3.164–67)

Macbeth's Caesarean rebirth has infected the entire nation with his nullified and self-alienated condition, and precludes any more natural births in the future. "Cruel are the times when we are traitors, / And do not know ourselves," the choral Rosse tells Lady Macduff moments before she and her babes are slaughtered (4.2.18–19). Disruptions of succession converted individual mothers and the mother-country into tombs in *Richard III* (4.1.53; 4.4.138, 423) and *Richard II* (2.1.51, 83), and now the same transaction threatens Scotland's future.

But eventually Scotland, like Macduff, is rescued from the dead maternal womb and begins a new generation of life. Macduff's role as the spearhead of this vengeful revival becomes an emblem of the fact that Macbeth is destroyed by the unlineal, unnatural provenance of his own royal identity. Macbeth is able to achieve his bloody rebirth only by performing a regicide; Macduff is able to perform his regicide, according to the prophecies, only because of his Caesarean origins. Macduff is, in this sense, the fulfillment of Macbeth's foolish wish to replace natural succession with abrupt violence. Macbeth again resembles Richard III, in serving as the sacrifice by which his nation restores its damaged lineal health, and Macduff is a suitable blade-wielding hierophant. When a society must purge a sin that has injured its fertility, it generally sacrifices a figure onto whom all the sin is projected, often a temporary mock-king; the executioner is generally a liminal figure who partly reflects or partly contracts the victim's particular taint.[39]

A group of paradoxically mighty infants resume the process of generation as Macbeth's enemies.[40] From the corrupt jumble of nature's germains in the witches' cauldron arise miraculously two such symbols of procreation's determination to survive and destroy the barren tyrant. The crowned babe, suggesting the rightful heir Malcolm, and the bloody babe, suggesting the Caesarean child Macduff, represent several things on other levels: the inheriting children Macbeth cannot have, the potential heirs Macbeth has sought to kill, the Oedipal children who typically abuse the father who was himself an Oedipal criminal, and the wounded regenerative order as a whole.[41] For Macbeth as for Richard III, the failure to eradicate all such heirs, and relatedly the failure to terminate all such cycles, generates a nemesis that returns to destroy him. As in Greek and Christian myths, at least one heir escapes the tyrant's defensive Slaughter of the Innocents, and the army that defeats Macbeth consists of "Siward's son, / And many unrough youths that even now / Protest their first of manhood" (5.2.9–11). Once again Macbeth has succeeded only in interrupting a cycle he sought to override completely, and when it resumes he finds himself trapped in an unnatural generational isolation (5.3.24–26), with no child of his own to succeed him.

Macbeth is not only the bad ruler of Freudian myth, who deprives others such as Macduff and Banquo of their reproductive rights; he is also the bad ruler of fisher-king myths, whose own reproductive impotence causes his nation's crops to fail. The repression and vengeful return of human generation in the play is closely paralleled by a repression and return of the seasonal forces of vegetative life. The parallel has several revealing precedents:

> The first religious poet of Greece, Hesiod . . . tells us that when men do justice [their crops flourish and] "their wives bear children that are like their parents." So, on the other hand, when a sin has been committed—such as the unconscious incest of Oedipus—all Nature is poisoned by the offence of man. The land of Thebes "Wasteth in the fruitless buds of earth, / In parchèd herds, and travail without birth / Of dying women."[42]

The Oedipal archetype, apparently from the very first, has been associated with a punitive collapse of nature's various regenerative cycles. In *2 Henry IV*, the haunted country is England rather than Thebes, but the ghosts are similar. Gloucester mentions "Unfather'd heirs and loathly births of nature. / The seasons change their manners, as the year / Had found some months asleep and leap'd them over" (4.4.121–24). A few lines later, Prince Hal confirms the Oedipal character of this disturbance by stealing his sleeping father's unlineal crown. This blight began, according to the Gardener, when Richard II allowed the "prodigal weight" of "unruly children" to ruin a tree, and allowed "The noisome weeds" to "suck / The soil's fertility from wholesome flowers" (*Richard II*, 3.4.29–45). The natural order is only temporarily salvaged when Hal conquers France in deference to his forefathers, thereby acquiring a new world of vegetative and procreative fertility. The more lasting solution is the return of Richmond, who supposedly unites and renews the White and Red Roses.

The same correspondences appear in *Macbeth*, where the savior returns accompanied by his nation's foliage, and by young men determined "To dew the sovereign flower and drown the weeds" on their "march towards Birnan" (5.2.30–31). When Duncan arrives at Macbeth's castle, he is associated not only with the martlet's procreative aspects, but also with its role as a "guest of summer" (1.6.3). Conversely, Macbeth describes his usurping reign by adjacent metonymies that suggest vegetative and procreative sterility respectively : "Upon my head they plac'd a fruitless crown, / And put a barren sceptre in my gripe, / Thence to be wrench'd with an unlineal hand, / No son of mine succeeding" (3.1.60–63). He returns to the witches hoping for a revision of this prophecy, but the visions they conjure only serve to reinforce it. As early as 1746, John Upton perceived the brutally literal level of these portents:

> The armed head represents symbolically Macbeth's head cut off and brought to Malcolm by Macduff. The bloody child is Macduff untimely ripp'd from his mother's womb. The child with a crown on his head, and a bough in his hand, is the royal Malcolm, who ordered his soldiers to hew them down a bough and bear it before them to Dunsinane.[43]

Having been lured by the witches across the threshold from reality into a fairy tale where words and imagination have an absolute efficacy, Macbeth overlooks this literal level of the portents, as he and other rash wishers overlook the literal level of their wishes; "the letter kills," as theologians warned, and the literal components of these apparitions emerge to kill Macbeth. Of course the armed head "knows thy thought," if it is actually his own head; it is an "unknown power" only to the extent that his own conscientious imagination is (4.1.69). The bloody babe is so overdetermined as a symbol that it resists any careful reading. The child's bough is all too easily interpreted as a symbol of regenerative nature, the rightful heir's sceptre that will replace Macbeth's "fruitless" one.

Yet there is a level on which this symbolic reading of Malcolm's return remains valuable, because even the literal advance of Birnan's branches symbolizes the unified nature that engulfs its betrayer. Dunsinane Castle, as a prize of Macbeth's ambition, represents on one level all of man's futile stays against his mortal limitations. It symbolizes for Shakespeare what Ozymandias' statue symbolized for Shelley, and the advancing branches are the equivalent of Shelley's centuries of sandstorms. In the form of Birnan wood, the balance of nature springs back against the kingly enclave man has manufactured against it; the wood, on this level, represents the endlessly persistent forces that erode humanity's efforts to make the world conform to its desires and reflect its consciousness. To build the castle in the primeval forest, to establish human sovereignty, land was cleared; eventually nature will reforest that land. The fact that civilization rapidly deforested Scotland in the era of the historical Macbeth makes the symbolism all the more plausible and evocative.[44] The camouflaged advance on Dunsinane provides an accelerated emblem for the futility of humanity's ambitious projects, an ethical lesson presented by a sort of time-lapse photography.

Several critics have commented that this advance resembles a

Maying festival, in which the young people carry green branches to chase out the tyrannical winter.[45] Such an association, however subliminal, would serve to reinforce our sense that we are witnessing nature's cyclical victory over its barren enemies. What I am suggesting is that Shakespeare has grounded his warning against ambition in a parable applicable to the entire history of human civilization, and not just to the cycle of any given year, just as the confrontation between Hal and the Lord Chief Justice in *2 Henry IV* is applicable to much more than the reformation of a single unruly son. Shakespeare thus reinforces the power of the specific confrontations, and at the same time reminds us of their universal relevance; the hazards of ambition are an essential component in human experience, all human experience.

The shift in the moral balance from the history plays to *Macbeth*—the shift that makes *Macbeth* a tragedy—is visible in the difference between these two primal confrontations. We may not be entirely delighted with Hal's submission to the Lord Chief Justice and his banishment of Falstaff, but we sense that it is a choice we have all made, and that it is finally not only compatible with our humanity, but necessary for its survival. But, inasmuch as Macbeth's ambition may represent the essential projects of humanity, the very essence of our identity as *homo faber*—the creature who shapes his environment, with words and other tools, to his desires—the destruction of Macbeth by that fated moving wood can please us as humane justice on only the most superficial level. Conventional goodness is victorious, but it defeats an evil that Shakespeare invites us to recognize as a plausible extension of the things that make us human, and its weapons are the instruments of our oppression as well as our salvation. Shakespeare may have suggested all the natural concomitants to the political hierarchy in the history plays to remind people of the deep sinfulness and foolishness of attempting to overthrow that hierarchy; he may simply have been dramatizing the Elizabethan propaganda typified by the passages quoted earlier from Hooker and from the "Exhortation Concerning Good Order." But at some point Shakespeare recognized the logical counterpart to the argument that rebellion can arise only from a failure to recognize the seamless and providential character of the world's order. To dislike anything about nature is to lose sight of the essential principle defending the sovereign's authority over the will of his individual subjects. If all levels of the established order are so intricately linked, then repercussions may travel upward from lesser violations of that order, as well as downward from greater ones. If political ambition entails a parallel distortion of every other natural system, then we are all implicated in an array of crimes including regicide by our casual individual resentment of some inconvenient bad weather, and by our imperative resistance as a species to the landscape and the climate, a resistance palpably evinced by our houses and garments.

The notion that human beings are necessarily ambitious has substantial precedents in Renaissance philosophy. Petrarch argues that the specific need for shelter and clothing authorizes humanity's more general aspirations to surpass its given condition. As opposed to the lower animals, who "are allotted whatever is given them at birth and no more," man's naked frailties indicate that God wants him to achieve and acquire "as much as he is able in his acute genius to attain by living and thinking."[46] Similarly, to Bovillus, as Ernst Cassirer explains it,

> freedom simply means that man does not receive his being ready-made from nature, as do the other entities, nor does he, so to speak, get it as a permanent fief; but rather that he must acquire it, must *form* it through *virtus* and *ars* . . . If he falls prey to the vice of inertia—the medieval *acedia*— he can sink down to the level at which only naked existence remains to him . . . The man of nature, simple *homo*, must become the man of art.[47]

In *Macbeth* Shakespeare gives us glimpses of the dark converse of this glorious art, this grand transformation. What if man's greatest and most characteristic quality is trapped in a world where it can express itself only as sin, or at least where its natural activity will be perceived and punished as a violation of natural law by a jealous paternal God? This was the belief of the Gnostics, who felt that some higher God had planted a spark of his own divinity in each person, but that we have been trapped into a natural world inimical to that divine essence by a lower and envious God-the-Father. To the Gnostics, according to Hans Jonas,

> It is almost by exaggeration that the divinity of cosmic order is turned into the opposite of divine. Order and law is the cosmos here too, but rigid and inimical order, tyrannical and evil law, devoid of meaning and goodness, alien to the purposes of man and to his inner essence, no object for his communication and affirmation.

> The blemish of nature lies not in any deficiency of order, but in the all too pervading completeness of it. Far from

> chaos, the creation of the demiurge, unenlightened as it
> is, is still a system of law. But cosmic law, once worshiped
> as the expression of a reason with which man's reason
> can communicate in the act of cognition, is now seen
> only in its aspect of compulsion which thwarts man's
> freedom.[48]

The cosmic order thus appears in its aspect of *heimarmene*, a Fate
morally congruent with Mosaic law and opposed to the human essence, rather than *pronoia*, a true Providence. From such a viewpoint, Macbeth's steadfast opposition to, and destruction by, a unified system of nature would mark him as a martyr rather than a
sinner.

Even his diseases, from the Gnostic perspective, are the proper
tactics for opposing the Archons (the gods who rule this world) rather
than punishments imposed by those Archons; this is revisionistic
history on a grand theological scale. Macbeth's abstention from procreation, and his intimately related program of "uprooting" the heirs
of others, recalls part of the formula dying Gnostics recited to escape
the Archons, a sort of perverse last confession: "I have not sown
children to the Archon but have uprooted his roots." To the Gnostics, the Mosaic God's injunction to "be fruitful and multiply" was
an evil trick designed to entrap more of the divine sparks in his
labyrinth. Even Macbeth's murder of sleep in himself and in others
squares with the Gnostic project of awakening humanity from a
sleep imposed by the Archons through a soporific poison that made
us passive to this world's evils and forgetful of our true, more exalted
home. Ambition is equated with insomnia in Gnosticism as it is in
Shakespeare, but for the Gnostics that would have been an endorsement rather than a condemnation. The Gnostic is saved, not damned,
by the Call from the supernatural agency that answers to an inner
potential, as the witches' call answers to Macbeth's prior ambitions.

There are also elements here of the family romance, and of the
decomposition motif by which that romance expresses itself in fairy
tales as well as in psychotic delusions: a Gnostic's ambitions, apparently rebellions against the Father, are actually justified as ful-
fillments of his true heritage from the lost higher Father who rules
the greater realm.[49] The genetic identity is an obstacle to fulfillment
for the Gnostics, and not a truly divine dictation of identity. In
Valentinian Gnosticism, the Oedipal archetype emerges when the
mother conceals the truly divine spark from the lower God-the-
Father, and tricks him into leaving it "implanted in the human soul

and body, to be carried there as if in a womb until it had grown sufficiently to receive the Logos."[50] This Mother carries within her the seed by which the son reconceives himself, and she hides him (as Zeus and Moses were hidden) to protect him from the father's jealous and fearful wrath until the boy is strong enough to rebel successfully and thus reunite with her. To this extent, the Oedipal components of Macbeth's crime correspond to the Gnostic program.

The world of Macbeth thus moves closer to the world of Marlowe's Faustus, whose effort to find something above the mundane that answers to his aspiring mind becomes mired in the limits of the physical universe. The lower God has taught us to perceive as Satanic the voices—Macbeth's witches, Faustus' Mephistopheles—that urge us to fulfill the transcendent within us; he has also learned how to imitate the grandeur of such voices when he chooses, for the purpose of luring us more deeply into the wordly labyrinth. When the witches implicitly laugh at Macbeth's defeat, as when the gods silently laugh at the defeat of Coriolanus (5.3.183–85), we may easily and chillingly sense that a spiteful conspiracy has triumphed over the ambition that is intrinsic to our humanity. What makes this even more horrifying is the recognition that this conspiracy has triumphed in the name of a "nature" we had been taught to revere as our mother, and to believe functioned in perfect harmony with our needs.

Nevertheless, on the play's primary level, the return of Birnan wood to Dunsinane serves the human good as well as the natural order. A virtuous new human generation accompanies these moving branches, and is protected by them. Malcolm restores to Scotland the same combination of blessings that the flower-strewing Perdita brings into the artificial winter of Sicilia, making her as welcome "As is the spring to th' earth" (5.1.152). Macbeth cannot embrace this renewed vegetation as Leontes does, because in this adult fairy tale nature returns not in forgiveness, as a gift, but in vengeance, as a weapon. When the cycle he has briefly suppressed resumes its natural flow, Macbeth is stranded outside it. Even while this new spring burgeons, he becomes the yellowed creature of autumn, and "ripe for shaking" (5.3.23, 4.3.238). As the Gardener remarks about Richard II, "He that hath suffered this disordered spring / Hath now himself met with the fall of leaf" (3.4.48–49).

Time, which Macbeth would not trust to bring the prophecies to fruition, thus becomes his enemy. For him, as for Tennyson's Tithonus, the fact that the cycles of days, seasons, and generations continue all around him only makes his own steady decay more

Foolish Wishes and the Tragedy of *Macbeth*

painful. Macbeth finds himself on a linear course into winter, while his wife retreats into a ritualistic repetition of yesterdays, until he loses her entirely:

> She should have died hereafter;
> There would have been a time for such a word.
> To-morrow, and to-morrow, and to-morrow,
> Creeps in this petty pace from day to day,
> To the last syllable of recorded time;
> And all our yesterdays have lighted fools
> The way to dusty death. Out, out, brief candle!
> Life's but a walking shadow . . .   (5.5.17–24)

With the loss of his wife, Macbeth's hopes for diurnal or generational renewal disappear. In this Shakespeare seems to be building on a Jacobean commonplace. Richard Brathwait's *The Prodigals Teares* suggests the same associations: "I know Lord, that the candle of the wicked . . . .shalbe soone put out . . . his faire and fruitfull fieldes laid waste, his treasures rifled, his pastures with all his hierds dispersed, and his children utterly rooted out and extinguished."[51] Nehemiah Rogers' prodigal-son tract provides a similar analogue to Macbeth's resigned conclusion that "Life's but a walking shadow," asserting that any existence devoid of spiritual growth and regeneration is "but a shadow of life."[52] Macbeth's phrase also alludes ominously, unwittingly, to his earlier characterization of Banquo's ghost as a "horrible shadow" (3.4.105). Both Banquo's shade and Birnan wood return as the ghosts of the natural life his royal aspirations have murdered, and as the fathers of the natural renewal he has failed to kill.

Macbeth's resigned conclusion, however, becomes a literal as well as a figurative truth. This speech is closely bracketed by revelations about the movement of Birnan wood. Specifically, less than forty lines before Macbeth dismisses life as a walking shadow, Malcolm tells his soldiers each to "hew him down a bough, / And bear't before him, thereby shall we shadow / The numbers of our host" (5.4.4–6). In its emblematic march on Dunsinane, in other words, life actually *is* a walking shadow. Malcolm's stratagem, Macbeth's verbal metaphor, and Shakespeare's visual emblem, all agree on that point. Macbeth has not foreseen either Malcolm's military tactic or Shakespeare's artistic device, but most important, he has again failed to perceive the literal as well as the figurative meaning of a phrase, a phrase that subsequently becomes all too prophetic. The world, like the witches, palters with him in a double sense (5.8.20). His very resignation to the hollowness of life actually invites life's true power to rise up against him, in a bitterly ironic reshaping of his own metaphor; again Macbeth becomes the fairy-tale figure whose unenlightened words return to haunt him. This complicated play on the notion of the walking shadow recapitulates in small the tragedy's central transaction. Macbeth's lack of faith in the natural cycles led to the rash wish that deprived him of cyclical regeneration; here, his lack of faith in life leads to a rash observation that unwittingly invites his death at hands of Malcolm's forces.

Cut off from his natural roots, Macbeth becomes a lifeless head on a pike (5.8.26), while Malcolm, festooned with green branches, takes his place. A contemporary of Shakespeare proposes a similar fate for his own murderous, incestuous, and overreaching protagonist:

> God would not permit him to enjoy that wealth, which
> to purchase had made him violate the lawes both divine,
> and humane, and prophane the most Sacred bonds that
> are in nature; [but] he that by just labours, and lawfull
> industries, gathers up any thing shall see his goods prosper
> like a tree planted neere the current of waters, which
> brings forth fruite in its season.[53]

The wages of sin are death, and the reward for cancelling the bonds of nature is at best an absence of life.

Malcolm, nominated as the new fisher-king by the procreative order itself, promises to reward his loyalists and to undertake all the tasks "Which would be newly planted with the time" (5.9.30–31). This represents a return to natural continuity, not only in the character of the metaphor he employs, but also in the history of that metaphor. He assumes his hereditary place while using the same figuration his father used at the start of the play to thank *his* loyalists. As nature is a metaphor for heredity in this play, so is it a hereditary metaphor. With the big war that made ambition virtue successfully concluded, Duncan told Macbeth,

> I have begun to plant thee, and will labor
> To make thee full of growing. Noble Banquo,
> That hast no less deserv'd, nor must be known
> No less to have done so, let me infold thee
> And hold thee to my heart.
> *Banquo*   There if I grow,
> The harvest is your own.   (1.4.28–33)

Foolish Wishes and the Tragedy of *Macbeth*

The witches know better than the egalitarian Duncan: Banquo shall be "Lesser than Macbeth, and greater" (1.3.65) when his grains grow and Macbeth's do not, and this exchange suggests the reasons for that distinction. By accepting Duncan's vegetative metaphor, Banquo acknowledges his dependence on Duncan's fertility, and thus becomes eligible for the role as "the root and father / Of many kings" that the witches promised him (3.1.5–6). By agreeing to surrender his fruits to the throne, he reserves a place for his scions on the throne.

Macbeth, in contrast, describes his "duties" as Duncan's "children" rather than as Duncan's "harvest," as if he expected his Caesarean deeds to win him a place in the royal family (1.4.24–25). That expectation becomes more obvious a few lines later in his violent response to Duncan's naming of Malcolm as heir to the throne.[54] Macbeth must pretend to accept what is duly planted with the time, while secretly undermining it as the traditionally parricidal serpent:

> *Lady Macbeth*   To beguile the time,
> Look like the time; bear welcome in your eye,
> Your hand, your tongue; look like th' innocent flower,
> But be the serpent under't.   (1.5.63–66)

Macbeth thus subverts the harvest Duncan promises. As soon as the regicide has been performed, the Porter, pretending to welcome the newly damned to hell, first hypothesizes his guest as "a farmer, that hang'd himself on th' expectation of plenty" (2.3.4–5). This paradoxical farmer destroyed himself because a healthy, orderly harvest and reseeding thwarted his selfish speculations: Macbeth's hope that the death of a royal line will legitimize his unnatural succession parallels the farmer's hope that scarcity will drive up the price of his hoarded grain. This correlation gains conviction from the similarly damning flaws of the Porter's other guests, who are all "caught out by overreaching themselves."[55] So, of course, is Macbeth, whose ambition has converted the blessings of nature into a curse.

Macbeth's attack on Banquo, like his attack on Duncan, arises from the extension of the planting metaphor into generational continuity. Banquo confronts the witches with characteristic confidence in the natural order:

> If you can look into the seeds of time,
> And say which grain will grow, and which will not,
> Speak then to me, who neither beg nor fear
> Your favors nor your hate.   (1.3.58–61)

Moral philosophers from Pelagius to Pico to Ralegh to Iago have used the selective cultivation of seeds as a metaphor for the legitimate range of self-improvement, self-cultivation.[56] Shakespeare, rather more conservative in his view of human aspiration, has Banquo leave not only the seeding, but also the choice of which seeds will grow, in the hands of God alone. He may therefore become "the root and father" of a new royal family tree (3.1.5). Macbeth has sacrificed his otherworldly hopes for worldly glory, only to find that he has no one to whom he may bequeath his costly acquisition; D'Amville, in Tourneur's *The Atheist's Tragedy*, makes much the same complaint, after a similar set of violations (4.2.36–39). But Shakespeare manipulates the vegetative metaphors to make the unity of divine and natural rules more vivid. Macbeth specifically complains about ruining his soul "To make them kings—the seeds of Banquo kings!" (3.1.69), unaware that his primal violation of nature necessarily entailed a loss of succession as well as virtue. This fear of seedlings, plausibly a premonition of the attack on his castle by shoots from Birnan wood, compels Macbeth to strike down Duncan and Banquo in the hope that their scions, Malcolm and Fleance, will then be destroyed. He has not reckoned with the proverbial truth Ben Jonson expresses in his *Discoveries*: "Severity represseth a few, but it irritates more. The lopping of trees makes the boughes shoote out thicker."[57]

Precisely that truth is driven home to Macbeth, on both the figurative and the literal levels, when Birnan wood begins its advance. But until it does, Macbeth supposes himself secure, because he has again failed to connect a figurative level with a literal one. His confidence that he can uproot these family trees is based on a literal reading of the witches' prophecy that he cannot be defeated until the trees of Birnan move, which he supposes is impossible:

> That will never be.
> Who can impress the forest, bid the tree
> Unfix his earth-bound root? Sweet bodements! good!
> Rebellious dead, rise never till the wood
> Of Birnan rise, and our high-plac'd Macbeth
> Shall live the lease of nature, pay his breath
> To time and mortal custom.   (4.1.94–100)

Either roots can be extirpated or they cannot; but because a family tree is a metaphor and a Birnan tree is real, Macbeth characteristically fails to see the contradiction in his hopes. Having broken the lease of nature, he can hardly expect to enforce it in his own defense;

time and mortal custom, which he sought to subdue to his will, subdue him instead. All that remains of Macbeth's natural foundation, all that grows to fill his oversized royal robes, is what he sees disturbing his wife's rest: "a rooted sorrow" (5.3.41). For her as for the barren women of the history plays, sorrow is the only thing that retains a regenerative basis. Macduff, too, was cut off at the root, but according to Rosse, he retained some feeling for "The fits o' th' season" (4.2.17), understood the principle of cyclical growth. Macbeth evidently does not: the plants he lops off inevitably send up new shoots, culminating in the forest that envelops his castle. At the end of the play the impotent fisher-king is a lifeless head on a wooden pole, like an old tree that has dropped no seedlings, disappearing one spring in the eternal forest, vengefully excluded by the regenerative cycles his ambition sought to suppress.

Disunity, Nullity, and the Tragedy of Manhood

In shattering the unity of these regenerative cycles, Macbeth shatters the unity of his own identity. He cannot attack outer nature without attacking inner nature, and the two employ remarkably similar methods of retribution. Macbeth's foolish wish to alienate his hereditary self, like his wish to alienate cyclical nature, is granted only temporarily; in both cases the alienated natural part persists outside of him and destroys him by returning once he has lost the capacity to reassimilate it. To the extent that Macbeth retains any stable self at all, it is a severely divided one; his triumphant departure from the circumference of his hereditary identity proves as Pyrrhic as his victory over natural regeneration. His mismanagement of the Oedipal crisis, implied in his bloody and sexualized attempt to steal a new identity, appropriately correlates with a mismanagement of the pre-Oedipal tasks of coordinating the senses and differentiating a unitary self from his environment.

In the early part of the play, this disintegration expresses itself largely as a dialectic of id and superego, as it did in the Henry IV plays. In fairy tales it is usually a parent who becomes divided into morally polarized halves, a loving mother and a wicked stepmother, a protective woodsman and a ravenous wolf.[58] In *Hamlet* and *Coriolanus* Shakespeare has similarly divided the father-figures in a way that answers to the psychic needs of the title characters. But Macbeth, like Prince Hal, represents in himself a divided son, inhabited by the extremes of filial loyalty and Oedipal rebelliousness. By encompassing these polar identities in a single figure over time, Shakespeare creates a schematic of the psychological mechanism, as first the conscientious superego, then the appetitive id, seeks to mold the protagonist's ego in its own image. The Macbeth of act one, like the Hal of Part One, heroically defeats those who rebel against the father's sovereign authority. The hints that Hal's symmetrical conquest of Hotspur is essentially a self-conquest have parallels in Macbeth's defeat of Norway, and even in the syntax Rosse uses to describe that confrontation: Norway was threatening to overcome Duncan's forces until Macbeth

> Confronted him with self-comparisons,
> Point against point, rebellious arm 'gainst arm,
> Curbing his lavish spirit.   (1.2.55–57)

The lack of clearly defined antecedents allows us to imagine that, in suppressing Norway, Macbeth is curbing his own lavish spirit, as the repressive model suggests. Even the momentary confusion induced by the fact that "rebellious arm," as the first of the pair, should normally refer to the subject Macbeth rather than the object Norway, contributes to this suggestion. This is not to say that the fight is merely a metaphor, any more than Hal's fight with Hotspur was merely a metaphor; but to undertake these battles, Hal and Macbeth had first to overcome a strongly implied impulse to overthrow the king they are protecting. (The witches remind Macbeth of unspeakable "things forgotten"—1.3.150.) The actual battles therefore recapitulate the psychological struggle that necessarily preceded them, and Shakespeare portrays the physical struggles in a way that permits them to serve as allegories, as well as consequences, of the accompanying psychological struggles. The mirror effect in Rosse's rhetoric is therefore quite purposeful: rebel and loyalist are diametrically opposed, but as the play goes on to demonstrate, they are by the same token virtually identical. They are so deeply entangled in each other, and so deeply ambivalent about each other, that the Sergeant's initial simile comparing the armies to "two spent swimmers that do cling together / And choke their art" is stunningly appropriate. (1.2.8–9).

Macbeth's relationship to the Thane of Cawdor provides a clear example of this pattern. The fact that Macbeth himself becomes "that most disloyal traitor, / The Thane of Cawdor" (1.2.52–53) shortly after defeating him is stark evidence that it is easy to pass through that looking glass, and become one's own mighty opposite. In this light, the Thane of Cawdor's surprisingly noble and loyal behavior at his execution (1.4.1–11) becomes suggestive: he seems to have compelled Macbeth to exchange his heroic loyalty for the Thane's rebelliousness, much as Hal forces Hotspur to "exchange / His glorious deeds for my indignities" in *1 Henry IV* (3.2.145–46). Hal attributes his reformation in *2 Henry IV* to a similar transaction— "My father is gone wild into his grave; / For in his tomb lie my affections, / And with his spirits sadly I survive" (5.2.123–25)—and we may justly fear that the opposite exchange has taken place at the Thane of Cawdor's death. Whether another such metempsychosis of the spirit of rebellion looms at the end of the play (as Roman Polanski's film version implies) is unclear, but it is evident enough that the id and its ambitions never completely disappear this side of death.

King Duncan comes close to recognizing Macbeth's resemblance to the rebels, or a least Shakespeare focuses the dramatic irony by giving Duncan words that hint at the terrible truth he is fatally overlooking:

> *Duncan* No more that Thane of Cawdor shall deceive
>   Our bosom interest. Go pronounce his present death,
>   And with his former title greet Macbeth.
> *Rosse* I'll see it done.
> *Duncan* What he hath lost, noble Macbeth hath won.
>
> (1.2.63–67).

This new Thane of Cawdor will renew the betrayal of Duncan's "absolute trust," which is again based on outward shows of loyalty (1.4.11–14). By giving Macbeth this new identity, Duncan helps the witches establish the ambitious momentum that eventually destroys both men; his words echo the witches' remark about what is "lost and won" from the previous scene, and anticipate their greeting of Macbeth by his new title in the following scene. What the original Thane of Cawdor hath lost, furthermore, includes his feigned loyalty and his rebellion, both of which Macbeth now seems to inherit. Macbeth then receives news from the witches of his forthcoming succession to the throne that should be Duncan's, and immediately encounters Rosse, who tells him,

> The King hath happily receiv'd, Macbeth,
> The news of thy success; and when he reads
> Thy personal venture in the rebels' fight,
> His wonders and his praises do contend
> Which should be thine or his.   (1.3.89–93)

Perhaps this is overinterpreting the speech, but it would be characteristic of Duncan to misread Macbeth as the rebel's moral opposite when he is merely their mirror-image, to overlook the moment when Macbeth crosses that thin line between creatures of the superego and creatures of the id.

Shakespeare portrays this moral degeneration in Macbeth by some extensions of the psychomachia. Macbeth's great speech dissuading himself from the murder is practically the pure voice of the superego. He overwhelms his forbidden desires with arguments of practicality, of social custom, and of religious stricture, until the desire itself almost disappears. Bound by political pragmatism, by civilized roles as kinsman, subject, and host, and by heavenly justice, Macbeth has

> no spur
> To prick the sides of my intent, but only
> Vaulting ambition, which o'erleaps itself,
> And falls on th' other—
> *(Enter Lady Macbeth)* (1.7.25–28)

Shakespeare, probably drawing on a tradition including Plato's *Phaedrus* and several Renaissance equestrian statues, often uses the horse as a symbol for the Elizabethan equivalent of the id.[59] Macbeth has this horse under control until his wife, who embodies his evil ambitions, arrives to "spur" it on with her own passions (see 1.6.23). She brushes aside the superego's arguments about public honors, humane restraint, and practical consequences, with the typical arguments of the id: "Art thou afeard / To be the same in thine own act and valor / As thou art in desire?" The real man, she adds, does not let " 'I dare not' wait upon 'I would',", and she relies on wine to help her evade the guilt of acting those desires (1.7.31–72). Macbeth is aroused, perhaps even sexually aroused, by these arguments, and begins to complete them on his own (1.7.72–82). As her husband yields to the id, Lady Macbeth gradually becomes superfluous, much in the way Lear's Fool becomes superfluous: when the protagonist internalizes the companion's voice, the companion can disappear from the stage. Once we recognize the fool at work in Lear, or the id at work in Macbeth, Shakespeare can eliminate the reified figure of the inward tendency, and focus our attention on the dialectic within the protagonist's identity.

That dialectic within Macbeth comes sharply into focus at the moment of Duncan's murder, amid new evidence of Macbeth's potential for self-alienation. Ambition, particularly such usurping ambition as Richard III and Macbeth display, constitutes a rash wish to move out of one identity into another; at the moment of regicide and unnatural rebirth, we see how costly the granting of this wish will be for Macbeth's integrity. In *Civilization and Its Discontents* Freud describes the merging of identities lovers sometimes feel, and the way that emulation can spill over into psychosis:

> Pathology has made us acquainted with a great number of states in which the boundary lines between the ego and the external world become uncertain or in which they are actually drawn incorrectly. There are cases in which parts of a person's own body, even portions of his own mental life . . . appear alien to him and as not belonging to his ego; there are other cases in which he ascribes to the external world things that clearly originate in his own ego and that ought to be acknowledged by it.[60]

The increasing disagreement between the two murderers over whether to spare Clarence in *Richard III* foreshadows the schizophrenia that eventually divides Richard into the brutal voice of ambition and the conscientious voice of his familial origins.[61] In *Macbeth*, a briefer but more intense contrast in the reaction of the two grooms to the murder seems to be Macbeth's own projection of his id and his superego onto those twinned inert figures. "There's one did laugh in 's sleep," Macbeth tells his wife, "and one cried, 'Murther!' " (2.2.20); he hears the delighted voice of gratified ambition alongside the horrified voice of the social conscience. Macbeth's own speeches, as Traversi has observed, become increasingly jolting and discontinuous as he prepares for the regicide.[62] At the moment of the murder, it seems to me, the breakdown culminates in Macbeth's inability to know his own voice, inward or outward, from that of the grooms. Like Freud's textbook psychotic, he projects aspects of his physical as well as his mental life onto others. Again, the point is not simply to suggest a correspondence between Freud's and Shakespeare's portrayals of pathology. Instead, as in my treatment of the Oedipal patterns, my purpose is to demonstrate that Shakespeare discovered a correspondence between the psychology of the ambitious individual and the transaction by which ambition earns its talionic punishment. The personal psychology is dramatically useful in itself, but its metaphoric link to the symbolic pattern surrounding ambition lends conviction (and at times ambivalence) to Shakespeare's cautionary moral. The rash wish not to be oneself, for the usurper as for the psychotic, inevitably imposes the torments of self-alienation and divided identity.

Macbeth's inability to say "Amen" may be another symptom of his increasing inability to know the boundary between himself and others, expressed again in a failure to distinguish his own voice from those of the grooms:

> One cried, "God bless us!" and "Amen!" the other,
> As they had seen me with these hangman's hands.
> List'ning their fear, I could not say "Amen,"
> When they did say "God bless us!"   (2.2.24–27)

"Consider it not so deeply," is Lady Macbeth's reply, but perhaps he should consider it more deeply. The idea that the grooms were shocked by his hands stands revealingly adjacent to his own horrified and distancing epithet for those hands; he may also be projecting his fear onto the grooms, as the ones onto whom the guilt must be publicly projected. By setting the scene off-stage, and providing it only through Macbeth's narration, Shakespeare leaves us room for such speculations; we only know what he perceived, not what was there, and all the voices we hear are spoken through his voice. Macbeth says he heard "God bless us" from one source and then "Amen" from "the other." When his narration subtly changes two lines later, implying now that both grooms "did say 'God bless us!',"" we may suppose he is merely treating the "Amen" as the second groom's joining in the plea for blessing; but we may alternatively suspect that the alienated "other" who answered "Amen" was Macbeth himself, or at least the pious part of Macbeth that his dagger had just severed from the rest of him forever. Shakespeare's presentation of the grooms as a pair should make us skeptical of the reported break in symmetry; and Macbeth's distraught emphasis on his failure to say "Amen" should remind us that the damnation Macbeth suffers hereafter is largely a damnation of self-alienation. He is decapitated when we last see him, not pulled into a hell-mouth. The idea that Macbeth perceives himself unable to speak his "Amen" precisely because he has already suffered this peculiar damnation fits well with both the Christian analogy and the play's atmosphere of demonic, paradoxical entrapment. Macbeth resumes his narration with the "Sleep no more" speech, which is usually understood as the projection of Macbeth's inner guilt; I am merely including a few earlier lines in that conscientious projection, an inclusion that would contribute to the play's persistent blurring of the distinctions between characters and its persistent moral ironies. We may even wonder if the uneasy sleep Macbeth attributes to the heavily drugged grooms is not a presentiment of the punitive insomnia about to descend on him. Lady Macbeth is right to ask, at the end of her husband's narration, "Who was it that thus cried?" (2.2.41).

Macbeth ends the scene with the revealing observation that "To know my deed, 'twere best not know myself" (2.2.70). His deed is very much an unknowing of himself, and it burdens him with what he terms a "restless ecstasy," a disquieting removal from his own reality (3.2.22). Scotland temporarily suffers the same disease—Rosse says that the weeping in the "poor country, / Almost afraid to know itself" seems to be "A modern ecstasy" (4.3.164–70)—but the body politic regains its unity under Malcolm. Despite a long Aesculapian struggle, Macbeth's body natural never achieves such reunification; his dream of becoming "Whole as the marble" by solidifying his royal identity dissolves into the nightmare (and the regicidal/suicidal nightmares) of self-alienation.

Macbeth invites this bodily fragmentation as part of his preparation to build a royal new self, only to discover on yet another level that "What's done cannot be undone" (5.2.68). From his first instigation by the witches, Macbeth finds his hair unfixed, his heart at war with his ribs "Against the use of nature," and his entire "single state of man" badly shaken (1.3.134–40). This points ahead to the end of the play, when his "better part of man" is cowed by the "double sense" of the witches, who set Macduff's tongue and Macbeth's ear at odds with Macbeth's hope, leading to his decapitation (5.8.17–27). Macbeth requests total darkness so that his eye may wink at his regicidal hand until the deed is done (1.4.51–53). As he advances toward Duncan's bed-chamber, Macbeth achieves this self-alienation, but in a way diametrically opposed to his desires. The dagger appears bloodily to his fearful eye before the crime is done, and will not serve as a weapon in his hand. His brain no longer knows which of his senses to trust, nor does he even fully trust his own brain:

> Art thou not, fatal vision, sensible
> To feeling as to sight? or art thou but
> A dagger of the mind, a false creation,
> Proceeding from the heat-oppressed brain?
> . . . . .
> Mine eyes are made the fools o' th' other senses,
> Or else worth all the rest. I see thee still;
> And on thy blade and dudgeon gouts of blood,
> Which was not so before. (2.1.36–47)

Macbeth then seems to watch his own approach to Duncan from some viewpoint outside of himself, describing the way "Murther . . . towards his design / Moves like a ghost" (2.1.52–56). To our even more removed faculties, the progress toward murder appears to be a fading into insubstantiality, as the haunting figure of Macbeth watches his own ghost follow its dagger, which follows the ghost of that dagger, into Duncan's chamber.

Lady Macbeth, too, suffers the bitter ramifications of her desire to divorce the murdering instrument from the perception of the murder (1.5.50–52). Instead of dispelling the horror, the rash wish merely displaces it in time, making it all the more burdensome. The dagger shows Macbeth the blood before the deed rather than after; Lady Macbeth becomes blind, not to the spilling of Duncan's blood, but rather to the fact that it has been washed away. The "gilt" of blood on her hand becomes the "guilt" of blood that mars her sleep, as her overly facile pun invites it to do (2.2.53–54). She dismisses Macbeth's perception of Banquo's ghost as "the very painting of your fear" (3.4.60), but she too finds herself haunted into revealing her secret by the frightening, unnatural persistence of the man she has killed; she is painted with the illusion of his blood as much as she had earlier painted the grooms with the illusion of guilt. When she tells her terrified husband after that murder that " 'tis the eye of childhood / That fears a painted devil" (2.2.51–52), we may recognize two more levels of irony. All three components of the line have latent secondary meanings that combine to foretell her fate. Since the verb "to fear" often meant "to frighten" in Elizabethan usage (see 2 Henry IV, 4.4.121), her words may unconsciously predict or even invite the gaze of the emblematic infants that eventually terrifies these blood-painted devils, "this dead butcher and his fiend-like queen" (5.9.35). But on a level closer to the line's obvious meaning, she may be unwittingly foretelling her regressive acquisition of an "eye of childhood" that is terrified by the blood painted on her fiend-like hands. Both husband and wife, then, find their eyes made the fools of their other senses, through a series of self-alienations they foolishly demanded.

Macbeth struggles to reunite, or at least to coordinate, the disjunct parts of himself, but it is not easily done.[63] When he brings his hands and his eyes back together after separating them to facilitate his regicide, they are at war with each other: "What hands are here? Hah! they pluck out mine eyes" (2.2.56). Six scenes later, he is still trying to reconcile these factions: "Strange things I have in head, that will to hand" (3.4.138). The heart, too, must be realigned with that hangman's hand:

> From this moment
> The very firstlings of my heart shall be
> The firstlings of my hand. And even now,
> To crown my thoughts with acts, be it thought and done.
>
> (4.1.146–59)

One critic has mentioned that "firstlings" could refer to first-born offspring as well as other sorts of first results.[64] My corollary to that observation is that these firstlings can be created only by marrying the heart to the hand; Macbeth is trying to unite in unholy matrimony a husband and wife that were truly one flesh before his self-alienating deed, hoping thereby to bequeath the throne to descendants of his body rather than of Banquo's, whom he is here plotting to murder. But it is merely an arranged marriage, not a natural union of intimacy. As in Richard III, where all that tongue and heart have in common is that "both are false" (1.2.194), here in Macbeth "False face must hide what the false heart doth know" (1.7.82); though married under the name of "false," the parts of the body remain alien and even opposite to each other.[65]

This inner dissension has parallels in the dissension within Macbeth's marriage, within Macbeth's army, and within Macbeth's kingdom; all these divisions conspire to destroy him, as they conspire to destroy Richard III. Queen Elizabeth's translation of Boethius warns that such a divided self can prove fatal:

> as in beastes we see, when they ingender, & be made of lyfe & body, then it is a Creature. But when this unitie makes a separation, then they are divided, perish & decay. This body allso when hit remayns in one forme & joyntes of lyms, then humayn shape is seene. But if distract or partid in twoo they be, then they leave their unitie which made them be . . . every thing shall last while it is one, but when it leaves that order, it perishith.[66]

Shakespeare portrays that perishing as a lesson in the hazards of ambition. Like Richard III before him or Coriolanus after, Macbeth cannot bring full force to bear on the civil war he fights, because he must simultaneously fight a civil war within his own psyche. We can hardly be surprised when we hear that "The tyrant's people on both sides do fight" (5.7.25), since his various faculties are at war among themselves. Such a divided creature stands little chance against the unifying "passion" driving Malcolm's forces, a passion Malcolm describes as a "Child of integrity" (4.3.115).

Lost in a maze of divisions, Richard III, Macbeth, and Coriolanus all try to cut their way out with the physical valor that first endorsed their ambitions; but this time the laws of heredity will not yield to the Caesarean assertion. Shakespeare repeatedly indicates that the new identity can be neither safely resigned nor permanently established. Richard and Macbeth are stranded halfway across that river of blood, equally unable to advance or retreat (4.2.65; 3.4.135–37); so, in effect, is Coriolanus (4.5.99, 5.3.186–91). As philosophers from Bovillus to Sartre have suggested, human beings cannot avoid a guilt-ridden divorce from their original selves, and any efforts at reconciliation will only call up the painful awareness of inward division. Only by pushing ahead, instead of looking back, can the new self achieve its own integrity.[67] The identity of evil tyrant urges Macbeth to enter it, much as De Flores urges Beatrice-Joanna to complete her corruption by uniting with him in *The Changeling*, again by a murder and a seduction that are virtually inextricable from each other:

> Push, fly not to your birth, but settle you
> In what the act has made you; y'are no more now.
> You must forget your parentage to me;
> Y'are the deed's creature; by that name
> You lost your first condition, and I challenge you,
> As peace and innocency has turn'd you out
> And made you one with me.[68]

Macbeth tells his wife that "We are yet but young in deed" (3.5.143), as if he too believed they had been reborn as the deed's creatures, and would outgrow their fear of ghosts and the dark as this unnatural new identity matured. But the transition from Lady Macbeth's consoling "what's done is done" (3.2.12) to her sleep-walking "What's done cannot be undone" (5.1.68) reveals that the deed was not a completion, but rather the irreparable loss of an original state. Macbeth, too, searches desperately for a way either to confirm or relinquish his royal identity, to relieve the agonies of an ambitiously divided self, but he can neither advance nor retreat far enough to reunify himself. He seeks out a battle that "Will cheer me ever, or disseat me now" (5.3.21), but even in that battle he finds that "There is nor flying hence, nor tarrying here" (5.5.47).

The various names that hover around Macbeth are another important index to the divisions in his identity. In making Macduff the agent of regeneration's vengeance against Macbeth, Shakespeare may be exploiting the historically founded overlap between the two men's names, which is the "Mac" that marks both names as patronymics. What Macduff represents, to the degree that he mirrors and opposes Macbeth, is the hereditary component of Macbeth's identity that his ambitions drive him to abandon; it is highly appropriate that Macduff ends Macbeth's reign while fighting on behalf of the generational order. By the same token, the Thane of Cawdor's sharing of his name with Macbeth stands for the malleability of identity to a pre-existent model, a model the ambitious man may conquer by force. Macbeth drifts into the original Thane's regicidal project as well as his possessions and his name, as if his reborn being were an infantile *tabula rasa*, wholly subservient to the first markings made on it. This promotion, of course, is what gives credence to the witches' prophecy and thereby induces Macbeth to believe that he can also seize and assimilate the identity of king. Macduff and the Thane of Cawdor, then, stand partly for Macbeth's lineal and unlineal identities, and the division of his name between theirs is an early indication of the division of his selfhood.

As in the history plays, the sheer multiplication of names is in itself an indication of such a division, brought on by an unnatural manipulation of political roles. Macbeth "deserves" the name "brave Macbeth," as the Sergeant says, but he moves beyond his deserts in becoming "King, Cawdor, Glamis, all," as Banquo complains (1.2.16, 3.1.1). The fact that this represents a fragmentation of identity and not merely an acquisition of property becomes clear at the moment of the regicide, when a voice that is and is not Macbeth cries, "Macbeth does murther sleep" and "Glamis hath murther'd sleep, and therefore Cawdor / Shall sleep no more, Macbeth shall sleep no more" (2.2.33–40). The parsing of tenses reveals a succession of people living restlessly in a single body, a series of demonic possessions rather than any gradation of the self. With the various parts of that body simultaneously at war with each other, insomnia seems almost inevitable: even when he sleeps alone, his bed is crowded with strangers.

Macbeth tries to restore the organic integrity of names as he tries to restore the organic integrity of his body. In inciting the murderers against Banquo, who forbids Macbeth to establish his name of king as a lineal name, Macbeth proposes a return to the most stable and primitive system of naming: the naming of things and creatures according to their uses and their physical qualities.[69] Macbeth begins the provocation, as his wife began her provocation of him, by a sarcastic and murderous definition of manhood:

First Murderer   We are men, my liege.
Macbeth Ay, in the catalogue ye go for men,
  As hounds and greyhounds, mungrels, spaniels, curs,
  Shoughs, water-rugs, and demi-wolves are clipt
  All by the name of dogs; the valued file
  Distinguishes the swift, the slow, the subtle,
  The house-keeper, the hunter, every one,
  According to the gift which bounteous nature
  Hath in him clos'd; whereby he does receive
  Particular addition, from the bill
  That writes them all alike: and so of men.   (3.1.90–100)

But Macbeth is himself the one who has wrested names loose from the order that "bounteous nature" provided, even degrading the name of man to include that of murderer; in tearing the great bond, he has also shuffled the valued file. Since he has prompted nature to revoke the gifts it had closed in him, furthermore, he should by his own analysis be nameless. When the witches mix various parts of various creatures in their cauldron, they claim to be performing "A deed without a name" (4.1.49). In committing the regicide that similarly jumbles the components of identity, Macbeth too performs a deed that cannot be named (2.3.64–65, 84).[70] He has overthrown the hereditary system that led Duncan to "name" Malcolm as "The Prince of Cumberland" (1.4.38–39), and it remains in disarray until the new generation of noblemen are "nam'd" as earls by Malcolm, whom they have restored to the throne (5.9.29–30). Intriguingly, Macbeth is not named in that final speech, and is mentioned by name only twice in the entire fifth act, once by himself, quoting the witches. Instead, he is known by epithets such as "tyrant," "hell-hound," and "butcher"; his name has gone the way of his legitimate identity, divided and conquered.

  Garments, like names, are an outward sign of identity, and the pattern of ill-fitting clothing explicated by Caroline Spurgeon contributes to the play's study of the flexibility (or rather the inflexibility) of the self.[71] When Rosse speculates that Macbeth will probably become king, Macduff replies that "He is already nam'd, and gone to Scone / To be invested" (2.4.31–32); but names and vestments, for Macbeth as for other usurpers, are a poor substitute for a lineal right to the throne. When the regicide upsets the normal demarcations of identity, names and garments cease to be stable and superficial appendages to selfhood, perhaps for the same reason that unstable societies structure their systems of naming and dressing so carefully.

Foolish Wishes and the Tragedy of *Macbeth*

In the absence of more substantial factors, these systems determine identity. The Elizabethan sumptuary laws represented an effort to repress social mobility: they indicated a fear that a glorified costume could actually create a glorified person, against the dictates of social caste.[72]

Ambitious figures in Shakespeare generally suppose that one can indeed change one's identity as one changes a garment, simply by choosing the best one and putting it on. The Biblical notion of "putting off the old man and putting on the new man who is created according to justice"[73] becomes literalized and twisted into the creation of a *gente nuovo* by any costume he can steal. In the process of rebirth, the garments become baptismal robes accompanying the process of renaming. But the original identity, like original sin at the first baptism, can only be partly eradicated. The futility, even the grotesquery, of Macbeth's royal costuming confirms this principle.

As long as Macbeth remains relatively innocent of ambition, he recognizes names and garments as equally superficial signs that one may wear without assimilating them. When first hailed by Rosse as Thane of Cawdor, Macbeth asks, "why do you dress me / In borrowed robes?" (1.3.108–09). Banquo's excuse for Macbeth's subsequent reverie emphasizes the same distinction: "New honors come upon him, / Like our strange garments, cleave not to their mould / But with the aid of use" (1.3.144–46). This same metaphor, designed as an innocent excuse for what must be, to Banquo, a suspicious reverie, appears again when Macbeth tries to keep himself innocent of the ambitious deeds which occupied that reverie. Macbeth resists his wife's urgings to regicide by reminding her that

> I have bought
> Golden opinions from all sorts of people,
> Which would be worn now in their newest gloss,
> Not cast aside so soon. (1.7.32–35)

Lady Macbeth counters this argument, as Coriolanus counters Volumnia's similar argument, by insisting that garments are not a precarious costume, but rather an intimate part of a malleable selfhood.

In consenting to perform the regicide, Macbeth also assents to his wife's interpretation of clothing's transforming power, and the lesser concession suggests some of the costs of the greater. Lady Macbeth says he is already "dress'd" in royal hopes (1.7.35–36), and insists he gain an identity to match that costume. Having sought to make himself king by stealing the royal robes—an action significantly

128

hollow in *Cymbeline* and *The Tempest* as well as the Henry IV plays—Macbeth loses his ability to distinguish between garments and inner reality. By relying too much on clothing, as Montaigne warns, we may lose a part of ourselves.[74] The man who seeks to include a garment as part of his identity cannot afterwards be sure that any part of his identity is more than a garment; Macbeth thus sets himself on the grim path toward his "poor player" soliloquy. Even Macbeth's description of Duncan's "silver skin lac'd with his golden blood" and the grooms' daggers "Unmannerly breech'd with gore" (2.3.112–16), which has disturbed critics up through Cleanth Brooks's elaborate defense, may serve to suggest that Macbeth can no longer distinguish human identity from garments.[75] Even blood, traditionally a symbol of a person's most inward, hereditary, and characteristic aspects, here becomes confused with Duncan's royal costume and the grooms' presumably sloppy breeches.

Banquo, standing as always in moral contrast to Macbeth, urges that the murder be investigated as soon as "we have our naked frailties hid" (2.3.126). Seven lines later Macbeth endorses that suggestion, but in doing so he revealingly broadens the connotative range of the garment imagery: "Let's briefly put on manly readiness." Banquo's remark suggests a humble definition of man, draped to cover, not to eradicate, his fallen frailties; Macbeth assumes that men put on their valor with their costumes. Petrarch's belief that humanity's need for clothing validates its desire to transcend its natural state becomes in Shakespeare a fear that an excessive reliance on clothing indicates an excessive belief in the viability of self-transformation. As we might expect after the storm scene in *King Lear*, Shakespeare displays in *Macbeth* a mistrust of both the sumptuous garments designed to exalt the wearer and the Pelagian notions Petrarch derives from such garments. Subsequent events prove that Macduff was right to be concerned "Lest our old robes sit easier than our new!" (2.4.38). Macbeth takes over the throne, but he is not "every inch a king" as Lear is even when costumed only in wildflowers (*King Lear*, 4.6.80, 107). Macbeth's aspirations are too great for his birth, and his moral stature too small for his title, so his garments remain foreign to him in every dimension: "He cannot buckle his distemper'd cause / Within the belt of rule," but at the same time he feels "his title / Hang loose about him, like a giant's robe / Upon a dwarfish thief" (5.2.15–16, 20–22). Garments finally assert, rather than cure, the discomfort and futility of ambition.

The idea that one may have the name and the costume of an

exalted person, and yet not be that person, points inescapably back to the dramatic medium itself. The frequent references to playing and acting that surround Macbeth remind us that his ambitious identity is as hollow and evanescent as the insubstantial pageant before us. Macbeth and his wife find theatrical imagery slipping into the very language they use to promote and defend their royal identity and its authenticity. She urges him to fulfill his ambitious desires "in thine own act," hoping he has the nerve to "play false" and "perform" the murder. These compromising metaphors invade Macbeth's speech as well, after he has performed his regicidal act. He promises to "play the humble host" at a feast for Banquo, even while his killers act out a murder plot that, like a play trying to evade the censors, must be hastily written and performed: "Strange things I have in head, that will to hand, / Which must be acted ere they may be scann'd" (3.4.138–39).

But Macbeth lacks the necessary *sprezzatura* to disguise the merely theatrical character of his roles as gracious host and legitimate king, and the enemies of his reign review his performance brutally. Banquo fears that Macbeth has "play'dst most foully" for his exalted roles (3.1.1–6). When Rosse remarks on the unnatural darkness brought on by the regicide, he associates it more explicitly with the conversion of the world into a stage, by an allusion to the theatrical "heavens" looming over the actors in an Elizabethan playhouse: "Thou seest the heavens, as troubled with man's act, / Threatens his bloody stage" (2.4.5–6). The bloody melodrama is endangered by the violent disapproval of its cosmic audience, and Macbeth's own life sinks into darkness as such a fustian performance:

> Out, out, brief candle!
> Life's but a walking shadow, a poor player,
> That struts and frets his hour upon the stage,
> And then is heard no more. It is a tale
> Told by an idiot, full of sound and fury,
> Signifying nothing.   (5.5.23–28)

Another rash wish, this time the wish that identities could be exchanged as easily as theatrical roles, thus receives its bitter fulfillment. Macbeth and his wife are tormented by the equivalent of stagefright, perpetually terrified of forgetting their lines and thereby revealing the distance between the mere actor and the grand part he or she pretends to embody: "To alter favor ever is to fear," as Lady Macbeth warns (1.5.72).

An even greater fear lurks behind Macbeth's stage-fright, though:

the fear, not that the real person beneath the role will be discovered, but rather that there will be no real person left beneath that role. Lionel Trilling traces back to the Renaissance the idea that "impersonation leads to the negation of self."[76] When the insubstantial pageant fades and the sound and fury subside, the actors themselves will become nothing; Macbeth is "signifying nothing" to us in the way a zero does. When the tomorrows will no longer be mocked, and the "fairest show" (1.7.81) crumbles around the poor player, Macbeth is left with an inner void. He remarks, at his wife's death, that he no longer needs to disguise his horror: he no longer has any inward sentiment to repress. He has only now become the hollow shell of a simulated person that some critics have claimed Shakespearean characters must always be.[77] Having managed "To crown my thoughts with acts" as he had promised (4.1.149), Macbeth discovers that the crown is merely an acting prop, and the royal identity itself merely an indulged idea, a show as evanescent as an ambitious daydream. The usurper, here as in the history plays, seems to become invisible, an absence rather than a presence.

By misdefining his "manhood" at his wife's instigation, Macbeth loses not only his procreative manliness, but also his human selfhood. As in *King Lear*, the disruptions of legacy and obedience create a terrifying nothingness by upsetting any reliable definitions of humanity. Albany reminds Goneril, who mocks his manliness by comparing him to a cat, that "Striving to better, oft we mar what's well" (4.2.68, 1.4.346). Banquo expresses the same fear about his manly honor, determined to "lose none / In seeking to augment it," and thereby refuses to be seduced into any conspiracy with Macbeth against Duncan (2.1.26–27). In the *Rape of Lucrece* Shakespeare portrays Tarquin (whose footsteps Macbeth envisions himself following at 2.1.55 on the way to the regicide) as precisely such a foolish trader, unloosing his own great "bond" through an "ambitious foul infirmity" that leads him to "Make something nothing by augmenting it," to "forsake" and therefore "bankrout" himself by a Pyrrhic conquest of his desires.[78] For Macbeth, as for Albany, the issue arises when he finds that defending his king has lowered his manliness in his wife's eyes to the level of

> the poor cat i' th' adage?
>
> *Macbeth*   Prithee, peace!
>   I dare do all that may become a man;
>   Who dares do more is none.
> *Lady Macbeth*   What beast was't then

> That made you break this enterprise to me?
> When you durst do it, then you were a man;
> And to be more than what you were, you would
> Be so much more the man. Nor time, nor place,
> Did then adhere, and yet you would make both:
> They have made themselves, and that their fitness now
> Does unmake you.
>
> (1.7.45–54)

Macbeth, ironically, is all too truly "unmade" by the circumstances that encourage him to commit this crime, just as Richard II is forced to "undo" himself into "nothing" by another unnatural transfer of the royal identity. Lady Macbeth equates manhood with a perpetual self-promotion, in a sinister translation of the spirit of Prometheus, Pelagius, Pico, and Petrarch; the same arguments will appear in the mouth of Coriolanus. But Shakespeare's warning that this is a foolish exchange, that self-promotion is only a guise for self-annihilation, rests in the definition of manhood Macbeth offers but fails to uphold; in daring to do more than becomes a man, Macbeth does in fact become none. Macbeth repeatedly verges on inadvertent truthfulness after the murder—critics often cite his proclamation that "the wine of life is drawn" and his own life cursed as a result of Duncan's murder (2.3.91–96)—and he may be doing so again a few lines later. Having killed the grooms in a moment that fuses true madness and calculated treachery, he justifies his deed with a revealing rhetorical question: "Who can be wise, amaz'd, temp'rate, and furious, / Loyal, and neutral, in a moment? No man" (2.3.108–09). In his circumspect show of furious and empty loyalty, Macbeth becomes the human nullity he describes; his evil duplicity leaves him fittingly with no real identity. We may recall Iago's revealingly ironic response when Emilia speculates that "some eternal villain" has deliberately roused Othello's jealousy: "Fie, there is no such man" (4.2.130, 134). Both men deny their deeds by putting them outside of mankind's moral range, but both are therefore actually confessing that their own humanity is lost. We sense a hungry and diabolically charged void beneath Iago's duplicity as we do beneath Macbeth's, and both point us toward a Machiavellian world where acting eliminates the core of moral being.[79] Queen Elizabeth's translation of Boethius states it simply: "whom transformed thou seest with vice, thou mayst not suppose him a man."[80]

The danger that manhood will be nullified, in an ontological as well as a sexual sense, gains coherence from the persistent comparison between Macbeth and Macduff. Macbeth's speech to the murderers includes an attempt to change the definition of manhood by which he has doomed himself to nullity; as for the Captain in *King Lear*, who is on a similar assignment (5.3.39), manhood is redefined for these thugs as demanding rather than excluding their murderous pursuit of promotion and self-interest (3.1.85–105). Macduff reasserts the limiting definition of manhood, the humane definition of humanity, when he too is urged to avenge "like a man" the wrong someone has done to his family and his future hopes. "I shall do so," Macduff answers, "But I must also feel it as a man . . . naught that I am, / Not for their own demerits, but for mine, / Fell slaughter on their souls" (4.3.220–27). Both "naught" and "demerit" are used as moral rather than ontological terms here, but both define evil as the deficiency of some good, an absence that has here nullified his procreative powers. If his Caesarean lack of "the natural touch" (4.2.10) caused him to attack Macbeth rather than defend his own family, then it is fitting that he regain his status as fully, feelingly human by choosing to mourn his family before seeking vengeance. Macduff is again the perfect counterpart to Macbeth, who has nullified his original manhood through a violent rebirth that subordinated family feeling to vindictiveness.

As Macbeth had feared, his "Vaulting ambition" has propelled him into a void, and Shakespeare insists that only a restored lineal identity can restore existence to someone whom ambition has nullified.[81] "To be thus is nothing," Macbeth all too accurately warns himself, "But to be safely thus." To gain such safety, to make his "I" again "perfect" and "whole" (3.4.20–21), he must loot the successive "royalty of nature" that is stored in Banquo. When he instigates the murderers with claims that Banquo has "beggar'd yours for ever" (3.1.90), he is merely projecting his own motives, and he perverts his own manhood as much as theirs in doing so. Macbeth practically makes himself a ghost by making Banquo one; such a deed negates rather than establishes manhood in its perpetrator as well as its victim. "Are you a man?" Lady Macbeth demands as her husband stands terrified by Banquo's specter, and she concludes that he is not, describing him as "quite unmann'd in folly." Her sarcasm is directed at his manliness rather than his existence, but the connection is reaffirmed when Macbeth tries to excuse his outburst as "a strange infirmity, which is nothing / To those that know me." A ghastly nothingness seems to be part of this secret infirmity, which bursts out again a few lines later. Despite his boast of manly daring, Macbeth himself is "a man again" only when the ghost disappears, as if it were an indicator of his ontological as well as moral failure. He became a ghost on the way to murdering Duncan (2.1.56), and now he is forced to encounter Banquo in a shadowy world belonging only to the two of them, becoming deathly pale and demonically possessed in the process (3.4.109–15).

Lady Macbeth seems to recognize that these murders are actually suicides, that the draining of another's blood is really an emptying of oneself, despite her efforts to bolster her husband's courage. A Jacobean tract warns that God designed envy of those more exalted "to be a plague unto it selfe" which "will quickly consume a man";[82] ambition ravins up its own life's means. Lady Macbeth acknowledges in soliloquy that the regicide was such an ontological and economic blunder, a costly acquisition of "Nought" that leaves them "without content" in either sense of the word:[83]

> Nought's had, all's spent,
> Where our desire is got without content;
> 'Tis safer to be that which we destroy
> Than by destruction dwell in doubtful joy.　　　　(3.2.4–7)

The idea of being "spent" by the achievement of a "desire" that fails to provide "content" points back to the association between the regicide and a sexual act, and indicates that Lady Macbeth, like her husband thirty lines later, is brooding about the symptomatic emptiness of her womb, which leaves the future to Banquo. All their deed achieves is a sickly reconception of Macbeth; Shakespeare's radical shortening of the historical Macbeth's reign makes that rebirth seem more like a stillbirth. Lady Macbeth has abjured her womanhood, as her husband becomes no man, and it is not surprising that the life they share, sexual and otherwise, is essentially an emptiness. Her speech subliminally suggests that they are themselves "that which we destroy," as in her husband's confused dreams about both committing and suffering regicide. When Macduff blames the deed on "Those that Macbeth hath slain" (2.4.23), meaning the grooms, the dramatic irony alerts us to a figurative suicide.[84]

A similar transaction appears occasionally in the literature and philosophy of Shakespeare's *milieu*, and with a suggestive ambivalence. One Jacobean prodigal-son tract warns that the greedy

> tumble in their bed, and take no rest,
> For such men in affliction ever are,
> And when they seem t'have most, then have they least,
> With mindes perplexed horror still opprest;

134

For this to Rich-men for a curse is sent,
Much they enjoy, but little with content.[85]

While the general moral is commonplace, the association of horrified insomnia, bankruptcy by unnatural acquisitiveness, and a loss of "content" is strikingly close to *Macbeth*. But the same costs that attach to man's greed may attach to his efforts to achieve the divinity for which he was designed. According to the Renaissance philosopher Bartolomeo Facio—and here Facio anticipates modern theorists of desire—"affected by the desire of attaining that good which is felt to be missing, it is impossible to be of a peaceful state of mind, but one is always anxious."[86] Human misery similarly rises out of human dignity in the Puritan doctrine that identifies divine election by the constant fear that one has not been elected.

If man is such an enigmatic mixture of glory and disgrace as Renaissance writers portrayed him, if he is so committed to the quest for the ideal that his search to fill an inner void makes him perpetually protean and uneasy, then Macbeth's foolishly chosen ordeal may serve as an allegory for the ordeal the world imposes on us all. Macbeth's archetypal crime has its shadows in our own psyches, and its punishments do as well, in our guilt, our nightmares, and our self-alienation. Pico della Mirandola suggested that God's special gift to Adam was the obligation to choose his own shape and engineer his own spiritual rebirth; Petrarch similarly justified the human impulse to transform the self by pointing to God's omissions in creating mankind, which oblige us to arm and clothe ourselves to survive. To make a new identity may be a crime against nature, but it is in our nature to make new identities. Macbeth's guilt, on this level, resembles the specter of existential bad faith. Lionel Trilling discusses the painfully delusive "idea that somewhere under all the roles there is Me, that poor old ultimate actuality, who, when all the roles have been played, would like to murmur, 'Off, off, you lendings!' and settle down with his own original actual self."[87] But such inner domesticity is precisely what Macbeth knows he "must not look to have" after he has destroyed his hereditary self and replaced it with borrowed robes (5.3.26). Jean-Paul Sartre, like Trilling, warns that while a person's humanity consists essentially in the self-consciousness and in the acts (in either sense) by which he makes himself known to the world, he will be perpetually haunted by guilt for not returning to some posited authentic self. This resembles the transaction between the adopted and hereditary identities in Shakespeare. And if the schism in Shakespeare's ambitious figures has such similar symptoms to the Sartrean schism, we may extrapolate that it has a similar inevitability. From the viewpoint of existential atheism, as well as that of Gnostic religion,[88] malcontents such as Macbeth are victims of their own humanity, rather than their own inhumanity. Our repugnance at Macbeth's deeds is softened by the recognition that they reflect our own, and whatever repugnance that recognition arouses toward our own conduct may lead us to resent the disproportionate guilt imposed by a world that palters with us, too, in a double sense.

This entrapment of profoundly human qualities in a situation that renders them destructive is highly characteristic of Shakespearean tragedy as A. C. Bradley describes it.[89] Like the warrior Othello enmeshed in Venetian intrigue, like the intellectual Hamlet compelled to violent action, like the blunt Coriolanus involved in politics, Macbeth finds his heroic quality—the ambitious violence that wins him praise in the opening scenes—converted to a fatal flaw. In a broader sense, like the Romantic tragic hero, Macbeth finds that a purely human instinct for greatness may be called a sin, or be channeled into a crime, by a world morally incompatible with his "aspiring mind." Tragedy, it has been suggested, cannot thrive in a world ruled by a unitary, benevolent, and just God;[90] something greater than man must contradict or divide what is great in man. Macbeth is not simply a justly punished sinner against a providential Christian order; he is also the unwitting victim of a repressive and divided godhead like that overseeing Greek tragedy. The play's secondary, figurative level takes place in a Classical era, in which the gods could be jealous of human aspiration or could issue mixed instructions. The temporal gap between these two worlds corresponds to an ethical discrepancy that may help to explain our ambivalent responses to Macbeth's downfall. In the Homeric world, according to Francis Cornford, "the one primary stuff, called 'Nature' . . . is a *moral* order, in the sense that transgression of its boundaries, the plundering of one element by another to make an individual thing, is injustice, unrighteousness . . . Birth is a crime, and growth an aggravated robbery."[91] This is, in effect, another version of original sin, in which the very act of coming into being implicates each person in an evil and fatal disobedience. The "Olympian morality" suggests that an act of heroic transcendence may lift a man briefly above the natural order, but "there is a strong sense that such feats are undesirable and dangerous," and that passing "certain destined bounds" provokes "an instant *nemesis*."[92]

Elizabethan and Jacobean tragedy shows its classical roots most clearly in its focus on this dialectic of transcendence and repression. J. M. R. Margeson's *The Origins of English Tragedy* describes the social order and a talionic natural law in conspiracy against heroic determinations:

> From the point of view of society, those who refuse to accept things as they are, or who attack the normal continuity of society as a disruptive force, deserve to be punished, whether their intentions are noble or evil. From the point of view of the tragic hero, the demands of society are wrong and must meet the headlong assault of the brave or defiant individual. Beyond both of these, in Elizabethan tragedy as in Greek tragedy, is an unchanging law which ensures that error reaps its proper reward and that human purpose is frustrated by its egocentric demands.

Margeson later attributes the intensity of Elizabethan and Jacobean tragedy to "the exuberant energy of the age, which glorified the boldness of man in his search after power, glory, love, or revenge, and yet which was checked severely by the weight of forces opposed to such desires in fate or providence, or in society."[93] The "rebellion of the human spirit against limitations" in Chapman is a good example of this tension,[94] but the clearest analogues to Macbeth are Marlowe's overreachers. They are rebels against God, but their rebellion generally expresses itself against the limitations imposed on ambition by the hereditary order, and we derive from their experience as from Macbeth's the sense that the godhead has actually demanded the violations it subsequently punishes.[95] Richard III has been called a tragic figure because he sets his individual will against historical inevitability; Macbeth, refusing "To kiss the ground before young Malcolm's feet" (5.8.28), pits his ambitious identity against the hereditary order that the history plays sought to equate with historical inevitability.[96]

Shakespeare establishes the tragic foundations of *Macbeth*, then, in a Renaissance version of a classical situation. Among the problems native to tragedy, he emphasizes those of birth, ambition, and identity, perhaps because the possibilities and imperatives of individual aspiration were so active in his time. The Florentine philosophers, with their emphasis on free will, are certainly part of the story. Another part is the much debated revolution in social mobility and individual self-consciousness that focused people's attention on the problems of defining and limiting the self. Burckhardt and his followers describe the liberation of the individual in the Renaissance by broader "choices of conduct and philosophy," a process that "did reach England in Shakespeare's time."[97] More recently, Lawrence Stone has explored evidence of such a change in Elizabethan social structures, and Michel Foucault has speculated on relevant changes in epistemology and the scientific method.[98] Alvin Kernan describes Shakespeare's "Henriad" as a depiction of "the passage from the Middle Ages to the Renaissance," characterized by this same loss of systemic certainty: "In political and social terms it is the movement from feudalism and hierarchy to the national state and individualism. In psychological terms, it is a passage from a situation in which a man knows with certainty who he is to an existential condition in which any identity is only a temporary role."[99]

In exploring these consequences of Henry IV's usurpation, Shakespeare may have come across a way to use political ambition as a truly tragic error, by making it represent the crisis of identity facing every thinking Elizabethan. On a political level, the very increase in mobility that invited the lowly and disinherited to try to improve their status provoked the society to repress such mobility in the ways it still could. Many men less famous than the Earl of Essex, and many who sought advancement in less extreme and dramatic ways, suffered badly enough from the mixed commands of that changing social godhead. On a psychological level, the structures that formerly told people who they were, that gave them stable and satisfactory roles, had largely crumbled, but the hereditary order retained a sort of posthumous reflex that punished those who were obliged to fabricate roles of their own. On the broadest cultural level, the Renaissance appetite for glory and dominion over nature by science and exploration collided with the Reformation's increasing insistence on human imbecility—physical, moral, and intellectual. Like the moments depicted in Greek tragedy, the Elizabethan moment may have been a difficult one in which to avoid offending one god or the other. People were strictly admonished, "To thine own self be true," at a time when their former means of subsistence had been disrupted (by enclosures, manufacturing, urbanization), and when the emergent Cartesian self-consciousness suggested that "there is no certainty that the self is identical throughout a lifetime, or even that there is only one existing at a time."[100]

Shakespeare's technique for portraying ambition in the history plays, turning a political situation into an allegory for the accompanying psychological transaction, may have had a foundation in an historical situation that presented the psyche with extraordinary dilemmas. If the Elizabethan era was truly a time when a "change in man's consciousness of himself" marked "that mysterious moment when the old fabric is undone and the new only beginning to be woven,"[101] then it is hardly surprising that Shakespeare became concerned with the tragic fall of those whom the old fabric would no longer support, and the new fabric was unprepared to catch. *Macbeth* is the story of such a fall, a story that contains deep within it a sympathetic parable about the experiences of those who were suffering the same sort of fall in a less bloody but no less fated manner. Stephen Greenblatt's *Renaissance Self-Fashioning* concludes that "in our culture to abandon self-fashioning is to abandon the craving for freedom, and to let go of one's stubborn hold upon selfhood, even selfhood conceived as a fiction, is to die."[102] Macbeth, presented with the clearest of moral choices, has in one sense no choice at all, and in that sense he evokes the sympathy, and empathy, that a tragic hero must.

Perhaps I am overstating the sympathetic qualities Shakespeare gives Macbeth; perhaps, in advocating such sympathy, I am simply sharing in Macbeth's characteristic error, failing to read the brutally literal level of the cautionary portent sketched in blood before me. Macbeth, after all, is not really an infant seeking a first identity or a displaced worker seeking a new job; he is the murderer of a good king, and a blasphemer against God's natural order. But even the horrifyingly literal level of the play's action could conceivably suggest a sense in which Macbeth is compelled to perform his ambitious self-fashioning, and in which we may all be implicated in his crimes. In *Totem and Taboo*, Freud argues that all men feel some residual guilt from his version of original sin, the primal Oedipal crisis represented by the patricide in the Primal Horde, a fantasy that became reality. This guilt is reawakened in each young male by his own Oedipal conflicts, and could presumably be exacerbated by such re-enactments of that deed as *Macbeth*, particularly because of the way the Macbeth-Banquo contrast warns that a fantasy we witness (such as a play) can easily become our own terrible reality. This is a "Mousetrap" to catch the conscience of patricidal princes. A principal reason for this uprising, in the Primal Horde as in the modern family, is the father's exercise of exclusive sexual rights; unless they overthrew the primal sovereign, the young men were doomed to genetic extinction. But even if the rebellion was necessary for survival, it was nonetheless fraught with guilt and fear, even as the necessary betrayal of the primal self is fraught with existential *angst*. Virtually the entire human race, according to Freud's theory, owes its existence to a primal ancestor's mutiny against the sovereign's

Foolish Wishes and the Tragedy of *Macbeth*

reproductive prohibitions. Each human being, furthermore, must re-
enact the rebellion, at least metaphorically: even the compromises
by which we substitute a mate for the forbidden parent, or form by
inward resistance independent selves, are figurative ways of salvag-
ing the Oedipal ambitions from their literal defeat. Freud insists that
the guilt from an Oedipal fantasy can be just as real as from an
Oedipal deed, and our guilty fantasies meet Macbeth's literal deeds
in the uneasy territory the witches and Shakespeare establish between the two. A psychoanalyst writes that "Without the guilty
deed of parricide there is no autonomous self," and yet "from the
viewpoint of received morality, individuality . . . is a virtue, a *sum-
mum bonum*, at any rate in modern Western civilizations. To live
among these paradoxes appears to be our fate for the time being."[103]
The same tragic dilemma generates the fate of Macbeth; Shakespeare
again works effectively as our contemporary.

Another aspect of the primal dilemma, the choice between patricide and suicide, recurs in *Macbeth*. As in the Oedipus story and
related classical and Christian stories of the Slaughter of the Innocents, the boy will attack the father because the father has attacked
the boy because the boy was destined to attack the father. A similar
vicious cycle appears in *1 Henry IV* (5.1.30–71, 5.2.1–25), where the
king and the Percies each feel obliged to attack because they each
know that fear of attack will oblige the other to attack. In Akira
Kurosawa's brilliant film version of *Macbeth*, "Throne of Blood,"
Lady Macbeth pressures her reluctant husband by pointing out that,
when the king hears that Macbeth is prophesied to replace him, he
will try to kill Macbeth first; this is one of several moments where
Kurosawa seems conscious of the symbolic patterns I have been
describing.[104]

For the sons in the Primal Horde described by Freud, as for Macbeth, the guilt attached to the murder is all the greater because they
love the sovereign father, and wish above all to become like him;
that mimetic desire is what spurs the crime. But to avoid converting
society into an endless series of tyrannicides, the sons must participate equally in that overthrow, and share equally in the spoils of
the victory; they therefore feast together, on a symbolic version of
the father's flesh, and establish an incest taboo to preclude competition for sexual rights to the family's females.[105] But when Macbeth characteristically elevates his typical Oedipal fantasy into the
realm of physical reality, he does so with the collaboration only of
the sinister mother-figure, Lady Macbeth. His attempt at a communal feast therefore collapses in horror (3.4), and collapses, appropriately enough, because he has been waging war on the procreative

140

rights of Banquo, who refused to take part in the conspiracy to kill Duncan and displace his offspring. By attacking Banquo, Fleance, and Macduff's family, Macbeth becomes a new version of the primal tyrant who forbids anyone other than himself to reproduce. He is therefore overthrown by a group of young men who assert and represent both the rights of lineage and the energies of puberty: "Siward's son, / And many unrough youths that even now / Protest their first of manhood" (5.2.8–10). Like Cronus in Greek myth, like unruly sons who become strict fathers, like the rebel Bullingbrook who becomes an imperious king, Macbeth must expect that his crime will be repeated against him by a new generation seeking access to the benefits of regeneration; his efforts to prevent that repetition, like those of the other bad fathers, only make it more inevitable and more ferocious when it occurs.

The story of Macbeth explores the destructive potential of our most basic impulses, and reminds us of the consequent fragility of the social order, which must cling to nature's more durable order for survival. But while endorsing to that extent the Elizabethan homilies quoted at the beginning of this chapter, the play also insists that the hierarchical system must always conflict with the individual human will, which eludes its repressors and slips into view through nightmares, Freudian slips, and foolish wishes, all of which subserve the primal rebellion in *Macbeth*. Margeson observes that "The emphasis in classical tragedy and in much Elizabethan tragedy upon the greatness of the tragic hero strongly suggests an anthropological background of the leader sacrificed or cast out of society for his defiance of the gods, which is secretly to be admired for its courage, but feared and publicly condemned for its blasphemy."[106] Macbeth's greatness need not be goodness to generate a tragedy. His struggle conforms to several tragic archetypes, all of them analogous to each other, and all of them relevant to Shakespeare's metaphorical analysis of ambition's hazards. It is a Promethean struggle against a Gnostic sort of God-Father who shows himself as a repressively orderly nature; an Oedipal struggle to unseat the primal sovereign, the success of which makes Macbeth both the envy and the enemy of the other young men; and a symbolically fraught struggle to reshape identity in ways his patrimony forbids. Macbeth fulfills his thriftless desires, and the inevitable result is his tragedy. To the extent that we all share in such foolish wishes and such ambitious reshapings of ourselves and our worlds—and I have tried to suggest that we all do—we all share deeply in the flaw we publicly condemn, and his tragedy is ours.

~III

Martial Ambition
and the Family Romance
in *Coriolanus*

C ORIOLANUS ASPIRES to replace his limited hereditary identity with an ideal martial one, to transform himself from
a merely human creature, made of flesh, appetite, and compassion,
into a virtually divine warrior, made of steel, honor, and wrath. The
story of Coriolanus' journey from a natural to an artificial self has
epic attributes. It begins *in medias res*; it implicitly involves the
hero's temporary death, his visitation by a spirit from the underworld
who informs his quest, and his battle with the gods; and from one
viewpoint it becomes, like the Virgilian epic, a story of national
reconsecration. The end of the journey marks the salvation of the
Roman people and the maturation of Roman democracy. But Coriolanus is trapped in a genre, as well as a city, whose ethos he can
neither understand nor accommodate; he naively awaits the un-
ambiguous endorsement of his heroic exertions that the complex
world of Shakespearean tragedy, like the complex world of Rome,
refuses to provide. He mistakenly supposes that his is an epic mission, that he is fighting for Rome's survival in striving for martial
perfection; whereas in fact, the valorous principles he identifies with
his city will finally demand that he destroy that city. He dies in
exile, and the Rome he had been fighting for dies with him, if indeed
it ever existed. Coriolanus' tragic dilemma, and his tragic solitude,
arise from his misconceptions about the mores of Rome. He imagines that he is fulfilling his natural identity as the offspring of his
mother and his motherland, but his course is so completely unnatural that it eventually turns him against family and city alike.

As in the history plays and *Macbeth*, the hazards of ambition first reveal themselves in *Coriolanus* on a political level; but Shakespeare again insists that the political strife is only one manifestation of the profound derangement generated by unfilial aspirations, however well intended. The protagonist's disruption of the political order is both cause and effect of a disruption in his hereditary identity; social conflict becomes a symbol as well as a consequence of the ambitious man's Oedipal conflict with his father-figures, and his fatal conflict with his natural self. The ambiguous heritage provided by Coriolanus' two-faced mother and absent father makes it almost impossible for him to play the strictly filial role that Shakespeare's universe demands. In the earlier plays, the defiance of lineal succession found a resonant analogue in what psychoanalysts call "the family romance, in which the child . . . imagines himself not to be the son of his parents, so that his desires may be more acceptable."[1] He invents parents who endorse rather than forbid his quest for a transcendent, usually royal, identity. If pressed, the child will claim that he is a changeling (as Henry IV wishes Hal were), that his real parents died (as Hamlet's ennobling father did), or that they underwent apotheosis (as does the totem-father posited by Freud). In *Coriolanus* this pattern is at least as prominent as it is in the earlier plays, but considerably more complex. The family romance seems almost to be inverted. The fantastic parents are all too easily mistaken for the real ones, by Coriolanus and by the audience as well. The nominal and visible family endorses his martial ambitions, while the family that would forbid them is fictional or dead or irretrievably dispersed. The only fathers Coriolanus acknowledges are his fellow-soldier Cominius and his fellow-patrician Menenius, both of whom resemble and encourage the heroic identity he is constructing. The visible mothers are Volumnia and Rome, both of whom share and praise his martial deeds. His only apparent sibling is Aufidius, a rival twin who seems to confirm Coriolanus' notion of himself as a pure creature of warfare. His only son is also a creature of proud ferocity, apparently by inheritance.

The fact that Coriolanus is destroyed as an ambitious violator of his hereditary nature is therefore a bitter surprise to him, and to us it provides the tragic spectacle of human aspiration entrapped by the confusing and finally contradictory instructions of a divided godhead. The mixed commands of the gods that confound the tragic hero in this play have correspondences in the mixed interests of a constituency that confound a politician, the mixed messages of a family that confound a child, and the mixed elements of human selfhood that confound any of us who claim it is our "nature, / Not to be other than one thing," as Aufidius says Coriolanus does (4.7.41–42). The world appears, as it does in *Macbeth*, as a sort of maternal temptress, inviting and then punishing Coriolanus' ambition as it does Macbeth's; the self-transformation can neither be completed nor reversed. Early in the plays, both protagonists achieve a form of Caesarean rebirth, but discover that it has not freed them from their hereditary constrictions, and a later attempt to complete the escape becomes a suicidal crime against the natural order.

This chapter considers the way Coriolanus' ambition is transformed from a glorious fulfillment of his familial identity to a fatal defiance of it. The various elements in that transformation are by their nature inextricable from each other; the unitary quality of the family ruins Coriolanus' quest as the unitary quality of the natural order defeats Macbeth. But I will focus in turn on each of the major elements, show how they change, and show how those changes mark the reborn Coriolanus as an enemy to human nature as well as an "enemy to the people" (3.3.118). Neither Cominius nor Menenius is truly his father, and he never manages to prove the identity his name and Aufidius' flattery offer him as "son and heir to Mars" (4.5.192); instead, the play gradually implies that the place of Coriolanus' invisible father is filled by the Roman citizenry, who bequeath to him the burden of common humanity he so violently resists. The concentric wombs of Rome and Volumnia temporarily support his martial transcendence, but only to the extent that it suits their interests, and Coriolanus finds his martial aspect bewilderingly disowned by both mothers when its principles conflict with their pragmatism. Aufidius proves to be not a twin brother, but merely a deceptive mirror who completes the destruction of Coriolanus by swerving from honorable martial opposition. Even Coriolanus' son, like the sons of other Oedipal figures, becomes literally and figuratively a weapon against his father.

The typical boy's struggles to rival the father, to differentiate himself from the mother, and to reshape himself according to an ideal male alter ego, all appear in Coriolanus' struggles for a transcendent identity; but his efforts are baffled by the corruption of those psychic objects. The merely human family betrays him on all sides in the process of reincorporating him into their limiting bodies natural and their limiting body politic. Coriolanus battles these competing versions of himself—the Roman citizen, the extension of Volumnia's body, and the mighty martial opposite—each of which offers him a different way of (literally or figuratively) reconceiving himself. His relationship to his hereditary and ideal selves is enacted in his confrontations with these three crucial elements of his world. Whether or not Coriolanus is on some level conscious of the symbolic importance of these encounters, we deepen our perception of the play by recognizing that importance. Shakespeare has crafted around his hero a political, familial, and martial situation that allows the hero's every ambitious action to generate a visual or rhetorical metaphor revealing the hazards of ambition.

Coriolanus and the Citizenry

The outlines of Shakespeare's myth of ambition are more strikingly visible in *Coriolanus* than in the earlier plays, perhaps because here they stand independent of the similar talionic outlines of Elizabethan propaganda against regicide, outlines so familiar and so transparently the product of political expediency that we barely bother to notice them. Ambition itself is on trial now, not as an avatar of usurpation, not even as an obviously sinful impulse, but as an independent ethical phenomenon. Many critics do treat *Coriolanus* as a political play but, significantly, they cannot agree on its politics. "Modern critics, echoing Coleridge's notes . . . have for the most part celebrated 'the wonderful philosophic impartiality in Shakespeare's politics.' "[2] Among the critics who do take sides, as many argue that Shakespeare values the refinement permitted by elitism as believe he claims precedence for the basic human needs of the masses: the dilemma is probably as old as politics itself.[3] But as Edward Dowden suggested over a century ago, "the central and vivifying element in the play is not a political problem, but an individual character and life. The tragic struggle of the play is not that of patricians with plebeians, but of Coriolanus with his own self."[4] The equipoise of the two political beliefs, from this perspective, reflects the balance Shakespeare characteristically maintains concerning the moral paradox of ambition: the noble impulse produces heights of heroism that we are loath to forfeit, but the persistent and sensible demands of common humanity (including the ambitious man's own humanity) naturally erode and undermine those heights. The Roman state's struggle to determine its politics, in other words, here parallels Coriolanus' struggle to determine his true identity.

This parallel is not merely a literary conceit; each of the struggles necessarily affects the other. If we take Coriolanus' fierce and unwavering opposition to the common people at face value, as the play's basic motivating conflict, we will be watching Coriolanus' play rather than Shakespeare's. As A. C. Bradley argues, "the type

145

of tragedy in which the hero opposes to a hostile force an undivided soul, is not the Shakespearean type."[5] In the plays about usurpation, Shakespeare uses the political situation to reflect or symbolize the protagonist's inner condition. Coriolanus' case differs crucially: he becomes almost his own playwright, manufacturing a particular sort of political crisis to express or authenticate the inner condition he desires to adopt. Shakespeare's commonplace becomes Coriolanus' self-aggrandizing, self-purifying metaphor. In the early seventeenth century, according to Michael Walzer, "Puritan ministers, extraordinarily sensitive to the dangers of disorder and wickedness, developed the moral authoritarianism of their theology into a theory of secular repression."[6] Coriolanus similarly converts his obsessive worship of heroic purity into social theory. The closest Shakespearean equivalent is the Puritanical Angelo in *Measure for Measure*, who "scarce confesses / That his blood flows" (1.3.51–52), and reflects that inner repression in a doomed program of political severity. The Roman plays of other playwrights—Jonson's *Sejanus* and *Cataline* for example—also portray leaders whose aristocratic ideals inform their political authority. But none of these playwrights explores the psychological implications of the correlation as Shakespeare does in *Coriolanus*.

Coriolanus turns to politics as a way of describing and enforcing a difficult internal distinction. This unconscious strategy has many suggestive analogues in life and literature. Authoritarian minds, according to T. W. Adorno's studies, "are generally devoid of introspection and insight and tend to project their own unacceptable qualities upon their opponents."[7] Coriolanus' determination that the aristocracy should suppress the citizenry is partly a projection of his effort to establish an internal aristocracy, a selective version of himself. The common people serve him as a metaphor for the internal taints of common human heritage. Delmore Schwartz, in his poetic representation of the play, says Coriolanus is "offended by their being, / Nursing in mind, older than any thought, / A hatred of all who issue sweat, urine, / Or excrement."[8] The purely hostile force, as Bradley's theory would suggest, proves to be an alienated aspect of the hero himself. Stephen Greenblatt argues that, in the Renaissance, "Self-fashioning is achieved in relation to something perceived as alien, strange, or hostile. This threatening Other . . . must be discovered or invented in order to be attacked and destroyed."[9] Certainly the relationship between Coriolanus and the Roman citizenry resembles the typical relationship between literary figures and their Doppelgänger. One theorist writes that the Self and the Other reveal their affinity "by inexplicable emotional reactions to each other, usually antagonism but often attraction (perhaps always, at some level, both); by insistent preoccupation with each other that may be quite unwilled by either or even consciously willed against by both." He adds that the Doppelgänger usually constitutes for the first self, as I think the citizenry does for Coriolanus, "the self that has been left behind . . . or otherwise excluded from the first self's self-conception; he is the self that must be come to terms with."[10]

Coriolanus' refusal to come to terms with the plebeians, then, corresponds to a revulsion from the bodily functions he shares with them. To become the ideal Roman hero he envisions, he must suppress not only the hunger, but also the fears, the vacillations, and even the affability normal to the human condition. Roman heroism requires a sort of metonymy of the self: it demands that a man's strictest martial aspect be allowed to stand for the entire man. The warrior must become his sword: silent, invulnerable, devoted entirely to combat. A 1599 translation of Cartari's mythography reports that "the people of Scithia hung up a sword in the middle of a temple, and worshipped it as the Image of Mars."[11] The Romans worship "Martius" by such a metonymy, which makes him first figuratively, then literally, into a sword: Lartius praises him as a "noble fellow! / Who sensibly outdares his senseless sword, / And when it bows, stand'st up" (1.4.52–54), and a hundred lines later the Roman soldiers wave their swords, then hoist Coriolanus in the air instead, and he asks, "Make you a sword of me?" (1.6.76). He is a harder and truer weapon than the weapons themselves.

Lawrence Danson argues convincingly that Coriolanus engineers this transformation in order to maintain a posture of "inhuman" purity. By resorting to metonymy, "Coriolanus denies in himself those contradictions (or, from another point of view, complexities) which mark lesser mortals."[12] However admirable this purity may be, it is as unsustainable in the world of Shakespeare's plays as any other denial of one's limiting heritage; that is how Coriolanus' heroism becomes tragic. Lucien Goldmann suggests that

> tragic thought merely poses the problem of a tension between a radically unsatisfactory world and an individual self that demands absolute authenticity. It does so, as Lukàcs writes, "with a strength that eliminates and destroys everything until this extreme affirmation of the self . . . endows everything it meets with a hard, steel-like autonomy: it then goes beyond itself."[13]

Coriolanus' steel-like autonomy is a device for self-transcendence. In North's translation of Plutarch, Shakespeare's primary source, Coriolanus "esteemed armour to no purpose, unles one were naturally armed within. Moreover he dyd so exercise his bodie to hardnes . . . that no man could ever cast him."[14] Several critics have observed that Coriolanus is often associated with metallic objects during the play.[15] What these critics neglect to observe is that Coriolanus himself, in his disdain for human frailty, is usually the one who insists on the association. He urges his army to advance "With hearts more proof than shields" (1.4.25), and tells the pleading Romans that "Mine ears against your suits are stronger than / Your gates against my force" (5.2.88–89). The others who describe him this way in the play do so in response to this deliberate rhetorical assertion of hardness (5.2.110–11, 5.4.18–21). Critics such as D. J. Enright who remark sadly, "If only we were persuaded that there is something inside him which is not reflected in his armour," perceive, however unsympathetically, exactly what Coriolanus wants them to perceive.[16] They read literally the metonymy by which he distinguishes himself from common humanity, and therefore overlook the tensions implicit in his struggle, however misguided, to enforce that metonymy.

The metonymy of the sword, which allows Coriolanus to deny any participation in the common processes of human flesh, provides an attractive alternative to the metonymy of Menenius' belly fable, which implicates him organically in the system of lesser mortals. To maintain his metallic identity, however, Coriolanus must be continually in battle; as Edmund tells the Captain in *King Lear*, "to be tender-minded / Does not become a sword" (5.3.31–32). Coriolanus' tendency to convert domestic situations into battlefields therefore serves a dual purpose: it emphasizes his rejection of the cooperative humanity which constitutes the Roman body politic, and it renews a metonymic identity which underscores and legitimizes that rejection. What was true for a Puritan seeking salvation is equally true for Coriolanus in his quest for transcendence of a different sort: any truce in the war for that victory, or any complacency that the evil had already been defeated, is itself a damning defeat. Coriolanus seeks in actual war what the Puritans first sought in spiritual war: a new identity through "a new world of discipline and work in which medieval hierarchy and patriarchy, organismic feeling, and corporate association are left far behind."[17] To affirm his ambitious identity, Coriolanus must fight off the limitations implicit in all of these systems: Menenius' organic metaphor, the

Chain of Being, the genetic family, and his own mortal patrimony. He attempts this " 'steeling' of character" as revolutionaries from the Puritans to the Bolsheviks have done: by discovering an outward enemy that corresponds to the enemy within, and fomenting a war against him that allows a new moral order in identity as well as politics.[18]

Constant and deliberate conflict marks Coriolanus' relationship with his Roman compatriots. His speeches to the citizens emphasize his bitter opposition to them and their ways, and they of course reciprocate. The central rhetorical devices in these exchanges are parallel constructions and sharp, balanced antitheses; though he claims to prefer action to words, Coriolanus consistently seeks out verbal structures that define a division and contrast between him and his plebeian audience when violence is forbidden. As the First Officer describes it,

> he seeks their hate with greater devotion than they can render it him, and leaves nothing undone that may fully discover him their opposite. Now, to seem to affect the malice and displeasure of the people is as bad as that which he dislikes, to flatter them for their love.
>
> (2.2.18–23)

Coriolanus is determined to "discover him their opposite," in every sense, and his efforts betray a willingness to manufacture distinction and enmity, as Voltaire says man manufactures his God, in case it might not already exist. He sets up the citizenry as a mirror-reversal of himself which, like Dorian Gray's portrait, draws off his mortal aspects. The same parallelism marks his descriptions of his relationship with Aufidius, whom he seeks to retain as the opposite sort of mirror, the ennobling exemplar. But these mirrors will prove deceptive: Coriolanus' frailties, like Dorian Gray's, are returned to him in force as soon as he loses his distinction from the mortal mirror, and he is destroyed by the real Aufidius, who lay in ambush behind the delusive mirror. In this sense, Aufidius and the citizenry are to Coriolanus what the Thane of Cawdor and Macduff are to Macbeth: the first of each pair is an alternative identity that the protagonist ambitiously seeks to assimilate and stands for the malleability of identity to a pre-existent model, while the second of each pair is a natural identity that resists any such assimilation and stands for the persistence of the hereditary self.

Coriolanus promises his mother that he will "exceed the common" (4.1.32), a phrase suggesting the unity between his opposition

to commonness and his opposition to the commoners. The First
Citizen is right that the patricians feel "our sufferance is a gain to
them" (1.2.22). Greatness, for Coriolanus, depends on getting clear
of the people and of what they represent:

> Who deserves greatness
> Deserves your hate; and your affections are
> A sick man's appetite, who desires most that
> Which would increase his evil. He that depends
> Upon your favors swims with fins of lead.   (1.1.176–80)

These metaphors assert something more complex than mere superiority. The common people represent something far more intimate
than a bad example: they are bodily afflictions that threaten his very
survival. To share organically in their body politic is to become sick;
to bathe the ideal self in their reverence is to drown it. Their food
and their praise are deadening weights on the journey to transcendence. Willard Farnham argues that Elizabethan tragedy depends on
the contrast between the "spiritual nobility" of the hero and the
"grossness" of the physical world in which he is obliged, to his
detriment, to live.[19] With opposite sympathies, an Elizabethan mor-
alist observes the same conflict: God gives man bodily afflictions
"to keepe this proud creature in his obedience, and to make him
acknowlege his creator."[20] Coriolanus' claims to self-authorship and
to steel-like autonomy both assist and require an evasion of gross
mortal physicality; whether that evasion, or that physicality, is a
more serious increase of Coriolanus' "evil" hangs in the balance
with the entire question of ambition's moral valence.

Food is a central focus for this ambivalence in the play, not only
because it was a political focal point in both Coriolanus' time and
Shakespeare's (there were massive corn riots in the English Midlands
about the time the play was being written), but also because it is a
natural focal point for questions about human transcendence. The
acquisition and digestion of food are absolutely necessary for human
existence, but they also necessarily degrade that existence. The subject invites us to weigh the greatness and the foolishness of abjuring
a natural aspect of human life in order to concentrate on its nobler
aspects, as in the practice of fasting for spiritual ends. The moral
imperative of surpassing our beastly need for food, and the natural
impossibility of doing so, correspond to the heroic imperative of
surpassing the hereditary bodily self, and the tragic impossibility of
doing so.

Food has traditionally determined the status, degraded or exalted, of those who eat it. According to several myths current in Shakespeare's milieu, figures such as Prosperpina who taste the food of the underworld, or of some other enchanted world, must remain there forever. Roman food threatens Coriolanus with an analogous entrapment. Coriolanus' journey to transcendence, like Odysseus' journey of return, demands that he avoid consuming the forbidden fruit consumed by his compatriots: the lotus will enthrall him into complacency, the banquet of Circe will evoke his bestial attributes, the cattle of Helios will call down divine vengeance against his mission. The need to eat at all, as Janet Adelman suggests, would seem to mark Coriolanus as part and product of common humanity. She deduces that Coriolanus rejects the plebeians' food in order to establish oral self-sufficiency, as if he were exorcising an infantile feeding-trauma.[21] My suggestion, conversely, is that he establishes such self-sufficiency to avoid entanglement with the plebeians. But either interpretation points toward the same evasion of an organic system that compromises his claim to pure martial nobility.

In accepting food produced by the plebeians, Coriolanus would compromise himself both politically and symbolically. Menenius' belly fable implicitly converts the Proserpina and Odysseus stories into a social principle. By accepting the lowly creatures' sustenance, Coriolanus would inevitably become bound to them and limited by them, as he is "bound to 's mother" and therefore limited in his heroic conquests (5.3.159) as a result of accepting her feedings (3.2.129). Menenius compares the aristocracy to a stomach that receives the fruits of the other members' labors, and could neither exist nor function without them; in return for their service, the stomach must therefore yield them its finest products. Coriolanus must either move outside of this fable by rejecting the food, or else concede that his martial heroism derives from, and belongs to, common humanity. Menenius warns the citizens that, when they "digest . . . rightly" their true relationship to the senators,

> you shall find
> No public benefit which you receive
> But it proceeds or comes from them to you,
> And no way from yourselves. (1.1.150–54)

Precisely this warning, though he apparently has not heard it, applies to Coriolanus when he seeks the public benefit of the consulship, which he must beg from the mouths of the citizens. He, like the belly in the fable, would be obliged to "minister / Unto the appetite and affection common / Of the whole body" (1.1.103–05). Rather than thus surrender his autonomy and his transcendence, he spits out arrogant tirades, fomenting civil war. In this sense, he has "Rebell'd against the belly" (1.1.97) as much as the lowly members do in Menenius' fable: his rejection of feeding is implicitly a war on the organic unity of the state, and vice versa.

There is a less apparent but no less important aspect of food-symbolism that nurtures rather than poisons Coriolanus' transcendence. The culmination of Tantalus' ambition is his effort to steal some of the gods' food, which would make him immortal. Zeus attempts to immortalize his demigod son Hercules by tricking Juno into suckling him with some of her divine milk. This latter case is particuarly intriguing in terms of *Coriolanus* because Coriolanus and Volumnia correspond in several ways to Hercules and Juno, and Coriolanus seems to receive a tentative sort of immortality from Volumnia's breasts. "Thy valiantness was mine," she tells him, "thou suck'st it from me" (3.2.129). Caius Martius may be a son of the valiant god Mars in name and deeds, but myth made Romulus the god's actual offspring, and made him another version of the boy who is exposed to death by a fearful usurper, but who survives to overthrow that wicked father-surrogate. Romulus survived to found Rome only because he was suckled by a she-wolf (a creature sacred to Mars), or perhaps by a sinister woman, since as North's Plutarch indicates, "the Latines doe call with one selfe name shee woulfes *Lupas*, & women that geve their bodyes to all commers."[22] The combination of rapacious wolf and sinister woman appears in Volumnia, who is presented as the mother of Rome, and who conspires Oedipally with her son to overthrow the paternal community and its mediocrity, through his god-like martial practices. She feeds Coriolanus in a way that evokes his identities as son of Mars and as the primal Roman. As she starves herself with feeding, using only anger as her meat (4.2.50–51), so she implicitly demands that Coriolanus feed himself on the blood of Rome's enemies:

> The breasts of Hecuba,
> When she did suckle Hector, look'd not lovelier
> Than Hector's forehead when it spit forth blood
> At Grecian sword, contemning.   (1.3.40–43)

Coriolanus has succeeded in feeding himself in this fashion—he tells Aufidius that he has "Drawn tuns of blood out of thy country's breast" (4.5.99)—and he is allowed to believe for some time that these deeds have rendered him as essential to the Roman state as Mars's son Romulus, and as free from any limiting mortal patrimony. Food is not invariably a mortal trap, then, and starvation not the only course that Coriolanus pursues; food, if properly selected, may apparently serve as a means of enforcing one's own apotheosis.

Such immortalizing food, however, is always a forbidden fruit, whether for Tantalus, for Hercules, or for Adam and Eve. The apple that looks so appealing in *Paradise Lost* leaves its eaters spitting ashes, bitterly disappointed, having assured not their immortality but rather their mortality. Coriolanus' temptation to deify himself, like the temptation of others to crown themselves in the earlier plays, proves to be a fatal delusion. After he has starved himself of one sort of food and carved himself another, Coriolanus discovers that the exalting transformation promised him has not taken place. His sense of betrayal when his mother insists that he is merely a man and should submit to the paternal citizenry, and when that citizenry insists that he does not belong in Rome, is overwhelming. He complains to Volumnia, "You were us'd to load me / With precepts that would make invincible / The heart that conn'd them" (4.1.9–11), but as he departs into exile she no longer feeds him any of these immortalizing martial principles. Recent psychoanalytic arguments such as Adelman's have described Volumnia as a stingy nurse to her son, and claim that this stinginess has deformed him into an oral-agressive personality. That interpretation seems to me defensible only to the extent that it reinforces this more basic mythological argument, in which Volumnia characteristically offers her son the flattering identity he seeks, provided he will behave nobly and fight for Rome. When he turns against her political program, and especially when he threatens to become a destroyer rather than a founder of Rome, she warns him that he will make his name cursed rather than worshiped (5.3.142–48).[23] She breaks from the Oedipal conspiracy and retracts his identity as a divinely fed Romulus, just as she retracts the other flatteries she had offered to motivate him toward her goals.

Coriolanus turns to Aufidius to replace this immortalizing sustenance, as he turns to Aufidius to reaffirm the threatened martial principles that defined his god-like identity. Aufidius promptly serves him a feast at which he is worshiped "as if he were son and heir to Mars" (4.5.192), but like everything else in Coriolanus' stay with the Volsces, this is merely a dangerously delusive mirror-image of what he experienced in Rome. Aufidius is the host, but he intends to consume rather than feed the body and blood of his quasi-divine guest. This is a perverted Last Supper then, before the martyr's mortality is feelingly enforced on him, and the embrace is the embrace of Judas. Aufidius drives Coriolanus back into a confrontation with his merely human identity, represented by his mortal family, and once that humanity has been demonstrated, Aufidius declares his own *Ecce Homo*: when Coriolanus calls on Mars to defend his claim to greatness, Aufidius scoffs, "Name not the god, thou boy of tears!" (5.6.99–100).

Until these betrayals occur, however, Coriolanus regulates his identity by a figurative regulation of his diet. By remaining at war, he remains a lonely sword rather than a cooperative bodily organ. By refusing to nurse on the milk of human kindness, he spares himself any visitings of compassion, which Pierre de La Primaudaye defined in 1594 as "a like sense and feeling of evil and of griefe, as if we our selves suffered that which we see others endure, by reason of that conjunction which we ought to have one with another, as members of one and the same body."[24] War frees him from any obligation to feel such compassion, and frees him to feed himself on the blood his sword draws. When he hears that "the Volsces are in arms," he replies, "I am glad on't, then we shall ha' means to vent / Our musty superfluity" (1.1.224–26). The war that will allow Coriolanus to resume his martial identity immediately appeals to him as a way of eliminating Romans as well as Volsces, and elimination, as his own metaphor makes evident, is very much what he has in mind. Two historical notes become relevant here. René Girard remarks, in a very different context, that men in the seventeenth century put tremendous emphasis on the idea of expulsion, which included the expulsion of wrath as well as the expulsion of excrement.[25] Keith Thomas observes that the Elizabethans believed it unhealthy to retain digestive gasses;[26] they must be vented promptly, as Menenius vents them in his famous belch (1.1.108). To Coriolanus, the common people are such gasses; they are the "sick man's appetite" and the poison cramping the body politic, stinking from the poorness of their diet (1.1.60, 2.1.236, 4.6.98). After the plebeians have "vented their complainings" (1.1.209), they are granted concessions of food for the body natural and power in the body politic, concessions that Coriolanus says "nourish'd disobedience, fed / The ruin of the state" by allowing a monstrous appetite that tends to "lick / The sweet that is their poison" to "digest / The Senate's courtesy" (3.1.116–57). In yielding, he warns,

> we nourish 'gainst our Senate
> The cockle of rebellion, insolence, sedition,
> Which we ourselves have plough'd for, sow'd, and scatter'd,
> By mingling them with us. (3.1.69–72)

They are a harvest entirely of chaff, which promises only indigestion to the body politic until war again divides the noble from the lowly, that which sustains the muscular state from that which merely inhabits it. In North's version of this story, the Roman aristocrats plan this war to rid the city "of many mutinous and seditious persones, being the superfluous ill humours that grevously fedde this disease."[27]

Menenius' fable claims that the aristocratic belly retains only the chaff and sends out the kernel to nourish the commonalty. Coriolanus, conversely, envisions the body politic eliminating the chaff digestively, and thereby eliminating the common people. Menenius' effort to excuse Coriolanus' hard words to the citizenry by claiming that he "is ill school'd / In bolted language; meal and bran together / He throws without distinction" (3.1.319–21) is misleading at best; he insults them precisely because he is a compulsive winnower. When Coriolanus returns from his banishment intent on destroying Rome, the patricians unwittingly concede that the terms of their justifying fable have been reversed. Cominius reports that, while Coriolanus regrets the imminent death of his noble former countrymen,

> He could not stay to pick them in a pile
> Of noisome musty chaff. He said 'twas folly,
> For one poor grain or two, to leave unburnt
> And still to nose th' offense.

Menenius interprets this allegory more testily than he did the earlier one: "we are the grains, / You are the musty chaff, and you are smelt / Above the moon. We must be burnt for you" (5.1.25–32). Coriolanus' references to "Our musty superfluity" (1.1.226) and "musty chaff" are revealingly similar. Both stand for the stench of mortal decay he constantly strives to evacuate from his system. War permits him to move into a martial identity as a sword that takes precedence over his common mortal functions, the chaff of his being, and the same conflagration helps eliminate the common people, who serve as metaphors for those unwanted mortal aspects. Fire traditionally serves this self-purifying project, and it is fire Coriolanus persistently threatens to use against Roman corruption. Thomas à Kempis, for example, urges God to burn our souls "in the lively flame that wasteth al grosse filthinesse, that after they be cleane sundred from the body, they may be coupled with an everlasting and most sweete bonde to heavenly beauty. And we severed from oure selves, may be changed like right lovers into the beloved."[28] Coriolanus takes this fiery god-making role onto himself, hoping to destroy by purgative or purgatory the degrading mirror of the Roman citizenry, and by the same fiery means to render himself eligible for assumption into the ennobling mirror-figures of Aufidius, Hercules, and Mars.

When Prince Hal battles Hotspur, we are invited to recognize the conquest of an inner rebel that necessarily preceded the outward combat. In *Coriolanus* we are given a much more elaborate description of the hero's conquest of his inner frailties that necessarily precedes the actual warfare. Coriolanus changes from man to sword, and his conflict against his cowardly compatriots is an acting-out of that transformation, an externalized struggle that mediates between his conquest of his own fears and his conquest of the Volsces. He goes to war against the common Romans in the very process of going to war alongside them. As Coriolanus leaves behind the chaff of his vulnerable bodily being, he also wants to discard the musty and cowardly chaff of Rome, culling from his army to assist him only those who "think brave death outweighs bad life" (1.6.71). This points suggestively to Ripa's *Iconologie*, which portrays Democracy as a bundle of stalks of wheat, with the stalks representing the masses "who have more ambition for their survival than for their honors."[29] Against this chaff, the enemies of his moral ideal, Coriolanus lights the fires of holy war and purification even while they are nominally his allies: "Mend and charge home, / Or, by the fires of heaven, I'll leave the foe / And make my wars on you" (1.4.38–40). His "murder of all parts of the self that do not fit into the preconceived image"[30] thus expresses itself outwardly, through the established metaphors of grain and chaff and burning. Coriolanus enters battles, as Volumnia reports, "Like to a harvest-man that's task'd to mow / Or all or lose his hire" (1.3.36–37), and the winnowing of that harvest is an essential part of the task.

The analogue between the sorting of grain and moral selection dates back at least as far as the Bible, reappearing in Dante's portrayal of the world as a threshing-floor and in Petrarch's assertion that men "are the grain fields of God to be winnowed in the plains of judgement."[31] It receives extensive treatment in Francis Quarles' 1635 emblem-book, which describes the world as "a Heape" of "yet unwinnowed graine" that is "lodg'd with chaffe" as "The good with bad; the noble with the vile" are sadly mixed in the human realm:

> The wordly wisdome of the foolish man
>   Is like a Sive, that does, alone retaine
> The grosser substance of the worthlesse Bran;

> But thou, my soule, let thy brave thoughts disdaine
> So course a purchace; O, be thou a Fan
>   To purge the Chaffe, and keep the winnow'd Graine;
>   Make cleane thy thoughts, and dresse thy mixt desires;
>   Thou art heav'ns Tasker; and thy GOD requires
> The purest of thy Floore, as well as of thy fires.[32]

Coriolanus is very much this sort of self-purifying Tasker, wielding his sword as alternately a fan or a fire; his "brave thoughts disdaine" Menenius' corporate fable, which would make him precisely such a foolish sieve full of bran. In his quest for a martial apotheosis, Coriolanus blows or burns away the bodily attributes and their analogues in the body politic that would compromise his heroic transformation. Ambition is an idealized form of digestion. We know he has failed in this quest when he cannot bring himself to purge Rome with fire, and must therefore return to Corioli and "appear before the people, hoping / To purge himself with words" (5.6.7–8). It is a revealing sort of defeat for a man who had mocked the people who "vented their complainings" (1.1.209).

Coriolanus attempts to make himself a demigod by rejecting all of his animal attributes, but the play insists on the precariousness of any such transformation. He may project his bestial characteristics out into the mirror of the Roman populace, but the play constantly threatens him with reminders that a mirror is finally only a representation of oneself. The very people he has described as poisons in the body politic find it easy enough to turn precisely that accusation against him: one man's purgative is another man's poison, particularly if he is what is being purged (3.1.219–22). Coriolanus' arrogant autonomy reminds us, perhaps deliberately, of Aristotle's maxim that "He that cannot abide to live in company, or through sufficiency hath need of nothing, is not esteemed a part or member of a Cittie, but is either a beast or a God."[33] The risk for Coriolanus, as for Leontes in *The Winter's Tale*, is that a failed leap toward godliness may plunge a man into something strongly resembling beastliness. C. S. Lewis remarks:

> Christians had always held that a man was a composite creature, *animal rationale*, and that it lay in his own choice to be governed by his reason or his animality. But that choice could produce order or disorder only within the limits assigned to him by the hierarchy of being. He could become a saint but not an angel: a swinish man but not a pig. The Florentines, on the other hand, sometimes ap-

pear to think that Man can become any kind of creature he pleases.[34]

Coriolanus seems to believe, in a pagan way, that he can force his own apotheosis by a sheer exertion of might and will. On the other hand, his program of insults against the citizenry suggests a conservative view of humanity's nature as a whole: he seems to believe that locating such animal attributes as fear, hunger, and odor in the citizens will propel his own nature up to the superhuman in counterpoise. He facilitates his self-elevation by a system of counterweights. Richard II applies the same physical principle to human advancement in comparing his abdication and Henry's anointment to the linked movements of two buckets in a well (4.1.183–89). As a political rule, this is almost universal: taking sovereignty almost always involves throwing someone into a dungeon. Coriolanus is trapped in a bad marriage with his own morally ambivalent humanity, and he deals with the ensuing conflicts as unhappily married people often do: "In those combats where they think they confront one another, it is really against the self that each one struggles, projecting into the partner that part of the self which is repudiated; instead of living out the ambiguities of their situation, each tries to make the other bear the abjection and tries to reserve the honor for the self."[35]

Coriolanus' rhetoric reveals his effort to enforce such distinctions, but also reveals their fragility. At the moments when language fails or betrays him, his natural frailities reach out in the form of a Doppelgänger to reclaim him, as nature reaches out to reclaim Macbeth. When the balanced antitheses by which he distinguishes himself from the citizenry collapse, they all too often prove to be merely mirror-reversals that turn his eyes onto the dark and grained spots in his own soul. His first speech to the plebeian mob is loaded with accusatory animal imagery, but is also revealingly mirror-like:

> What would you have, you curs,
> That like nor peace nor war? The one affrights you,
> The other makes you proud. He that trusts to you,
> Where he should find you lions, finds you hares;
> Where foxes, geese. (1.1.168–72)

Depending on how we understand the parallelism, we may hear Coriolanus inadvertently but accurately accuse himself: peace affrights him, as we have seen, and war makes him proud. A more dangerous slip, again with a suggestion of mirroring, occurs when

Coriolanus urges "the mutable, rank-scented meiny" to "Regard me as I do not flatter, and / Therein behold themselves" (3.1.66–68). He means that he is holding a mirror up to their unattractive nature, through his insults, but on a secondary level his words imply that he is himself a reflection of their unflattering nature.[36]

His accusatory animal imagery, like his poison imagery, returns to haunt him by implicating him in the very categories he has condemned. In scorning the common people in the passage above as "geese" (and at 1.4.34 as "souls of geese") for fleeing battles, he prepares a bitter irony for his own downfall. Ready to destroy Rome, he insists he will 'never / Be such a gosling to obey instinct" (5.3.34–35), but when his mother describes him as a creature that "she, poor hen . . . cluck'd . . . to the wars" (5.3.162–63), he reverts to instinct and retreats from the battle himself. Such moments, where glimpses of unwilling self-recognition undermine the blustering intention, foreshadow not only the fact of Coriolanus' defeat, but also its nature. Freudian slips are moments when fallibility and repressed nature combine to break through a socially acceptable utterance. Even the moment of silence in which he takes his mother's hand and resigns his conquest may be considered as such a slip, on a grand scale; in that silence his repressed natural self reasserts itself against his rhetorical and violent assertions of a public ideal.

To explore the play's range of animal epithets would be neither brief nor original;[37] but it is worth noting that they erupt most vehemently at the moments when the citizens threaten to eclipse Coriolanus' heroism, as if he were suggesting that everything but the animal in humanity would disappear with the failure of his quest. The robe he wears to beg the consulship is "woolvish" (2.3.115), and when he fails to wear it humbly enough, Volumnia says he is banished by "cats" following the "foxship" of the tribunes (4.2.34, 18). Menenius says that the senators themselves became "beasts" in allowing the citizens to "hoot" Coriolanus away, turning Rome into the monster he had feared it would become (4.6.121–23, 3.1.288–92). Coriolanus himself, at his banishment, calls the citizenry "the beast with many heads" that "butts me away" (4.1.1–2), led by an "old goat" (3.1.176). The traditional aristocratic device of justifying one's elevation by positioning oneself against the mere animality of the lower classes is fully at work here.

The accusations of animality are persistently linked to accusations of multiplicity and of sickness, perhaps because Coriolanus seeks an individual exemption from the common world of bodily humanity. The people are a "multiplying spawn," a "common cry of curs," a school of "minnows," a "herd" (2.2.78, 3.3.120, 3.1.88, 3.2.32).[38] When this herd threatens to taint his Roman valor with their cowardice, Coriolanus furiously couples their fear with disease as well as animal multiplicity:

> All the contagion of the south light on you,
> You shames of Rome! you herd of—Biles and plagues
> Plaster you o'er, that you may be abhorr'd
> Farther than seen, and one infect another
> Against the wind a mile!   (1.4.30–34)

Menenius picks up the association a few scenes later, refusing to talk to the people's tribunes, because their "conversation would infect my brain, being the herdsmen of the beastly plebeians" (2.1.94–95). Coriolanus distinguishes himself from these multiple decaying bodies by identifying with his solitary sword, and the other patricians similarly grant him distinction from the common "scabs" (1.1.166) by saying that his martial deeds have made him "A carbuncle entire" (1.4.55), a hard and unitary jewel. But the word "carbuncle" signified to the Elizabethans not only a red jewel, but also the subcutaneous infection that resembles that jewel; Coriolanus is again entangled in his own nasty metaphor, becoming a virulent version of the "scabs" he disdains, as a direct result of his rhetorical and martial efforts to surpass them. Lear makes the problem explicit when he rages at Goneril,

> But yet thou art my flesh, my blood, my daughter—
> Or rather a disease that's in my flesh,
> Which I must needs call mine: thou art a boil,
> A plague-sore, or embossed carbuncle,
> In my corrupted blood.   (King Lear, 2.4.221–25)

The carbuncle is a sickness arising from within, and Coriolanus assaults the citizens as a way of externalizing, and thus resisting, an internal contaminant. Like Lear, he insists that the disease is in his flesh but not exactly of it. To deny the frailty of his own flesh, Coriolanus must deny any kinship with these other sons of Adam and their mortality. His scars therefore embarrass him; his grandeur, like Lear's, is compromised when he "smells of mortality" (King Lear, 4.6.133). It is not surprising that he detests begging the people's voices and displaying his scars to them; the scabrous rebels in his body natural and those in the body politic combine at the marketplace to threaten his transcendence with reminders of his mortality.

Coriolanus' angry exchange with the tribune Junius Brutus, after

the people have withdrawn their endorsement, reveals the tactics
and also the dangers of Coriolanus' self-elevation:

> As for my country I have shed my blood,
> Not fearing outward force, so shall my lungs
> Coin words till their decay against those measles
> Which we disdain should tetter us, yet sought
> The very way to catch them.
> *Brutus*   You speak a' th' people
> As if you were a god, to punish; not
> A man of their infirmity.   (3.1.76–82)

He fears the enmity of the people no more than the enmity of the
Volsces; what he does fear is a subversion, political or psychological,
that will compromise his hard purity, that will make his lungs a
habitation of disease rather than a metal-stamping machine. The
tribune states concisely a crucial paradox of ambition in answering
this politicized denial of the flesh. To use Montaigne's terms, how
can a man raise himself above his own humanity? Or, to use the
anti-Pelagian terms of the Reformation, how can a creature himself
imperfect hope to construct a perfect selfhood, or even hope to know
what perfection would be? The tribune reminds Coriolanus, as other
Jacobean plays such as *Bartholomew Fair* and *The Tempest* remind
their protagonists and audiences, that no mortal man can safely judge
and punish the frailties of others. Judge not, the tribune here suggests, that ye be not judged. Later in the scene, in fact, both tribunes
condemn Coriolanus through the same metaphor (and the same
metonymic device) Coriolanus uses against the plebeians: "He's a
disease," Sicinius declares, "that must be cut away" (3.1.293; similarly 3.1.219–21, 3.1.309–10). This is an accusation Coriolanus desperately struggles to disprove through the rest of the play. When he
finally believes himself "full quit of those my banishers," he declares
himself "No more infected with my country's love," prepared to
eradicate "my cank'red country" (4.5.83; 5.6.71; 4.5.91). The scabrous carbuncle has apparently been healed. Cominius reports, "He
is their god; he leads them like a thing / Made by some other deity
than Nature, / That shapes man better" (4.6.90–92).

Cominius' diagnosis of superhuman health may, however, be
skewed by his partisan attitude and by his desire to frighten the
tribunes. His insistence that Coriolanus *is* a god must be weighed
against the tribune's dubious subjunctive, "As if you *were* a god."
This too may be a factional rather than a factual remark. Brutus and
Sicinius, as tribunes of the people, are appropriate critics of Corio-

lanus' godly transformation. Their political function is to insist that the patricians remember the needs of the plebeians, and their corresponding symbolic function is to insist on Coriolanus' debt to his common human attributes. If Coriolanus' political repressiveness is largely a macrocosmic projection of his effort to silence his own bodily needs, then the tribunes can best protect their constituency by constantly reminding Coriolanus of his humanity. Prospero is reminded of his own humanity, and hence of his obligation to be tolerant, in the same two ways: by Ariel, who asserts it verbally, and by Caliban, who becomes its external representation (5.1.20,275). According to Menenius' microcosmic fable, the tribunes represent the common element, the merely human voice, in Coriolanus' ruling nobility; they forbid him to isolate his greatness from mortal taints in the body natural, just as they limit the Senate's repressiveness in the body politic. The unflattering counselors, here as in Duke Senior's speech in *As You Like It* (2.1.10–11), are the bodily afflictions " 'That feelingly persuade me what I am.' "

The tribune Brutus is therefore an incisive critic of Coriolanus' claim to godhead. His political position and the play's symbolic system combine to grant him an intimate insight into the hero's workings, of a sort usually permitted only to a hero's Doppelgänger. When everyone else accepts Coriolanus' martial apotheosis, Brutus remains stubbornly in the subjunctive, complaining that, since his defeat of the Volsces, Coriolanus has been treated

> As if that whatsoever god who leads him
> Were slily crept into his human powers,
> And gave him graceful posture.

> (2.1.219–21)

It is one thing to believe that Coriolanus is following a divine example, another to suppose that imitation has become incarnation. The assumption of deity into Coriolanus' body has been treated as less of an incongruity than the draping of that body with "the napless vesture of humility" (2.1.234; cf. 4.5.151), as if the hero were now more god than man. The play of course takes place in a pre-Christian world, but to its audience such pride would have seemed quintessentially Satanic, and the description of this incarnation would have made an alert Elizabethan audience even more uneasy. The phrase "whatsoever god" is emphatically unspecific, and the phrase "slily crept" can best be explained as an allusion (by Shakespeare rather than Brutus) to Satan's assumption of the serpent's form, which gave it "graceful posture." Early English dramatizations of the Fall

simply dressed up one of the actors in a serpentine costume, thereby accidentally reviving the rabbinic belief
that the snake originally walked like a man. This device . . . created a somewhat ambiguous figure who could
have been mistaken for an angel as well as a snake. Consequently in several versions of the episode Eve seems to
have been under the impression that the intruder was in
fact a messenger from Heaven.[39]

When the gods laugh mockingly at the fatal humiliation of Coriolanus' proud quest (5.3.183–85), we may suspect that Coriolanus
has committed a similar error. Supernatural visitors in Elizabethan
and Jacobean plays, most commonly the ghosts in revenge tragedies,
tend to be morally ambiguous at best. Coriolanus' association with
a "serpent" (1.8.3), a "viper" (3.1.262, 285), and a "dragon" (4.1.30,
5.4.13)—the traditional analogues to the Satanic snake—makes his
supernatural visitor seem at least as untrustworthy. The effort to
deny the human frailties brought on by the Fall—and I will argue
that the same warning attaches to ambition in *The Winter's Tale*—
threatens to repeat that Fall rather than repair it.

Elizabethan and Jacobean political and theological writers repeatedly associated ambitious resistance to a limiting human hierarchy with a Satanic dragon. Malynes' *Saint George for England*
(1601) argues that societies where "every member thereof doth live
contentedly and proportionably in his vocation" are often "brought
to confusion and utter destruction by means of this Dragon," a
monster of pride that disdains such organic unity, "whereunto ambition is annexed which moveth sedition and civil war."[40] Thomas
Floyd, in *The Picture of a perfit Common wealth* (1600), characterizes this ambition in terms strikingly similar to those in which
Junius Brutus characterizes the "whatsoever god": "Ambition is a
serpent, which pryeth into every mans thoghts, & slily insinuateth
her selfe into the bowels of men."[41] This description is also intriguingly similar to the way Northumberland is assigned to "secretly
into the bosom creep" of the Archbishop of York in *1 Henry IV*
(1.3.266) to enlist him in the rebel cause. Stephen Batman's *Batman
uppon Bartholme* suggests a correlation between Coriolanus' metonymic effort to transcend humanity, as a carbuncle or a dragon,
and the similarly humiliated project of Satan himself:

For the first Angell was beautified as a precious
stone . . . because he in an undue manner coveted high-
nesse, that belonged not to him, therefore by a right decree

> he felle downe into a lowe place . . . For he is called a
> Serpent or a Dragon.[42]

The martially possessed Coriolanus cannot, however, be identified with the Satanic serpent completely:

> Patristic commentators had claimed that Satan entered
> the snake . . . because its tortuous windings accorded with
> his devious nature. According to most medieval authors,
> on the contrary, the Devil chose the serpent because it
> was peculiarly fitted to deceive Eve by virtue of its ap-
> pearance, its "lady visage."[43]

Neither sly complexity nor winsome femininity suggest Coriolanus
in the least. The god who chose to insinuate himself into Coriolanus'
form would be blunt and warlike. One candidate is of course the
god of war himself, and Coriolanus is worshiped in Antium "as if
he were son and heir to Mars" (4.5.192), just as he is worshiped in
Rome "as if" he were the new embodiment of the "whatsoever god."
It is worth noting that the worship in Antium is actually a very
dangerous deception, and we may infer that the visitation of deity
in Rome is equally delusive and destructive. Another possibility is
Hercules; we know from *Antony and Cleopatra* that Shakespeare
envisions Hercules as a god who travels with a warrior until he
compromises his martial purity (4.3.16–17). The two plays are connected in several ways,[44] and the god who flees from Antony may
creep into the form of Coriolanus until he is obliged to flee again
for shame. Moreover, an early seventeenth-century translation of
Philostratus reports that Juno made the demigod Hercules destroy
his mortal family by sending "hideous hundred-headed serpents,
who crept insensibly into the most inward chambers of his stomach
and brain; where, playing their games at their pleasure, they trans-
ported him so far out of himself that he killed his own children and
his wife."[45] The terms again resemble the serpentine insinuation of
Coriolanus, which exalts him, too, out of himself and to the brink
of the same proud crime. The fact that Coriolanus, unlike Hercules,
cannot complete the eradication of his mortal family, only confirms
the notion that Coriolanus fails to attain the status of the demigod
on whom he models himself. The point is not that Coriolanus stands
for the god Mars, or the devil Satan, or the demigod Hercules. The
point instead is that, by maintaining this ambiguity of allusion,
Shakespeare maintains his characteristic ambivalence about ambi-

tion: whether a person can or should transcend his humanity remains a crucial and unresolved question.

Sicinius, the other tribune, has his own insights about Coriolanus' ambition. He recognizes Coriolanus' proud resistance to the idea that his ultimate identity, as consul, should be a filial derivation from the common people, and again the insight expresses itself as an "As if": Coriolanus demands the people's voices "As if he did contemn what he requested / Should be in them to give" (2.2.157–58). As Albany warns Goneril, who is also scornfully replacing filial obedience with filial violence, "That nature which contemns it origin" invites disorder and death (4.2.32–36). Essentially the same conflict occurs in Macbeth, who cannot enjoy his unnatural personal and political identities "When all that is within him does condemn / Itself for being there" (5.2.24–25). In all three cases, the disdainful and violent rejection of a limiting patrimony is actually a dangerous rejection of one's own natural existence; in scorning the citizenry and their power to give him an identity, Coriolanus is scorning his origin, his nature, and his own belly. The figurative patricide is therefore also a figurative suicide. The tribune Brutus remarks that, in a confrontation with the plebeians, Coriolanus' proud heart will work with them "to break his neck" (3.3.28–30); and when Coriolanus resists the praising of his martial deeds to the citizenry, Cominius replies that "If 'gainst yourself you be incens'd, we'll put you / (Like one that means his proper harm) in manacles" (1.9.56–57). These mock-precautions against suicide suggest all too accurately the dynamics of Coriolanus' pride.

Sicinius makes another remark about Coriolanus' pride that describes it as, if not a self-destruction, at least a self-*askesis*, an unnatural amputation of one's unwanted attributes:

> Such a nature,
> Tickled with good success, disdains the shadow
> Which he treads on at noon. But I do wonder
> His insolence can brook to be commanded
> Under Cominius. (1.1.259–63)

The cynical explanation Brutus offers in reply misses the point: Coriolanus is willing to act as an obedient son to any father-figure who defines him as a martial creature, which the general Cominius certainly does as long as Coriolanus remains on the Roman side. But the man who disdains the invisible shadow beneath his feet is making untenable distinctions and desperately investing them with moral significance. As in the political disdain that prompts Sicinius' observation, Coriolanus seems to be searching for external modes in which to express (and thereby figuratively enforce) a rejection of the things of darkness that cannot be assaulted internally. Several Renaissance emblems set up an analogy between the noon-time sun, which allows no shadow, and pure virtue, which allows no taint.[46] The shadow, of course, is a standard metaphor for the tenacious Doppelgänger: Coriolanus' pride makes him fight against an inaccessible specter, an inverted version of himself which is firmly rooted in the earth.

After Coriolanus' pride has led to his banishment, Sicinius again suggests the way Coriolanus has disassembled himself in the effort to advance himself:

> I would he had continued to his country
> As he began, and not unknit himself
> The noble knot he made.   (4.2.30–32)

In breaking free from Rome, he opens a path to both glory and destruction. The knot is traditionally a symbol of human complications, and when Cleopatra begs the serpent to untie "this knot intrinsicate / Of life" (5.2.304–05), her plea recalls legends promising sovereignty to anyone who can loose the Gordian knot.[47] Her escape from Caesar is a victory, but also a suicide; and Coriolanus' effort to seize a sovereignty that would eradicate his complex humanity requires that he too undo what Donne's "The Extasie" calls "That subtile knot, which makes us man" (line 64), a knot that is limited by our mortal bodies. An Elizabethan pamphlet warns that a rebellious spirit "Brings them to naught, that seketh Civill warres," and concludes that the only way to avoid such nullification is to "Knit fast the knotte" binding the individual to his surrounding body-politic.[48] Coriolanus, as Sicinius notes, does quite the opposite, eventually becoming "a kind of nothing" (5.1.13) by cutting the umbilical knot binding him to his human heritage and the body politic of Rome.

Coriolanus' dangerous rebellion against the body politic, then, is largely an extension of his dangerous rebellion against the body natural, and both entail a claim to self-authorship that defies the rights of the paternal authorities. Filial allegiance is as tenuously compatible with Coriolanus' ambition as it is with the ambitions of Richard III and Henry IV. The final step to sovereignty reveals ambition's true opposition to family, and subsequently the usurpers cannot acknowledge any obligation to Buckingham or the Percies, because a real royal identity can derive only from God and not from man (1 Henry IV, 1.3.11–20). Coriolanus seems similarly aware that the idea of sovereign exaltation cannot be reconciled with the idea of human dependency: Sicinius describes him as "affecting one sole throne, / Without assistance" (4.6.32–33). Shakespeare goes to considerable trouble to show us the newly triumphant Coriolanus forgetting the name, and thereby perhaps permitting the execution, of the old Volscian who had formerly lodged him and cared for him.[49] When the father-figures Cominius and Menenius try to dissuade Coriolanus from burning Rome, he renounces his former identity as their son, apparently because they are opposing both his absolute martial principles and the conflagration that, by burning away the taints of his derivation, will permit his apotheosis as son of Mars (5.1.3–17, 5.2.63–72). North's Plutarch suggests that Coriolanus' fatherless upbringing "taught us by experience, that orphanage bringeth many discommodities to a childe, but doth not hinder him to become an honest man, and to excell in vertue above the common sorte."[50] Shakespeare's version of the story seems to indicate that orphanage might actually help: to accomplish uncommon things, Coriolanus must accept no common father.

This resistance to the father is generally a necessity for those who hope to surpass the merely human. Otto Rank, citing the maxim from Mark 6:4 that a holy man lacks honor only "in his own country and in his father's house," observes that the hero in the myths of many cultures seems to be intrinsically at war with his derivation, and that "There seems to be a certain necessity for the prophet to deny his parents."[51] The absence of any visible father might seem for a while to make Coriolanus' family romance, his claim to an exalted heritage, all the easier to sustain; but it gradually becomes clear, to us as to him, that the lack of a single real father subjugates him to a world of shadow-fathers. The father who is no one man, but lurks awaiting recognition in every man, places his son decisively in the midst of common human ancestry. The patrimony becomes literally a mediocrity, an amorphous mass of all human qualities—an even heavier burden on the metonymic quest for heroic purity than derivation from, say, a Scythian shepherd would be. Tamburlaine, "That fiery thirster after sovereignty," is the obvious dramatic ancestor of Coriolanus' determination to overreach his parentage with the voluntarist assertions of his sword. When Cosroe asks, "What means this devilish shepherd, to aspire / With such a giantly presumption?" Meander answers,

> Some powers divine, or else infernal, mix'd
> Their angry seeds at his conception;
> For he was never sprung of human race,

> Since with the spirit of his fearful pride,
> He dares so doubtlessly resolve of rule,
> And by profession be ambitious.

Ortygius then adds that, whatever sort of "god, or fiend, or spirit of the earth / Or monster turned to a manly shape" Tamburlaine proves to be, they must oppose him.[52] But the *libido dominandi* that Harry Levin sees underlying Tamburlaine's proud soldiership[53] becomes in Coriolanus something more like the *libido excellendi* that the Jansenists blamed for the Fall of Adam and Eve; the desire to conquer becomes in Shakespeare merely one expression of the desire to transcend. Since some power divine or else infernal slyly crept into his manly shape, Coriolanus has sought to claim derivation from some superhuman seed, even at the risk at becoming both the seducing serpent and the seduced human being in a new Fall.

On a symbolic level, this quest for excellence generates libido in a more modern sense of the word. Through the phallic assertion of his sword, Coriolanus seeks to father a new self. The violent refusal to recognize or defer to the paternal sovereign, and the insistence instead on reshaping oneself according to one's own desires, carries heavy Oedipal overtones, as it does in the history plays, in *Macbeth*, and even in Milton's Satan. For Coriolanus to resist the element of common humanity within him, the literal mediocrity that is his universal patrimony, would be Oedipal defiance of every man in the world; but that is precisely what he is willing to undertake, free from the degrading "assistance" of the Roman citizenry, inside the walls of Corioles. He emerges from that womb by his own force, bloody and renamed; a new self, untainted by the common paternity of Rome, has apparently been born. A Jacobean tract asserts that "By the first birth, wee may say to corruption, thou art my father, and to the wormes, yee are my brethren and sisters. But by the second, we have God for our Father."[54] Coriolanus' rebirth is as much physical as spiritual, and it allows him to claim an incorruptibility of the flesh, derived from the god Mars.

Coriolanus' struggle at the gates of Corioles, as Cominius describes it, evokes images of both a phallus penetrating a hymen and an infant fighting its way from the womb into the world:

> from face to foot
> He was a thing of blood, whose every motion
> Was tim'd with dying cries. Alone he ent'red
> The mortal gate of th' city.   (2.2.108–11)

One critic argues that the play's most persistent and pivotal images are bloody men and gateways, and notes that Coriolanus often either propels himself or is propelled bloodily through those gates.[55] Gates were a common seventeenth-century metaphor for the vagina, and psychoanalysts have discovered that "The symbol of entering through doors occurs commonly in dreams and fantasies; usually it symbolizes birth."[56] Conversely, the process of birth was sometimes described in the seventeenth century as a heroic battle against a womb that had begun to constrict and starve its growing inhabitant, as Rome constricts and starves the heroic Coriolanus: "the Infant then as it were undertaking of himselfe a beginning of motion, striveth to free himselfe from the prison and dungeon wherein he was restrayned; kicking therefore he breaketh the membranes wherein he was inwrapped, and arming himselfe with strong violence maketh way for his inlargement with all the strength and contention that he may."[57]

This passage suggests the motif of the soldier's self-induced Caesarean birth, and Shakespeare links the rebirth of Coriolanus, as he does the rebirth of Macbeth, to that motif. While Coriolanus is shut inside Corioles' gates, Lartius addresses to him a somewhat premature eulogy:

> with thy grim looks and
> The thunder-like percussion of thy sounds,
> Thou mad'st thine enemies shake, as if the world
> Were feverous and did tremble.   (1.4.58–61)

The essential themes of autochthonic rebirth are sounded here. Glendower claimed that "the earth did shake when I was born," and Hotspur replies with the suggestion that he must merely have been a venting of its diseased vapors (1 Henry IV, 3.1.20–34). Tamburlaine's heroic rebirth, surpassing the constraints of his mortal parentage, is also compared to the rumblings of wind that shake the earth in their struggle for passage to the surface. The comparison to thunder, which marks this kind of transformation in classical and Renaissance literature, appears again some fifty lines later, when the reborn Coriolanus encounters the paternal Cominius. Using Shakespeare's familiar coining metaphor, generally invoked to describe the resemblance of a son to his father, Cominius notes Coriolanus' resemblance to Coriolanus. This suggestion that Coriolanus has fathered himself in this rebirth is strengthened by the fact that both Cominius and Coriolanus elsewhere describe Coriolanus as such a coin-stamp (2.2.107, 3.1.78; see also 1.3.32):

> He has the stamp of Martius, and I have
> Before-time seen him thus.
> *Coriolanus*   Come I too late?
> *Cominius* The shepherd knows not thunder from a tabor
>   More than I know the sound of Martius' tongue
>   From every meaner man.
> *Coriolanus*   Come I too late?
> *Cominius* Ay, if you come not in the blood of others,
>   But mantled in your own.
> *Coriolanus*   O! let me clip ye
>   In arms as sound as when I woo'd, in heart
>   As merry as when our nuptial day was done
>   And tapers burnt to bedward!   (1.6.23–32)

The question of whether the blood on the Caesarean infant is his own is common enough among concerned new fathers, crucially ambiguous in *Macbeth*,[58] and directly answered by Coriolanus when he confronts Aufidius shortly after this conversation: " 'Tis not my blood / Wherein thou seest me mask'd" (1.8.9–10). The Caesarean operation has been performed in time to save the overgrown child from death within Corioles' walls, and it has evidently been performed before, on a lesser scale, in Coriolanus' previous battles. Each act of war has been a gesture toward a martial rebirth.

What makes this occasion different from the "before-times" when Cominius has "seen him thus" is the heavily symbolic enclosure inside the enemy's gates. The entrapment and escape combines an archetypal heroic motif of death and rebirth with the Shakespearean metaphor of Oedipal rape and Caesarean section. Several critics have remarked on the strange and striking sexual elements in Coriolanus' comparison of the battle to a wedding night, and in Cominius' subsequent description of that battle.[59] These elements seem to me to reveal a relationship between physical love and physical death that is unusually intimate and intricate even for the Elizabethans. The standard quibble linking dying to orgasm is not merely a joke for Coriolanus, but a highly symbolic and characteristic association. The blood-lust by which he creates his ideal martial self is a twisted version of the lust that leads to normal procreation. The sword that carves its passage back out of the womblike city may have served as a phallic weapon on the way in, allowing Coriolanus to function as the "author of himself" he aspires to become (5.3.36). For Coriolanus, killing is a means of self-procreation that entails in turn the killing of a limiting father-figure.

The saga of the archetypal hero, as Rank describes it, thus correlates with the saga of the boy's psyche as Freud and Jung describe it: he moves from an intense emulation of the progenitor to the grand defiant "fantasy of being one's own son." The essential component for Rank is not Oedipal sexuality as such, but rather this "fantasy of being born again, to which the incest motive is subordinated."[60] As Rank's mythography suggests, the hero is often reborn out of an enclosure believed to be a coffin before it proves to be a womb; here Caius Martius is eulogized as dead before returning miraculously, and heroically, into life (1.4.52–62). Some societies impose a similar ritual on their adolescents, defusing the dangerously "liminal" transition from dependent child to independent adult by making them into two separate identities.[61] Killing others (like a pubescent hunter killing his first game) is not enough to establish a wholly new identity; Coriolanus' entire hereditary self must die inside those walls in order to beget an autonomous self. The incident at Corioles represents a conflation of rituals: the former Caius Martius dies, in either sense, to further the conception, in either sense, of Coriolanus.

This pattern has literary antecedents as well as anthropological analogues. In *Much Ado About Nothing, As You Like It, The Winter's Tale,* and *Cymbeline,* Shakespeare allows his heroines to escape former identies that hinder their proper marriages by swooning into temporary, figurative deaths. The heroine's temporary death in *Romeo and Juliet* is a failed example of this technique, since it was designed to free her from the obstacles presented by her familial identity and to revive her as the child of the mediating Friar Lawrence. Coriolanus' struggle to evade the limitations imposed by his first birth bears some resemblance to Juliet's ordeal, as he is enclosed, eulogized, and reborn in a way that proves truly deadly. There may be an even deeper resemblance to the apparent death and the figurative rebirths of Oedipus, as a modern critic describes them:

> The act of exposure, like casting adrift in a chest, or ritual immersion, seems to be an attempt to inaugurate an "absolute beginning" (Delcourt, 1944, 56); the time-lag which prevents this beginning from coinciding with birth will show later, in each of the myth's episodes, that it is above all a desire for an indefinitely renewed origin.[62]

The need to renew the bloody act of rebirth becomes both more direct and more broadly metaphorical in *Coriolanus* than in the stories of regicide. Killing is itself the generative force of this glorious new identity, and unless he is continually carving out that Caesarean passage, Coriolanus will be smotheringly reabsorbed by his original nature, by the Roman womb.

While Coriolanus' enclosure at Corioles recalls several elements of the Oedipal archetype, one important element is missing: his actual mother. The fact that the womb he here assaults and escapes is not Volumnia's may explain why this victory eventually fails Coriolanus as an "absolute beginning" and obliges him to begin his quest all over again. Janet Adelman's recent interpretation of this attack parallels mine to a considerable extent: "For the assault on Corioli is both a rape and a rebirth: the underlying fantasy is that intercourse is a literal return to the womb, from which one is reborn, one's own author. The fantasy of self-authorship is complete when Coriolanus is given his new name, earned by his own actions."[63] But Adelman does not follow this point to its logical conclusion. If the fantasy is a literal, sexualized return to the womb, then that womb should be his mother's, and he must strike against Rome's gates and Volumnia's body to fulfill it. The assault on Corioles, then, is a displaced expression of his real desire, and inevitably it proves an *incomplete* replacement of identity, an unsatisfying release of repressed impulses. Like Macbeth, whose first Caesarean rebirth fails to free him from loyal subservience, Coriolanus finds himself still subordinate to the will of the common father and therefore turns his violence against Rome itself.

The latent sexual relationship between Coriolanus and Volumnia is suggested clearly enough, and it frequently threatens to cross the boundary into an explicitly Oedipal attachment. Like Lady Macbeth, Volumnia provokes the man to his figurative patricide, through which she can gain vicarious honor and power, by a sinister melding of the roles of wife and mother. In older versions of the story, which Shakespeare apparently knew, Volumnia was the name of Coriolanus' wife.[64] From her very first lines, Shakespeare's Volumnia vacillates disconcertingly between her two roles: "If my son were my husband, I should freelier rejoice in that absence wherein he won honor than in the embracements of his bed where he would show most love" (1.3.1–5). This implies that her son is actually her husband more than Virgilia's: his sexualized martial violence, which Volumnia here gives precedence over normal love-making, is shared with his mother rather than with his wife. Some psychoanalytic critics have described Coriolanus' martial agression as Oedipal aggression that Volumnia has deflected: she uses the battlefield to desexualize their relationship.[65] Others argue that "Coriolanus' military victories are presented as reflexes to his relationship with Volumnia, who regards her son as a kind of sexual surrogate": she uses the battlefield to sexualize their relationship.[66] I suspect the confusion arises from the fact that the Oedipal aggression and the martial aggression are both aspects of the effort to create a new and ideal Coriolanus; again, by reading the Oedipal situation in Shakespeare as a metaphor for ambition rather than a psychoanalytic case-study, we can turn the disease of apparent contradictions into the commodity of symbolic meaning. Lust becomes confused with blood-lust in this play, because they are both part of a single endeavor.[67]

The ambitious endeavor to recreate himself as a creature of pure martial nobility eventually, and inevitably, leads Coriolanus to attack his own mother-country and his own mother's body. Volumnia's strategy of provoking her son to impressive deeds by implicitly sexualizing their relationship threatens her very survival when he can no longer be deflected into surrogate satisfactions of the ambitious desires she has roused. Janet Adelman treats the attack on Rome as an abstract enforcement of dominance, rather than as an extension of his sexualized attack on Corioles: "For Coriolanus can become author of himself only by first becoming author of his mother, as he attempts to do here: by becoming in effect a god, dispensing life and death (5.4.24–25), so that he can finally stand alone."[68] Certainly Coriolanus' determination to become "author of himself" resembles Descartes' conclusion that "if I were . . . the author of my own being . . . I would be God himself."[69] But people have an efficient cause as well as a first cause; they are authored by fathers more directly than by God, and Coriolanus' sexualized assault on his mother would usurp the father's role more clearly than it would God's.

In fact, the idea that this should be a godly spiritual rebirth rather than a physical re-use of the mother's womb is precisely what Coriolanus overlooks. Elizabethan moralists allowed, even encouraged, men to seek rebirth as children of a higher Father, but they took pains to distinguish that project from a literal reunion with the mother's womb. One Elizabethan Prodigal Son tract recalls Paul's testimony that "Hee separated mee from my mothers wombe, and called me by his grace."[70] Coriolanus tries, by an analogous separation, to authenticate the "graceful posture" visited on him by the "whatsover god," but we are less confident of that god's benevolence. Nehemiah Rogers' Jacobean tract makes the distinction more explicit: "As to live a naturall life, there must be a generation according to the flesh: so if thou wouldest attaine to live this life of the Spirit, thou must of necessitie be brought to a second birth: Not to be turned into our mothers womb againe (as *Nicodemus* thought) but as Christ saith, we must be borne of the will of his Father."[71] Coriolanus, like this ideal Christian, defies the fleshly corruption of his common humanity, his original mortal family, by submitting to the will of a posited higher father who is in heaven or at least on Olympus. But, like Nicodemus, Coriolanus has trouble distinguishing a purely figurative action from a physical one. He marches back from exile determined to re-father himself in the maternal body natural of Volumnia and the maternal body politic of Rome. In this he resembles Seneca's Oedipus rather than an ideal Christian:

> A bloody wretch, a wretched child that sits in father's seat
> And mother's bed defiles, O wretch, and enters in again
> In places whence he came from once, and doubleth so her pain,
> Whilst that he fills the hapless womb wherein himself did lie
> With graceless seed, and causes her twice childbirth's pangs to try.[72]

On the stage, Coriolanus' violent return to the gates of Rome that had ejected him would surely recall the scene at the gates of Corioles. The physical situation, even the set, would presumably suggest a connection, and the language repeats the themes of rape and heroic Caesarean rebirth that were evoked at Corioles. Addressing the Volscians, Coriolanus boasts that he made a "bloody passage" leading "even to / The gates of Rome" (5.6.75–76), but his boast is rendered hollow by his failure to carve his passage through those gates. He had scorned the common Romans after the victory at Corioles because "when the navel of the state was touch'd, / They would not thread the gates" (3.1.123–34), and after his retreat from the gates of Rome, Coriolanus is susceptible to the same suggestive accusation. The reason his assault on Rome fails where his assault on Corioles succeeded may be essentially the same reason Adelman and other critics have failed to connect the two assaults: because the Oedipal aspects of Coriolanus' quest have become unacceptably explicit. The gates retain their parturient significance: they are the legs between which the bloody child emerges. When Volumnia stands between them and announces,

> thou shalt no sooner
> March to assault thy country than to tread

(Trust to't, thou shalt not) on thy mother's womb
That brought thee to this world   (5.3.122–25)

the Oedipal implications become almost unbearably vivid. The terms "assault" and "tread" both serve elsewhere in Shakespeare as euphemisms for sexual intercourse, as does the broader implicit metaphor of attacking a city's gates; "country" was also a common sexual pun, all the clearer here because it is set up in parallel with "womb."[73] As critics or as audiences we tend to avert our eyes from such virulent vulgarity—which is precisely the point. Our aversion helps us to understand, and even implicates us in, Coriolanus' defeat: how can he be expected to perform an act that we can hardly stand to recognize? Lady Macbeth fails to perform her sexualized killing because the victim resembles her father; Coriolanus here fails because the victim really is his mother. Volumnia subverts her son's ambitious project by forcing him to confront its latent Oedipal content: Shakespeare, by the same device, arouses and defines our powerful ambivalences toward that project.

Volumnia, in this sense, swerves selfishly from the role of Jocasta, by forcing on her son the horrible recognition he urges her to suppress. She has all along been modulating the sexual innuendo to keep Coriolanus subliminally motivated toward her goals. Such manipulative promises of love were presumably as common in Shakespeare's time as in others, and their portrayal on stage would have been equally evocative, whether or not they had yet been scientifically described. In seeking to complete the martial identity she offered him, Coriolanus in effect demands that she pay what she promised. With an invincible army to assist him in rape and rapine—whether those crimes appear as actual sexual and material theft, or as a looting of the storehouse of ideal selfhood—he no longer needs to pursue his desires indirectly. So Volumnia changes her graceless coyness to outright vulgarity, imploding the hidden sexuality of her son's attack. She blunts the assault, as victims of attempted rape sometimes do, by a degree of literalism that turns fantasy into disgust. Volumnia herself becomes a sort of psychoanalytic critic of the hazards of ambition, explicating to her son the underlying Oedipal metaphor that forbids him to complete his perfect new identity. "Tell me not / Wherein I seem unnatural," he pleads with her (5.3.83–84), but that is precisely what she does tell him, and she tells it in such a way that his long appetite for unnaturalness changes into aversion.

Coriolanus' culminating Oedipal crime falls disastrously short of completion. His failure to act as a pure martial creature, on pure martial principles, coincides with this symbolically sexual failure, because both represent the failure of his quest for self-overcoming. One critic argues that, in Shakespeare's Henry VI plays, the murderous conflict between father and son becomes "Shakespeare's metaphor for civil war in all its manifestations."[74] Conversely, in *Coriolanus* as in *Macbeth*, civil war becomes Shakespeare's metaphor for that Oedipal sort of conflict. Whereas the father-son struggle was the embodiment and culmination of the civil wars in *3 Henry VI*, civil war is now the embodiment and culmination of a long, essentially Oedipal struggle. Ends and means, in other words, are reversed in the movement from the histories to the tragedies: denying one's own nature is now the essential purpose of the political struggle, rather than a grim necessity in a political project. The germinal tragic idea in *Richard III* thus achieves its full flowering. Before beginning his ambitious project, Coriolanus should perhaps have been warned as the Oracle warns Seneca's proud Oedipus:

> And, as for thee, thou shalt not long in quiet state endure,
> But with thyself wage war thou shalt, and war thou shalt
>   procure
> Unto thy children dear, and creep again thou shalt into thy
>   mother's womb.[75]

Coriolanus fails to assault his and Rome's progeny, and fails to reenter the figurative womb, because he cannot win an inner civil war against his own limiting humanity; he cannot win that internal war, conversely, because he cannot eradicate his family and give himself rebirth.

The way Shakespeare portrays the consequences of this failure to overrun Rome and Volumnia suggestively parallels the way psychoanalysts portray an Oedipal son's deepest fears. As in the classic castration fantasy, Coriolanus finds that his mother has rejected and publicly reprimanded the advances she had seemed to invite. The Volscian citizens consequently perform what the Roman citizenry had threatened, dismembering Coriolanus in a rage of familial vengeance (5.6.120–22). Having returned him to the status of "boy," they sacrifice him as if he were an archetypal social criminal, as he well may be.[76] We may recognize, in retrospect, that the citizenry have borne a remarkable resemblance to the castrating father-figure throughout Coriolanus' struggle for rebirth. As Freud and Rank suggest, the Doppelgänger in literature typically ruins the hero's attempts to take a lover, and thereby forestalls his effort to break free from his family; the Doppelgänger, in these functions, stands for the castrating father.[77] This notion fits nicely, not only with my suggestion that the citizens are both Doppelgänger and figurative father to Coriolanus, but also with my suggestion that his effort to overcome those limiting figures is an Oedipal effort to re-father the self.

Coriolanus' gestures toward such a rebirth early in the play are tenaciously haunted by threats of figurative castration from the citizenry. The fact that their lack of steely firmness in general hinders his effort to define an ideal martial self corresponds to the fact that their failure to "stand fast" in support of him hinders his penetration of Corioles' gates and the glorious rape it entails (1.4.41). The cowardly patrimony they bestow on him impedes his progress toward identity with his sword, progress that the play repeatedly describes as a movement into sexual manhood, an Oedipal tumescence (1.3.2–17; 1.6.29–32; 2.2.87–101; 4.5.106–18). His castration anxiety increases when he is obliged to submit these martial deeds, with their sexual overtones, for the citizenry's approval. By assuming the gown of humility, he is abjuring the pride in which he forged his sword-like manhood, and in that gown he is supposed to show his wounds so that the people may "put our tongues into those wounds" (2.3.6–7). A boy's castration anxiety, according to Freudian theory, arises from his assumption that the vagina is merely the wound left after castration by a jealous father.[78] A poem often attributed to Shakespeare himself, in *The Passionate Pilgrim* collection (IX, lines 12–14), plays explicitly and uneasily on the idea that the vagina is a "wound." In naming Coriolanus as consul, fathering that new identity with their tongues, the citizens assume the phallic role. His struggle to transcend the bodies natural and politic of Rome generally represents itself as a phallic assertion; in seeking a Roman office and public approval, in showing his bodily injuries, Coriolanus becomes instead a passive female object of phallic assertion. Instead of being possessed by a martial "whatsoever god," he declares that he now must be possessed by

> Some harlot's spirit! My throat of war be turn'd,
> Which quier'd with my drum, into a pipe
> Small as an eunuch, or the virgin voice
> That babies lull asleep! (3.2.111–15)

"The voyce of men," as Stephen Batman remarks, "when they be gelded, chaungeth, and be as the voyce of women";[79] this seems to be precisely what is happening to Coriolanus.

If such concepts as "absence" carry connotations of castration anxiety in Shakespeare and in psychoanalytic theory, as one critic has recently suggested,[80] then it is appropriate that the nullity threatening Shakespeare's ambitious protagonists appears alongside the Oedipal implications of their ambitions. The talionic ontology of the plays, which suggests that a man who rejects his given being becomes nothing, is aligned with an Oedipal myth about paternal reprisal. As sin (according to a conventional theology) leads to privation of being, the Oedipal sin implicit in ambition leads to a figurative nullification of one's procreative powers. The ambitious protagonist abuses his identity and virility when he seeks to defeat and replace his hereditary self by defeating and replacing his father. Shakespeare's ambitious figures might speak of their father-figures as Donne speaks of love: "He ruin'd mee, and I am rebegot / Of absence, darknesse, death; things which are not."[81]

Coriolanus can be read as a history of the Oedipal ruination that obliges the hero to construct a new self out of absence, shadows, death, and nothingness. The martial Coriolanus makes love to his mother in an "absence wherein he won honor" (1.3.3–4), and when he pursues that honor further, against the will of the citizenry, he becomes a manly knot unknit (4.2.30–32). He dismisses his honorable accomplishments as "nothings" that he cannot bear to have proclaimed publicly (2.2.75–77), and when Cominius tries to stall Coriolanus' advance on Rome by asserting his paternal role, he discovers that

> Coriolanus
> He would not answer to; forbade all names;
> He was a kind of nothing, titleless,
> Till he had forg'd himself a name a' th' fire
> Of burning Rome. (5.1.11–15)

Coriolanus plans to repeat and improve the process that won him his agnomen. To do so, he must reshape himself according to his heart's desire, becoming "What his breast forges" (3.1.257): the avenging sword that is his metonymic model, forged from steel and fire. But the word "forge" had its other, less Promethean, meaning in Shakespeare's time and writings.[82] The metallic selfhood Coriolanus "coins" and "stamps" into being may be merely a counterfeit. A forged sovereign, as in *Hamlet* (4.2.30–32) and the other plays of usurpation, is potentially "a thing—of nothing." Like the other forged sovereigns, Coriolanus discovers that seizing a new name only renders his outward identity, as well as his inward one, multiple and evanescent. After his feat at Corioles, he is "By deed-achieving honor

178

newly nam'd," and given "the whole name of the war" (2.1.173, 135); he has achieved the "good report" that Volumnia was willing to exchange for her son's natural life (1.3.20–21). He returns as "Martius Caius Coriolanus, whom / We met here both to thank and to remember / With honors like himself" (2.2.46–48). In a sense Menenius is thanking the Coriolanus who has been born, and memorializing the Caius Martius who is therefore dead. His identity has receded into a simile; he is merely a reflection of his honors, and a symbol of the absence in which he won them. Coriolanus seems to acknowledge as much when he promises his friends and family, after the citizens have banished him, that they will hear of him only "what is like me formerly" (4.1.53).[83]

All such surrogate identities, where simulation replaces procreation, are fragile, hollow, and transient. As Aufidius proves at the end of the play, "good report" and "Coriolanus" are alternative identities that collapse as soon as one ceases to uphold them. Coriolanus complains after his banishment that the Romans have rewarded his deeds "But with that surname—a good memory" (4.5.71), and all that finally survives of him is the "noble memory" (5.6.153) represented by the play that bears his surname. The man who is remembered lacks the human substance of the man who was dismembered; in acting the role in which his mother has cast him, he has become more an actor than a person. Lionel Trilling suggests that the alienated man's efforts at integrity and autonomy may fail "to the extent that he is scarcely a self at all, but, rather, a reiterated impersonation."[84] Stephen Greenblatt observes a sort of "repetition compulsion" in Marlowe's heroes, a condition reinforced by the dramatic medium, that compels them to renew their identities and even their existence by repeating the self-constituting act.[85] The self must become an artifice to avoid fading into nothingness. A similar compulsion haunts Shakespeare's ambitious figures: in their lives as in the medium through which we witness them, identity becomes an eerily detached imitation of the actions previously associated with the self. Any semblance of the spontaneous continuity normal to human identity is counterfeit. To retain his throne, Macbeth must commit versions of the regicide again and again; Coriolanus must foment one sexualized battle after another to persist as a purely martial creature. When they cease to play their roles, the plays that kept them alive end also, and they are consumed by a nature in which they have forfeited their place.

Coriolanus' natural self, along with his family names, dies inside Corioles' walls, as he wills it; but he seems not to have considered the costs of living in an artificial self, which exists only by a sort of ontological prosthesis. Returning from the battle, he compares his wife's tears to those of a widow (2.1.178), unaware of how fitting the comparison may actually be. Menenius, trying to save Coriolanus from the angry plebeians, describes Coriolanus' body as a churchyard full of graves (3.3.49–51). The wages of unfilial ambition is a sort of death-in-life, and as Coriolanus strides defiantly into the exile imposed by the paternal commonalty, we may think of the Jacobean Prodigal Son tracts which warn that such proud young men "are but dead corpses" until they return humbly to their fathers.[86] Coriolanus' own rhetoric is infested with suggestions that the self replacing this dead one after his battles is merely a poor player, a painted canvas, or a verbal construct. He tells the Volscian servant that he dwells "Under the canopy" (4.5.38), a phrase that suggests his whole world has become a theater;[87] the suggestion recurs in his complaint about laughter from "the heavens" (5.3.183–85). He says his performance was a flawed "act" that nonetheless allowed him to make a new self "mask'd" in blood (1.9.18–19; 1.8.8–10). He urges his soldiers, "If any such be here / (As it were sin to doubt) that love this painting / Wherein you see me smear'd; if any fear / Lesser his person than an ill report," then "Let him . . . follow Martius" (1.6.67–75). They will be following him, his diction inadvertently warns, not only into battle, but also into merely verbal or visual representations of the self. The official Elizabethan "Sermon of Good Works annexed unto Faith" warns about the fatal limitations of such substitutions: "Even as the picture graven or painted is but a dead representation of the thing itself, and is without life, or any manner of moving; so be the works of all unfaithful persons before God: they do appear to be lively works, and indeed they be but dead."[88]

What Coriolanus opposes to this danger is a version of the fiery ambition of Prometheus, who according to an Elizabethan mythographer "by degrees contrived a picture, / And gave life to the same with fyre that he stole fro the heavens."[89] A comtemporary medical text even cites examples of children born resembling a picture the mother was watching at the moment of conception,[90] and Volumnia seems to have worked at developing such an artificially valorous offspring:

> I, considering how honor would become such a person,
> that it was no better than picture-like to hang by th' wall,
> if renown made it not stir, was pleas'd to let him seek
> danger where he was like to find fame.   (1.3.9–13)

Volumnia here contradicts the threats implied in the substitution of "honors" and "painting" for a natural self, by arguing that honor augments a person, and that peaceful passivity, not martial ambition, creates a merely painted identity. She in effect shields him from the hazards of ambition by suggesting that his valor is part of his birth, part of what marks him as his mother's son.

Coriolanus and Volumnia

Coriolanus' conspiracy with his mother shapes the physical and rhetorical tactics of his war against a limiting human patrimony, but it finally leads to his physical and rhetorical surrender. Her implicit argument, against the threat of mere theatricalism, that Coriolanus' martial self is his true self, typifies her contribution; she provides some lineal foundation for his combative bluster, but when his purposes stray from hers, she enforces the hollowness and fragility of his reborn identity with a bitter finality.

Coriolanus is betrayed by the illusion that he can achieve martial perfection without departing from the maternal embrace of Volumnia and Rome. Some recent psychoanalytic observations provide intriguing analogues to his betrayal. If it is true that, "While the boy's sense of *self* begins in union with the feminine, his sense of *masculinity* arises against it,"[91] then Coriolanus' quest for a wholly masculine self reaches a contradiction, an inevitable impasse, at the gates of Rome. A premature or exaggerated Oedipal hostility may blind a boy to the fact that "one componet of the castration threat is maternal in origin," the threat "to engulf the emerging ego into the original unity."[92] The father's threatened damage to the male genitalia is, from this viewpoint, secondary to the pre-Oedipal damage to the masculine psyche from a failure to "disidentify" from the mother and "counteridentify" with the father.[93]

This insidious danger of maternal engulfment, hinted at only vaguely in *Macbeth*, becomes a crucial hazard of ambition in *Coriolanus*.[94] During the long Oedipal struggle depicted in the first part of this chapter, Coriolanus is deluded by his mother's militarism into overlooking the importance of its other, pre-Oedipal, aspect. In willingly identifying with Volumnia, for the sake of defying the paternal citizenry he cannot respect, Coriolanus behaves much like the child in the family romance: "with the child's realization of the fact that the father is always uncertain, whereas the mother is very certain—the family romance undergoes a peculiar restriction; it is satisfied with ennobling the father, while the descent from the mother is no longer questioned, but accepted as an unalterable fact."[95] Indeed, as I suggested at the start of the chapter, Coriolanus is under the understandable illusion that his family romance need not be wholly a fantasy, since his father is truly absent and his mother apparently an embodiment of everything he aspires to become. He has no objection to the fact that Volumnia contributes to, and takes credit for, his rebirth as the son of Mars at Corioles. Philemon Holland's 1601 translation of Pliny declares "that those men are fortunate 'whose birth costeth their mothers life, and part from their mothers by meanes of incision.' "[96] Only at the end of the play, when he is forbidden to wield his sword against the spectral umbilical cord by which he remains "bound to 's mother" (5.3.159), does Coriolanus understand how unfortunate he was in having a merely figurative Caesarean birth rather than a real one.

The Oedipal conspiracy is a sensible strategy, both for the young man seeking liberty and for the author describing that quest. Harold Bloom, discussing the efforts of modern poets to escape the constrictions of their literary patrimonies, argues that the pursuit of independence is "necessarily Oedipal; reject your parents vehemently enough, and you will become a belated version of them, but compound with their reality, and you may partly free yourself."[97] Hereditary nature is too powerful to be openly defied, but it can be partly subverted by conspiracy with the mother, a pattern suggested by the stories of Zeus and Oedipus as well as Coriolanus. When he tries to pull completely free from his parentage at the end of the play, Coriolanus loses his mother's cooperation and becomes the "boy" the paternal masses dismember. As with Hal and Macbeth, Shakespeare here uses his intuitions about developmental psychology to make the men in his audience subliminally identify with the protagonist, and to make his crisis represent man's experience of ambition in all its manifestations.

Rome and Volumnia deliberately make it difficult for Coriolanus to recognize that he must escape their wombs if he is to fulfill his martial inspiration. They injure him by convincing him that he will be fulfilling his martial aspect when he will actually be betraying it, in lying to gain the consulship, and later in retreating from the gates of Rome; but they injure him in a deeper way by leading him to believe that he will be fulfilling his hereditary aspect in the great martial deeds that necessarily oppose his human heritage. His fatal confusion about the actual nature of his patrimony adds a note of sour irony, but also a note of tragic entrapment, to his downfall. The noble father-figures Cominius and Menenius misleadingly associate Roman nature with heroic valor. Cominius congratulates the army after the defeat of Corioles for fighting "Like Romans" (1.6.2). Menenius praises Cominius' fellow-general Titus Lartius as "true-bred!" for his eagerness to fight the Volsces (1.1.243); the compliment seems to refer to both martial nature and aristocratic ancestry, a conflation that was doubtless encouraging to Coriolanus, who seeks to parlay his having been "bred i' th' wars" (3.1.318) into an ennobling new line of descent. Menenius cites that breeding in his defense of Coriolanus' bluntness toward the citizenry, and warns against the prospect

> That our renowned Rome, whose gratitude
> Towards her deserved children is enroll'd
> In Jove's own book, like an unnatural dam
> Should now eat up her own! (3.1.289–92)

The fiercely proud Coriolanus is the true offspring of Rome, the citizens its bestial anomaly. Coriolanus uses a similar premise to protest his humiliation by those citizens:

> I would they were barbarians, as they are,
> Though in Rome litter'd; not Romans, as they are not,
> Though calved i' th' porch o' th' Capitol. (3.1.237–39)

The sheer rhetorical effort of this distinction, driving Coriolanus back to his characteristic animal imagery and antithetical constructions, suggests its deep importance to him. Imagining her son in battle, Volumnia supposes that precisely this issue will be on his lips:

> Methinks I see him stamp thus, and call thus:
> "Come on, you cowards, you were got in fear,
> Though you were born in Rome!" (1.3.32–34)

To be a true Roman, the patricians all assure each other, is to be part of a martial aristocracy.

The patricians therefore portray Rome as a parent whose legitimate children are naturally harder, braver, and more self-denying than the offspring of common humanity. Rome as a society, in all of Shakespeare's Roman plays, worships the repression of fleshly frailties,[98] and in *Coriolanus* Shakespeare explores the dangers and hypocrisies of such a religion. His main source for the play mentions that "in those dayes, valliantnes was honoured in Rome above all other vertues."[99] Coriolanus seems to be the quintessential child of this Rome: his mother is figuratively the city's mother, "our patroness, the life of Rome!" (5.5.1), and his figurative father is all the city's men. He serves both the body natural and the body politic that shaped him, and serves them according to their proclaimed principles; why, then, should he be punished as rebels against the hereditary order are punished in Shakespeare's other plays?

But the argument that Coriolanus "is actually the logical end result of the Roman system of values"[100] cannot finally absolve him of denying heredity any more than it absolves him of bloodlust. The notion that Romans are born valorous and self-denying may be indispensable in molding and motivating the city's armies, but it need not therefore be true. Shakespeare's martial chauvinism in the history plays, and the martial chauvinism of his Henry V, seem designed more for use-value than for truth-value. The repeated Volscian invasions demonstrate the need for Roman soldiers to aspire toward an ideal of indomitability, but Shakespeare makes it clear that those soldiers rarely reach that ideal. So Coriolanus' identity may be derivative, but as the details of the play's rhetoric indicate, he is derivative from a myth rather than from a human father.[101] His only valid defense against the charge of unnaturalness, then, may be a plea of entrapment: the patricians have urged this ideal upon him, as if it were natural, and his mother has seductively offered to assist in its birth and nurture.

When Coriolanus performs according to the patricians' script, he becomes an idol through whom they live out their fantasy of Roman nature. His tragedy is his failure to comprehend that the script is truly theatrical, that the society (like so many) need not and does not entirely believe its useful patriotic slogans. He never considers that the serpentine "whatsoever god" who so demonically encourages, exploits, and then destroys his transcendence may be Hobbes's Leviathan, the society itself. The political hypocrisy of the tribunes obviously contributes to Coriolanus' destruction, but the hypocrisy of the patricians makes an even more insidious contribution. The contradictions inherent in Rome's patriotic myth entrap Coriolanus at least as harmfully as the conflicts inherent in Rome's class system; he is caught between natural and ideal versions of himself, as much as between populist and elitist political forces. These schisms render him a schizoid figure, possessor and possessed, through the classic mechanism of the double bind. The political task the aristocrats set him demands that he efface the very characteristics which, they claimed, marked him as Rome's legitimate offspring. To obey his human parent-figures, he must defy Rome's paternal character; to lead the city as consul, he must suppress in himself that city's vaunted traits. Patriotic myths are usually outdated, and Shakespeare's tragic heroes are often men who are great in a way their world no longer rewards. Coriolanus confronts his entire society with the granting of its foolish wish: the purest embodiment of their boasted social values threatens to destroy the society completely.

Rome and Volumnia, having made this monster, contend that he is only what their precepts have made him, and that he should therefore change as their needs do. Throughout the play, Volumnia and Coriolanus indirectly debate these issues. Is his martial idealism an expression of his nature or an imposition of her nurture? Does he owe fealty primarily to his god-like principles, or to his human context? When Volumnia imagines Coriolanus stamping and calling his soldiers cowards (1.3.32–34), she is savoring vicariously an assertion of the Roman fantasy, but she is also boasting a proprietary interest in that assertion. The assertive lines are in her own words, and the supposed speaker is the flesh of her own flesh, or perhaps the metal of her own metal. When we see Coriolanus rage according to her prediciton (3.1.237–39), we may suspect he is merely following her script, rather than expressing any spontaneous and self-generated sentiment. On the other hand, she may be counterfeiting such authority by imitating what she knows to be his concerns and characteristics. Clearly they say and do the same things, but it is hard to tell which is the model and which the imitation.

The question does not demand an answer until the middle of the play. At first the goals of Coriolanus, his mother, and Rome, coincide in the defeat of the Volsces. His various possible motives—personal pride, national duty, filial obedience, aristocratic principles, valorous nature—have not yet had occasion to conflict. But though the conflict remains latent, the play's first evaluation of Coriolanus suggests it will prove important:

> *Second Citizen* Consider you what services he has done for his country?
> *First Citizen* Very well, and could be content to give him good report for't, but that he pays himself with being proud.
> *Second Citizen* Nay, but speak not maliciously.
> *First Citizen* I say unto you, what he hath done famously, he did it to that end. Though soft-conscienc'd men can be content to say it was for his country, he did it to please his mother, and to be partly proud, which he is, even to the altitude of his virtue.
> *Second Citizen* What he cannot help in his nature, you account a vice in him.   (1.1.32–42)

Moral evaluation must await more discriminating tests. For the moment, his proud martial "nature" still coincides with the will of the bodies natural and politic that gave him birth, suggesting a solid grounding in the hereditary order.

But Volumnia's excited and proprietary description of these martial accomplishments inadvertently links them to the ephemeral subjectivity that haunts ambitious deeds in Shakespeare. Richard III, by promising to make Tyrrel "inheritor of thy desire" (4.3.34) if he will murder the princes, takes control over the inheritance of his own *desideratum*. Similarly, Volumnia, hoping that Coriolanus' martial deeds will propel him into the consulship, tells him:

> I have lived
> To see inherited my very wishes
> And the buildings of my fancy; only
> There's one thing wanting, which I doubt not but
> Our Rome will cast upon thee.
> *Coriolanus*   Know, good mother,
> I had rather be their servant in my way
> Than sway with them in theirs.   (2.1.198–204)

Whether or not Coriolanus will continue to identify himself with that "fancy" when it entails derivation from the citizenry as well as from Volumnia is a fatal crux of the play's movement. To live as the inheritance of Volumnia's wishes, a sort of immaculate conception of martial principles resembling his own, would suit him very well. But to seek "the inheritance of their loves" (3.2.68) in the form of the consulship, a gross conception of the people's venting tongues, threatens both the autonomy and the purity toward which he aspires. Both the source and the conduct of the office would degrade him; both its acquisition and its exercise require the very harmony, deference, and fraternity that his ambition forbids him.

A close study of act 3, scene 2, in which Volumnia convinces Coriolanus to renew his plea for the consulship, reveals a submerged but intense rhetorical struggle over his true identity and obligations. In less than a hundred and fifty lines, Volumnia's definition of Coriolanus as the child of her womb and Rome's subverts and overcomes Coriolanus' definition of himself as the child of a god and of his martial principles. At first the new discrepancy of goals and definitions bewilders Coriolanus: "I muse my mother / Does not approve me further, who was wont / To call them woolen vassals." (3.2.7–9). Volumnia was apparently referring to the plebeians' humble garments—the equivalent of the humble "gown" (2.2.137) in which she now urges him to plead. Recognizing his confusion and her contradiction, Volumnia tries to reconcile the two ideas of the self by sophistry and careful qualifications:

> You are too absolute,
> Though therein you can never be too noble,
> But when extremities speak. I have heard you say
> Honor and policy, like unsever'd friends,
> I' th' war do grow together; grant that, and tell me
> In peace what each of them by th' other lose
> That they combine not there.
>
> Coriolanus   Tush, tush!
> Menenius   A good demand.   (3.2.39–45)

The audience would have been likely to sympathize with Coriolanus' response more than with Menenius'. Shakespeare makes Volumnia's rhetoric suspiciously strenuous and involuted here, and Elizabethans were trained to distrust as well as admire skillfully manipulative oratory.[102] Her terms, furthermore, invite a sharp answer: Coriolanus has everything to lose by such a combination. Coriolanus and Audifius, as honor and policy, seem to maintain an unsevered friendship in war; but when Volumnia prompts Coriolanus to a peace she claims combines honor and policy (and in fact involves neither) at the end of the play, he loses both honor and life to his martial ally's policy. In Corioles as in Rome, it is the ungainly mixture of political pragmatism and martial pride that enrages the people against Coriolanus.

Volumnia, to prevent this objection, disguises the distinction between martial and political behavior. When she resumes her speech, the word "honor," which has hypnotic power over Coriolanus, seems somehow to refer to the very qualities diametrically opposed to it in the first set of syllogisms. An evasive "it" serves as a cover for this shell-game:

> If it be honor in your wars to seem
> The same you are not, which, for your best ends,
> You adopt your policy, how is it less or worse
> That it shall hold companionship in peace
> With honor, as in war, since that to both
> It stands in like request?
>
> Coriolanus   Why force you this?

Coriolanus' irritable question, like Regan's similar "Why is this reason'd?" in *King Lear* (5.1.28), exposes the breathless overexertion of Volumnia's syntax. The most important rhetorical maneuver in her speech involves the clause "to seem / The same you are not." This has none of the ontological vagueness of Iago's "I am not what I am" (1.1.65); she offers her son a clear and desirable way of distinguishing a real from an artificial self. Volumnia's analogy allows Coriolanus, in obeying her, to assert that any political gesture toward common humanity constitutes a false identity, a "seeming" deviation from his true honorable self. Her wording concedes that the blunt martial creature is the real Coriolanus, and suggests that his very discomfort in acting the humble political role would confirm that fact. Since Coriolanus is alert enough to sense that Volumnia is "forcing" a confusion of honor and policy, Volumnia answers by heightening the distinction, so that the political aspect is too far below the honorable aspect to taint it:

> Because that now it lies you on to speak
> To th' people; not by your own instruction,
> Nor by th' matter which your heart prompts you,
> But with such words that are but roted in
> Your tongue, though but bastards, and syllables
> Of no allowance, to your bosom's truth.
> Now, this no more dishonors you at all
> Than to take in a town with gentle words,
> Which else would put you to your fortune and
> The hazard of much blood.
> I would dissemble with my nature where
> My fortunes and my friends at stake requir'd
> I should do so in honor. I am in this
> Your wife, your son, these senators, the nobles.   (3.2.52–65)

Again, subsequent events indicate that her advice does not apply well to her son: his final dishonor results from his bastardized efforts to take in towns with gentle words. Again, she agrees to define his proud martial identity as his "nature" if he will agree to dissemble with that nature, and moves "honor" into a category where it correlates with his domestic duties. She also sweetens this advice with subliminal pseudosexual inducements. To "dishonor" someone, as the play later reminds us, may mean to assault that person sexually (4.6.83); Volumnia here assures Coriolanus that submitting his wounds to the plebeians' tongues will not constitute such a "dishonor." Instead, any filial attitudes he displays toward the citizenry in assuming the humble gown will be "but bastards." This characterization, in effect, assures Coriolanus that his proud martial principles constitute his real formative father, and therefore perhaps her real husband. By such seductive flattery, which includes declaring herself "in this / Your wife" before listing her additional roles as son and political ally, she hopes to win his tacit approval for a brief exploitative flirtation with the paternal commonalty.

Volumnia seems to be playing a standard maternal role in the mythic Oedipal situation, trying to disguise the son's threat to the father until the son is strong enough to overthrow that father. She urges him, until the people grant him the consulship, to "say to them, / Thou art their soldier," and to promise to "frame / Thyself, forsooth, hereafter theirs, so far / As thou hast power and person" (3.2.80–86). This sounds more like filial subjugation than political compromise, but it is necessary if Coriolanus is to win "the inheritance of their loves" (3.2.68). Volumnia's phrase certainly refers to a struggle over a patrimony, and it may be part of a loose allusion to the struggle over Isaac's patrimony in Genesis 25–27. Esau was born moments before his twin brother Jacob (to whom he bore almost no resemblance) but sold his birthright to Jacob for a meal; Coriolanus claims that the citizens' unprincipled devotion to their bellies disinherits them (his outwardly dissimilar kindred) as Rome's true children. Rebecca conspires with her youngest son against the will of her husband, Isaac, who prefers Esau. By dressing Jacob in Esau's garments and in furs that make him resemble his hirsute brother, Rebecca tricks the blind Isaac into speaking his blessing onto Jacob instead. This corresponds to Volumnia's disguising of Coriolanus in the uncharacteristic woolen gown of humility, until the people have granted their verbal endorsement to the son they do not love. Jacob subsequently flees his brother's vengeful anger, but retains the blessing and thrives in another city. Coriolanus' brief theft of "the inheritance of their loves," with its tragic aftermath, is thus a failed version of Jacob's triumph over the hereditary order.

The notion that Coriolanus' filial pleas to the citizenry will be merely an act, consisting of superficial costuming and speech-making, is exploited by both Coriolanus and Volumnia. The theatrical metaphor, which usually in Shakespeare reveals the hollowness and transience of an ambitious identity, is here used to dismiss any humbling performance as merely an hour upon the stage, leaving the proud self as the true one.[103] Coriolanus first resorts to this tactic when Menenius presents the humbling gown as if it were part of a hereditary identity, a "form" descending on Coriolanus as part of the apostolic succession to the consulship:

Pray you go fit you to the custom, and
Take to you, as your predecessors have,

> Your honor with your form.
> *Coriolanus*   It is a part
> That I shall blush in acting, and might well
> Be taken from the people.   (2.2.142–46)

Standing in the despised gown, he offers the people "my hat" rather than "my heart," and promises only that he "will counterfeit the bewitchment of some popular man" (2.3.99–102). This phrase suggests a degrading alternative to his possession by the "whatsoever god"; he seems to be insisting that his appearance as a common man, rather than as a martial god, is alien to his true nature. At the moment when derivation from the paternal citizenry threatens to taint him, Coriolanus finds a verbal formula that reasserts his derivation from Mars. As soon as he is allowed to escape the gown and the marketplace, he does so: "Knowing myself again," he will "Repair to th' Senate-house" (2.3.147–48). His brief inability to know himself suggests that this bewitchment, like Macbeth's, causes a dangerous failure of the boundaries between clothing and selfhood. In Sonnet 111, Shakespeare expresses a similar concern that Fortune

> did not better for my life provide
> Than public means which public manners breeds.
> Thence comes it that my name receives a brand,
> And almost thence my nature is subdu'd
> To what it works in, like the dyer's hand.

Coriolanus therefore shields his nature from the public context, using the theatrical metaphor to explain his failure to be convincingly humble: it is a role he is proud to act badly.

In act 3, scene 2, however, Volumnia threatens to destroy that defense unless Coriolanus performs his plea for the consulship in better faith. She describes his outbursts of pride as the poor player's insignificant sound and fury, and implies that the real man grows quietly at the center of the Roman womb. Coriolanus is on the defensive concerning his true moral "nature," and Volumnia suggests that he protests too much:

> *Coriolanus* Why did you wish me milder? Would you have me
> False to my nature? Rather say, I play
> The man I am.
> *Volumnia*   O, sir, sir, sir,
> I would have had you put your power well on
> Before you had worn it out.
> *Coriolanus*   Let go.

Volumnia You might have been enough the man you are,
   With striving less to be so.   (3.2.14–20)

When Coriolanus scoffs at the idea that he is merely "playing" the role of martial hero, Volumnia replies that his overplaying the role makes people question its solidity, and may even indicate that he doubts it himself, like people whose sexual insecurities cause them ostentatiously to overplay their sexuality.

Some parallels between this exchange and a conversation in *Macbeth* suggest the polarities of Shakespeare's thought concerning a man's ability to transform himself by deeds and garments. Volumnia's argument that honor consists of accepting a given place in the social hierarchy, and that Coriolanus should therefore restrain his violent opposition to the paternal citizenry, resembles Macbeth's argument against attacking the paternal Duncan:

> He hath honor'd me of late, and I have bought
> Golden opinions from all sorts of people,
> Which would be worn now in their newest gloss,
> Not cast aside so soon.
> *Lady Macbeth*   Was the hope drunk
> Wherein you dress'd yourself?   (1.7.32–36)

Coriolanus' resistance may be translated into a similar reply: why struggle into the humble robe of political office if one's real hope is to transform oneself entirely into a suit of armor, and thereby transcend all derivation? Furthermore, Volumnia's argument that Coriolanus has been compromising rather than improving his manhood by striving so hard to demonstrate it resembles Macbeth's assertion here that he dares "do all that may become a man; / Who dares do more is none" (1.7.46–47). Lady Macbeth replies that manhood consists of a constant self-overcoming: "to be more than what you were, you would / Be so much more the man" (1.7.50–51). Coriolanus, according to Plutarch, sustained his manly honor on the same principle: "he strained still to passe him selfe in manlines . . . being desirous to shewe a daylie increase of his valliantnes . . . ."[104] For Lady Macbeth and Coriolanus, passivity and constancy do not preserve identity, but rather make it stagnant. In this regard their position resembles that of Pico and Petrarch, who argue that humanity's normal and rightful condition is its constant struggle for improvement, and who cite the need for clothing as justification for more inward sorts of transformation. Macbeth and Volumnia's remarks, in contrast, recall those of the conservative Elizabethan moralists on the same issues. Naturally I do not mean to credit these characters with schooling and interest in Renaissance philosophy, but Shakespeare endows them with arguments that suggest the philosophical premises underlying their positions on superficial political decisions. The very fact that Shakespeare grants his characters such unrealistic concern with the essential philosophical issues supports my belief that the plays entail an ethical study of ambition, and that Shakespeare intended some portion of his audience to be conscious of that analysis.

In *Coriolanus* as in *Macbeth*, domestic sentiment is the great enforcer of the limiting and static definition of humanity, perhaps because it places man in a familial context and makes him part of a shared human experience. Coriolanus' ambitions are finally ruined by the pity and obligation roused in him toward his family, just as Macbeth is briefly restrained from his regicide, Lady Macbeth from helping him perform it, and Macduff from avenging it, by the emotional bonds of the family (*Macbeth*, 1.5.17; 1.7.21; 2.2.12–13; 4.3.214–23). Macduff redefines manhood from the capacity to kill to the capacity to feel for the death of loved ones; Volumnia, the embodied force of family, performs a similar redefinition. She reminds us of her dispute with her son by making the simple statement he is obliged, and bitterly unwilling, to make:

> *Sicinius*   Are you mankind?
> *Volumnia* Ay, fool, is that a shame? Note but this fool.
>   Was not a man my father?   (4.2.16–18)

Shakespeare allows her to twist this challenge to her femininity into a challenge to her humanity, so we can see the radical contrast between her dismissal of the idea that a filial human identity could be an embarrassment, and her son's intense embarrassment by precisely such a generally human derivation.

The moment when Coriolanus agrees to beg the identity of consul from the citizenry is the moment he most needs reassurance that this filial mildness will be merely an act, that he has not merely been playing the man he is. Volumnia and Cominius emphasize this escape-clause in his political contract with common humanity when Coriolanus insists, perhaps with a little pride, that they

>   have put me now to such a part which never
>   I shall discharge to th' life.
> *Cominius*   Come, come, we'll prompt you.
> *Volumnia* I prithee now, sweet son, as thou hast said

192

> My praises made thee first a soldier, so,
> To have my praise for this, perform a part
> Thou hast not done before.
> *Coriolanus*   Well, I must do't.
> Away, my disposition, and possess me
> Some harlot's spirit!   (3.2.105–12)

Volumnia again exploits rhetoric to create an illusory parallel, a faulty syllogism: the fact that her praise molded his martial identity does not mean that any pursuit of her praise will necessarily be a pursuit of an honorable ideal. She also reminds him that his humility will be no more derivative than his martial pride, since she has given birth to both. Coriolanus seems to be aware of these manipulations, though unable to resist them successfully. He does not accuse her of changing her praising voice, but he certainly implies its degradation in describing the transformation of his own "throat of war" into a girl's or eunuch's voice (3.2.112–15). He does not yet deny his derivation from her, but he does refer to his proud martial aspect as "my disposition," leaving her as the creator only of this new humility. If she is nurturing a "harlot's spirit" within him, then she resembles the harlot who nurtures Romulus in one interpretation of the myth, rather than the she-wolf whose nurture contributes to Romulus' greatness in the other interpretation of the myth. He defends his sense that manhood equals unyielding pride by portraying betrayal of his aristocratic principles as a movement into the female or emasculate.

If this first section of Coriolanus' speech echoes the opening speech of *Richard III*, describing an effeminate and musical world in which his blunt martial talents have no place, the next section of the speech comes closer to the self-dramatizing rant of Richard II before his mirror, describing an atomized world in which he has no identity. Shakespearean characters who lose their hereditary identities often disappear into a meaningless multiplicity of theatrical roles. Richard II emphasizes the natural inviolability of his royal identity by equating its loss with such a fragmentation; Coriolanus makes the same sort of implicit claim for his proud martial identity. In *Troilus and Cressida*, Aeneas asks the proud Achilles, tarnished by pacifism, what his name is if not Achilles; when he replies, "If not Achilles, nothing" (4.5.76), the latter alternative seems all too plausible. If one fails to "act like" the person one "is," as Sartre argues, then where can identity be perceived or defined at all? Coriolanus' fear of being tainted like the dyer's hand has been overruled; now

Martial Ambition and the Family Romance

he indirectly suggests the other danger of accepting the mendicant role, a danger Volumnia's use of the theatrical metaphor can only aggravate. He expands his objection from Plato's idea that "the soul of the actor is deteriorated by identification with such morally inferior characters as he impersonates" to Rousseau's idea that "by engaging in impersonation at all the actor diminishes his own existence as a person."[105] It becomes hard to tell whether Coriolanus is being degraded or disintegrated by the part he is playing: he becomes the victim of so many invasive metonymies that the belly fable he had resisted seems to be consuming him. The very body of this chimerical new Coriolanus (like the bodies of the usurpers in the earlier plays) is a tangle:

> The smiles of knaves
> Tent in my cheeks, and schoolboys' tears take up
> The glasses of my sight! A beggar's tongue
> Make motion through my lips, and my arm'd knees,
> Who bow'd but in my stirrup, bend like his
> That hath receiv'd an alms! I will not do't,
> Lest I surcease to honor mine own truth,
> And by my body's action teach my mind
> A most inherent baseness.
> Volumnia   At thy choice then.
> To beg of thee, it is my more dishonor
> Than thou of them.   (3.2.115–25)

The fear of degradation described by Plato, and the fear of disintegration described by Rousseau, here become the same fear: Coriolanus is afraid that he will lose himself—in other words, that he will find himself—among these degrading others. Volumnia replies that it is entirely futile for him to resist dishonor from these others, because that resistance is a dishonor to her which is naturally contagious to her son:

> Do as thou list;
> Thy valiantness was mine, thou suck'st it from me;
> But owe thy pride thyself.
> Coriolanus   Pray be content.
> Mother, I am going to the market-place;
> Chide me no more. I'll mountebank their loves,
> Cog their hearts from them, and come home belov'd
> Of all the trades in Rome. Look, I am going.   (3.2.128–34)

His blunt phallic assertion has given way to a coy feminine court-ship, and his heroic bluster has collapsed into the frightened and apologetic tone of a helpless little boy yielding obedience to his angry mother. "Do your will" (3.2.137) is all she replies, but of course, like that angry mother, she knows he will have to do her will and not his own. Coriolanus even defines his mild submission to the plebeians' anticipated insults as "mine honor" (3.2.144), as her rhe-torical trickery had suggested. She has provided this surrender with the pretext of a pragmatic, theatrical simulation of the common humanity to which he was born; and she has skillfully located the distinction, not between Coriolanus as an obedient child and Cor-iolanus as an autonomous warrior, but rather between a valiant man she has shaped and a merely proud one he is becoming. The scene ends with Volumnia in full control.

Volumnia cannot, however, invest him with her political desires and skills, and his conciliatory rhetoric at the marketplace soon explodes into a typical combative rage. He finally shouts that the citizens who have banished him "do corrupt my air—I banish you!" and heads off for the "world elsewhere" from which they are ban-ished by their human limitations (3.3.123, 135). With this excla-mation, he echoes what Valla's *De vero bono* calls "the best saying: For me the *patria* is wherever the good is."[106] The idea of martial honor by which he defines Rome travels with him, and implicit in this revisionistic definition of the *patria* is a similar redefinition of the patriarch: the father is whoever provides the best precedent for martial virtue. A recent study of the Oedipus myth finds the "theme of moving to another country" very frequently associated with the boy who is conceived by his mother in apparent consort with a god, and then exposed to supposed death by a fearful human father-figure. That boy then begins a new life of heroic exploits "during which a more or less accidental parricde takes place," made possible by a latency period of "dissociation and distancing" that allows the hero ignorance (at least on the conscious level) of the kinship that makes his deed so reprehensible.[107] Coriolanus can complete his heroic self-overcoming, his superhuman rebirth, only by denying his former genetic context as well as his former national context; he must deny all kinship with the maternal city, and its paternal citizenry who exposed him in the wilds, if he is to push his sword through that city's gates as a rapist, and raise his sword against those citizens as a killer. Ambition, as John Byshop commented in 1577, "breaketh all bandes of pietie towards friendes, parentes, children, countrie"[108]— or at least it must try to. The distancing of his exile permits him to wage war, and war, as La Primaudaye remarks, frees man from his compassionate obligation to acknowledge bodily kinship with others.[109] Coriolanus turns away the martial father-figure Cominius, and the conventional rhetorical appeal by the political father-figure Menenius fails dismally. As the defeated Menenius departs, Coriolanus boasts, "Wife, mother, child, I know not" (5.2.82). He seems overeager to claim victory in a battle he has not yet fought. Those three have an actual familial call on him, where Cominius and Menenius had only a figurative one; and they have a leader in Volumnia whose rhetorical skills are better suited to this task than Menenius' homiletic tendencies.

The tragic crisis of act 5, scene 3, renews the rhetorical struggle between Volumnia and Coriolanus that took shape in act 3, scene 2, much as Coriolanus' assault on Rome renews his symbolic rape of Corioles. Coriolanus' transcendence of his human context, which he boasts is already complete, receives its most stringent analysis and therefore its most decisive defeat. As Francis Bacon warns, "let not a man trust his victory over his nature too far; for nature will lie buried a great time, and yet revive upon the occasion, or temptation; like as it was with Aesop's damsel, turned from a cat to a woman, who sat very demurely at the board's end till a mouse ran before her."[110] When his family parades in, Coriolanus' god-like bearing immediately falters; he shifts in his seat, fearing he will be "tempted to infringe my vow" (5.3.20). Genetic heritage, in the form of these relatives, reasserts itself against Coriolanus' ambition as regenerative nature does against Macbeth in the form of Birnan wood, and Volumnia's commentary on the reassertion clarifies its import and heightens its power. She is the temptation that reclaims him for hereditary nature, as the mouse is the temptation that reclaims the woman in Aesop's fable for her animal nature. A psychoanalyst argues that

> the whole process of becoming masculine is at risk in the little boy from the day of birth on; his still-to-be-created masculinity is endangered by the primary, profound, primeval oneness with mother, a blissful experience that serves, buried but active in the core of one's identity, as a focus which, throughout life, can attract one to regress ... That is the threat lying latent in masculinity.[111]

That threat Volumnia awakens, knowing as usual precisely where the heart-strings—and the puppet-strings—of her ambitious son can be reached. As La Primaudaye wrote in 1594, "Men are of that nature, that they cannot acknowledge what they are themselves, or what they have received of God, except they bee brought backe to that first dust and earth, out of which they are taken, even to their first creation and generation."[112] Volumnia is the primal earth-mother who imposes this acknowledgment on Coriolanus. His tragic *anagnorisis*, like that of Oedipus, is less a recognition of his family than a ruinous recognition of himself through that family's agency.

Coriolanus struggles with himself as he narrates the approach of the generational web that threatens him with both moral and developmental regression:

> My wife comes foremost; then the honor'd mould
> Wherein this trunk was fram'd, and in her hand
> The grandchild to her blood. But out, affection,
> All bond and privilege of nature, break!
> Let it be virtuous to be obstinate.
> What is that curtsy worth? or those doves' eyes,
> Which can make gods forsworn? I melt, and am not
> Of stronger earth than others. My mother bows,
> As if Olympus to a molehill should
> In supplication nod; and my young boy
> Hath an aspect of intercession, which
> Great Nature cries, "Deny not." Let the Volsces
> Plough Rome and harrow Italy, I'll never
> Be such a gosling to obey instinct, but stand
> As if a man were author of himself,
> And knew no other kin.
> Virgilia   My lord and husband!
> Coriolanus These eyes are not the same I wore in Rome.
>
> (5.3.22–38)

This remark recalls the transformed Henry V, coldly denying his degrading bonds to the grossly corporal Falstaff; but Coriolanus' version of "Presume not that I am the thing I was" is not the last word as it is in *2 Henry IV* (5.5.56). Both the hereditary and the ambitious selves look out of Coriolanus' eyes, and both speak in his voice as well; his speech, like those of Richard III and Macbeth, sounds more like a debate between two opposing voices than like the voice of any single man. He vacillates wildly between conceding that he shares his flesh with others and is made of the same earth, and denying any such kinship, denying even that he retains the same faculties he was born with. He uses the comparison to a "gosling" to distance himself from animal "instinct" childish dependency;

but he now claims only a simulation of autogenous status, through the same "as if" construction the tribunes used to question his claim to godhead (2.1.219; 3.1.81). His earlier claim not to "know" his family (5.2.82) has therefore retreated into the subjunctive. By declaring that such familial pleas "can make gods forsworn" and by identifying Volumnia with Olympus, Coriolanus seems to be preparing terms whereby yielding to these pleas and returning to Volumnia will confirm rather than contradict his god-like status. Anticipating defeat, he seeks to describe it as fairly honorable.

Coriolanus is now willing to describe his imminent surrender as a return to virtue, even if that necessitates describing it as a return to his true natural identity:

> Like a dull actor now
> I have forgot my part, and I am out,
> Even to a full disgrace. Best of my flesh,
> Forgive my tyranny.   (5.3.40–43)

Having lost command of his god-like "*graceful* posture" (2.1.221), he finds himself in "dis*grace*," and what had been a heroically possessing god becomes merely a forgettable theatrical script. The theatrical metaphor turns entirely against him: where earlier he had willingly been a bad actor, unable to simulate common humanity, he now unwillingly becomes too poor a player to simulate heroic purity. Since the bonds of flesh are taking precedence over the martial role, Coriolanus tries to insist that they are the best of flesh, that his wife's kiss will undo his exile and compensate for the revenge he must abjure, that the obedience he must show to his mother will be more dutiful "Than that of common sons" and shown toward "the most noble mother of the world" (5.3.44–52). His mother is in a sense the mother of the world here, as his father is in a sense universal, and he can only make the best of his consequent identity as *filius terrae*, a son of the earth.[113]

Volumnia seizes this concession to emphasize the "duty" that is properly owed "Between the child and parent," and when he acknowledges that duty, she rewards him with a pat on the head that also reiterates the lesson: "Thou art my warrior, / I holp to frame thee" (5.3.55–63). This echoes the moment in act 3, scene 2, when she obliges him to tell the citizens that "Thou art their soldier," and to "frame / Thyself, forsooth, hereafter theirs" (3.2.80–85). The explicitly filial character of this new subjugation confirms our sense that his subjugation to the citizenry was essentially filial as well. Volumnia then makes Coriolanus acknowledge his wife, and he acknowledges her first in terms of her family and her city (5.3.64–65), the very identifying marks he had been striving to eradicate in himself. Having pushed Coriolanus into this corner, Volumnia forces him to acknowledge his child as well, and she uses very much the same technique Paulina uses in *The Winter's Tale* to force Leontes to acknowledge his child and therefore his flawed bodily humanity:

> *Volumnia* This is a poor epitome of yours,
>   Which by th' interpretation of full time
>   May show like all yourself.

Coriolanus again struggles to make his familial entanglement an endorsement of his ambition, rather than attempting to deny such entanglement as he had before: he prays that "The gods of soldiers" may "inform" his son's "Thoughts with nobleness" so that his son will become an "unvulnerable" warrior, "Saving those that eye thee" as if he were "a great sea-mark" (5.3.68–75). By making Mars a father or godfather to the boy, Coriolanus claims his own place in the divine martial succession, and his obligation to save those who are now eyeing him becomes a way of confirming rather than disproving his martial invulnerability and constancy.

Coriolanus, who had echoed Lear and Macbeth in his willingness to shatter the "bonds of nature" only sixty lines earlier, now pleads with his mother to "Tell me not / Wherein I seem unnatural" (5.3.83–84). But that is precisely what her generational parade emphasizes, accusing him of "Making the mother, wife, and child to see / The son, the husband, and the father tearing / His country's bowels out" (5.3.101–03). She goes on to complain that this Caesarean action leaves them painfully divided between their desire that he survive and their desire that their motherland survive. But the division enforces itself most painfully against Coriolanus' devotion to a pure martial identity. As Lawrence Danson argues, "in being thus true to 'himself,' he is being false to another self who is a son, a husband, a father, a Roman."[114] The final element is a metaphorical extension of the first three. By returning to Menenius' anthropomorphic metaphor for the state, which makes it a single body with digestive bowels, Volumnia includes Rome in the hereditary trinity Coriolanus is obliged to worship and obey. Coriolanus rejected the fable that made the state a macrocosm of a man, because of what it implied about his own manhood. To accept the figuration justifying the isolation of the aristocracy in the national system, he would have to concede that an analogue of the citizenry populates another territory within his "single state of man," and he openly denies that such impurities exist, even in his digestive tract. Coriolanus again resembles the Puritan extremists, who could not afford to confront the reciprocal of the microcosmic metaphor for the state, and who therefore dissociated themselves "from the three crucial forms of traditional relationship: hierarchy, organic connection, and family. For in the images of political fatherhood, body politic, and great chain, the old order found its symbolic expression and made its appeal for the emotional loyalty of its members." The repression of the flawed old Adam within each of us, for Coriolanus as for the Puritans, required that they permit no compromising "intervention of nature, blood, or patriarchy with all their affective and emotional connotations."[115]

Volumnia engineers precisely such an emotional intervention. The shaken Coriolanus has tried to accept some partial compromise, agreeing to acknowledge his attachment to his family if they will "not say / For that, 'Forgive our Romans' " (5.3.42–44); but she refuses to make distinctions among these various "natural" obligations, these different sorts of entangling alliances. The limiting parental complex stands united against his autogenous ambitions:

> If I cannot persuade thee
> Rather to show a noble grace to both parts
> Than seek the end of one, thou shalt no sooner
> March to assault thy country than to tread
> (Trust to't, thou shalt not) on thy mother's womb
> That brought thee to this world.

Determined to seek the end of one part of himself, he cannot afford to compromise between it and his other, martial aspect. But Virgilia and young Martius each chime in, stating their roles as the hereditary carriers of Coriolanus' unhereditary martial glory, and Coriolanus retreats in bewilderment, "Not of a woman's tenderness to be, / Requires nor child nor woman's face to see" (5.3.129–30). This pronouncement may be a little disingenuous: their tender childishness and femininity affect him less than the generational context they represent. No random woman or child could have unsettled his integrity: although he resists admitting it, the genetic circumscription he sought to evade has recaptured him. Despite Volumnia's characteristically conciliatory manipulation of some crucial words— she associates "a noble grace" with the proposed compromise, rather than with a strict martial posture—the suitors are at their most assertive, and their least tender, in the passage that shakes him. But he would rather concede himself again emasculated, into "a woman's tenderness," than concede that his manhood and his hereditary identity are one and the same.

Instead of portraying the emasculation of Coriolanus as merely a dramatic pretense, as she does in act 3, scene 2, Volumnia now portrays his masculine displays as merely a role, merely affectation and mimesis on a grand scale:

> Thou hast affected the fine strains of honor,
> To imitate the graces of the gods:
> To tear with thunder the wide cheeks a' th' air,
> And yet to charge thy sulphur with a bolt
> That should but rive an oak. (5.3.149–53)

The martial performance in which he acquires his god-like graceful posture (through a typically thunderous Caesarean stroke) may be dismissed as merely so much sound and fury, unless it culminates in a resubmission to Rome. His noble manhood will otherwise be "dogg'd" and "wip'd . . . out" by the curses survivors and historians will place on his name (5.3.142–48).[116] Coriolanus will become Aristotle's uncivil beast, "a very dog to the commonalty" (1.1.28–29), rather than Aristotle's uncivil god.

Volumnia follows these warnings with another evocation of the encompassing familial trinity to which he owes both his human feeling and his martial toughness (5.3.155–64). Like the kneeling Lear, she calls down vengeance from the heavens against filial ingratitude:

> Say my request's unjust,
> And spurn me back; but if it be not so,
> Thou art not honest, and the gods will plague thee
> That thou restrain'st from me the duty which
> To a mother's part belongs.—He turns away.
> Down, ladies, let us shame him with our knees.
> To his surname Coriolanus 'longs more pride
> Than pity to our prayers. (5.3.164–71)

He belongs to his mother, she implies, more than his agnomen belongs to him; Aufidius makes precisely the same point in completing the fatal humiliation Volumnia has begun. Ambition and pity wrestle for Coriolanus' soul here, and as in *The Merchant of Venice*, *Measure for Measure*, *Macbeth*, and *The Tempest*, pity and mercy represent the element of common humanity urged against the proud dreams of power. As Shylock discovers at the trial, as Angelo learns from Isabella, as Lady Macbeth recognizes beside the sleeping Duncan, as Prospero is prompted by Ariel to admit, one must ignore the evidence of human kinship to enforce such sovereign dreams. Volumnia asserts that lesson decisively by a final, sarcastic dimissal of the generational trinity:

> Nay, behold 's!
> This boy, that cannot tell what he would have,
> But kneels and holds up hands for fellowship,
> Does reason our petition with more strength
> Than thou hast to deny't.—Come, let us go.
> This fellow had a Volscian to his mother;
> His wife is in Corioles, and his child
> Like him by chance.—Yet give us our dispatch.
> I am hush'd until our city be afire,
> And then I'll speak a little.
> (*Coriolanus holds her by the hand, silent*)
>
> *Coriolanus*   O, mother, mother!
> What have you done? Behold, the heavens do ope,
> The gods look down, and this unnatural scene
> They laugh at.   (5.3.173–85)

What she has done is simple and deadly: she has ended the long struggle, fought with proud words and violent deeds, to construct a martial creature who transcends his familial context. In taking her hand, Coriolanus mirrors the pose of his own son and rejoins the generational chain of humanity; the same action by which he implicitly agrees to make peace represents an abandonment of the cause for which he made war. In the moment of silence that signals the end of the martial conflict, the long rhetorical conflict over the viability of ambition fades into the background as well, and we retreat to the broader perspective of the gods. As long as she could use these conflicts to propel her son toward the goals they shared, Volumnia kept them active; but when he opposes her, and literalizes the sexual instigation she had manipulated rhetorically, she disarms him and his arguments with the silent facts of nature, awakening the latent recognition that any such struggle is both morally repugnant and ultimately futile. Aufidius had supposed that Coriolanus would "be to Rome / As is the aspray to the fish, who takes it / By sovereignty of nature" (4.7.33–35), but it is finally Rome who recaptures Coriolanus by the same method. As Francis Bacon suggests, echoing Horace, "Nature is often hidden, sometimes overcome, seldom extinguished. Force maketh nature more violent in the return; doctrine and discourse maketh nature less importune."[117] For Coriolanus, as for Macbeth and Leontes, the collapse of rhetoric into the literal and the visual is both cause and index of the collapse of ambition into nature; it is tempting to compare their dilemmas and their fates, in this regard, with those of their creator.[118] Virgilia, whom Coriolanus hails as "My gracious silence" (2.1.175), is an embodiment of his meeker and more tender attributes that await him each time the noise of conflict subsides. When he silently clasps his mother's hand, their verbal contest suddenly seems like a petty, distracting quarrel, and we are back with the gods, observing a more basic truth: the deterministic nature that preempts debate.

Shakespeare's moral endorsement of this deterministic power is at least as ambivalent in *Coriolanus* as it is in *Macbeth*. Coriolanus' gods, like Macbeth's witches, laugh at the protagonist because his proud quest for freedom has been trapped from the start in a deterministic paradox. The construction of a supernatural self runs up against the dark side of Polixenes' aphoristic assertion that "Nature is made better by no mean / But nature makes that mean" (*The Winter's Tale*, 4.4.89–90). The man seeking to exalt himself in Shakespeare finds this a burdensome truth: his degrading means, his inner conflicts, render him (like the usurper Claudius) a "limed soul, that, struggling to be free, / Art more engag'd" (*Hamlet*, 3.3.68–69). As Claudius can repent only with the same soul that chose to murder, Coriolanus can construct a martial machine only from the mortal womb that bred him, and the mortal food that fed him. Is it perfect justice, or a cruel trick, to use the ambiguities of human nature as a moral enforcer against the aspirations that nature generates? Montaigne may have been correct in asserting that a man's desire to "raise himself above himself" is "absurd"; but what kind of a god is it who traps the human will in such a dangerous farce? As in *Macbeth*, the almost Gnostic alienation of the human essence from the seamless natural order raises questions about Shakespeare's approval of the limiting system he shows so rigidly enforced. To the extent that we perceive Coriolanus' martial purity as the expression of an inner greatness, we regret the degraded world that ruins and punishes his effort to realize that ideal. But to the extent that we perceive his effort as arising from a repellently childish or sexualized subservience to his blood- and power-thirsty mother (a subservience she helps him mistake for a true will to glory), we regret only a misuse of parenthood, not any frustration of greatness.

A man's failure in such a deterministic universe invites a range of responses, depending on the viewpoint and the values of the observer. On a generic level, Coriolanus' fall would seem typically comic from the perspective of a young Roman lover. He is the blustering figure who tries to impose honorable death and a denial of all bodily appetites on everyone; his frustrated departure from Rome, promising vengeance, resembles Malvolio's flight at the end of *Twelfth Night*; and his reassimilation into his family, accompanied by a final acknowledgment of his own human frailty, which compels him to mercy, has analogues in almost every happy ending Shakespeare wrote. On a philosophical level, apologists for the Elizabethan order endorse such determinism as part of a benevolent chain-of-being. The Renaissance philosopher Valla comments "not only on the 'goodness' of 'nature' but on its potency and inescapability and resourcefulness in functioning through all the myriad disguises men invent for it."[119] In the context of a tragedy, or in the hands of a playwright more openly rebellious and Promethean than Shakespeare, such as Marlowe, this very adaptability can easily appear as a demonic repression of greatness. Shakespeare leaves us in an undefined middle ground between the sort of demonic conspiracy that seems to destroy Faustus, and the "demonized" world that, Lukács argues, frustrates by sheer mediocrity and neutrality the quest for heroism in novels such as *Don Quixote*.[120] Shakespeare takes advantage of the difficulty of distinguishing nature's thoughtless resistance to aberrations from the gods' punishment of hubristic aspirations: in a work focusing on the hero's struggle toward transcendence, a passive but stable nature will inevitably take on the semblance of a jealously punitive force. As Shakespeare protects *King Lear* from simplification or censorship by making it hard to tell whether the gods are malevolent or merely absent, so he protects his treatment of the hazards of ambition: we can neither prove nor disprove a divine conspiracy concealed behind the natural order's repressive impact.

The gods who laugh at Coriolanus' downfall may or may not have engineered it. "Tragedy is a game," Lukács argues, in which "God is nothing more than a spectator."[121] But Coriolanus' laughing gods do not quite correspond to the play's audience, gazing down from the level known as "the heavens" in the Elizabethan theater, though we may be struck as those gods are by the emptiness of the roles played out beneath us. We may even feel ourselves another object of the gods' laughter, when we realize that the ambitious struggle we have been following so intensely has never stood a chance of success. Nor are these gods the ones Volumnia summons to "plague" her ungrateful son. No *deus ex machina* descends to smite Coriolanus, because, as Aristotle recommends, the moral structure resolves itself without superhuman interference: Coriolanus' own assertions of freedom, and steps toward freedom, rebound to destroy him.

If the laughing gods have appeared anywhere else in the play, they have appeared within Coriolanus. The "whatsoever god" who possesses Coriolanus has Satanic overtones, as I have suggested. One major line of Renaissance theological thought saw represented in Lucifer's fall "all the absurdities, all the hopeless revolts against God and His world-order, and all the illusions of possible victory to which highly-gifted human spirits so often abandon themselves."[122] Coriolanus' early virtue (like that of Macbeth) is despoiled by an idea of greatness that enters him seductively, promising him exaltation over common humanity, only to leave him in his merely human form to be punished for his transgression. If Coriolanus is a damned figure, as man or serpentine dragon, he is a damned figure with such a pure and naive faith in his gods that, in the moment of his martyrdom, he can call out to Mars asking why Mars has forsaken him. Could the Bibical serpent himself have known (when even the rational humans may have been confused) that his possession was a damnation rather than a holy visitation? Shakespeare drops hints throughout the play that the gods who shaped the martial Coriolanus—the sword made flesh, to amend a Biblical phrase—may have been Tempters rather than Creators. After his conquest of Corioles, Coriolanus jokes that "The gods begin to mock me. I, that now / Refus'd most princely gifts, am bound to beg / Of my lord general" for the redemption of the old man who had formerly sheltered Coriolanus and had now been taken prisoner by his army (1.9.79–87); this adumbrates his effort to protect his Roman family, which leads to the gods' laughter and his subjugation to Aufidius. He supposes his mother has "petition'd all the gods / For my prosperity" (2.1.170–71), but those petitions backfire as badly as such petitions do in King Lear (5.2.4; 5.3.257). Coriolanus returns against his country "dragon-like," propelled by "the spleen / of all the under fiends," until even his new allies wonder "what witchcraft's in him" that his vengeful project runs so smoothly (4.7.23, 4.5.91–92, 4.7.2). Only when this vengeance is fatally baffled can we recognize the likeliest import of these demonic hints: the god-like voices that inspired him may simply have been fattening his ambition for a more satisfying kill. Shakespeare, perhaps building from some hints in North's Plutarch,[123] implies that his hero may be seduced and abandoned, instigated and punished, by a single superhuman force. If that is so, then the gods laugh not at man's folly, as innocent spectators, but rather at man's destruction, as cruelly jealous demons.

Aufidius finally forbids Coriolanus to call on his tutelary god Mars and dismisses Coriolanus as a "boy of tears" (5.6.100). Where the Volsces had formerly made him "sweat with wrath" (1.4.27), Coriolanus must now claim that his family makes his "eyes . . . sweat compassion" (5.3.196), but such rhetorical gestures toward sustaining his muscular manhood cannot erase our perception of a defeated boy. His regression, which began with the compromise of the manly identity won precociously in battle, now approaches its fitting conclusion. He will be carried, covered with his own blood, through one more gate to end the play: the image suggests the retraction of his natural birth, and the stillbirth of his ambitious identity. Instead of undergoing a Caesarean liberation, the child must die to preserve the integrity of the womb and the life of the mother. The fact that this stillbirth takes place at Corioles' gates rather than Rome's suggests that, although he has failed as a father to himself, Coriolanus has put some distance between himself and his common Roman patrimony. He manages to prove, in the last flurry of heroic violence characteristic of Shakespeare's tragic heroes, his assertion that his fate is necessarily very different from Rome's fate (5.3.186–89); by fulfilling his own prophecy, he usurps a little of the womb's deterministic power. But these fine distinctions, these small victories, are essentially all that remains of his physically and rhetorically violent struggle to escape the constrictions of his birth, a struggle that dominates the play's action and imagery.

Coriolanus and Aufidius

Coriolanus' alternative to identification with either of his parents is identification with Tullus Aufidius, whether as twin brother, as Doppelgänger, as mirror-reflection, or as ego-ideal. Again the process is suggestively analogous to a child's psychological development. According to Peter Blos, the adolescent trying to escape a painful attachment to his parents "has recourse to the usual mechanism of mourning: he identifies with them, or one of them. But he does this indirectly, by merging narcissistically with persons who can mirror him as that parent once did. In effect, he recapitulates the symbiotic merger with the mother preceding separation and individuation."[124] When his mother Volumnia and his mother-city Rome betray the martial identity he thought he shared with them, Coriolanus seeks another version of that affirmation from Aufidius, with whom he also supposes he shares that martial ideal. This resembles a standard phase described by psychoanalysts in a boy's growth "in which he perceives another person as separate, but only as a mirror of himself, or a projection of his own feelings, or a substitute for his frustrated ideal grandiose self."[125] As Coriolanus fatally delays his differentiation from his mother, under the illusion that her purpose mirrors his, so he understands too late his separateness from Aufidius in body and intention. His determination to project his ego-ideal onto his martial enemy, to perceive that enemy as his mirror-image, allows that enemy to plot against him undetected.

After escaping the centripetal pull of the maternal figures, the boy struggles toward a counteridentification with a masculine model. Coriolanus finds a model who is the seeming opposite of his cowardly common Roman father: a warlike noble Volscian. Rather than recognize the reflection of his own humanity in the citizenry, Coriolanus seeks instead to align himself with an ideal other, hoping to absorb from that other, by mimesis and osmosis, the martial qualities he cannot perfect by and within himself. In this hope, Coriolanus again resembles the Puritans: "Instead of saying, Who am I? to the mirror image, the Puritan says to himself, or to it, Here is who I am, or intend to be."[126] But this effort to conjure or confirm the ideal new self with mirrors proves no more reliable than the effort to do so with rebirth, and the two efforts combine to destroy Coriolanus. The duplication Coriolanus seeks becomes merely Aufidius' duplicity; Coriolanus' attempt to isolate his martial aspects by union with his martial counterpart becomes merely schizophrenia; and the city where Coriolanus gained and hoped to reassert his autogenous martial identity becomes merely a deadly replica of the degrading city he fled. The deceptiveness, schizophrenia, and claustrophobia that typify mirror-romances turn Coriolanus' attachment to Aufidius into a fatal disease.[127]

From the first mention of Aufidius, Coriolanus displays a peculiar hunger for him: he tells Cominius that the Volsces

> have a leader,
> Tullus Aufidius, that will put you to't.
> I sin in envying his nobility;
> And were I any thing but what I am,
> I would wish me only he.
> *Cominius*　　　　　　　　You have fought together?
> *Coriolanus* Were half to half the world by th' ears, and he
> Upon my party, I'd revolt, to make
> Only my wars with him. He is a lion
> That I am proud to hunt.　　　　　　　(1.1.228–36)

His yearning to confront his Doppelgänger sounds suspiciously like his yearning to confront the citizenry, in a reciprocal form. Even the animal imagery, used to justify his assaults on the citizenry, reappears here in a complimentary form to justify his assaults on Aufidius. His desire for a cause to visit Aufidius and "oppose his hatred fully" (3.1.19–20) resembles his approach to the citizenry: he "seeks their hate" and strives to "discover him their opposite" (2.2.18–21). The parallels between these two forces of otherness suggest two things. First, they lead us to suspect that the same ambitious mechanisms are at work in the artificial exaltation of Aufidius as in the artificial degradation of the citizenry. Second, they warn us that Aufidius may resemble the citizenry a great deal more than Coriolanus suspects, and may join the mob in entrapping and degrading Coriolanus' martial identity.

Coriolanus' determination to keep Aufidius symmetrically opposed, expressed in such images "half to half the world by th' ears," blurs the distinction between a mirror-image and a true other disquietingly. The similarity between Coriolanus' "were I any thing but what I am, / I would wish me only he," and Iago's "Were I the Moor, I would not be Iago: / In following him, I follow but myself" (Othello, 1.1.57–58) is rightly disturbing. In both cases the peculiar phrasing indicates a peculiar desire that threatens the borderline between self and other. Aufidius reciprocates Coriolanus' emulative remark later in the first act, in a speech which heightens our uneasy sense that the relationship between these individuals has edged toward a relationship between mirror-images:

> I would I were a Roman, for I cannot,
> Being a Volsce, be that I am. Condition?
> What good condition can a treaty find
> I' th' part that is at mercy? Five times, Martius,
> I have fought with thee; so often hast thou beat me;
> And wouldst do so, I think, should we encounter
> As often as we eat. By th' elements,
> If e'er again I meet him beard to beard,
> He's mine, or I am his. Mine emulation
> Hath not that honor in't it had; for where
> I thought to crush him in an equal force,
> True sword to sword, I'll potch at him some way,
> Or wrath or craft may get him.   (1.10.4–16)

To break this symmetrical pattern, in which he seems doomed to remain the dim reflection and not the commanding subject, Aufidius will transform himself from real to delusive mirror, "fly out of" his valorous identity into a secret program of treachery (1.10.17–19). Jealous of the dominant soldier's simpler greatness, Aufidius will use an appearance of honor to insinuate and subvert that soldier's image of himself. Aufidius' situation, as that last sentence describes it, connects him with Iago at a level deeper than his merely verbal echoes of the earlier villain (*Othello*, 2.1.250, 1.1.65, 3.3.480). Both men seem driven by a gnawing suspicion that they have lost themselves, been inwardly dishonored, and they try to recapture selfhood from the men they dimly perceive as the thieves. Both attempts are essentially seductions, but in both cases the homosexual overtones may easily be misinterpreted.

Othello and Coriolanus submit to these secret tricksters for opposite reasons. Othello strives to become a Venetian, and heeds Iago's counsel because Iago is a native; Coriolanus strives to eradicate his Roman origins, and turns to Aufidius because Aufidius is a foreigner. As Aufidius "cannot, / Being a Volsce, be that I am," so Coriolanus cannot, being a Roman, be what he chooses to be. As Una Ellis-Fermor suggests, "The preoccupation with his rival Aufidius, which appears early in the play, may be but another indication of this restless search for an ideal objective; Aufidius becomes in some sort a focus, though but a nebulous one, for this desire for splendour of life that the summit of achievement in Rome could never offer."[128] This strikes me as entirely right; the crucial question it leaves unanswered is why that summit should be unattainable in Rome but visible through Aufidius. My suggestion is that Coriolanus perceives Aufidius as a reflection of his own martial honor, unhindered by any compromising physical or political derivation from Volumnia or Rome. Since he sees Aufidius only in battle, he can understand him as a purely martial entity, devoid of the domestic attributes Coriolanus disdains in himself.

Coriolanus' need to believe that such an ideal being exists, and may be seized like a foreign country, absorbed like a hunter's prey, causes him to mistake a mirror reflecting his own desires for a window showing Aufidius. The bait is also the blind, and from behind it, Aufidius makes easy prey of his old rival.[129] Even the rhetoric Aufidius uses to describe his plot is deceptively mirrorlike: "One fire drives out one fire; one nail, one nail; / Rights by rights fouler, strengths by strengths do fail" (4.7.54–55). His verbal symmetries seem to imply that he will remain Coriolanus' noble opposite, but in fact he will merely hold up a mirror and allow Coriolanus to defeat himself. The result is a Coriolanus who has been "cut i' th' middle, and but one half of what he was yesterday," as the servant had feared Aufidius would be (4.5.197–98). When he is banished, Coriolanus promises that he "will or exceed the common or be caught / With cautelous baits and practice" (4.1.32–33), and we eventually realize that the alternatives are not mutually exclusive: his very determination to exceed the common, to eradicate the taint of the Roman citizenry, renders him vulnerable to Aufidius' treachery. He tells Aufidius,

> if
> I had fear'd death, of all the men i' th' world
> I would have 'voided thee; but in mere spite,
> To be full quit of those my banishers,
> Stand I before thee here. (4.5.80–84)

The clearest antecedent is Macbeth's speech to Macduff:

> Of all men else I have avoided thee.
> But get thee back, my soul is too much charg'd
> With blood of thine already. (5.8.4–6)

To hold his new identity in safety, Macbeth must destroy this mirror of its unnaturally late and bloody birth, but the conscience and the prophecy which threaten that new identity dissuade him from the confrontation. Coriolanus, who has similarly "Drawn tuns of blood out of thy country's breast" (4.5.99), must submit to his deadliest enemy if he is to eradicate the threats to his new identity.

Coriolanus therefore arrives in Antium as a sort of free agent and assures himself that he has left behind his former attachments. He is determined to generate an autonomous new self, or to recover the unity of his former self, by merger with his former rival; and although he cannot clearly articulate that mission, he narrates his arrival in terms that associate procreation with the ambivalent intimacy of two people who seem to be divided only by heritage, perhaps only by a mirror:

> O world, thy slippery turns! Friend now fast sworn,
> Whose double bosoms seems to wear one heart,
> Whose hours, whose bed, whose meal and exercise
> Are still together, who twin, as 'twere, in love
> Unseparable, shall within this hour,
> On a dissension of a doit, break out
> To bitterest enmity; so, fellest foes,
> Whose passions and whose plots have broke their sleep
> To take the one the other, by some chance,
> Some trick not worth an egg, shall grow dear friends
> And interjoin their issues. So with me,
> My birthplace hate I, and my love's upon

This enemy town. I'll enter. If he slay me,
He does fair justice; if he give me way,
I'll do his country service.   (4.4.12–26)

Love and hate are two sides of the same coin, and may be exchanged
in an instant. The Elizabethan pun on "slaying" in the final lines,
reinforced by the speech's dual theme and by the sexual puns on
"entering" another set of gates that may "give me way" to "do
. . . service" to "his country," stresses the proximity of amorous and
murderous embraces. This proximity has become an axiom of modern psychology: "Aggressivity is intimately linked to identification,
notably in paranoia, where the subject's persecutors may turn out
to be those with whom he had once identified himself: the other
we fear is often the other we love."[130]

Coriolanus shifts the mode of his identification with Aufidius
from hate to love, from martial to sexual aggression, hoping to generate a new identity embodying the heroism they have in common.
But he cannot evade the influence of his derivation so easily. In
flipping the coin of enmity and emulation, Coriolanus inadvertently
re-identifies himself with the Roman citizenry whose persecution
he had been combating and fleeing. As Coriolanus felt himself con-
taminated by the citizens and their food, so Aufidius feels his "val-
or's poison'd" by Coriolanus (1.10.17); yet as the citizens had to beg
food from Coriolanus, so Coriolanus must beg from Aufidius. The
citizens briefly accepted Coriolanus' badly counterfeited humility
because he fulfilled the ideal martial type they desired to identify
with Rome. Coriolanus believes Aufidius' flatteries because he fulfills the ideal martial type Coriolanus desires to identify with himself. Coriolanus and Aufidius alike conclude that they can end the
poisonous taint only by murdering its carriers; but, in the attempt,
they only end up tainting their valor more seriously. The brave new
world Coriolanus sought among the Volsces turns out to be merely
another chamber in the confining labyrinth, a mirror of the very
associations he fled Rome to escape.

There are some suggestions that the Volscian world offers Coriolanus an ennobled version of what he experienced in Rome, but
those improvements turn out to be deceptions. Coriolanus' quest
for the consulship had overtones of sexual courtship: it required that
the tribunes show a "loving motion toward the common body" in
endorsing his candidacy, and necessitated Menenius' warning that
Coriolanus "loves your people, / But tie him not to be their bedfellow" (2.2.53, 64–65). When Aufidius embraces Coriolanus more ea-

gerly than he first took his wife to bed (4.5.115–18), he offers the
alternative sort of marriage Coriolanus desires, a sort of dynastic or
eugenic marriage of martial nobilities. The notion that this soldierly
embrace—the standard of chivalric expression of mutual emulation—offers a nobler alternative to the rebirth offered by the consulship is confirmed in several other ways. Instead of deriving an
identity from common humanity, Coriolanus now hears Aufidius
declare that

> If Jupiter
> Should from yond cloud speak divine things,
> And say, " 'Tis true," I'd not believe them more
> Than thee, all-noble Martius.   (4.5.103–06)

It is again as if Coriolanus may become, not the all-common product
of the Roman citizens' "voices," but instead the all-noble word of
a god made flesh. In defeating Corioles, Coriolanus was allowed to
rename himself according to his deeds, but Rome's domestic forces
still denied him the privilege of defining "The man I am" (3.2.16).
In yielding to Corioles, however, his power of self-renaming includes
precisely such a self-definition: "If, Tullus, / Not yet thou know'st
me, and, seeing me, dost not / Think me for the man I am, necessity /
Commands me name myself" (4.5.54–57).

   This welcome necessity brings with it another, less pleasant one.
Coriolanus has become like Marlowe's self-fashioning heroes, who
become "virtually autochthonous, their names and identities given
by no one but themselves" and can therefore continue to exist "only
by virtue of constantly renewed acts of will."[131] When Coriolanus
fails to renew his act of will at Rome's gates, fails to establish himself
as an autochthonous "author of himself," Aufidius retracts all that
he had given. He refuses Coriolanus both the name and the manhood
Coriolanus had claimed, calling him now "Caius Martius" and "boy"
(5.6.86–103). Even the martial marriage is annulled, revealing it as
merely a pretext for seduction and abandonment. Instead of offering
himself as the host (in either sense) at a supper consecrated to the
martial ideal, Aufidius refuses Coriolanus the "remission" that "lies /
In Volscian breasts"—the same "breasts" on which Coriolanus had
formerly fed himself (4.5.188, 99; 5.2.84–85)—determined that Coriolanus should be instead "by his own alms empoison'd" (5.6.10).
Coriolanus' oral incorporation of Aufidius was, as psychoanalytic
theory suggests, an expression of emulation, an effort to absorb his
identity;[132] now Coriolanus' charitable concession of his identity
with the Roman body politic obliges him to ingest the chaff he

previously characterized as poison. It is not surprising that Volumnia is at pains to deny that saving Rome would be "poisonous of your honor" (5.3.135), since that is precisely what it will be.

The causes and effects of Aufidius' treachery toward Coriolanus are perhaps most clearly evident in their pseudosexual relationship. Coriolanus arrives in Antium assuming that Aufidius will either kill him or else accept him as fully as a woman accepts a man, allowing him to "enter" and "do service" to Aufidius' "country" (4.4.24–26). His dominance in their encounters "beard to beard" and "sword to sword" (1.10.11, 15; 3.1.13) have encouraged Coriolanus to believe that he may seize the masculine role in their alliance. He had carried an "Amazonian chin" into battle, and proved his manhood in a series of victories that culminated in his conversion into a sword (2.2.91, 96–97; 1.6.76). But Aufidius intends to subvert that manhood and reclaim his own manly honor. In the process, Aufidius performs the figurative castration Coriolanus feared from the Roman citizenry, transmitting to Coriolanus his own inability to penetrate the gates of Rome and thus fulfill his martial project.

Before Coriolanus arrives in Antium, a Roman remarks that his country is vulnerable to Volscian conquest, since "the fittest time to corrupt a man's wife is when she's fall'n out with her husband" (4.3.32–33). At this point we assume that Rome is the wife, susceptible to assault in the absence of Coriolanus' sword. But as we watch Coriolanus, having fallen out with the Roman citizenry, being corrupted by Aufidius, who "makes a mistress of him" (4.5.194–95), we may sense him slipping from the masculine to the feminine role. In his almost grotesquely sexual greeting of his former foe, Aufidius, gripping his sword as he speaks, portrays himself rhetorically as the phallic lance and as the "arm" furiously assaulting Coriolanus' hewn-out "target'"

> Let me twine
> Mine arms about that body, where against
> My grained ash an hundred times hath broke,
> And scarr'd the moon with splinters. Here I cleep
> The anvil of my sword, and do contest
> As hotly and as nobly with thy love
> As ever in ambitious strength I did
> Contend against thy valor. Know thou first,
> I lov'd the maid I married; never man
> Sigh'd truer breath; but that I see thee here,
> Thou noble thing, more dances my rapt heart

> Than when I first my wedded mistress saw
> Bestride my threshold. Why, thou Mars, I tell thee,
> We have a power on foot; and I had purpose
> Once more to hew thy target from thy brawn,
> Or lose mine arm for't. Thou hast beat me out
> Twelve several times, and I have nightly since
> Dreamt of encounters 'twixt thyself and me;
> We have been down together in my sleep,
> Unbuckling helms, fisting each other's throat,
> And wak'd half dead with nothing.　　　　(4.5.106–26)

The suggestiveness here is unrelenting. Aufidius is a sort of unwitting Renaissance love-poet, describing love, as the period's lyricists so often did, by comparing it to warfare. He is ostensibly inverting that conventional metaphor, describing acts of war by barely subliminal comparisons to acts of love; but in the speech, as in the dream it describes, the subliminal sexual content overwhelms the ostensible martial topic. The choking intimacy of this encounter recalls Aufidius' first remarks about Coriolanus, concerning their encounters "beard to beard" and "sword to sword," and recalls even more vividly Coriolanus' first remarks about Aufidius, portraying "half to half the world by th' ears." As when Macbeth confronts Macdonwald's forces (1.2.8–9, 56), the rhetoric evokes a struggle between two forces not really distinct enough to strike out freely; and in both cases that struggle represents the mirrorlike complicity of two identities lost in a limbo between total opposition and total identification.

The homosexual overtones may therefore be interpreted figuratively, as relevant to an ontological rather than a sexual crisis; those overtones, like the Oedipal overtones elsewhere, have more to do with a desire for a new identity than with conventional physical desire. The physical entanglement of the two men, which makes them more than one person but fewer than two, may suggest some form of physical penetration, "the beast with two backs" as Iago describes it (1.1.116–17); but Aufidius implies that their encounters, martial or amorous, have always stopped short of such a conclusion. Their deeds and desires point instead to a psychological interpenetration which, like the soldierly embrace of Suffolk and York described in *Henry V* (4.6.11–27), could be easily but wrongly perceived as homosexuality. Psychoanalysts have defined a "pseudosexuality" that has more to do with self-definition than with libidinal drives.[133] In some cases, a man's aggressive homosexual advances may evince a secret craving "for a primitive merger with a mirror image of himself."[134] The hidden desire actually conceals an even deeper and more forbidden desire: the desire to redefine the self. Shakespeare again makes a psychoanalytic commonplace—that a domineering mother and an absent father create a homosexual and Oedipally unresolved son[135]—serve on a symbolic level. Volumnia's dominance and the father's dispersion impel Coriolanus toward his figuratively homosexual and Oedipal actions. The violations of the various taboos point to the violation of hereditary identity.

The homosexual aggression, like the Oedipal aggression, subserves the procreation of a new Coriolanus; he returns to Rome determined to replace Roman heredity with his own mirror-like-nesses. Virgilia and Volumnia warn the tribunes that, once free from the constraints of local loyalty, Coriolanus would "make an end of thy posterity," "Bastards and all" (4.2.23–27). The common offspring the tribunes create, even such "bastards" of commonness and nobility as they make of the Senate and almost make of Coriolanus (3.1.108 3.2.56), must give way to Coriolanus' new martial self and his new martial family. Cominius reports that he returns like a god, shaped by some supernatural diety, and that his soldiers "follow him / Against us brats with no less confidence / Than boys pursuing summer butterflies" (4.6.90–95). Valeria and Volumnia earlier observe Coriolanus' son pursuing summer butterflies with the same violent intent, and remark on the resemblance this reveals to his violent father (1.3.57–66). Coriolanus' army therefore becomes a figuration, and a multiplication, of his natural progeny. He, like the god who made him, seems to shape men better than nature: the process resembles modern fantasies of cloning, or classical myths about sowing dragons' teeth, creating instant armies of perfect soldiers.

If Coriolanus were truly a loyal "heir to Mars" (4.5.118, 192) rather than a rebellious heir to man, then his martial alliance with Aufidius would be a redemptively filial act that could rightly restore his procreative powers. But the play indicates that he has only aggravated his dangerous status as an Oedipal son by marching with the Volsces against Rome. As Coriolanus advances against his fatherland, the tribune Sicinius characteristically seeks consolation in the idea that the continuity of human identity cannot be so quickly overcome, recalling that Coriolanus "lov'd his mother dearly" and asking,

I'st possible that so short a time can alter the condition of a man?
Menenius There is a difference between a grub and a butterfly,

yet your butterfly was a grub. This Martius is grown from man
to dragon: he has wings, he's more than a creeping thing.

(5.4.9–15)

Menenius intends his analogy to imply that Coriolanus has tran-
scended his hereditary identity as if it were merely a chrysalis state,
but he thereby associates Coriolanus' ambitious new identity with
a butterfly—the very creature Coriolanus' literal and figurative sons
tear to pieces.[136] When his literal son helps turn him back from the
gates of Rome, he falls into the hands of his figurative Volscian sons,
who virtually "Tear him to pieces" (5.6.120). In the very moment
of Oedipal triumph described by Menenius, the seeds of Oedipal
vengeance begin to grow. Jacobean moralists attempted to warn young
men about this sort of legacy of filial violence: "Art thou a disobedient child unto thy parents? . . . Be thou assured, who ever thou
art, that there is a just God in heaven, who (if ever he bestow posterity on thee) may withhold his grace from them, & suffer them to
be as disobedient, scornefull, theevish, undutifull to thee as now
thou art to thine."[137] Shakespeare's treatments of ambition contain
a similar warning: the man who defies the will of his father or his
king may bring in time a similar defiance from his own son or
subjects. When Volumnia tries to halt Coriolanus' assault on Rome
by pointing to his son, who may eventually "show all like yourself"
(5.3.70), she may be warning him as much as awakening his paternal
tenderness. The warning is strengthened when, after the women
announce that Coriolanus will have to tread upon them to enter
Rome, young Martius announces, " 'A shall not tread on me; / I'll
run away till I am bigger, but then I'll fight" (5.3.127–28). He thus
becomes a version of the archetypal exposed child who survives to
overthrow the father, particularly a father who was himself banished
as a patricidal threat.

Volumnia ruins Coriolanus' quest by dislodging the mirror-figure
of Aufidius, by whom Coriolanus becomes autogenous, and replacing him with the mirror-figure of young Martius, by whom Coriolanus is further entangled in the procreative order.[138] When he finally
mirrors his son by standing silently holding Volumnia's hand, we
know she has succeeded. The artificial mirroring process by which
he was going to recreate himself and overthrow his heritage has been
reassimilated by hereditary nature. This reassimilation does not,
however, entail the reconciliation of Coriolanus' hereditary and ambitious selves; he is fatally torn between his commitments to each
of them. Coriolanus stands mesmerized between the mirror of young

Martius and the mirror of Aufidius, unable to make the two reflect
the same image of himself. He tries desperately to salvage his resemblance to Aufidius in the moment of surrender to the Roman
family:

> Now, good Aufidius,
> Were you in my stead, would you have heard
> A mother less? or granted less, Aufidius?
> *Aufidius* I was mov'd withal.
> *Coriolanus*   I dare be sworn you were.
>
> (5.3.191–94)

But Aufidius now knows the worth of Coriolanus' oaths, and is
moved only to spite:

> I am glad thou hast set thy mercy and thy honor
> At difference in thee. Out of that I'll work
> Myself a former fortune.   (5.3.200–02)

Coriolanus' engrossment of honor had reduced Aufidius to a creature
of policy. Now that Coriolanus is making "conditions" (5.3.205)—
precisely what disgraced Aufidius "I' th' part that is at mercy" (1.10.7)—
Aufidius can recapture some martial pre-eminence. Aufidius knows
that the martial attributes are virtually part of his rival's "nature"
(4.7.10; 5.6.24), and is pleased to see a contradictory sort of nature
roused in him as well; for Coriolanus as for the usurpers in the
earlier plays, the merciful hereditary self and the brutal ambitious
self are trapped in a deadly and irresolvable stalemate. In the play's
opening scene, Coriolanus portrays mercy as the only obstacle between his sword and the winnowing of the world into pure nobility:

> Would the nobility lay aside their ruth
> And let me use my sword, I'd make a quarry
> With thousands of these quarter'd slaves.   (1.1.197–99)

The Volscians slaughter him because mercy has again sheathed the
sword that wished to destroy the embodiments of his human heritage. The common human attributes Volumnia reawakens in Coriolanus, like the common human beings in the Roman body-politic,
gain a voice in decisions formerly made exclusively by nobility; the
arousal of Coriolanus' pity for his family is compromising in a way
analogous to the appointment of tribunes for the common people.
The personal and political facets of the ambitious project remain
deeply interwoven, and each is here lured into an inherently fatal
compromise.

Coriolanus is very much aware of the dangers of compromise on the political level, but Shakespeare leaves it to us to see the analogous personal dangers. Coriolanus warns that the establishment of tribunes brings a sickening element into the voice and the food of Rome—two of his usual concerns—and that it therefore

> makes the consuls base; and my soul aches
> To know, when two authorities are up,
> Neither supreme, how soon confusion
> May enter 'twixt the gap of both, and take
> The one by th' other.   (3.1.103–12)

Coriolanus is confused by the conflict between the authority of the Roman womb and his claim to be "author of himself"; Aufidius, uncomfortably sharing his martial authority with Coriolanus, enters that very gap to destroy him. The Third Conspirator describes the political situation in Corioles to Aufidius in much the same terms: "The people will remain uncertain, whilst / 'Twixt you there's difference; but the fall of either / Makes the survivor heir of all" (5.6.16–18). So Aufidius deftly sends Coriolanus stumbling into the abyss between his two identities, between the human being and the divine purity toward which he aspires. When the spirit was entirely willing, it could exalt the weak flesh to its own level. Coriolanus triumphed in battle because "his doubled spirit / Requick'ned what in flesh was fatigate" (2.2.116–17; see also 2.1.136). But when his "double bosoms" (4.4.13) lead him to Antium, the doubling, as the verbal shading implies, has become ambivalence rather than synergy.

As his tirade against political compromise proceeds, Coriolanus continues to describe unwittingly the dangers of a compromised identity. Unless the nobler part can dominate the baser, whether in Roman politics or in Coriolanus' psyche, the division precludes any stability. He swears by "both divine and human" objects that the "double worship" of a bicameral government yields so much power to "general ignorance" that the result is "unstable slightness." He adds that the "dishonor" of allowing the tribunes to dictate the Senate's actions

> bereaves the state
> Of that integrity which should become't;
> Not having the power to do the good it would,
> For th' ill which doth control't.   (3.1.141–61)

Coriolanus later suffers exactly this sort of helpless loss of honor and integrity by letting his hereditary human aspect dictate his actions. Aufidius finds him an unreliable ally—as divided governments tend to be—and so submits his unstable slightness to the general ignorance of the Volsces. In proving himself neither entirely "divine" nor merely "human," Coriolanus proves unable to finish the martial project he cannot afford to resign; the divisions ambition has made in his identity are reflected in the political divisions that drive him from Rome, and in the divided obligations that cripple him when he tries to return there as a Volscian. He abandoned his homeland to escape his hereditary self, but his failure to complete the adopted self finally prevents his acceptance in a new homeland. Having constructed a political conflict at home to express his self-overcoming, he is destroyed by a political conflict abroad when he surrenders that self-overcoming. To go back, in identity or in politics, is as tedious and dangerous as go o'er.

The tragedy of Coriolanus to this extent resembles the tragedy of Macbeth, obeying Hegel's rule that tragic conflict arises from the irreconcilable orders of two godheads, two imperious principles. My previous chapter suggested that Shakespeare displaces one level of *Macbeth* to a classical era so that Macbeth's existential imperatives can encounter the nemesis of "Olympian morality"; in *Coriolanus* Shakespeare does the opposite, allowing the hero's classical *virtus* to encounter the Christian doctrine of humility. The two godheads at war within Coriolanus are, in this sense, the alternative characterizations of the proud "whatsoever god" who insinuates his identity: it could be Hercules, the glorious martial demigod, or it could be Satan, the evil fallen angel. In another sense, Coriolanus is torn between the rules of the Furies, who avenge crimes against kinship, and those of Prometheus, who urges humanity to assert its fiery freedom from the limits its makers impose. The dilemma even makes itself felt on the psychoanalytic level: Coriolanus must be a bad son, either to his human father-figures in Rome or to his godly father-figure Mars. A. C. Bradley's theory, that Shakespeare's tragic heroes are destroyed by quality virtually inseparable from the greatness by which they merit our attention,[139] is a version of Hegel's rule; and Coriolanus' blunt determination to create an autonomous and invulnerable self out of the mortal flesh he inherits, and within the mortal world he inhabits, is that sort of ambivalent quality. "The tragic God," according to Lucien Goldmann, manifests his "paradoxical nature" in "the demand for absolute values and . . . the impossibility of ever satisfying this demand in the real world."[140] If there is a god who, acting through Volumnia, demands concessions to one's mere humanity, then there is also Lukács' sort of tragic god who, acting through Aufidius, "mercilessly punishes the slightest hint of infidelity towards the quest for Essence."[141]

Volumnia seems almost to be in league with Aufidius, as Rome seems to be in league with Antium, to trap Coriolanus between identities and between worlds.[142] She, like Aufidius, encourages his martial endeavors only until it suits her purposes to stop him. She turns him away from Rome's gates by reminding him that he was born of her blood and labor; Aufidius then accuses him of slighting his obligation to "the blood and labor" the Volsces have invested in his rebirth (5.6.46–47). These conflicts cause not only Coriolanus' political double-dealing, but also his inward dividedness, by a mechanism like the one R. D. Laing describes in the schizophrenic: "The malignant influence which he fails to withstand commonly masks itself in benevolence," but it is always "a pressure exerted by society through the agency of the family . . . which is directly responsible for the ontological break, the 'divided self' of schizophrenia."[143] Volumnia has turned the ideas of name and fame she had given him against themselves, trapped his filial identity in a hopeless Oedipal paradox, and forced him finally to confront the rabble of both cities, who accord only in calling him "traitor." He tries to revel in the embattled solitude these accusations reinforce, but he grows increasingly aware of an inner treason matching the political one; he cannot shut himself off from his accusers because part of the accusation arises from within himself. As he is fatally attainted for treason in Rome and then in Corioles, so is he fatally divorced from his inherited and then his ambitious identities. He has betrayed them both, and therefore has no spiritual home to return to, as he has no physical retreat.

Coriolanus finally stands transfixed between the degrading and the ideal mirrors, half-recognizing himself in each, lost between the two things he can no longer be. A mob of Volsces murder him for his political betrayal; but when his spirit was integral, he vanquished the whole of Corioles by himself. The defeat that enforces on him his vulnerable humanity is possible only because his vulnerable humanity has already been aroused within him. *Coriolanus* thus becomes neither the martial epic Coriolanus desired to inhabit nor the comic refutation of that ambition desired by the tribunes, but rather a tragically ambivalent morality play. The hero is torn between the diabolical debasement of bodily pleasures and the godlike exaltation of pure virtue—or perhaps, conversely, between the forgiveness that is divine and the pride that is satanic. As "The devils whom Faustus served" finally tear him apart (5.3.8), so Coriolanus is fatally divided, spiritually by the flight of the "whatsoever god" he has betrayed, and physically by a herd of commoners: "Tear him to pieces! Do it presently!—He kill'd my son!—My daughter!—He kill'd my cousin Marcus!—He kill'd my father!" (5.6.120–22). The net that ensnares the ambitious man has an appropriate character. Common humanity makes a sacrificial claim on him; and it does so on the basis of kinship, on behalf of the demands of common blood. A name like his own patronymic Martius slips in among those being avenged. His martial self has victimized both his hereditary self and its analogues in the common people; and they in turn collaborate to kill that martial self, which his mother has already prompted to a sort of preparatory suicide. No final flurry of swordsmanship can cut a new hero free from the unrelenting context of common, generational humanity, which here returns him to his mother earth.

~IV

Ambition and Original Sin
in *The Winter's Tale*

*T*HE *WINTER'S TALE* provides a useful epilogue and a happy
ending to my study of tragic ambition, much as *Henry V*
did to my study of historical ambition. In both cases, the destructive
elements from the earlier plays remain in view, as a foil for the
disrupted nation's healthy assimilation of the ambitious impulse
and its return to normal generation. This is not to say that *The
Winter's Tale* is as logical a successor to *Macbeth* and *Coriolanus*
as *Henry V* is to *Henry IV*. But the recurrence of the ambitious
stigmata in the very different case of Leontes helps us focus on the
analogy between his error and those of his tragic predecessors: all
dangerous and futile denials of filial limitations are, for Shakespeare,
versions of the basic ambitious violation.

This focus in turn, helps us recognize Leontes' evasion of his fallen
heritage as a precipitator of the play's crisis. The figure of the constraining father becomes increasingly metaphorical and universal in
the movement from the history plays' struggles over royal lineage
to Macbeth's murder of a paternal monarch, and then to Coriolanus'
repression of the citizenry whose mediocrity fills the paternal void
in his family history. This progression reaches its logical extreme
in the figure of Adam, who in *The Winter's Tale* haunts the stage
like a recessive version of old Hamlet's ghost, implicitly admonishing his children to "Remember me!" in remembering the burdensome and even fatal task his fall bequeathed to them. By recognizing
the talionic pattern governing all these cases of filial overreaching,
we can unite *The Winter's Tale*'s theology and its psychology—
which critics have studied extensively but separately—into a co-

herent message about the risks and the values of moral and cultural refinement. The political dilemma of Bullingbrook, obliged to overreach his place in the hierarchy in seeking to maintain it, evolves into the tragic ambivalences of Macbeth and Coriolanus, who are punished as inhuman for pursuing aspirations essential to the human spirit; in *The Winter's Tale,* these conflicts reappear as the Reformation paradox that made an acknowledgment of depravity and helplessness the necessary foundation for any ascent toward virtue. Leontes' presumptuous attempt to turn Sicilia into Eden renders him more bestial than angelic. But *The Winter's Tale* resolves this paradox, which limits the holiness a pious soul can deliberately attain, by another paradox, which bestows complete holiness on that flawed soul. The divided godhead that lured the earlier protagonists into impossible dilemmas becomes the paradoxically unified Christian godhead that allows Leontes to reunify his hereditary and ideal selves; Christ's humble obedience to his Father's will atones for the primal ambition that condemned humanity to the hereditary burden of original sin.

Closing the circle of this book's argument with an example at once eccentric and logically conclusive allows me to open my central idea to new possibilities. The interpretive pattern this book has been describing may be appropriately and usefully applied to themes (such as original sin) and protagonists (such as Leontes) not usually associated with ambition or its pseudo-sexual analogues. The overreaching in *The Winter's Tale* is more a broad representation of human aspiration than it is a specific case of ambition in its usual sense, and the ambitious pattern illuminates only one facet of the play's structural and ethical complexity. It is of course not my intention here to force, diffuse, or simplistically moralize the argument of either my book or Shakespeare's play. But the very fact that a version of the ethical pattern recurs in so distinct an instance clarifies the ethical foundations of Shakespeare's treatment of more conventional ambitions in the political plays. The extent to which this play's crisis resembles those of the earlier works provides a measure of how central the burdens of hereditary identity are to Shakespeare's understanding of ambition, since those burdens are the main point of correspondence between *The Winter's Tale* and its precursors; conversely, it provides a measure of how central the burdens of original sin are to Leontes' disintegration, since that is the one clear connection to the pattern of paternal vengeance.

The Winter's Tale also provides a more tolerant view of ambition and a more genial perspective on its hazards than my study of the earlier plays has attributed to Shakespeare. The fact that Coriolanus' struggle for personal virtue meets the same obstacles as Macbeth's struggle for wrongful political advancement should give us pause. The superficial moral has resembled the primitivism of Montaigne's later essays, granting the natural order both ethical and practical superiority over human art, human desire, and human discipline. But what becomes of this moral—"that we cannot go wrong by following Nature, that the sovereign principle is to conform to her"— if we believe that "the seed . . . implanted in every man who is not denatured" is inherited vice (as Protestant theology insisted) rather than instinctive virtue (as Montaigne argued)?[1]

Orthodox Elizabethan thought maintained that human concord with nature was impossible, and that human nature was evil, because of the Fall from the Garden; the effort to alter one's "nature" toward some public ideal was therefore more a duty than a crime.[2] The new Reformed Christianity, even more than the old Catholic beliefs, portrayed humanity as so profoundly corrupted that an artificial self would almost surely be preferable to the hereditary one. The connotation of the word "artificial," in fact, was as positive in the Elizabethan court as it is negative today.[3] Why then should heroic ambitions in Shakespearean drama always be doomed to retribution, always be portrayed as an empty theatricality undermined and even avenged by a mediocre natural order? Why should the self-regulating "new man"—a Puritan ideal—repeatedly take the sinister form of Shakespeare's Italianate villains? Are Shakespeare's plays so virulently anti-Pelagian that self-discipline and self-improvement must always appear as futile and mortal sins?

The Winter's Tale helps to answer these questions by distinguishing between unrealistic efforts to replace a limited human identity, and necessary efforts to regulate human nature and compensate for natural limitations. In terms of ambition, the transition from the pessimism of the tragedies to the optimism of the romances is a shift of emphasis rather than principle: Shakespeare turns from showing the world's punishment of unnatural aspirations to showing its endorsement of humble progress within the bounds of nature. By re-establishing art's foundation in nature, and correspondingly virtue's foundations in the frailties that are "Hereditary ours" (1.2.75), *The Winter's Tale* grants Leontes precisely what the histories and tragedies refuse their protagonists: safe passage back from the identity their ambitions have created, back into a place in regenerative nature and the divine favor it represents. In portraying the separation and reconciliation of families, the romances often portray the separation and reconciliation of hereditary and ambitious identities as well. The symbolic death of the self, like the deaths of relatives in the plots, proves to be a reversible illusion; the adopted self, like the adopted families in the plots, proves to be hereditary after all.

In the earlier plays, the protagonists are torn between their hereditary obligations to two father-figures who issue contradictory commands about their identities and obligations. Bullingbrook cannot respect both Gaunt's heritage and Richard's; Coriolanus must betray either the exalted or the common figurations of his absent father. Leontes is torn between the heritage of Adam, which makes him a sinner, and the heritage of God, which obliges him to purity. But in learning to acknowledge the limiting father Adam, Leontes learns how to ease that burdensome patrimony, through a penitent recognition of the natural grace that still inhabits the fallen world, and through a penitent plea for the supernatural Grace through which God reclaims his prodigal sons. He gains, through the greatest humility, what Shakespeare's protagonists had craved in their greatest ambitions: an identity at once filial and perfect.

Sicilia, Civility, and Eden

Leontes' ambition, like Macbeth's or Richard III's, entails a murderous attack on the royal embodiment of grace-in-nature—in this case, Polixenes.[4] Such an assault arises almost inevitably from the ambitious man's assault on his own human nature. As in the tragedies, the compromising forces of nature—in this case, sexuality and time, sin and death—return vengefully against the man who sought to deny their power. Coriolanus' quest for manly autonomy sends him weeping into his mother's arms; Leontes' quest for purity, amity, and social refinement leaves him plotting murders and ranting obsessively about barnyard sexuality. Procreative renewal, and its cyclical analogues in sleep and seasonal change, again desert the man who disdains the constraining order of which they are a part. A passage in a recent book aptly summarizes Leontes' error and its consequences: "Having wished to act as a god, he became like the irrational animals. The sin is greater than one can imagine. It has devastated the human family."[5]

The passage is not from a book about Shakespeare, however, but from a synopsis of Augustine's views about the Fall and original sin. The consequences of Leontes' overreaching persistently suggest a renewal of the consequences of the Fall: his own evolving sinfulness and mistrust of providence, his son's mortality, his wife's extreme suffering in childbirth, the harsh onset of seasons, and even the enmity between Antigonus and the bear. The preceding chapters have discussed the ways that aspects of Renaissance aspiration, whether toward political power or toward manly martial virtue, encounter the stubborn barriers of heritage—the constraints imposed by the conservative patriarchal order and by the limited natures of the individual fathers themselves. But the most important constraint on the aspiring minds of the Renaissance, the obstacle most often cited by their cautioning contemporaries, was the legacy of original sin bequeathed to each of us by our first father, Adam. Leontes defies this paternal constraint as foolishly as the other ambitious figures deny theirs, and suffers the same deranging consequences. The denial of the father's limiting legacy (the Fall) and the usurpation of the father's exclusive role (as unfallen man) trap the protagonist in an endless winter's tale. Northrop Frye observes that, in the tragic "Mythos of Autumn," when the hero disturbs "a balance in nature . . . *nemesis* happens, and happens impersonally, unaffected, as *Oedipus Tyrannus* illustrates, by the moral quality of human motivation involved."[6] But here the moral quality finally does affect the conduct of the nemesis: where the gods laugh at the ruined projects they have inspired in Macbeth and Coriolanus, the Christian God here redeems Leontes' family romance by intervening as the true father. In seeking the ultimate expansion of his cautionary pattern, Shakespeare has necessarily softened it.

Shakespeare would have had good reason to treat ambition in the context of original sin. His contemporaries such as Sir Walter Ralegh closely associated ambition with original sin.[7] Freudian theory, of which Shakespeare seems to have been so sharply prescient, views original sin as yet another mythic recollection of the patricide in the Primal Horde, the guilt of which is similarly passed on to each young man as his emergent sexuality arouses his own disobedient impulses.[8] Even Augustinian theory described original sin as a transaction suggestively similar to the one Shakespeare attaches to ambition: Adam was primarily guilty of "a sin of pride, a determined will to be like the gods. Man turned away from his creator [and therefore] became a bundle of contradictory tendencies, divided, scattered, a stranger to himself."[9] In his proud attempt to retract the Fall and deny his patrimony, Leontes necessarily repeats the Fall, and suffers the same self-alienation as Shakespeare's other unruly sons.

Leontes' error is not finally so different in character from the errors of those previous miscreants. In 1606, Edward Forset wrote that, as a man may ceaselessly attempt a further dilatation or extention of his nature (as to bee like unto God himselfe:) so doeth oft times a Soveraigne (haughtily conceyted of the likenesse he hath with his ordainer) strive . . . to bee extended beyond the compasse of any limitation. . . . as the one hath ever since beene stinted . . . by the organs of the body (the which to seeke to exceed is a renouncing of humilitie, yea a forgetting of our humane imbecilitie . . .) [similarly a monarch has limits] the which who so is not contented with, is accounted blamable of a presumptuous & unjust usurpation beyond the bounds to him assigned.[10]

Where Richard III, Henry IV, and Macbeth commit the usual political sort of usurpation, Leontes commits this figurative sort. The treacherous illusion of an ideal self, which earlier ambitious figures pursue in shedding the blood of others, Leontes presumes to recognize in his own royal blood. The Renaissance conceived of kingship as the divine creation of a man above men, potentially unmatched in wisdom and symbolically immortal in body, a conception that could easily promote moral as well as political arrogance in a monarch. One of the official Elizabethan sermons warns against such presumption, urging us all "to remember our mortal and earthly generation, which we have all of him that was first made: and that all men, as well kings as subjects, come into this world, and go out of the same, in like sort."[11] Another sermon warns that the attempt to override original sin is, paradoxically, itself a consequence of original sin, trapping Leontes' ambitions in the same sort of deterministic maze that frustrated the earlier ambitious figures: since Adam's Fall, "all that came of him have been so blinded through original sin, that they have been ever ready to fall from God and his law, and to invent a new way unto salvation by works of their own device."[12] Macbeth and Coriolanus seek to transcend their compromising births by becoming children of their deeds; Leontes tries to expunge his fallen taints by virtuous conduct, by acts of will that are supposed to mark him as "born again." Biology remains destiny in The Winter's Tale, a Lamarckian biology in which a trait such as fallenness can be passed on with the force of genetic fact. So the sharp superficial differences between political, martial, and theological ambition disappear at a deeper symbolic level. It is no mere coincidence that Pelagius and Luther, who represent the extreme opposite positions on man's ability to reshape himself and control his worldly destiny, also represent the extreme positions on the possibility of overcoming original sin.[13]

Original Sin in *The Winter's Tale*

This theological framing of the play may seem overly dry and abstract: Shakespeare was a playwright rather than a theologian, more concerned with human behavior than with doctrinal issues. But the issue of original sin would have seemed far less distant to Shakespeare's audience than it does to us, and he builds onto that doctrinal framework all the flesh-and-blood choices of human life: how to give gifts and compliments, how to treat families and guests, even how to take meals, pleasures, and rest. A proud misconception of human perfectibility can lead to the mismanagement of any of these activities. Since they cannot eradicate the fallen appetites underlying human misconduct, excessive prohibitions only encourage such misconduct to flourish in secret.

This is as true of individual self-censorship as of organized social repression. Shakespeare again suggests a parallel between conventional moralizations about political ambition, and his own anatomy of ambition's workings in the individual. Machiavelli warns his prince that "A man who wishes to make a profession of goodness in everything must necessarily come to grief among so many who are not good."[14] In *The Winter's Tale* as in *Coriolanus*, Shakespeare compresses the political pattern, whereby the idealistic prince is destroyed by his flawed subjects, into the microcosm of a single tragic character, whose higher faculties dictate an ideal identity that is destroyed by the unruly components of his own hereditary humanity. In *Civilization and Its Discontents*, Freud warns that the overly ambitious superego of either a psyche or a state actually promotes the id's rebellion, by demanding firmer controls than the ego can maintain.[15] As tyranny breeds rebellion, so an unrealistic severity of the puritanical or exalted instincts breeds violence from the animal attributes it seeks to eradicate, whether we echo Freud in calling those attributes the id, or the Elizabethans in calling them *peccatum originatum*, the residual depravity of original sin. As a 1573 tract explains, Elizabethans were not expected to become perfect, but rather "To mortifie themselves as nyghe as nature can."[16] Fallen men best combat their weaknesses, not by denying their existence, but rather by building upon that cracked foundation with due respect for its seismic instability. The aspiration to radical innocence can be a sin of moral complacency, and as such an ally of sin in less subtle forms: such an aspiration promotes jealousy, attempted murder, and blasphemy in Sicilia. Renaissance mistrust of such presumption is well exemplified by Charles Trinkaus' paraphrase of Valla: "moral idealism . . . in the end is a hypocritical unwillingness to accept the presence of the hedonistic motives in oneself, and a fastidiousness concerning the ordinary life of mankind. To impose the brake of convention on the storm of nature is fruitless and vain."[17]

The elaborate manners of the Sicilian court represent such a delusive convention (though more Epicurean than Stoic), and the storm of nature that overwhelms Leontes arises from a fastidious denial of ordinary fallen sexuality. Polixenes' memorable narrative of his boyhood with Leontes prepares us to understand this presumption, through the rest of the play, in specifically Christian terms:

> *Polixenes*   We were, fair queen,
>   Two lads that thought there was no more behind
>   But such a day to-morrow as to-day,
>   And to be boy eternal.
> *Hermione*   Was not my lord
>   The verier wag o' th' two?
> *Polixenes* We were as twinn'd lambs that did frisk i' th' sun,
>   And bleat the one at th' other. What we chang'd
>   Was innocence for innocence; we knew not
>   The doctrine of ill-doing, nor dream'd
>   That any did. Had we pursu'd that life,
>   And our weak spirits ne'er been higher rear'd
>   With stronger blood, we should have answer'd heaven
>   Boldly, "Not guilty"; the imposition clear'd,
>   Hereditary ours.   (1.2.62–75)

This is the first of several explicit "not guilty" pleas, proclamations of innocence that this precedent invites us to evaluate in terms of original sin. Critics disagree about whether Polixenes means that they would have pleaded innocent if not for the fact of original sin, or that they thought even original sin might be expunged by their childish innocence. Peter Lindenbaum argues for the latter reading, but concedes that it "makes less theological sense . . . (since it is impossible to plead 'not guilty' to original sin)."[18] But that is precisely the point: the error Polixenes attributes to his "boy eternal" frame of mind is the same error committed by Leontes in trying to extend that boyhood companionship indefinitely. The initial conflict between the kings seems so trivial, that the play threatens to become a treatise on house-guests. Polixenes feels he has stayed long enough, and Leontes politely asks him to stay longer. Many people have had such a dispute, and many have (like Leontes) become angrier with the guest for agreeing to stay than they would have been had he insisted on leaving. But Shakespeare uses Polixenes'

reminiscence of an Edenic delusion to suggest the impiety latent in
Leontes' good manners. By dismissing Polixenes' sensible concern
that he has burdened his hosts and ignored his royal responsibilities
long enough, Leontes is implicitly claiming that there will always
be "such a day to-morrow as to-day," and that no evil could possibly
have arisen to threaten the survival of Polixenes' kingdom or family.
Implicit in Leontes' plea for a longer stay is a renewal of that boyhood
plea of prelapsarian innocence.

Polixenes knows such a plea is no longer defensible, and his subjunctive presentation of it leads Hermione to posit, punningly, a
new Fall:

>   By this we gather
>   You have tripp'd since.
> *Polixenes*   O my most sacred lady,
>   Temptations have since then been born to 's: for
>   In those unfledg'd days was my wife a girl;
>   Your precious self had then not cross'd the eyes
>   Of my young playfellow.
> *Hermione*   Grace to boot!
>   Of this make no conclusion, lest you say
>   Your queen and I are devils.   (1.2.75–82)

No such conclusion is necessary, as Hermione presumably knows.[19]
Once the first devil induced the first Fall, the loss of innocence
became "Hereditary ours"; the violent expressions of concupiscence
at puberty are merely the emergence of a corruption present in us
all since our conception, and not the work of some new temptress.[20]
But Leontes, whether or not he overhears this particular conversation, seems to reach in earnest the conclusion his wife reaches in
jest. Having denied in his own mind that time and sexuality impinge
on his decorous court, Leontes inevitably mistakes their manifestations for active diabolical workings. If he and Polixenes were still
innocent at the start of this visit, then any discordant hints of concupiscence or mortality must be blamed on some recent evil seduction, and not on a passive inheritance of the primal seduction.
Hermione, who evokes his sexuality, and Polixenes, who warns about
evils bred in the passage of time, are the natural suspects when
Leontes seeks to arraign someone for ruining his Garden. Under
these psychological circumstances, Leontes' fantasy of a wicked seduction would seem to him the indisputable fact he insists it is. He
has simply deduced his verdict backward from his unexamined theological premise.

The language of the play often suggests a twisted re-enactment of events in Eden. John Anthony Williams argues that Leontes' denial of time and nature makes Sicilia resemble Richard II's untrimmed Garden of England:

> Uncultivated nature grows to wildness because it is fallen; it has succumbed to what Milton called the "ruins of our first parents" ["Of Education"]. The king is the husband-man who must clear away the "briers and darnell of appetite" [Book of the Courtier] from his state and his subjects.[21]

This duty Leontes disdains. Instead, he invites his court to believe that a thornless Eden is as near as the back gate. His determination to keep Polixenes under the same roof as the lovely Hermione month after month is an act of denial, of moral overreaching, similar in type if not in degree to Prospero's determination to lodge Caliban with the lovely Miranda. Polixenes knows that women can be a temptation when they cross a man's eye (1.2.77–80), and knows therefore how to resist it; but (like Prospero) Leontes at first provokes the bestial "thing of darkness" within himself by denying it is his. Leontes sends Hermione off alone with Polixenes, commanding her, "How thou lov'st us, show in our brother's welcome." Hermione overlooks his odd phrasing, which allows a standard exhortation to hospitality to be read as a redirection of her wifely affections, and answers,

> If you would seek us,
> We are yours i' th' garden. Shall 's attend you there?
> *Leontes* To your own bents dispose you; you'll be found,
> Be you beneath the sky. [*Aside*] I am angling now,
> Though you perceive me not how I give line.
> Go to, go to! (1.2.172–82)

Leontes has transformed himself from fisher-king to a diabolical version of Christ, the fisher of men. His bait is an apple of carnal knowledge, a temptation to be fruitful and multiply, which he offers to the pair's natural appetites; at the same time he becomes the garden's patriarchal judge. As his identity splits into its extremes of courteous generosity and ranting jealousy, Leontes makes himself both Satan and God in this new Fall. He gloats when he thinks he has exposed the moral frailties, the natural "bents" of the man and woman in the garden, knowing they cannot flee his judgment anywhere "beneath the sky." Eventually he claims the ability to de-

231

termine alone "the guilt or the purgation" that should follow on their behavior (3.2.7), a phrase generally glossed as meaning the legal guilt or exculpation, but which carries broader connotations—particularly when Leontes overrules Divine Judgment, in the form of the Delphic Oracle, to enforce his own.

In this re-enactment of the Fall Leontes studiously avoids the one role he must learn to accept: the sinning Adam. In Christian doctrine, the claim to autonomous godhead is quintessentially satanic. Similarly, in the zero-sum game that often thwarts ambition in Shakespearean drama, the quest for a godly identity tends to breed a satanic shadow-self that destroys its counterpart. In Eden, by most Renaissance interpretations, it was our first parents' determination to seize divinity that doomed them to mortality. In *The Winter's Tale*, Leontes' aspiration toward a pure sensibility seduces and corrupts itself, making him perceive ordinary human transactions as diabolical. His determination to view his world as unfallen makes him witness a renewed Fall, a distorted vision that proves self-fulfilling. He becomes his own serpent, "fork'd" and hissing with sibilants, by imagining himself a cuckold: "Thy mother plays, and I / Play too, but so disgrac'd a part, whose issue / Will hiss me to my grave...." (1.2.185–89). After trying to send Polixenes a poisoned drink, Leontes compares his acquisition of fatal knowledge—knowledge of "Good lost, and Evil got," as Milton puts it in *Paradise Lost* (X, 1072)—with drinking venom:[22]

> Alack, for lesser knowledge! how accurs'd
> In being so blest! There may be in the cup
> A spider steep'd, and one may drink; depart,
> And yet partake no venom (for his knowledge
> Is not infected).   (2.1.38–42)

The even-handed justice, as in *Macbeth*, commends the ingredients of our poisoned fangs to our own bodies.

Leontes fantasizes first his own unfallen condition, then the seduction that infects his garden, by the same psychological mechanism. Like Coriolanus, he has an alter ego, a foreign counterpart onto whom he projects his ideal self, and whom he then tries to embrace or even ingest.[23] At the same time, like Coriolanus, he projects those aspects of himself that hinder his quest for transcendence onto another, whom he tries to destroy. The boy Polixenes is the legitimizing mirror of his ambitions—a "twinn'd lamb" as Aufidius was a twinned lion—while the man Polixenes is the fabricated enemy of those ambitions. Most psychoanalytic interpretations of the play diagnose Leontes' jealousy as a displacement of his own repressed homosexual attraction to Polixenes; he supposedly tells himself preconsciously, "I don't love him; she does."[24] He dreams the adulterous act—"You had a bastard by Polixenes, and I but dream'd it" (3.2.83–94)—so that he can express his homosexual desire in an acceptably masked form, substituting his wife for himself. This seems to me to put the substitution on the wrong side of the bed: it makes more sense to suppose that he has replaced himself with Polixenes than that he has replaced himself with Hermione. Substituting Hermione would hardly be the way to make the scene morally acceptable, and we know for a fact that Leontes is replacing himself with Polixenes in interpreting this situation, because we know that Leontes truly performed the insemination he attributes to his friend. The waking mind's "secondary revision," as Freudian dream interretation suggests, is an excellent clue to the sleeping mind's symbolism. When Leontes chides Hermione that, in bestowing her sexual favors, "You have mistook, my lady, / Polixenes for Leontes" (2.1.81–82), he may again be accusing others of precisely what he is doing himself (as when he accuses others of poisoning drinks, disturbing his rest, or undermining his reign). The Leontes he witnessed fathering Perdita one night could have been so alien and repugnant to his rarified self-concept that he refused to recognize it as himself. So he escaped from the physical reality by changing it into a dream, then used the subjectivity of dreams to change his role from the perpetrator of concupiscence to its innocent victim. In aspiring to disown his animal nature, Leontes has created a divided self that can regard even its marital affections as evil and repugnant. Certainly the man who describes his wife's pregnancy as a swelling (2.1.62) perceives conjugal relations as a disease. One may of course argue that he hates the conception, the pregnancy, and the child simply because they are not his; but the play fits Shakespeare's deeper psychological patterns at least as well if we posit the opposite, that Leontes denies they are his because he hates the mortal frailties implied in the procreative process. This hatred connects the play's psychological and theological concerns. The concupiscence involved in the moment of conception, both Augustine and Aquinas assert, is the medium by which original sin is transmitted to each new child of Adam.[25]

Polixenes is an appropriate subject for Leontes' projection of his cruder natural aspects, because he is as much the king of unrefined nature as Leontes is the king of refined civilization. Shakespeare seems to have reversed the kingdoms of the two from his source

(Greene's *Pandosto*) to underscore this distinction.[26] Where Leontes denies the pressures of time, mortality, and procreation, Polixenes maintains a sensible perspective on them all. He fears what nine months might "breed" (1.2.12) back in his kingdom:

> Nine changes of the wat'ry star hath been
> The shepherd's note since we have left our throne
> Without a burthen. Time as long again
> Would be fill'd up, my brother, with our thanks. (1.2.1–4)

The procreative overtones of these nine lunar months of breeding are reinforced by Polixenes' diction. The idea of filling up that suggestive interval with thanks looks ahead to Hermione's plea later in the scene that the men "cram's with praise, and make's / As fat as tame things" (1.2.91–92). The word "burthen," furthermore, is used several times by Shakespeare to mean "the weight of a man's body during intercourse,"[27] and elsewhere in *The Winter's Tale* a "burthen" seems to be a full-grown fetus (4.4.263–64; cf. *Paradise Lost*, II, 767).

Polixenes recognizes the different seasons of the year and of a man's life. He reports that his son Florizel

> makes a July's day short as December,
> And with his varying childness cures in me
> Thoughts that would thick my blood. (1.2.169–71)

This is precisely the awareness of the curative role of generations, and of mortality's demand of such a cure, that is lacking in Sicilia. Like Macduff, Polixenes becomes a symbolic counterpart to the unnatural protagonist through a sensitivity to "The fits o' th' season" (*Macbeth*, 4.2.17). When he visits the sheep-shearing festival, he praises Perdita because "well you fit our ages / With flow'rs of winter" (4.4.78–79).

Leontes, in contrast, seems once to have known about seasonal renewal, but has forgotten the lesson in his dreams of immortality. When Hermione convinces Polixenes to stay longer, Leontes compares her successful speech to another gracious one:

> Why, that was when
> Three crabbed months had sour'd themselves to death,
> Ere I could make thee open thy white hand,
> And clap thyself my love; then didst thou utter,
> "I am yours forever."
> *Hermione*   'Tis Grace indeed. (1.2.101–05)

His language suggests a beautiful metaphor, Hermione's hand folded up through the three harsh, deadly months of winter, then opening up to renew life, a lily to the spring. But he misunderstands the nature of this Grace. By linking the metaphor to Hermione's promise of eternity—itself an overreaching version of "till death do us part"— he presumes that their marital spring will be eternal, and that the harsh seasons which man's Fall brought to his world will not invade his garden or his marriage.

If Leontes has not exactly forfeited the Garden of Eden, then, he has joined Shakespeare's other ambitious figures in forfeiting the garden of regenerative nature. The escape from a compromising natural legacy is again the punishment as well as the crime. The Oracle announces that "the King shall live without an heir, if that which is lost be not found" (3.2.135–36), and as in *Macbeth*, the babe who is victimized in the ambitious effort to abandon the natural order and the hereditary self becomes an empowered symbol of that lost order and that lost self. Polixenes tells Camillo,

> The King hath on him such a countenance
> As he had lost some province and a region
> Lov'd as he loves himself. Even now I met him
> With customary compliment, when he,
> Wafting his eyes to th' contrary and falling
> A lip of much contempt, speeds from me, and
> So leaves me to consider what is breeding
> That changes thus his manners.   (1.2.368–75)

Polixenes speaks more wisely than he knows. An overextension of manners has allowed a contrary force to go on "breeding" underneath—hate rather than love, and speechless animal passion rather than "customary compliment." Leontes, as his disdain to acknowledge Polixenes implies, has indeed lost a province "Lov'd as he loves himself": he has lost contact with his inner Bohemia, his own fallen nature, which unruled breeds trouble for them both.

When critics seek to explain the polite Leontes' explosion into animal rage, to consider for themselves "what is breeding / That changes thus his manners," they usually conclude with Camillo merely that " 'tis safer to / Avoid what's grown than question how 'tis born" (1.2.432–33). But to insist, with E. K. Chambers among others, that the play "will not have you apply too searching a psychology" because it is essentially a fairy tale, is to ignore both the psychological roots of fairy tales and the transformation Shakespeare works on that material.[28] The play's ethical pattern demands that all its supernatural events retain a foundation in human nature, and Leontes' inconsistent behavior is no exception. In fact, his "schizophrenia" follows R. D. Laing's model: as in *Coriolanus*, the ambitious man's destructive peculiarities arise from the schizoid tendencies of his society as a whole, divided between its reality and its chimerical ideal.

The exaggerated purity and artificiality of Sicilian language is a symptom that helps us trace this schizophrenia back to its source in moral idealism. In accusing Hermione of degrading his rarified court, Leontes calls her

> O thou thing!
> Which I'll not call a creature of thy place,
> Lest barbarism (making me the precedent)
> Should a like language use to all degrees,
> And mannerly distinguishment leave out
> Betwixt the prince and beggar.   (2.1.82–87)

He tries to uphold a verbal distinction—between queen and whore—even when he believes its real moral basis has collapsed. As language thus breaks loose from its foundations, in defense of decorum, Leontes' mannerly court identity breaks loose from his hereditary foundations. The linguistic schizophrenia parallels and even derives from the social one.

This symptomatic abuse of language begins in the play's opening scene, the sheer uneventfulness of which invites us to inspect it for other sorts of instructions about how to read the more substantial scenes that follow. The scene consists almost entirely of "customary compliment": all it conveys by way of exposition is that a king is visiting his old friend, another king who has a gallant son. The speakers here are a Bohemian and the most stable and realistic of the Sicilians, but they are functioning within their roles as courtiers in Leontes' palace, and their conversation therefore carries the germs of his court's disease.

Archidamus' promise that Camillo will see, when he visits Bohemia, "great difference betwixt our Bohemia and your Sicilia," is ominous because a "difference" often meant a conflict in Elizabethan usage, and the nations' names often serve as alternative names for the rulers themselves in the play; their conflict is what causes Camillo to visit Bohemia prematurely. Camillo's response that "this coming summer, the King of Sicilia means to pay Bohemia the visitation which he justly owes him" offers little reassurance, since he may decide he owes a vengeful visitation, like the one Hermione pays to Antigonus. This remark typifies the moral complacency of the Sicilian court: the benevolent meanings are so blithely assumed that they go unstated. Language itself may therefore be surprised by sin. By failing to reckon with the potential of evil, the possibility of as corrupt a reader as Leontes, such remarks (like the court as a whole) become susceptible to moral inversion by a single serpent, a single moment of evil interpretation. Once we perceive the first lines of this exchange in a negative way, the following speeches begin to sound like threats. Archidamus responds to the promise of a visitation with concern about how "our entertainment shall shame us." Language seems briefly to fail him in his search for words of sufficient praise and grandeur; when he finds such words, they prove to be the most disturbing yet: "we cannot with such magnificence— in so rare—I know not what to say—We will give you sleepy drinks, that your senses (unintelligent of our insufficience) may, though they cannot praise us, as little accuse us." In the following scene, Leontes urges Camillo to offer their guest Polixenes precisely this sort of shameful entertainment, using another silencing and soporific potion "To give mine enemy a lasting wink; / Which draught to me were cordial" (1.2.317–18).

When Archidamus asserts the reliability of his speech, Camillo answers with the most equivocal speech of them all, betrayed by his unmanageably high style:

> Sicilia cannot show himself overkind to Bohemia. They were train'd together in their childhoods; and there rooted betwixt them then such an affection, which cannot choose but branch now. Since their more mature dignities and royal necessities made separation of their society, their encounters (though not personal) hath been royally attorney'd with interchange of gifts, letters, loving embassies, that they have seem'd to be together, though absent; shook hands, as over a vast; and embrac'd as it were, from the ends of oppos'd winds. The heavens continue their loves!   (1.1.21–32)

The final exhortation prepares the same sort of cruel irony as Albany's "The gods defend her!" which immediately precedes Lear's entrance carrying Cordelia's body (5.3.257). The two kings, meeting as opposed winds, can be neither overkind nor entirely substantial to each other. They have branched away from their common natural root, and between them lies a terrible abyss that ceremony cannot safely bridge, perhaps because the rhetorical winds of ceremony partly constitute that abyss. They may fall into the void between them at any moment, and despite any physical proximity—fall, in fact, without knowing it. Leontes' rage will show how absent they may be from each other even when they seem to be together. Their society has itself become separation: Camillo's vague diction allows us to suspect that this loss of real contact, originated by the physical distance their royal duties required, persists in the majestic formality of their actual encounters.

Their quest for social exaltation, like quests for other sorts of exaltation in the other plays, has replaced human substance with a nullity. Polixenes tells his host that "like a cipher / (Yet standing in rich place), I multiply / With one 'We thank you' many thousands moe / That go before it" (1.2.6–9). This courteous remark, like those of Camillo and Archidamus, relies too much on a presumption about the cipher's substance and value, which the least shift in the rhetorical context could disturb. An early seventeenth-century poem warns,

> Though thanckfull hands and eyes may prove
> >Cyphers of love,
> >Yett, till some figure bee prefixt,
> As oos, by thousands or alone,
> >Stand all for none,
> >So, till our lookes and smiles bee mixt
> With further meaning, they amount
> To nothing by a just account.[29]

The smiles and thanks exchanged by the kings are such precarious ciphers, as Camillo's ambiguities have warned us. Royal ceremony cannot fully rectify the loss of "personal" identity in Shakespeare, as the history plays have demonstrated.[30]

Some of the ironies of Camillo's speech have already been noted by other critics, but their full import has not. Fitzroy Pyle insists that critics such as Derek Traversi who detect ambiguity here are mistaken, because if Camillo "were intended to imply the possibility of future dissention he would be far from happy about it."[31] But what Shakespeare intends to say and what Camillo intends to say are distinct issues. By having Camillo speak a truth he does not recognize, Shakespeare reinforces the notion that Sicilian decorum obstructs self-knowledge. The fact that Camillo intends to describe an ideal friendship is not only compatible with his speech's ironies; it actually adds a deeper level to those ironies. The unintentional ambiguities that foreshadow the conflict appear for the same reason

the conflict itself appears. The extreme politeness of the two courtiers, reflecting the excesses of the court in which they converse,
provides a perfect culture for the germs of monstrous misunderstanding to grow in. If Camillo and Archidamus were not using the
same courtly hyperbole that the kings use in the following scene,
then the adumbrations of the kings' conflict would never find room
to insinuate their speeches. Ornamented language resembles the
boy's sword described by Leontes, which may "prove (as ornament
oft does) too dangerous" (1.2.157–58).[32] Language overextended, as
Freud argues, often leaves space for the inadvertent expression of
plain and unpleasant truths. As the euphuistic language loses touch
with the basic meanings of its words, those meanings reassert themselves against the mannerly ambitions of Leontes, as they did (in
the deceptively literal prophecies) against the political ambitions of
Macbeth; the loss of touch with literal meaning corresponds to a
loss of touch with the hereditary confines of the self, and both invite
a nemesis. In linguistic terms, the lowly *paroles*, the individual
speech-acts, reassert themselves until they seem actually to overthrow the *langue*; the words rise up on behalf of their integrity and
alter the context that supposedly dictates their meaning. Accidental
puns are language's revenge against the speaker who demands too
much of it, destroying his aspiration toward an exalted meaning by
giving him more meanings than he desires, just as the divided self
is heredity's revenge against personal ambition. The lowlier aspect
of the word or self reappears and thus undermines the higher pretensions, and the undermining proves all the more mortifying because it does not dispel the speaker's or aspirer's commitment to
the pretense that is no longer tenable.

These verbal failures, which punish the linguistic aspect of Sicilia's cultural overreaching, help us to diagnose the ailment from
which they arise. Words participate in the vicious cycle of ambition,
punishing one act of filial defiance—Leontes' denial of Adam—with
their analogous rebellion against the language and the speakers that
generated them. The words in turn suffer the fate of such rebels:
their unfilial relation to their linguistic context and their speakers'
intentions costs them their coherence, dignity, and identity. The
grandiloquence reflects the grandiose social postures of the speakers,
and the collapse of the verbal artifice warns us that the speakers,
too, are on the brink of a mortifying fall. According to historians of
rhetoric, seventeenth-century writers came to mistrust the *genus
grande*, the elevated Asiatic-Ciceronian style of speech.[33] This mistrust is visible elsewhere in Jacobean drama, notably in Middleton's

The Changeling, where ugly sexual references arise repeatedly, like maggots, from the decaying fabric of courtly language. The higher a man tries to climb on that fabric, and the more weight he asks it to support, the likelier it is to send him plunging painfully down to the dirt of his original level. Such a plunge is part of Leontes' renewed Fall. While inhabiting the blunt, bestial aspect of his divided self, he cannot understand the courtly metaphors spoken around him. So Polixenes' announcement that, after a stay of nine lunar months, he is going to "multiply" by "standing" in a "rich place" could easily strike Leontes as a brazen public confession.[34] That Leontes misreads in this way becomes virtually unmistakable when Camillo tells him that Polixenes has agreed to remain longer "To satisfy your Highness and the entreaties / Of our most gracious mistress." Leontes rants, "*Satisfy?* / Th' entreaties of *your mistress? Satisfy?* Let that suffice" (1.2.232–35; emphases mine).

Leontes has become illiterate in the courtly *langue* that explains and disarms the sexual *paroles*. As Shakespeare demonstrates in *Henry V* (3.4.50–56), words that are polite in English become obscene if they are mistaken for French, and Leontes falls into an analogous hermeneutic schism. He perceives what might be expressions of sexuality—kisses for instance—apart from the social code that generates them and therefore defines their meaning. We see him on the stage watching his wife gaze fondly at Polixenes, hold his hand, perhaps even demurely kiss him. Such actions could be a legitimate basis for jealousy, except that they occur within a social artifice which boasts its immunity from "the doctrine of ill-doing" by encouraging them. If Leontes reads the behavior in front of him with the same brute literality he applies to Camillo's remarks about satisfying their mistress, then we need not wonder at the source of his suspicions.

Mark Van Doren describes Sicilia as a "frankly sensual place";[35] I suspect, on the contrary, that the Sicilians' elegantly sensual display deceives both them and us, by suggesting that sexuality has been safely sublimated into something more refined. The ostentatious liberalities of the host seem designed to insist that the baser impulses have been fully assimilated into the social artifice, that generosity will slake rather than heighten greed, and that civilized noblemen need not worry about playing with the fires of the id. But as Prospero learns from the rebellions of Antonio and Caliban, the fallen creature must not be led into temptation. Leontes' affected garden, like Prospero's island, finally serves to remind him that he is neither in Eden nor capable of staying there if he were. He now perceives sexual corruption in the very expressions of Platonic love by which he boasted of transcendence; his moral downfall evolves fittingly from his unsustainable moral pretense.

We can better understand the manner of this self-seduction by comparison to Othello, whose jealousy grows by a similarly over-literal and oversexual misreading of language and action. His incoherent outburst (4.1.35–44) contains many decontextualized echoes of crude sexual words from earlier polite conversations,[36] much as Leontes furiously echoes Camillo. Later in the scene, Iago sets Othello where he can witness Iago's provocative exchange with Cassio, but cannot hear the actual words that disarm the apparent abuses; Leontes watches Polixenes and Hermione from an analogous standpoint. Leontes differs crucially from Othello, however, because he serves as his own Iago. Several sets of strikingly parallel speeches between the two plays differ essentially in putting Leontes in both roles; compare, for example, *Othello*, 4.1.66–70 and 4.2.130–36, with *The Winter's Tale*, 1.2.192–96 and 2.1.141–43 respectively, with the ironies in both cases intact. If to some extent the Iago-Othello relationship becomes the psychomachia of a single person, divided into what is best and worst in his humanity, then to some extent Leontes has divided himself (as ambitious figures in Shakespeare tend to do) into two similarly polarized men. Leontes then creates his own false context, arouses and nurtures his own jealousy, and undermines his own marriage, reputation, and spiritual standing through a destructive ambition. Even the defenses of the slandered women are strikingly parallel efforts to put the evidence back in the context of the courtly system that encouraged it:

> *Desdemona*   I never did
>   Offend you in my life, never lov'd Cassio
>   But with such general warranty of heaven
>   As I might love.   (5.2.58–61)

> *Hermione* I lov'd him as in honor he requir'd;
>   With such a kind of love as might become
>   A lady like me; with a love even such,
>   So, and no other, as yourself commanded.   (3.2.63–66)

Leontes, like Othello and Lear, fails to recognize that the expressions of love generated by a social ceremony may actually amount to "nothing":

>   Is whispering nothing?
>   Is leaning cheek to cheek? is meeting noses?

. . . . .
>   Is this nothing?
> Why then the world and all that's in't is nothing,
> The covering sky is nothing, Bohemia nothing,
> My wife is nothing, nor nothing have these nothings,
> If this be nothing.   (1.2.284–95)

This is a desperate effort to stave off the sense of nullity that attacks ambitious figures in Shakespeare, but the obsessive iteration overwhelms the syllogistic denial, and the facts turn the syllogism against him. Again an overtaxed rhetoric rebels against its enslavement, at the same moment that human nature misreads and deflates an exaggerated code of courtesy. In his *Conversion of the Sinner*, Pascal explains that when the soul loses its temporal and spiritual bearings, it discovers with terror that "all it loves" has become "perishable as already corrupt or falling into corruption. . . . Hence comes the fact that the soul begins to consider as nothing everything which will return to nothingness, the heavens, the earth, its own spirit and body, its relatives, friends and enemies."[37] The recognition of mortality Leontes has been resisting insinuates his accusatory rage, feeding on his struggle to deny it. Ambition is again generating its own talionic and didactic nemesis. Soon the "ceremonious" Oracle induces the bodily death of Leontes' son, whose name (Mamillius) and nicknames ("egg" and "calf") mark him as a creature of regenerative nature; Leontes' denial of fallibility and mortality has rendered itself untenable. The essential message of the Delphic Oracle in this play is the message that, according to Plutarch, stood above the entry to the actual Delphic Oracle: "Know Thyself." When death arrives in the garden, the purgatorial fantasy Leontes was enforcing against Polixenes, Hermione, and Perdita loses its rationale, its premise. Leontes must recognize in himself all at once the fourfold wound that Aquinas attributed to original sin, consisting of malice, error, concupiscence, and mortality, a wound made all the more severe by his presumption of invulnerability.[38]

The nation, as in the earlier plays, suffers a briefer version of its monarch's foolish alienation from the natural order; but here the emphasis characteristically shifts from a defiance of the political hierarchy to a defiance of original sin. The self-dividing impact of Leontes' purgatorial project becomes more evident, and threatens to become contagious, when he demands Camillo's assistance in killing Polixenes: "Do't, and thou hast the one half of my heart; / Do't not, thou split'st thine own." Contemplating this unnatural choice,

Camillo refers to Leontes as "one / Who, in rebellion with himself, will have / All that are his so too. To do this deed, / Promotion follows" (1.2.348–56). Leontes has in fact been leading Camillo into temptation, into hazardous ambitions, by such promotions all along, nurturing in him an almost divine new identity: Leontes describes Camillo as a creature "whom I from meaner form / ... rear'd to worship" (1.2.313–14). This is conventional ambition, but it also clearly echoes Polixenes' explanation earlier in the scene that he and Leontes fell from innocence because their "weak spirits" were eventually "higher rear'd / With stronger blood" (1.2.72–73).

Leontes leads Camillo toward his theological sort of ambition by casting him as a perfect absolver of sin, remarking how often

> priest-like, thou
> Hast cleans'd my bosom: I from thee departed
> Thy penitent reform'd. But we have been
> Deceiv'd in thy integrity, deceiv'd
> In that which seems so. (1.2.237–41).

The word "integrity" seems to slip from its common meaning, as honesty, back to its Renaissance theological meaning, as the term for Adam's perfect capacity to resist evil through his unfallen will and reason. Leontes merely means that Camillo, who has been trusted so near his heart, should have told him about Hermione's supposedly well-known adultery; but the transition in this speech seems to imply that Camillo has negligently abdicated an ability to purge all sin from the court. That, at least, is the charge that Camillo seems primarily to be answering, in replying that any failings Leontes has observed can be explained as ordinary fallen human behavior, and not necessarily as malice, dishonesty, or some other form of deliberate misconduct:

> My gracious lord,
> I may be negligent, foolish, and fearful:
> In every one of these no man is free
> . . . . .
> these, my lord,
> Are such allow'd infirmities that honesty
> Is never free of. But beseech your Grace
> Be plainer with me, let me know my trespass
> By its own visage. If I then deny it,
> 'Tis none of mine. (1.2.249–67)

This conclusion enrages Leontes, since it runs entirely against the grain of his moral ambitions, and he accuses Camillo of being "a hovering temporizer, that / Canst with thine eyes at once see good and evil, / Inclining to them both" (1.2.302–04). Significantly, what Leontes intends as a bitter accusation may strike us as simply a description of a fallen man's normal condition, which he must recognize in order to regulate. Even the word "temporizer" implicitly accuses Camillo of accepting the temporality that Leontes tries vainly to resist.

The other members of the Sicilian court prove susceptible in varying degrees to the moral illness bequeathed them by their Adam-like patriarch. *The Winter's Tale* is of course a play and not a sermon, but the allusions to the difference between specific and general guilt, between adult and infant guilt, and between merit and grace are so persistent and so strategically placed that we must be conscious of the doctrine if we are to make proper use of the moral index Shakespeare is providing. Hermione and Paulina, for example, fail to match Camillo's doctrinal humility. When Hermione accuses Polixenes of casting her and his own wife as devils, by making them responsible for their husbands' loss of innocence, she overlooks a subtle but important distinction: women may be an efficient cause of men's concupiscence, but not the first cause. All seductions are merely the distant but inevitable echoes of the primal one. Hermione is not a trained theologian of course; she may even be playfully accusing Polixenes of the very doctrinal error I have attributed to her. But when she defends her daughter's innocence and her own, she revealingly omits Camillo's acknowledgment that claiming innocence to Leontes' charges in no way entails a claim to total innocence. Hermione's first speech in answer to the official accusation stresses heredity: she describes herself as "a great king's daughter, / The mother to a hopeful prince," and describes her cause as the defense, not of her individual life, but rather of the honor which is "a derivative from me to mine" (3.2.39–45). Her emphasis on heredity makes us more conscious of her failure elsewhere in the speech to acknowledge the corruption that is "Hereditary ours," derivative to her and hers from even such an exalted father. She begins by complaining that "it scarce shall boot me / To say 'Not guilty'," since her supposed lack of "integrity" is the premise of the trial (3.2.22–28). The precedent of Polixenes' abandoned "Not guilty" plea invites us to examine this one for theological error, and therefore directs our attention to the word "integrity." She is right to claim she has maintained her integrity, as opposed to dishonesty, just as she is right to claim innocence of Leontes' specific charges; but we have seen precedents warning us how easily and dangerously these exact claims can expand into moral presumption unless they are carefully defined.

Hermione uses several other theologically loaded terms in this speech, in ways that suggest an inadvertent tendency to claim precisely the rights and characteristics Adam surrendered by his Fall, and Leontes implicitly claims for his court. She portrays herself as the embodiment of "innocence," reminding Leontes "before Polixenes / Came to your court, how I was in your grace, / How merited to be so" (3.2.30–48). The notion that one could gain "grace" by "merit" was anathema to orthodox Christians, and advanced only by Pelagians who denied that original sin had any absolute impact of the individual's moral being. Furthermore, she claims an inaccurate parallel to Adam's situation in suggesting that she cannot have forfeited her lord's grace unless she sinned with the man he sent into the garden with her. Adam's sin with the woman his Lord introduced into his Garden undermines Hermione's innocence, integrity, and merit, whether or not she re-enacts the original crime. The official Elizabethan "Sermon of the Salvation of Mankind" warned people to trust only God's mercy, and not their own good works, "to obtain thereby God's grace and remission, as well of our original sin in baptism, as of all actual sin committed by us after our baptism."[39] Hermione muddles this distinction almost as badly in answering Leontes' charges as he does in concocting them. She closes her speech by insisting that she has not violated her honor "in act"— which is perfectly true—or in "will / That way inclining," which may be true regarding adultery with Polixenes, but which sounds like a broader denial of concupiscence, the fallen susceptibility of the human will (3.2.51–52). The echo of Leontes' absurd attack on Camillo for having a normal human will "Inclining to" both "good and evil" is clear enough, indicating that Hermione shares to some extent her husband's moral presumption.

Leontes and Hermione then argue briefly about whether she is partly accountable for the proverbial truth that the guilty are always wicked enough to deny their guilt; but they have already both confirmed the doctrinal maxim that original sin induces an evil tendency to deny original sin. Hermione concludes the dispute by saying, "More than mistress of / Which comes to me in name of fault, I must not / At all acknowledge" (3.2.59–61). This can be read as parallel to Camillo's defense, which admits to the common faults of fallenness while denying Leontes' specific charge. But since it leads directly into a defense of her love for Polixenes, her answer more likely means, "I must not admit being answerable for anything more than that [honorable love] which is now being called a fault."[40] Again the parallel with Camillo suggests a slight presumption in Hermione.

Hermione's assumption that guilt arises only from sinful deeds, and not from heredity itself, becomes clearer when she tells her infant daughter, " 'My poor prisoner, / I am innocent as you' " (2.2.25–27). An Elizabethan theologian would likely have added, as guilty too. She may be as innocent of worldly misconduct as the babe, but to an audience highly conscious of the sinfulness transmitted at conception, her phrasing would have seemed dangerously general. One of Pelagius' close associates was condemned for the shocking assertion that "new-born infants are in the same state as was Adam in innocence."[41] Intending to use her infant as a model of pure innocence, Hermione inadvertently reveals the one active sin she could reasonably be accused of: the sin of moral complacency.

Paulina's comments on the relative innocence of Hermione and Perdita closely echo Hermione's errors on the same subject. In demanding that the jailer release the infant Perdita from her mother's cell, Paulina approaches and then swerves perceptibly away from the problem of hereditary sin:

> This child was prisoner to the womb, and is
> By law and process of great Nature thence
> Freed and enfranchis'd, not a party to
> The anger of the King, nor guilty of
> (If any be) the trespass of the Queen.   (2.2.57–61)

This "not guilty" plea lacks the sharp qualifications it receives from Polixenes, who limits it to the illusions of childhood, and from Camillo, who limits it to one specific crime as opposed to others. Paulina simply means that, even if Hermione were guilty of adultery, the child would not be, and hence should not be imprisoned; but what she says is subtly yet importantly different. It may be only a careless error, but carelessness about this hereditary burden is the problem. The parenthetical "(If any be)" should certainly remind us of the "trespass" in which both the queen and her children are hereditarily implicated, a guilt supposedly communicated from parent to child prior to this "enfranchising" process of birth.[42] Paulina's evasion of this doctrine takes exactly the same revealing form as Eve's evasion of her Fall in *Paradise Lost*, where she urges Adam "To undergo with mee one Guilt, one Crime, / If any be, of tasting

246

this fair Fruit" (IX, 971–72). In both cases the rhetorical qualification suggests a will to forget the nature of original sin, whether in its primal or residual form.

To clarify Paulina's error, Shakespeare provides the Sicilian lords with sharply contrasting responses to Leontes' wild accusations. The limited "not guilty" plea is spoken by the lords together, in answer to the charge that Antigonus "set on" Paulina to plead for the infant: "My royal liege, / He is not guilty of her coming hither" (2.3.144–45). Even more striking is the First Lord's insistence "that the Queen is spotless / I' th' eyes of heaven and to you—I mean, / In this which you accuse her" (2.1.131–33). The fact that this lord draws back so hurriedly from the claim of heavenly purity he hears himself making reveals the boldness of Paulina's similar claim.

A pious defense concludes, not with a claim that heaven itself could find no taint, but rather with a plea that heavenly Grace forgive the taints it finds. Even in *The Merchant of Venice*, where Antonio (like Hermione and Perdita) is condemned only by a harsh literal doctrine, Shakespeare's heroine undertakes this humble sort of defense (4.1.184–202; cf. *Measure for Measure*, 2.2.73–77). But when Paulina presents the babe to Leontes, she describes Hermione as a "gracious innocent soul" (2.3.29)—all loaded words—and skirts the issue of the infant's hereditary sin in a way that calls our attention to it. She says Perdita is "So like you, 'tis the worse," a small-print version of what is now fully legible in the father; and she calls on the "good goddess Nature, which hast made it / So like to him that got it," not to replicate the father's moral form as accurately as it has his physical form (2.3.96–108). She is referring to his jealous temper, but we have seen that this temper is essentially an outgrowth of original sin itself, the latent evil that has become legible in the adult man because of just such a wish to exclude it. In acknowledging heredity, Paulina has symptomatically omitted the one degrading likeness all children inherit from their parents.

Paulina's plan—to recall Leontes from his destructively superhuman course by confronting him with a family resemblance—strongly resembles Volumnia's plan for retrieving Coriolanus. Paulina's statement of her intentions might serve as an epigraph for the family confrontation in *Coriolanus:* "We do not know / How he may soften at the sight o' th' child: / The silence often of pure innocence / Persuades where speaking fails" (2.2.37–40). The risks in the two plays are also similar. Coriolanus furiously destroys any reminders of his bodily mortality that do not destroy him first, and Leontes vows to eradicate the evidence of his procreative identity in the same way. As Coriolanus repeatedly insists on burning the Roman citizenry and later his own family, so Leontes five times orders the burning of Perdita and/or Hermione in act two, scene three—perhaps a kind of trial-by-fire, or purgatorial preparation, for entry to his supposedly unfallen realm. He threatens Paulina with the same fate, apparently on the grounds that she is "a mankind witch" managing the conspiracy to make him accept Perdita as the flesh of his flesh (2.3.114, 68). Part of his evidence for the epithet is her refusal to obey her husband; again Leontes mistakes the normal consequences of the Fall (Eve was conventionally understood as the first disobedient wife) for some diabolical evil currently at work in his court.

A war against the procreative order, as in the earlier plays, has become an inevitable concomitant of ambition, the war against the hereditary self. Leontes' family, like Niobe's in an Elizabethan emblem, seem to be slain "That mortall men, shoulde thinke from whence they came, / And not presume, nor puffe them up with pride."[43] After reconciling himself to his mortal fallibility, Leontes acknowledges this order of cause and effect, bemoaning

> The wrong I did myself; which was so much
> That heirless it hath made my kingdom, and
> Destroy'd the sweet'st companion that e'er man
> Bred his hopes out of. (5.1.9–12)

His self-betrayal has robbed Hermione, as she herself reports, of both the means to make life and the will to live. Instead she hopes for death, because she has lost her husband and first child, and because her new babe

> is from my breast
> (The innocent milk in it most innocent mouth)
> Hal'd out to murther; myself on every post
> Proclaim'd a strumpet; with immodest hatred
> The child-bed privilege denied. (3.2.99–103)

The assault on procreative order echoes *Macbeth*. When the king denies his hereditary limitations, whether as subject or as sinner, the entire nation endures a loss of issue. Antigonus even threatens to "geld" all his children, and thus in effect "glib myself," if Leontes' accusations prove correct (2.1.147–50).

The regenerative cycle of sleep again breaks down alongside that of procreation. Sleep may be particularly inimical to Leontes' ambition, because it becomes associated (as in *Hamlet*) with the entrance of the serpent sexuality into the garden. North's Plutarch, which Shakespeare had been using extensively, reports that Alexander the Great "did understand that he was mortall by these two things: to wit, sleepe and lust: for, from the weaknes of our nature proceedeth sleepe and sensualitie."[44] Leontes' moral idealism requires an unblinking vigilance against what Banquo calls "the cursed thoughts that nature / Gives way to in repose" (*Macbeth*, 2.1.8–9). He must especially avoid the pleasures of his bed, pleasures he apparently projects onto Polixenes in such a dream of wickedness. Leontes demands of those who question his accusation,

> Dost think I am so muddy, so unsettled,
> To appoint myself in this vexation, sully
> The purity and whiteness of my sheets
> (Which to preserve is sleep, which being spotted
> Is goads, thorns, nettles, tails of wasps)
> . . . . .
> Could man so blench?   (1.2.325–33)

But ambition makes men "no man" in Shakespeare, and Leontes tortures himself by splitting into two parts, one a punitive god, the other a sinful animal. Leontes' ambition entails a mortification of his fallen fleshly impulses; the garment in which he "appoints himself" resembles the ascetic's hair shirt. He has again unwittingly played his own Iago, who told Roderigo that people can regulate the "carnal stings" and "nettles" in the "garden" of themselves, then went on to plant these in Othello's Edenic bed and thereby ruined his sleep (1.3.320–32; 3.3.330–63). These same "thorns and thistles" invade Adam's garden as punishment for original sin (Genesis 3:18). In contrast, the amoral and sensual Autolycus can announce, "For the life to come, I sleep out the thought of it" (4.3.30).

Wakefulness may thus reflect an unnatural moral elevation in Leontes, as it does an unnatural political elevation in Shakespeare's usurpers. Alexander Ross's *Mystagogus Poeticus* remarks that "ambitious and tyrannicall spirits . . . have rest neither night nor day."[45] In his tyrannical phase, Leontes suffers this sort of insomnia: "Nor night, nor day, no rest. It is but weakness / To bear the matter thus— mere weakness" (2.3.1–2). In struggling to expunge original sin, he has merely contracted a severe version of it, as Luther describes it: "The holy Fathers have said that original sin is concupiscence (*fomes*), the law of the flesh, the law of the members, a weakness of nature, a tyrant, a congenital illness."[46] Leontes imagines he can regain "a moi'ty of my rest" by sending Perdita "to the fire" (2.3.8), just as Richard III hoped to regain his sleep by murdering the princes (4.2.73):

in both cases, the children prevent sleep because they are specters of the procreative system that constantly threatens to recall the men from their ambitious outposts. But neither man can cure his "congenital illness" simply by attacking its symptoms or symbols. Paulina works on the opposite assumption, hoping to bring Leontes back into contact with nature by showing him the new child who so resembles him. She associates the infant, as evidence of natural continuity, with the restoration of sleep:

> *Second Servant* Madam—he hath not slept to-night, commanded
> None should come at him.
> *Paulina*   Not so hot, good sir,
> I come to bring him sleep. 'Tis such as you,
> That creep like shadows by him, and do sigh
> At each his needless heavings, such as you
> Nourish the cause of his awaking. I
> Do come with words as medicinal as true,
> Honest as either, to purge him of that humor
> That presses him from sleep.   (2.3.31–39)

She offers the generational resemblance of the babe as a healthier substitute for the mirroring resemblance of these "shadows." Sleep in Shakespeare continues to depend on the natural integrity of the self, and therefore on acceptance of one's place in the hereditary order.

The seasonal cycle, as in *Macbeth*, withers along with nature's other regenerative cycles. Leontes' Edenic fantasies soon confront the postlapsarian reality of winter, and as Northrop Frye suggests, winter generally represents the reality of death. The fratricidal death of Adam's son, the shepherd Abel, first enforced that reality on humanity; and here Leontes' attempt on the life of his twin lamb Polixenes, and the death of his son Mamillius, renew the bitter lesson. The wintry barrenness that punished Macbeth now threatens, in Paulina's prophecy, to punish Leontes as well:[47]

>   A thousand knees,
> Ten thousand years together, naked, fasting,
> Upon a barren mountain, and still winter
> In storm perpetual, could not move the gods
> To look that way thou wert.   (3.2.210–15)

Leontes must now confront the darker side of the eternity he foolishly claimed for his court, not the eternal spring of Hermione's lily-like acceptance, but rather the lonely winter of the natural gods' vengeance, made eternal when his deadly rage leaves his son's winter's tale perpetually unfinished.

Fittingly, Leontes' life becomes suspended at precisely the same point as Mamillius' story, which is interrupted after telling us only that "There was a man . . . Dwelt by a churchyard" (2.1.29–30). The penitent Leontes vows to take up just such a residence for the remainder of his life, conceding in the process that he has become a new sort of fallen Adam, bringing mortality and perpetual guilt into the world:

> Prithee bring me
> To the dead bodies of my queen and son.
> One grave shall be for both; upon them shall
> The causes of their death appear (unto
> Our shame perpetual). Once a day I'll visit
> The chapel where they lie, and tears shed there
> Shall be my recreation. So long as nature
> Will bear up with this exercise, so long
> I daily vow to use it.   (3.2.234–42)

Not yet attuned to salvation by Grace, Leontes expects no resurrection to relieve his awesome burdens of mortality and guilt. But he is contrite for the sort of sin he knows he has committed, and therefore accepts a penance regulated by time and nature in which time does not seem to progress, nor nature provide any recreational impetus. His "rooted . . . affection" for Polixenes (1.1.23–24) and his "root[ed] opinion" about Hermione (2.3.90) had lost their natural basis, and all that thrives in his Garden is a version of Lady Macbeth's "rooted sorrow" (5.3.41). Leontes has moved from echoing the first stanza of Donne's "Twicknam Garden" to echoing the second:

> Blasted with sighs, and surrounded with teares,
>   Hither I come to seeke the spring,
>   And at mine eyes, and at mine eares
> Receive such balmes, as else cure every thing,
>   But O, selfe traytor, I do bring
> The spider love, which transubstantiates all,
>   And can convert Manna to gall,
> And that this place may thoroughly be thought
>   True Paradise, I have the serpent brought.
>
> 'Twere wholsomer for mee, that winter did
>   Benight the glory of this place,

> And that a grave frost did forbid
> These trees to laugh and mocke mee to my face;
> But that I may not this disgrace
> Indure, nor leave this garden, Love let mee
> Some sensless peece of this place bee;
> Make me a mandrake, so I may groane here,
> Or a stone fountaine, weeping out my yeare.[48]

But the play does not move on into the bitter paradoxes of Donne's final stanza, nor are we left, as in Shakespeare's tragedies, to watch the protagonist's alienation from self and nature take its deadly toll on him. Instead, we escape to a different world, with a complementary set of values, even a complementary set of errors. This natural garden redeems time and nature from the general curse that Leontes, by denying their reality, has brought them to; a figurative version of the Edenic Garden he sought to construct allows him to fulfill a figurative version of his ambitions without losing his place in God's order or in nature's.

Redemption and the Bohemian Garden

Immediately after Leontes resigns himself and his country to wintry stagnation, the scene shifts to an entire new world. The first three lines after his despairing vow tell us that we are in wild Bohemia, under an open sky, and tossed by swiftly changing weather. The shift of locale from one country to another is only the geographic aspect of this scene's highly complex transition, which is an exhilarating but frightening release from physical, spiritual, and temporal claustrophobia. The forces of nature Sicilia imprisoned and slandered lie waiting here in ambush, and attack the courtier Antigonus as the hapless emissary of that artificial world. Antigonus is carrying some dangerous baggage: his own version of Leontes' dream-induced doubt about Perdita's legitimacy (3.2.82–84; 3.3.16–46), and a ludicrously overcivilized notion of the workings of fallen nature. Taking up Perdita to begin the mission Leontes spitefully assigned him, Antigonus says,

> Come on, poor babe.
> Some powerful spirit instruct the kites and ravens
> To be thy nurses! Wolves and bears, they say,
> Casting their savageness aside, have done
> Like offices of pity. (2.3.185–89)

Such handsome notions do not apply, as the young shepherd mentions, when the creatures are hungry (3.3.130–31). A real bear soon enforces a more realistic idea of its character on the emissary, despite his distinctly Sicilian protest, reported by the young shepherd, that "his name was Antigonus, a nobleman." The bear, not impressed, then "mock'd him" and consumed him (3.3.96–101).

The brutality of the scene raises for the audience a question that has troubled Christian minds over the centuries: "But how did man so lose his mastery over creation that irrational animals can devour him? [Augustine's] answer is that the present state of mankind is the consequence of sin. In paradise it had been totally different, and man's forfeited powers will be restored to him at the time of the resurrection."[49] The devouring of Antigonus by the bear, like the devouring of Leontes by the wild beast within him, is fallen nature's appropriate (if harsh) response to the presumption of paradise. Antigonus is truly "gone for ever" (3.3.58), and Leontes will be trapped in a barren ritual until the babe spared by the bear returns from Bohemia, first to symbolize, then to inspire, the redemptive resurrection of Hermione. On the Bohemian shore, Antigonus has only a very marginal understanding of the regenerative force he holds in his arms. He expresses the hope that the money and documents he leaves with the child will "breed thee" (3.3.48), whereas her breeding will depend more on the kindly nature of the shepherds than on such civilized Sicilian artifacts. The shepherds soon arrive to bury Antigonus and nurture this "Blossom" (3.3.46) who receives from his death a new life.

The figure of Time itself follows this transitional scene, and speaking (like Duncan and Malcolm) in terms of "growth" and "planting," propels us into Bohemia's ongoing natural life. When Leontes accused Hermione and Polixenes of "wishing clocks more swift; / Hours, minutes; noon, midnight" (1.2.289–90), he simply meant that they eagerly awaited each night's adulterous pleasure; but in the context of his other implicit denials of time, we may infer on a secondary level that he was accusing them of accelerating time itself, thereby compromising the roles of boy eternal and eternal host by which he claimed immortality. As long as he holds his wife's seduction responsible for bringing sexuality into his garden, he may as well also hold it responsible for the intrusion of time. But his effort to deny and even overthrow Father Time proves as futile as the earlier filial rebellions, and the ambitious figure again sees even his normal patrimony threatened when the father retakes authority. When the figure of Time requests that we "imagine me, / Gentle spectators, that I now may be / In fair Bohemia," the phrasing implies more than a change of setting. Time itself, as the character of Leontes' crime invited, and as the character of his penance indicates, has virtually ceased to exist in Sicilia. With his wife's "death," Leontes, like Macbeth, disappears into a series of meaningless "to-morrows," and renewal takes place only outside his kingdom, among his more "natural" enemies.

But the transition to Bohemia is not simply a renaissance of nature; it is the first step in a rapprochement between nature and artifice. The second half of the play points less to the abandonment of custom and civility than to the redemption of those notions by rediscovering their foundations. By the same token, the tragic portrayal of an ambitious identity destroyed gives way to the romantic portrayal of an ambitious identity saved by the recovery of its hereditary basis. The choral figure of Time, the most conventional sort of theatrical artifice, serves to introduce the drama of nature. Time's boasted ability "To plant and o'erwhelm custom" resubordinates social habit to a regenerative process, and his offer to "give my scene such growing / As you had slept between" provides a dramatic transition by the very forces of maturation and restfulness that distinguish the new locale from the old. The self-defeating manners of Leontes' overextended hospitality stand in grim contrast to the basic hospitality of the shepherds, which is a spontaneous response to Perdita's real human needs. At the sheep-shearing festival, guests are greeted with flowers and food rather than prolonged encomia, and the hosts worry more about buying and preparing the meal than they do about "customary compliment."

The language of the play similarly supports the ethical pattern, regaining health as it regains contact with literal meanings. The rhetorical absurdity of the first scene, where the metaphors clash with their forgotten literal meanings, prepares the social absurdity of the second scene, where good manners, out of touch with their basic purpose, clash with the underlying human sentiments. The overpopulation of dead metaphors in Sicilian speech foreshadows and helps create the ghost-town of Leontes' penance. Ernest Schanzer points out that Polixenes' "poetic embroideries" comparing himself and Leontes to "twinn'd lambs" yield later in the play to the shepherds' practical discussions of real sheep, and that the figurative references to planting and growing in the first half of the play "reappear in the second half on a more literal level in the horticultural debate between Perdita and Polixenes."[50] The same rule may be applied to images of birth: "issue" is generally used metaphorically early in the play (2.2.43; 2.3.153; 3.1.22), but from the moment Antigonus arrives in Bohemia (3.3.43) to the final reconciliation (5.3.128), the term tends to refer to actual human offspring.

The play now appears to be systematically divided into two opposing camps:

Sicilia	Bohemia
city	country
art	nature
ceremony	spontaneity
social artifice	human nature
figurative language	literal language
age	youth
linear time	cyclical time
dreams	senses/sleep
acts 1–3	act 4

Such a chart reveals the range of levels on which Shakespeare creates the contrast we feel. And if Shakespeare had permitted Bohemia to wage a vengeful war to free Sicilia from its withered tyrant, the right hand column marching against the left, we would have a play strongly resembling *Macbeth* in its ethical pattern and symbolic action. But Shakespeare's last plays tend to resolve, by miraculous reconciliations, the same sorts of divisions and conflicts that prove fatal in plays written only a few years earlier. The romances find ways to defuse the tragic threats of usurpation, political naiveté, premature death, incest, and the illusion of adultery; and *The Winter's Tale* defuses the subtler threat of moral idealism that defeated Coriolanus. As families in the romances ultimately reunite after a long and hazardous separation, so do the two sets of values charted above, and so, therefore, do the adopted and hereditary identities.[51] Without the natural Bohemian basis, artificialities—manners, morals, language, marriage—become monstrosities. But with that basis, they become the "art / That Nature makes" which Polixenes defends so strongly (4.4.91–92), facets of the world's beauty, such as gillyvors, which only human endeavor can incite nature to produce.

The first scenes in Bohemia establish the opposed terms, and alert us to the need for a combination, by showing us a starkly natural world that is refreshing after three acts in Sicilia, but not altogether desirable in itself.[52] The depredations of the storm on the crew, the bear on Antigonus, even Autolycus on the clown, remind us that

255

Original Sin in *The Winter's Tale*

natural law can be as capricious and tyrannical as ceremonial law. Where Sicilia denies the forces of time, sexuality, and mortality, Bohemia is obsessed by them. The old shepherd's first speech begins by lamenting the misbehavior accompanying puberty, and ends with the deduction that Perdita is the product of heated fornication; he then calls his son over to "see a thing to talk on when thou art dead and rotten" (3.3.59–81). Sin and death are on the son's mind too. Seeing the gold left with Perdita, he tells his father, "if the sins of your youth are forgiven you, you're well to live" (3.3.120–21); he then talks about the drowning of the mariners, the eating of Antigonus, and the obligation to bury what is left of him. The figure of Time itself appears next, followed by Camillo's complaint that "It is fifteen years since I saw my country; though I have for the most part been air'd abroad, I desire to lay my bones there." Polixenes resists this plea with a similarly morbid figuration: " 'Tis a sickness denying thee any thing; a death to grant this" (4.2.2–6). Their conversation then turns to the illicit sexual motives that have apparently been drawing Florizel away from the court. Autolycus begins the following scene by singing about seasons, flowers, animals, and "tumbling in the hay," worrying about the prospect of hanging rather than about any "life to come."

By the time we arrive at act four, scene four, we may therefore be ready to regret the abandonment of the moral struggle that felt so oppressive in Sicilia. At the sheep-shearing festival, the chain of being seems to lie in a chaotic heap on the grass. Perdita speaks casually and publicly of Florizel's "Desire to breed by me" as if they belonged to some lower order of creation (4.4.103). Conversely, when she describes a flower closing at night and opening in the morning wet with dew, her wording fairly drips with overtones of human seduction and subsequent regrets: "The marigold, that goes to bed wi' th' sun, / And with him rises weeping" (4.4.105–06). Florizel's remarks show even less respect for hierarchies and solemnities:

> Apprehend
> Nothing but jollity. The gods themselves
> (Humbling their deities to love) have taken
> The shapes of beasts upon them. Jupiter
> Became a bull and bellow'd; the green Neptune
> A ram and bleated; and the fire-rob'd god,
> Golden Apollo, a poor humble swain,
> As I seem now. Their transformations
> Were never for a piece of beauty rarer,

Nor in a way so chaste, since my desires
Run not before mine honor, nor my lusts
Burn hotter than my faith.
Perdita   O but, sir,
Your resolution cannot hold when 'tis
Oppos'd (as it must be) by th' pow'r of the King.   (4.4.24–37)

She means that his intention to marry her must yield to his ceremonial duties, but his speech should also make her fear that his
resolution to respect her chastity "cannot hold when 'tis / Oppos'd
(as it must be)" by the appetitive power that Bohemia embodies.
The speech is laden with Freudian slips, most prominently the entire
comparison of his disguise to those of various gods who descended
from higher stature only long enough to seduce or rape maidens and
then abandoned them. Perdita should think carefully about her own
image of the marigold, which is left weeping after the sun takes her
to bed. Florizel hastens to cover his tracks in the second half of his
speech, but the lurking pun on "chaste" and the image of his desires
not running before his honor only further remind us of Apollo's
destructive pursuits of mortal maidens. At the same time, his diction
may remind us of Christ as a much purer sort of deity whose love
led him to humble his shape and walk among his inferiors. That
better sort of love, and the Incarnation by which it answers man's
Fall from Grace, are far beyond the ken of the Bohemians, who are
celebrating a merely natural sort of regeneration. Their innocent
ignorance of the need for Grace prepares us to appreciate the Christian aspects of Hermione's mock-incarnation, just as Leontes' willful
ignorance of the Fall's impact on nature prepares us to appreciate
the natural aspects of Hermione's survival.

The excesses that disturb the harmony of the sheep-shearing festival and prevent the marriage are opposite to the ones that disrupt
the Sicilian court and its central marriage. The faults in Florizel's
language and behavior are negatives of the same faults in Leontes,
and may therefore serve to redress the imbalance. The young man's
desire to eternize Perdita's graceful youth bears some resemblance
to Leontes' determination to remain "boy eternal" with Polixenes:

When you speak, sweet,
I'ld have you do it ever; when you sing,
I'ld have you buy and sell so; so give alms;
Pray so; and for the ord'ring your affairs,
To sing them too. When you do dance, I wish you
A wave o' th' sea, that you might ever do

> Nothing but that; move still, still so,
> And own no other function. Each your doing
> (So singular in each particular)
> Crowns what you are doing in the present deeds,
> That all your acts are queens.　　　　　　(4.4.136–46)

However greatly they differ in pleasantness and mental health, Florizel and Leontes alike become so entranced by a mundane representation of grace that they forget the need for otherworldly Grace. Natural affection can no more assure such perpetuation than ceremonial manners can: only the combination of the two, resulting in legitimate procreation, can perpetuate the youth and beauty of humankind. But if Florizel commits a version of the error that ruined Leontes' marriage—a neglect of the rule of Ecclesiastes, that each thing has its own time and season—his image of eternity as "A wave o' th' sea" suggests an awareness that this world offers eternity only through cyclical renewal and not through stasis. There may be no new thing under the sun, but each new wave or babe reproduces a former one as if it were new again—as the blossom Perdita reproduces her mother's lily-like betrothal. Perdita is playing three overlapping roles in this scene: she is partly a new bride, the symbol of human regeneration, partly Flora, the goddess of vegetative renewal (4.4.2), and partly Proserpina, the figure who connects the cyclical human escape from death with the cyclical return of vegetation. While playing these roles, she necessarily perceives death as only a normal and unthreatening counterpart to sexuality, and is utterly unshaken by the idea of Florizel's flower-strewn "dying," in either sense (4.4.129–32). So Florizel may be half-consciously acknowledging something essential and redemptive about Perdita, in the very sort of praise that represented Leontes' half-conscious decision to overlook the essential mortality of those closest to him.

In the last two lines of his speech, Florizel implies that physical "acts" take precedence for him over the ceremonial heritage of royalty—a heritage dismissed as "dreams" three times in this scene. Where Leontes dreams of rampant appetitive nature (3.2.82), the shepherd predicts (with inadvertent acuity) that the hidden princess Perdita will bring Florizel "that / Which he dreams not of," and the hidden prince Florizel promises Perdita "more than you can dream of yet" (4.4.179–80, 388). When her royal marriage seems doomed, Perdita announces, "This dream of mine / Being now awake, I'll queen it no inch farther" (4.4.448–49). The natural and sexual values the Sicilians repress, and the ceremonial and hierarchical values the

Bohemians repress, surface exactly where a psychoanalyst would expect repressed material to surface: in their respective dreams.

Perdita consistently represses the artificial on behalf of the natural, inverting her father's errors in the process. Florizel refuses to buy her any of Autolycus' finery, because "She prizes not such trifles as these are. / The gifts she looks from me are pack'd and lock'd / Up in my heart" (4.4.357–59). This is an admirable alternative to the hollowly gift-laden way love was formerly exchanged between the two royal families (1.1.24–31). Furthermore, if David Kaula is correct in claiming that Autolycus' trumpery represents Catholic relics and indulgences,[53] then Perdita's emphasis on gifts of faith is an admirable alternative and an appropriate corrective to her father's implicit belief in the saving power of worldly ornamentation. But the Puritanical mistrust of ornament can be carried too far, even in defense of nature. In expressing this same strict preference during the debate about the gillyvors, Perdita commits an inverted version of the error her father committed in rejecting her. He banished her as a "bastard," apparently because unrefined nature had a part in her making. She banishes these "blossoms" (the name Antigonus gave her) from her "garden" (the name the Sicilians gave the place where Leontes perceives the adultery) because she considers them adulterated by the artificial part of their creation. She desires such a mixture "No more than were I painted I would wish / This youth to say 'twere well, and only therefore / Desire to breed by me" (4.4.101–03). Cosmetics, revealingly popular with the women of the Sicilian court (2.1.8–15), may represent an ethical danger analogous to the other Sicilian excesses. As Ben Jonson writes, the thicker the lady is painted and ornamented with "th' adulteries of art," the safer it is to assume that underneath "All is not sweet, all is not sound."[54] In fact, Paulina characterizes Leontes' jealousy as that sort of extravagance: "Here's such ado to make no stain a stain / As passes coloring" (2.2.17–18).

But meretriciously painting over one's faults differs crucially from eliciting one's natural beauty by artificial additions, just as denying one's fallen nature differs crucially from nurturing one's remaining virtues by sensible social customs. By showing Perdita and Leontes overlooking these distinctions, *The Winter's Tale* urges us to remember them. The sheep-shearing scene evokes and then shatters the supposition that keeping in touch with agricultural nature corresponds to keeping in touch with hereditary nature. In the pastoral setting that Renaissance writers often used to espouse a primitivist ethic, Shakespeare compromises the apparent primitivist ethic of several earlier plays. Here human life and legacy can be as badly disrupted by a pure obedience to nature as by the pursuit of artificial ambitions. The dark undertones of *Macbeth* and *Coriolanus*, which resemble Florentine philosophy in suggesting that mere submission to nature is itself unnatural for human beings, become forthright and redemptive toward the end of *The Winter's Tale*. As Pico's *Oration* suggests, God's gift to Adam of choice and self-consciousness authorizes us to improve on our original nature, if such a thing can be said to exist at all; the same legacy of free will that permitted original sin to occur remains with us as an obligation to virtue. To respect our heritage is to battle our hereditary frailties.

Shakespeare hints at this paradox by making Florizel necessarily deny his royal patrimony in pursuing an exclusively natural passion, just as Leontes must deny his fallen patrimony to pursue a strictly artificial purity. As his ambush by the unconsidered guilt of Adam's accident renders Leontes a wild-acting "feather for each wind that blows" (2.3.154), so Florizel describes his father's intervention as "th' unthought-on accident" that "is guilty / To what we wildly do" as "flies / Of every wind that blows" (4.4.538–41). The verbal echoes where there is little parallel in meaning are Shakespeare's invitation to associate the two incidents. In fleeing the constraints that are, Polixenes would tell them both, hereditary theirs, Leontes and Florizel perform desexualized versions of the ambitious man's Oedipal crime, and briefly lose their procreative hopes as a result. Both attempt to defy and even replace their limiting fathers: Adam, who forbids Leontes to ignore his natural impulses, and Polixenes, who forbids Florizel to obey them. Where Leontes imagines himself as something like Adam, Florizel imagines himself as his own "heir" and as King of Bohemia, promising Perdita, "Or I'll be thine, my fair, / Or not my father's; for I cannot be / Mine own, nor anything to any, if / I be not thine" (4.4.42–45). Obviously he would not be much without being his father's as well: Shakespeare's plays are full of characters who become nullities, not "anything to any," by thus defying paternal authority. After the paternal force—this time the father himself—confronts him and forbids the marriage, Florizel reasserts this claim, but he sounds as if he were trying to reassure himself that his identity is still intact, like a man feeling himself after a bad fall: "Why look you so upon me? / I am but sorry, not afeard; delay'd, / But nothing alt'red. What I was, I am" (4.4.462–64). Fruitful marriage in Shakespeare generally requires a dutiful filial identity;[55] Florizel's loving promise effectively invites disaster to befall his engagement.

Redemption and the Bohemian Garden

Florizel's narrow devotion to natural values also determines the type of disaster that will occur. Where Leontes' devotion to artificial values caused the vengeful return of the old Adam within him, along with brute sexuality and mortality, Florizel's father spies on him from behind a theatrical artifice, then attacks him on behalf of ceremonial royalty. Polixenes bursts from behind his mask, threatening to punish in kind what he sees as Perdita's crime against decorum and his son's crime against succession:

> Mark your divorce, young sir,
> Whom son I dare not call. Thou art too base
> To be acknowledg'd. Thou, a sceptre's heir,
> That thus affects a sheep-hook!
> . . . . .
> I'll have thy beauty scratch'd with briers and made
> More homely than thy state. For thee, fond boy,
> If I may ever know thou dost but sigh
> That thou no more shall see this knack (as never
> I mean thou shalt), we'll bar thee from succession,
> Not hold thee of our blood, no, not our kin,
> Farre than Deucalion off.   (4.4.417–31)

In threatening to avenge these offenses, Polixenes virtually recommits them. Perdita's beauty is actually the proper representation of her royal birth; and forbidding her father's wish "To die upon the bed my father died, / To lie close by his honest bones" (4.4.455–56) can hardly serve the hereditary order. In the last part of his tirade, Polixenes makes the same sort of ethical error in disavowing his son—an act reminiscent of Leontes' disowning of Perdita—as his son made in disavowing him. This speech only serves to escalate the conflict in Florizel, who now echoes his father's parenthetical threat—"he shall miss me (as, in faith, I mean not / To see him any more)" (4.4.494–95)—and simultaneously (like Macbeth) sets the entire process of generation *against* his hereditary obligations. If he leaves Perdita at his father's command, "Let nature crush the sides o' th' earth together, / And mar the seeds within! Lift up thy looks. / From my succession wipe me, father, I / Am heir to my affection" (4.4.478–81). He cannot be heir to his natural affection any more than Leontes could be heir to his artificial affectations; his phrase recalls such failures of ambition to supplant heredity as Richard III's promise to make Tyrell "inheritor of thy desire," and Volumnia's announcement that she has seen in Coriolanus "inherited my very wishes."

Original Sin in *The Winter's Tale*

Camillo repeatedly interrupts Florizel's oaths with pleas for reason and reconsideration, as he did Leontes' tirades earlier. Throughout the play Camillo is the good and steady advisor, retaining the
balance between natural and artificial values that is lost in the two
kingdoms he serves, and leading an exodus to the opposite when
the imbalance precipitates a crisis. The parallels between these two
hasty departures suggest graphically the play's mistrust of both extremes. The first follows Leontes' plea that Polixenes stay yet longer
away from his homeland; the second follows Polixenes' similar appeal to Camillo, against similar objections. The Sicilian crisis emerges
when Leontes watches his wife and friend embrace, and murmurs,
" 'Tis far gone" (1.2.218); the Bohemian crisis surfaces when Polixenes watches Florizel and Perdita embrace, and whispers, "Is it not
too far gone? 'Tis time to part them" (4.4.344). Intriguingly, Camillo
is given a soliloquy on both occasions to weigh his choices, and each
time his decision to flee to the other kingdom is based on a perfect
balance of principled Sicilian philanthropy and pragmatic Bohemian
self-serving:

> If I could find example
> Of thousands that had struck anointed kings
> And flourish'd after, I'ld not do it; but since
> Nor brass nor stone nor parchment bears not one,
> Let villainy itself forswear't. (1.2.357–61)

> Now were I happy if
> His going I could frame to serve my turn,
> Save him from danger, do him love and honor,
> Purchase the sight again of dear Sicilia. (4.4.508–11)

Camillo is therefore precisely the counselor this couple needs in
its struggle to convert natural affection into a ceremonial bond. He
prescribes for them a theatrical ploy which both literally and symbolically assists their effort to reach Sicilia and there achieve marriage. Echoing the phrase "royally attorney'd" that typified the
overceremonious marriage of the two kingdoms at the start of the
play (1.1.27), Camillo promises to have the couple "royally appointed, as if / The scene you play were mine" (4.4.592–93). Perdita
sees that "the play so lies / That I must bear a part," and Florizel
adds, "Should I now meet my father, / He would not call me son."
(4.4.655–58). Camillo thus helps interrupt generational continuity,
but only for the sake of curing such a breach. By giving them roles

and disguises—they are not "like themselves" in the interim, as both Florizel and Leontes note (4.4.588, 5.1.88–89)—Camillo corrects their excessive naturalism, using the same theatrical device that led to their wedding's postponement. Such a correction symbolically qualifies them for entrance into Sicilia, where life has become the poor player's meaningless and monotonous hour upon the stage, just as it practically permitted their escape from Bohemia. Like the statue of Hermione, they are nature smuggled back into the dead kingdom under an artificial guise. The dramatic metaphor that haunted ambition in the earlier plays now serves as a corrective, bringing back the procreative order in a form the self-alienated king and kingdom can assimilate. As the Bohemian ships hastily set sail, they set a course back from the destructive extremes.

The new garments therefore disguise the young people's natures only for the purpose of restoring them to their fathers and their ceremonial identities. The notion that garments can lastingly change one's social standing, implicit in Lady Macbeth's and Volumnia's metaphors and evident in the period's sumptuary laws, here is located only in the clowns, where it can be pleasantly satirized. As Perdita's nobility shows through her peasant trappings, so Autolycus' baseness is evident even to the gullible Bohemians: the old shepherd concludes, "His garments are rich, but he wears them not handsomely" (4.4.731–50). Autolycus gains his revenge two scenes later, when the shepherds absurdly insist that their expensive new "robes" are themselves "gentlemen born" and make their wearers such. At the same time, the shepherds take their metaphorical greeting by the royal family as "brother" and "father" literally, a humorously disarming version of Leontes' overly literal reading of "customary compliment" earlier in the play. The shepherds' mistake also playfully disarms the ambitious "family romance" of earlier plays, in which people claimed to be part of an exalted lineage to which their original birth gave them no right. To have been "gentlemen born . . . any time these four hours" is, as Autolycus suggests, entirely ridiculous (5.2.125–45). But it is ridiculous in a way that distances the characteristic errors of ambition from the main characters' redemptive reunion.

We arrive back in Sicilia shortly before the first Bohemian ship, and we quickly recognize how badly Sicilia needs the reunion. The repetitive cycle of Leontes' mourning has not forestalled aging, and the Sicilian lords, worried about "his highness' fail of issue," open the scene by urging him to remarry:

> *Cleomines* Sir, you have done enough, and have perform'd
> A saint-like sorrow. No fault could you make
> Which you have not redeem'd; indeed paid down
> More penitence than done trespass. At the last
> Do as the heavens have done, forget your evil,
> With them, forgive yourself.   (5.1.1–6)

Paradoxically, this assurance that Leontes' penance has eradicated all his earlier faults actually indicates that those faults still infect the Sicilian court. The diction is relentless in its theological implications, which are all too similar to those of earlier remarks underestimating the residual burden of original sin. Cleomines credits his king with "saint-like" conduct that has already "redeem'd" every conceivable "fault," that has actually outweighed his primal "trespass." Such forgiveness belongs only to heaven, according to Elizabethan doctrine, but this speech makes Leontes a co-executor of God's elective Grace.[56] Cleomines' plea that Leontes "forget your evil" is another example of Sicilia's careless diction concerning innocence: he simply means that Leontes should now put his mistreatment of Hermione out of his mind, but his phrase reminds us that he mistreated her because he was determined to forget his evil in a more general sense.

But, under Paulina's guidance, Leontes is no more susceptible to his former sort of presumption than he is to his lords' entreaties for a new marriage. He tells Cleomines that his childlessness is the rightful punishment for his violation, and when Paulina reminds him that the mortal sin which destroyed his marriage is permanent in its effects, he accepts that the wages of his error is death, though that fruit is "bitter / Upon thy tongue as in my thought" (5.1.6–19). The reward for this new-found humility is the return of the lost regenerative flowers, Perdita and Florizel, a counterpart to the destructive return of "the seeds of Banquo" and those of Duncan to Macbeth's Scotland. In greeting the young couple, Leontes carefully acknowledges his own sinfulness and his kingdom's diseased mortality:

> The blessed gods
> Purge all infection from our air whilest you
> Do climate here! You have a holy father,
> A graceful gentleman, against whose person
> (So sacred as it is) I have done sin,
> For which the heavens, taking angry note,

Have left me issueless; and your father's bless'd
(As he from heaven merits it) with you,
Worthy his goodness.   (5.1.168–76)

Like the Sicilians discussing innocence earlier in the play, like Caliban dreaming of the heavens in *The Tempest* (3.2.140–43), Leontes
is groping with the darkened outlines of a Christian revelation, but
unable yet to see it face to face. Instead, he displaces onto Polixenes
the characteristics of the Christian God, the "sacred," "graceful"
and "holy father" whose "goodness" actually "merits" every conceivable "blessing," and "against whose person" Leontes has "done
sin." The theological emphasis of this passage is far too persistent
to be accidental, and what it suggests is Leontes' growing recognition
of his more abstract sin, though he cannot yet recognize its real
character or its real victim.

Leontes' first words to the young couple suggest that his moral
convalescence in other areas is similarly encouraging but incomplete:

Your mother was most true to wedlock, Prince,
For she did print your royal father off,
Conceiving you. Were I but twenty-one,
Your father's image is so hit in you
(His very air) that I should call you brother,
As I did him, and speak of something wildly
By us perform'd before. Most dearly welcome!
And your fair princess—goddess! O! alas,
I lost a couple, that 'twixt heaven and earth
Might thus have stood, begetting wonder, as
You, gracious couple, do; and then I lost
(All mine own folly) the society,
Amity too, of your brave father, whom
(Though bearing misery) I desire my life
Once more to look on him.   (5.1.124–38)

The first sentence acknowledges that a child's physical resemblance
to the husband proves the wife's fidelity—precisely what Leontes
refused to believe, in his deep mistrust of the senses, at Perdita's
birth. The last six lines submit "wonder" to the process of "begetting," and credit both to the "grac[e]" expressed in the couple's
bodily nobility. The final few lines clearly contrast with the Sicilians' former denial of time, suffering, and death, specifically as dis-
played in their patriotic but unrealistic attitude toward Mamillius:

Original Sin in *The Winter's Tale*

"They that went on crutches ere he was born desire yet their life to see him a man" (1.1.39–41). Faced with Florizel, Mamillius' parallel in age and role (1.2.163–72; 5.1.115–23), Leontes hopes only to survive in pain long enough to see the boy's father, not the boy's own maturity. Certainly the Leontes who declares himself "a friend" to the young couple's "desires" at the end of the scene accepts human sexuality better than the man who furiously rejected the idea that he could have fathered Perdita.

The middle part of his speech, however, indicates that Leontes' education on these points is not yet complete. He perceives Perdita as a "goddess"—what her costume at the sheep-shearing had made her—and places the couple " 'twixt heaven and earth." As he displaces his earlier godly role more humbly but still wrongly onto Polixenes, so he displaces his role as an immortal inhabitant of Eden onto this pair; good and lovely as they may be, they are not Adam and Eve any more than he and Hermione were. The hard-won generational distinction threatens to collapse in Leontes' impulse to embrace young Florizel as if he were the young Polixenes. Though for the moment Leontes keeps this impulse safely in the subjunctive, as Polixenes did his "not guilty" plea, we sense its appeal to him.

Later in the scene, the time-denying impulse returns and conquers him in a parallel case of substitution, a case clearly designed to make us morally mistrustful of such a tendency:

> *Florizel*   Beseech you, sir,
> Remember since you ow'd no more to time
> Than I do now. With thought of such affections,
> Step forth mine advocate. At your request
> My father will grant precious things as trifles.
> *Leontes* Would he do so, I'ld beg your precious mistress,
> Which he counts but a trifle.
> *Paulina*   Sir, my liege,
> Your eye hath too much youth in't. Not a month
> 'Fore your queen died, she was more worth such gazes
> Than what you look on now.
> *Leontes*   I thought of her,
> Even in those looks I made.   (5.1.218–28)

As plausible and sufficient as this reply may seem, it reveals the dangerous absurdity of a moral idealism that leads toward incest; indeed, in Shakespeare's source, the Leontes-figure tries to seduce his unrecognized daughter, and threatens her with rape when she resists him. Even with his only son dead, Leontes finds himself in

266

a sort of Oedipal struggle, because his desire to be "boy eternal" leads him to desire a girl-eternal version of his wife.

The same problem recurs when, on seeing the statue, Leontes protests,

> Hermione was not so much wrinkled, nothing
> So aged as this seems.
> *Polixenes*　　　　　　　　O, not by much,
> *Paulina* So much the more our carver's excellence,
> Which lets go by some sixteen years, and makes her
> As she liv'd now.　　　　　　　　　　　　　　(5.3.28–32)

He still tends to prefer the version of Hermione that time-denying art would conventionally strive to create, rather than the version nature would have created had she survived. But art and nature are so thoroughly interwoven in the symbolic presentation that Hermione and Perdita form a web of integrated identity, a safety net through which he cannot fall, because "the art itself is Nature," to use Polixenes' earlier formulation (4.4.97). The human Perdita is praised as static art, and only the supposed statue shows nature's progress. Where Macbeth could reunify himself neither by resolute advance nor by tedious retreat, Leontes finds a saving integration of natural and artificial identities every way he turns.

But only Perdita's return can rouse into life the latent nature in Leontes' and Hermione's artificial poses. Leontes declares the young couple "Welcome hither, / As is the spring to th' earth," and a servant calls Perdita "the most peerless piece of earth, I think, / That e'er the sun shone bright on" (5.1.151–52, 94–95). Paulina immediately chides the servant for forgetting Hermione "As every present time doth boast itself / Above a better gone," but Perdita is rightly time's choice to replace Hermione. The servant's poem, which Paulina bitterly reminds him had declared that Hermione " 'had not been, / Nor was not to be equall'd,' " was merely a typical piece of Sicilian art, emptily flattering the royal family with the illusion that it could overcome time. The very fact that the poem has itself been refuted by time is the most fitting commentary on it.

As the transplanting of Bohemia's flora restores Sicilia's natural foundation and thereby ends its unnaturally prolonged winter, the fantastic "winter's tale" regains a reality that allows it to progress toward a happier season. The stories of destructive and redemptive nature are repeatedly described as "like an old tale" (5.2.27–29, 61; 5.3.116–17), but they are also described in words that associate them with the procreative miracle that allows them to be true. The report that Leontes has "found his heir" is "Most true, if ever truth were pregnant by circumstance," and the story of Paulina's statue gives hope that "some new grace will be born" (5.2.29–31, 110–11; cf. 132). The play's ethical pattern forbids it to win its audience with unnatural events, as Autolycus' ballads about unnatural births and diets do. Instead, the restoration of naturally-born children and natural appetites makes the reunions so wonderful "that ballad-makers cannot be able to describe it" (5.2.24–25). The elements of fantasy and artificiality persist in these closing scenes, but in a form that allows Shakespeare to show they are actually part of a natural reality whose scope and worth (as in *Macbeth*) have been badly underrated, and whose miracles are so frequent and ubiquitous that we tend to overlook them. The characters on stage disable our suspicions that this is all merely an old tale or a magical conjuration, by echoing those suspicions and then putting them aside as the miracle of nature unfolds.

Act five, scene two, returns the linguistic arts to their natural basis, and prepares us for the statue's reconciliation of art and nature, by the way it describes the reunion of Sicilia with its Bohemian exiles. The play has moved from the courtiers' dangerous assumption, in the opening scene, that flowery language could fully embody their kings' mutual affection, to concessions by two Sicilian gentlemen that their words cannot adequately describe the wordless expressions of the kings' reunion (5.2.9–19, 42–58). Natural feeling, once smothered by ambitious language, is here protected from language by a double wall of humility. The Third Gentleman reports the next reunion in terms that suggest the convergence of artificial elements of identity with natural ones: he speaks of "unity in the proofs," which include Hermione's garment and Antigonus' letters as well as "the majesty of the creature in resemblance of the mother; the affection of nobleness which nature shows above her breeding; and many other evidences [that] proclaim her with all certainty, to be the King's daughter" (5.2.30–39). The association of nobleness with nature, and of majesty with hereditary physical appearance, suggests that the false distinctions that disrupted Bohemia are disappearing along with those that disrupted Sicilia.

In closing his description of the reunion scene, the Third Gentleman furthers our impression that art is being reincorporated into nature, by remarking that "Who was most marble there chang'd color" (5.2.89–90). This grand metaphor, like those of the play's opening speeches, will soon become much more literal than its speaker can anticipate; but this time the literal level provides reconciliation rather than "separation" (1.1.26). Four lines later, he informs us that the court have all gone to see the statue of Hermione, "a piece many years in doing and now newly perform'd by that rare Italian master Julio Romano, who, had he himself eternity and could put breath into his work, would beguile Nature of her custom, so perfectly he is her ape." This description recalls Leontes' promise in the preceding scene not to remarry "Unless another, / As like Hermione as is her picture, / Affront his eye," which will only be "when your first queen's again in breath," when the work of art becomes again a work of nature (5.1.73–84). But Julio Romano's potentially Promethean powers are kept safely in the subjunctive here, like Polixenes' earlier speculations on escaping original sin, or Leontes' recent ones on ignoring generational time. The Sicilian court has learned that cultural endeavors alone, however skillfully refined, can provide neither eternity nor natural life to inhabit it. The Gentleman adds, "Thither with all greediness of affection are they gone, and there they intend to sup" (5.2.102–03). The hearty affections and appetites that were Bohemia's great merits have returned to cold, abstemious Sicilia.

Paulina promptly puts this new naturalness to the test—a sort of Rorschach test—by presenting the statue for evaluation in a radically cultural and ceremonial context. The setting as well as the occasion encourage distant reverence rather than human interaction. We are not only in Sicilia but in a chapel, not only in a chapel but in an art gallery within that chapel, with the theater's own discovery-space curtain probably hiding the statue itself. This is typical of the benevolent misleadings performed by Shakespeare's comic heroines, such as Rosaline and Portia and Rosalind, who test the results of their educational programs under the most trying circumstances available, to be sure that the romantic maturity of a Berowne, Bassanio, or Orlando will last. Paulina wants the audience in general, and Leontes in particular, to acknowledge the beneficent natural basis for even the most artificial-seeming of phenomena. Before revealing the statue, she assures him that it "Excels whatever yet you look'd upon, / Or hand of man hath done" (5.3.16–17), which is a beautifully equivocal clue. It encourages and then forbids him to view the statue as a superhuman creation of human art; it forbids and then encourages him to view it as the divinely created woman he has known.

At first, in their eagerness for reunion with Hermione, Leontes and Perdita nearly fail the test: they choose the artificial basis for reunion, making themselves into companion statues instead of eliciting the statue's living humanity. Leontes says he feels "more stone than it," and observes Perdita "Standing like stone with thee" (5.3.37–42). When Perdita and Leontes yield in turn to a natural desire to kiss the statue, Paulina restrains them by asserting again—in hopes of curing entirely—the delusion that this woman is a work of static and cosmetic art rather than nature, and should be treated as such. These warnings challenge father and daughter to appreciate the "art / That Nature makes." Perdita, who earlier preferred natural to cosmetic colors, here has trouble telling the difference (5.3.46–48). Leontes asks,

> What fine chisel
> Could ever yet cut breath? Let no man mock me,
> For I will kiss her.
> *Paulina*   Good my lord, forbear.
> The ruddiness upon her lip is wet;
> You'll mar it if you kiss it; stain your own
> With oily painting. Shall I draw the curtain?   (5.3.78–83)

By kissing the statue, Leontes would not turn into a painted companion-piece; he would return fully to life, as her conjugal companion.

Leontes has earned such a transformation essentially by wishing for it. He no longer views conjugal relations as a mutual staining and marring, and retracts his implicit foolish wish for a pure, cold, unchanging version of his wife. Instead, like King Lear holding the dead Cordelia, he insists that a single breath of life in her would surpass all that human art can achieve, however fine its chisel. By insisting on staying with the statue, insisting that the curtain not fall on this imitation of life, Leontes makes the crucial choice for a living Hermione over an elegantly artificial one:

> *Paulina*   I'll draw the curtain.
> My lord's almost so far transported that
> He'll think anon it lives.
> *Leontes*   O sweet Paulina,
> Make me to think so twenty years together!
> No settled senses of the world can match
> The pleasure of that madness. Let't alone.
> *Paulina* I am sorry, sir, I have thus far stirr'd you; but
> I could afflict you farther.
> *Leontes*   Do, Paulina;
> For this affliction has a taste as sweet
> As any cordial comfort.   (5.3.68–77)

An appetite for life has replaced Leontes' life-denying madness of the first act, typified by the transition from the poisoned "cordials" he imagines drinking and serving Polixenes to this sweet and salutary one. He finds a value in affliction, a use for adversity, and leaves his "settled senses of the world" to restore Hermione's life rather than (as earlier) to destroy it. In making this choice for the statue, and in fondly making his visitors represent his lost children, he in effect wills his family back into existence; and he thereby becomes the natural self he "might . . . have been" that would have saved him from losing his family in the first place (5.1.176–78).

But to maintain the play's moral pattern, Shakespeare must emphasize that these fantasies come true because they have a basis in nature, and not solely because of Leontes' life-affirming imagination. He takes the trouble to explain that Paulina "hath privately twice or thrice a day, ever since the death of Hermione, visited that remov'd house" where the statue is lodged, and where the royal family now retreats "to sup" (5.2.103–07). We may infer in retrospect, after the statue awakens, that Paulina brought Hermione meals—a significant inference, because the play often uses eating as a symbol or synecdoche of ongoing natural life. From this perspective, it is dangerously wrong to indulge in the fantasy (as some critics do) that Hermione has essentially "come back to life. We do not, that is to say, seek to explain the impossible away. Instead, we gladly accept the impossibility for the sake of the symbolic pattern."[57] Shakespeare's didactic pattern, like Paulina's, demands natural explanations that dispel the tempting illusion of impossibility. Northrop Frye suggests that "in *The Winter's Tale* nature is associated, not with the credible, but with the incredible: nature as an order is subordinated to the nature that yearly confronts us with the impossible miracle of renewed life."[58] What we must remember is that the appearance of a new generation is finally as miraculous a phenomenon as the survival and reappearance of the old. As the witches induced Macbeth to forfeit regenerative nature in favor of supernatural tricks, so Shakespeare's and Paulina's plays lead us, together with Leontes, to overlook temporarily the miracle of "great creating Nature" (4.4.88) in our fascination with the apparent miracle of art, the enlivened statue. Only if our values shift in retrospect, and we come to respect food and shelter and human patience as the necessary basis for such impressive art, have we shared in Leontes' successful education.

Paulina therefore insists repeatedly that no one mistake her awakening of the statue for the black arts. She intends to restore the very

Original Sin in *The Winter's Tale*

sort of regenerative order that witchcraft subverted in Macbeth's Scotland, and were she to recreate Leontes' family by conjuration, she would contradict the lesson in obedience to nature. If supernatural Grace is at work here, and for complete salvation it must be, a sort of prevenient grace arising from nature rather than descending from above it must also contribute.[59] So Paulina declares that she is not "assisted / By wicked powers," that hers is not "unlawful business," and that her "spell is lawful" (5.3.90–105). If this is magic, it is magic of an allowed sort, and therefore similar to the play's allowed sort of ambition. The only kind of magic generally considered lawful in the Renaissance was "intransitive," intended not to impose on nature but rather to elicit the best qualities already inherent in people or objects.[60]

Earlier Leontes had demanded that Paulina be burnt as "A mankind witch" (2.3.68) for her efforts to make him acknowledge his paternity of Perdita. Now, confronting him with another instance of natural survival and his human kinship, Paulina is understandably fearful that it will again be dismissed as witchcraft. When he first sees that statue, Leontes clearly demonstrates the threat to Paulina's project:

> O royal piece,
> There's magic in thy majesty, which has
> My evils conjur'd to remembrance, and
> From thy admiring daughter took the spirits,
> Standing like stone with thee.   (5.3.38–42)

The living Hermione is here portrayed as a conjurer who revives past evils, steals people's spirits, turns them to stone as if she were a Medusa, and uses magic to simulate majesty—hardly a generous description of a woman who is standing passively, displaying the natural majesty of her birth. When the same majestic nature wins Florizel's heart for Perdita, Polixenes errs in strikingly similar terms, calling her an "enchantment" and a "fresh piece / Of excellent witchcraft" (4.4.434, 422–23).

Both women might well complain to the kings (as Othello does to the Senate at 1.6.169) that a noble nature is the only witchcraft they have used; but the very fact that they are thus accused demonstrates how easily the blessings of nature can be mistaken for strayings from nature. Since Eve, women have been accused of witchcraft merely for eliciting an amoral sexual impulse that men fear and deny in their own nature. Only when Leontes can make himself reach lovingly out for Hermione does he correct these characteristic errors:

> *Paulina*   Nay, present your hand.
> When she was young, you woo'd her; now, in age,
> Is she become the suitor?
> *Leontes*   O, she's warm!
> If this be magic, let it be an art
> Lawful as eating.   (5.3.107–11)

Paulina is reminding us, as she reminds Leontes, of the courtship that took place exactly a generation ago, when at last he clasped Hermione's flower-like hand in marriage (1.2.102–04). That cycle of winter and spring has repeated itself, yielding the nubile "Blossom" Perdita, and Leontes has regained the ability to appreciate such miracles of nature. His fond embrace of Hermione contrasts sharply with his earlier disgust at physical expressions of affection, and his endorsement of eating contrasts with his earlier revulsion from food and drink, which in him as in Coriolanus evinced an effort to deny his bodily frailties.

The kind of magic Leontes has implicitly left behind him is as important as the kind he now accepts. A man's impious effort to transcend his hereditary limitations was often associated in the sixteenth century with black magic. C. S. Lewis links an upsurge in magical practices during the period to a loosening in the chain-of-being hierarchy, a loosening that encouraged ambitious revisions of the self.[61] This is the sort of rough magic Leontes here abjures. In the first three acts, his courtly code served much the same purpose, and entailed much the same dangers, as Prospero's spells:

> Prospero's project, then, is no less than to purge the evil from the inhabitants of his world and restore them to goodness . . . But it is precisely this assumption of god-like powers and responsibilities by one who is in no way superhuman that precipitates the central problem of the play. Prospero [is] in a perilous position. . . . We need only remind ourselves that *"prospero"* is the Italian for *"faustus."*[62]

In fact, Leontes' efforts to evade the consequences of original sin do bear some disquieting resemblances to the exertions of that other great stage magician of the period, Marlowe's Faustus, whose

> adventure with the powers of darkness is thus characterized by the desire to escape the conditions imposed by

his religious heritage—which pictures man as a finite,
suffering, damned creature—and to improvise a new, om-
nipotent self which will not be subject to mortality . . . Faustus embodies the Renaissance notion that man
can infinitely improve and develop himself.[63]

The immortalizing magic implicitly attempted at the start of *The
Winter's Tale* and explicitly abjured at the end of it thus points us
back to the archetypal figure of hazardous ambition on the Renaissance stage.

The enlivening of a statue, furthermore, was a favorite exploit of
Hermetic magic. Several mythic and quasi-mythic figures supposedly committed precisely that crime, and the Renaissance treated
them as archetypes of unlawful human aspiration in general. Dae-
dalus and Simon Magus were renowned both for enlivening statues
and for flying, thus invading in two modes the domain of the gods
or God. The two deeds may appear in conjunction because both
symbolize the basic ambitious impulse to construct a new self that
(literally or figuratively) surpasses lowly humanity. The third figure
commonly accused of enlivening a statue is Prometheus, the greatest
archetype of humanity's aspiring spirit, who steals the tools of self-
reliance from the gods and endures their jealous vengeance.[64] Paulina's emphatic disavowal of magic in reviving Hermione may therefore represent a corrective to Leontes' moral error, even as it cures
the consequences of that error. She replaces an archetypal ambitious
deed, and the purely artificial identity it brings into the living world,
with a natural reality that proves no less rewarding in its outcome;
the spell she uses to return "that which is lost" to Leontes is, like
most curative magic, a reversed version of the spell that caused the
disappearance.

When the statue moves, Shakespeare's and Paulina's audiences
confront a *paradeigma:* we witness nature actually springing out of
the form of art. The statue may prove to be merely Hermione's
mortal body, but that body has proved praiseworthy when taken to
be skillfully carved stone. As there can be a natural art, so can there
be a humble ambition; the play can reject the supernaturalism of
magic, because it denies human limitations, without rejecting the
supernaturalism of Grace, which is a necessary repair of human
deficiencies. Now that the ambitious man's aspiration toward godhead is no longer a hero's pagan invasion of a divine privilege, but
instead a Christian submission to divine rules, Shakespeare can redress his tragic emphasis on the evils of ambition. Moral passivity,

like primitivism, can be overdone. There is an ethical middle ground between unproductively burying our talent for self-fashioning, and the unethical usury of that talent (Matthew 25:14–30, 21:12–13); there is a salvageable remnant of the divine form in the human, as there is a worthy piece of statuary in nature. Nicholas Cusanus, according to Cassirer, argues that "inasmuch as he develops and expresses every facet of his nature, man represents the divine in the form and within the limits of the human . . . only by doing that can he honour and love God within it and give evidence of the purity of his own origin."[65] The moral limitations placed on us by our impure origins as Adam's children must be balanced against the moral possibilities offered to us by our pure origins as God's children. Ambition is circumscribed, but also necessitated, by the burden of original sin. The effort to create a better self is desirable if it does not directly defy one's natural heritage; the *imitatio Christi* is admirable if one remains aware of the insurmountable distance between Christ and his figuration in one's own behavior. In *The Merchant of Venice,* Lorenzo and Jessica are not the great doomed lovers of myth and history, the music of Portia's servants is not the music of the spheres, the candle is not the sun, nor is the mortal master's goodness equal to the king of heaven's Atonement; but the love, the music, and the virtue will all be better for recognizing their resemblances and contributions to such greater schemes.

Hermione understands the distinction better than Leontes does. The deed for which she claims the name of Grace is her acceptance of his marriage proposal; as the statue, in whom "some new grace will be born," she again provides a human version of salvation, in the form of natural renewal (1.2.97–105; 5.2.110–11). In consenting to bear Leontes' children, she helps him toward a cyclical version of immortality. In forgiving him, she anticipates the Grace that will eventually forgive the trespasses arising from original sin, provided "You do awake your faith" (5.3.95). "Grace destroyes not nature, but onely rectifies it," according to one Jacobean author;[66] Hermione is in harmony with that sort of Grace, translating rather than usurping the sort provided by Heaven.

Leontes, in contrast, attempts to usurp Adam's integral identity and Christ's redemptive role, an ambition that succeeds only in making him a version of Eve and Satan. As he becomes both the seduced and the seducer in re-enacting the primal trespass, he comes to resemble Eve, who underestimated the impact of original sin, and Satan, who jealously inverts Christ's deeds in wishing to supplant Him. Like them, Leontes creates discord and death in seeking to replace a derivative self with one disobediently created out of ambition. Christ overcomes sin and death by precisely the opposite tactic, answering the errors of unfilial pride with the ultimate act of filial humility, replacing the evil aspiration to godhead with an assumption of the burdens of mortal flesh. So Christ is on several levels the victim of Leontes' offense, and it is appropriate that Leontes' primary human victim, and his primary human forgiver, becomes a human figuration of Christ. Hermione has been described as a Christ-figure, but the comparison may be taken even further than critics have taken it.[67] In descending from her pedestal, Hermione appears to sacrifice a perfect, immortal identity, and to take on a fleshly, mortal one—a combination of Incarnation and Resurrection that at once counterbalances the cause and relieves the consequences of Leontes' impiety.

Mamillius, too, undergoes a version of death and resurrection as part of Leontes' crime and rehabilitation. Like his mother, Mamillius can be restored to life only to the extent that nature permits, and in this case that is a fatal rather than a saving fact. A play that advocates solemnly recognizing our mortality can hardly permit some fairy-tale ending to efface the *memento mori* represented by Mamillius' and Antigonus' deaths. But the comic ending that marries Perdita and remarries Paulina reminds us that (as in Book Ten of *Paradise Lost*) the appropriate corrective to fallen man's time-bound condition, as well as his concupiscence, is married procreation that patiently awaits the final Resurrection which will end or redeem time and souls alike. Leontes can regain a son only through his daughter's marriage, and when he does, as Inga-Stina Ewbank comments, "Leontes has defeated time in that his lines of life are stretching into the future . . . Rather than a myth of immortality, then, this play is a probing into the human condition, and—as a whole as well as in details—it looks at what time means and does to man."[68] The play is finally a myth of *mortality*, a reminder of the frailties man cannot afford to deny without losing what Shakespeare's ambitious figure so often lose: both an integral hereditary identity, and lineal survival.

Leontes regains these things because the play's religious overtones replace the paternal jealousy of the natural and political orders in the earlier plays with the paternal benevolence of the Christian myth. The result is a redeemed version of the family romance that proved so destructive under the laughing gods in *Coriolanus*. Shakespeare again uses the common childhood intuition of having two fathers, one a lowly mortal and merely a foster-parent, the other royal or divine but somehow misplaced, to establish the divided authority whose conflicting commands often destroy tragic heroes. By original sin, we are all defined as disobedient children to God, doomed to the ultimate punishment; yet to move above that tainted and risky heritage, we must deny our first mortal father, Adam. But the Christian God is (as Freudian theory suggests all benevolent gods are) a dangerous paternal figure converted into a protective form and worshiped as such. This God, precisely because his Son has humbly sacrificed himself to the Father's will, is capable of rising above the jealous paternal reflex we have seen punishing ambition in earlier plays. Freud argues that the Christ myth is essentially another expiation of the patricide in the primal horde;[69] Christ's role, after all, is to atone for our primal filial disobedience, whether we call it the primal horde's patricide or original sin, so that we are spared its taint of guilt and its risk of vengeful paternal wrath. By the ultimate act of filial humility, Christ in effect retracts the archetypal ambitious misdeeds, drawing onto himself their punishment. The prophecy that threatens Sicilia as a result of Leontes' error thus comes to resemble the prophecy that saves all humanity from Adam's primal misdeed. Heaven's king will again have an heir when that which was lost in Adam is found in Christ: a human being who is capable of being both filial and immortal. The bifurcated godhead that confronted Shakespeare's tragic protagonists with an impossible choice between natural and exalted selves now becomes a unity of Father and Son that invites humanity to become both rightful heirs and perfect souls.

Shakespeare has transferred the field of aspiration from the political or martial to the theological, but the change of topic only confirms the poetic justice that rebukes ambition; the terms are quite different, but the punishment dictated by the ethical pattern still fits the crime. Even with these two entirely new sorts of fathers, Adam and God, the association of ambition with filial rebellion still shapes and justifies ambition's fate. In portraying the hazards of ambition, Shakespeare characteristically astonishes us with endless resonances, with the sense that he writes with a clear view of a universal order that we had mistaken for scattered phenomena devoid of deep moral consistency.

Shakespeare has come full circle from early comedies such as *Love's Labor's Lost*, which tell the story of unacknowledged human frailties driving repressed or repressive people into the feared but redemptive embrace of marriage. *The Winter's Tale* is partly a version of such plays, one with a more systematic theological basis for its mistrust of moral idealism. As in *Love's Labor's Lost,* men forget that their fallen condition bars them from Eden and attempt to construct—largely by physical abstentions and overblown courtly rhetoric—a society exempt from the lures of sexuality and the need for procreation.[70] In both cases the excessive cultural refinement causes natural desire to burgeon dangerously in secret; and when women invade the garden, as inevitably they do, the men's hypocrisy works its way to the surface. Procreation becomes the necessary figurative substitute for immortality in *The Winter's Tale,* as married chastity is for sexual innocence in *Love's Labor's Lost.* By taking its higher, theological perspective on the human situation, *The Winter's Tale* makes old Adam resemble the conventional comic *senex* or blocking father who (as in *Midsummer Night's Dream*) imposes his paternal authority through a narrow, repressive law that can be overcome by love. Nature endorses resistance to this sort of father, rather than punishing it as in the tragedies, and Christianity offers an escape to a better Father. *The Winter's Tale* is partly a rereading of the New Testament as festive comedy, as a measured and humane rebellion against the harsher paternal constraints.

Aspects of Leontes' ambition have roots also in the tragedies. Like Coriolanus, Leontes pursues his society's ideal with a naive perfectionism that his limiting human heritage, his generalized patrimony, cannot sustain. Like Macbeth, he uses the exalted role of king to try to legitimize and enforce his claim to transcendence, only to discover the entire natural order at war within and against him. But *The Winter's Tale* returns to the spirit of the early comedies in permitting the error to be remedied—not so much retracted as recast, so that a figurative version of the ideal role can be achieved after all.[71] The theatrical metaphor, so dangerous in the histories, so deadly in the tragedies, allows Kate the Curst to become Kate the Kind in Petruchio's show without losing her identity, allows Rosalind the girl to become Rosalind the wife without losing her modesty, and allows Portia to become her husband's shining redeemer without losing her humility toward God. For the royal family of Sicilia, as for these women, art makes it possible to become the best possible version of one's natural self, to find the exalted role to which one was born, but which has long been out of reach.

Shakespeare's tragedies of ambition generally resemble the Elizabethan prodigal-son stories, which heighten their cautionary impact by denying the son the forgiveness he receives in the New Testament. But like Jacobean writers who were reworking the Biblical story more explicitly, Shakespeare finally returns to the original forgiving version. Samuel Gardiner's *Portraiture of the Prodigal Sonne* shows the father granting his penitent son the untainted garment that Adam wore in Eden, and concludes, "God doth not utterlie cast off his children, and forsake his inheritance. But when the time commeth that they return to him he returneth to them, and bringeth all joy with him."[72] Returning to his own nature, reconciled to his fallen condition, Leontes retakes his Eve's hand, and his posterity extends toward Christ's renewal of humanity's Edenic purity. God the Father restores to us an identity that is both filial and perfect: by making us perfect, he renders us recognizable as his children before we were Adam's; and by making us his children, he cleanses away original sin and obviates the similarly unfilial sin of denying that legacy. The ambition that humility makes, like the "art / That Nature makes," is the source of salvation.

✎ Notes

Introduction

1. Michel de Montaigne, "Apology for Raymond Sebond," in *The Complete Essays of Montaigne*, trans. Donald M. Frame (Stanford: Stanford University Press, 1975), p. 457.

2. For more general studies of theatricalism within the plays, see Anne Righter, *Shakespeare and the Idea of the Play* (London: Chatto and Windus, 1962); and Thomas F. Van Laan, *Role-Playing in Shakespeare* (Toronto: University of Toronto Press, 1978).

3. *Sermons or Homilies Appointed to be Read in Churches in the Time of Queen Elizabeth of Famous Memory* (London: C. & J. Rivington, 1825), p. 650. Irving Ribner, *The English History Play in the Age of Shakespeare* (Princeton: Princeton University Press, 1957), p. 255, comments similarly that the word ambition "had a far wider meaning in the Renaissance than it has today. It signified a striving by man to rise above his legitimate position in the divinely created chain of being, and thus, in effect, was a rebellion against the will of God and an upsetting of the perfect harmony of creation."

4. Montaigne, *Complete Essays*, p. 428.

5. E. E. Cummings, "pity this busy monster, manunkind," lines 8–9, in *Complete Poems 1913–1962* (New York: Harcourt Brace Jovanovich, 1972), p. 554.

6. See discussions of this mythic pattern in Otto Rank, *The Myth of the Birth of the Hero*, trans. F. Robbins and Smith Ely Jelliffe (New York: Robert Brunner, 1952), passim; André Green, *The Tragic Effect*, trans. Alan Sheridan (New York: Cambridge University Press, 1979), pp. 199–202; Marjorie Garber, *Coming of Age in Shakespeare* (London: Methuen, 1981), p. 12, citing Mircea Eliade, *Rites and Symbols of Initiation*, trans. Willard

R. Trask (originally published as *Birth and Rebirth*) (1958; rpt. New York: Harper, 1975), pp. x–xiii.

7. Michael Neill, "Shakespeare's Halle of Mirrors: Play, Politics, and Psychology in *Richard III*," in *Shakespeare Studies* 8 (1975), 120, quoting Ficino's *Commentary*.

8. R. D. Laing, *The Divided Self* (London: Penguin, 1965), pp. 42–43; quoted by Neill, in *Shakespeare Studies* 8: 127, n. 11.

9. G. W. Hegel, *The Philosophy of Fine Art*, trans. F. P. B. Osmaston, rpt. in *Hegel on Tragedy*, ed. Anne and Henry Paolucci (Garden City, N.Y.: Doubleday, 1962), pp. 116–123.

10. Sigmund Freud, "Moses and Monotheism," in the Standard Edition of his *Works*, trans. James Strachey, XXIII (London: Hogarth Press, 1964), 87. See also Green, *Tragic Effect*, p. 46.

11. Hans Loewald, *Papers on Psychoanalysis* (New Haven: Yale University Press, 1980), p. 389, observes that "it is no exaggeration to say that the assumption of responsibility for one's own life and its conduct is in psychic reality tantamount to the murder of the parents, to the crime of parricide, and involves dealing with the guilt incurred thereby." Claude Lévi-Strauss, "The Structural Study of Myth," in his *Structural Anthropology*, trans. Claire Jacobson and Brooke Grundfest Schoepf (New York: Basic Books, 1963), pp. 214–217, describes an archetypal hero whose deformed birth correlates with an autochthonic origin, a threat of incest, a denial of bloodlines, and a related threat of parricide; cf. Fitzroy Raglan, *The Hero* (London: Methuen, 1936). W. H. Auden, *The Enchafed Flood* (New York: Random House, 1950), pp. 145–146, observes that in Ahab's proud revolt against dependency in *Moby-Dick*, "the sexual symbolism centres round incest and the Oedipus situation, because incest is the magic act of self-derivation, self-autonomy, with the annihilation of all rival power." R. E. Gajdusek, "Death, Incest, and the Triple Bond in the Later Plays of Shakespeare," *American Imago*, 31 (1974), 158, concludes, "The incest taboo is the transcultural device, the alarm, embedded in the psyche of man to alert him to the dangers of the loss of ego, of selfhood."

Meredith Skura, "Interpreting Posthumus' Dream from Above and Below," in *Representing Shakespeare*, ed. Murray M. Schwartz and Coppélia Kahn (Baltimore: Johns Hopkins University Press, 1980), p. 206, discusses the essential "conflict between family inheritance and personal individuality [which] is the universal drama that Freud saw in the specific fate of Oedipus. What psychoanalysis adds to the traditional Western understanding that the past shapes us is the idea that the past works on us unconsciously and in even stranger, less direct ways than it did for Oedipus, permeating our present lives without being literally true as it was for him." What my analysis hopes to add, in turn, is an explanation of the dramatic metaphor Shakespeare evolved from the specific fate of Oedipus to describe one pervasive burden of the past: the derivative familial identity that individual ambition necessarily opposes.

12. Sigmund Freud, *Totem and Taboo*, trans. James Strachey (New York: Norton, 1950), pp. 152–153, discusses the mythic pattern whereby vegetative divinities such as Attis, Adonis, and Tammuz consort and conspire with their Mother Earth and their mother-divinities, only to be castrated or killed by an embodiment of the father's jealousy.

13. Augustine, sermon 169, quoted by Peter Brown, *Religion and Society in the Age of St. Augustine* (London: Faber and Faber, 1972), p. 30, and by Stephen Greenblatt, *Renaissance Self-Fashioning* (Chicago: University of Chicago Press, 1980), p. 2.

14. See for example Sir Walter Raleigh, *The History of the World*, ed. C. A. Patrides (London: Macmillan, 1971), p. 142. This first-hand observer of the dangers of ambition in the Elizabethan world argues that Adam, "ambitious of a farther knowledge," was provoked to taste the forbidden fruit by Satan, who temptingly moistened it "with the liquor of the same ambition, by which himselfe perished for ever." He also accuses Adam, as Shakespeare indirectly accuses his ambitious victims of poetic justice, of "looking but slightly (as all his issues doe) into the miseries and sorrowes incident, and greatly affecting the supposed glorie which he might obtaine by tasting the fruit forbidden."

15. Alexander Nowell, *A Catechism Written in Latin*, trans. Thomas Norton, ed. G. E. Corrie (London: Parker Society, 1853); quoted by Ernest W. Talbert, *The Problem of Order* (Chapel Hill: University of North Carolina Press, 1962), p. 8.

16. Freud, *Totem*, pp. 125–161; he shows that the religious patterns can be read as a myth of good and bad sons, appeasing or enraging a punitive father. Paul N. Siegel, *Shakespearean Tragedy and the Elizabethan Compromise* (New York: New York University Press, 1957), pp. 88–89, remarks that "In the Elizabethan homilies Adam's disobedience of God, Lucifer's rebellion against Him, and Christ's sacrifice for the sake of mankind were repeatedly presented as basic patterns which men followed in their conduct." Shakespeare explores some of the secular implications of those patterns in politics and psychology. P. L. Robertson, "The Role of the Political Usurper: Macbeth and Boris Gudounov," *American Imago* 23 (1966), 95, observes, "The usurper's act appears to approximate the desire to kill the father who represents authority"—or, to put it the other way, the authority who represents the father.

17. Lionel Trilling, *Sincerity and Authenticity* (Cambridge: Harvard University Press, 1972), p. 16: "The original social meaning of the word 'villain' bears decisively upon its later moral meaning. The opprobrious term referred to the man who stood lowest in the scale of feudal society; the villain of plays and novels is characteristically a person who seeks to rise above the station to which he was born. He is not what he is."

18. See the final pages of chapter 2; also Thomas Greene, "The Flexibility of the Self in Renaissance Literature," in *The Disciplines of Criticism*, ed. Peter Demetz, Thomas Greene, and Lowry Nelson, Jr. (New Haven: Yale

University Press, 1968), pp. 241–264; and Greenblatt, *Renaissance Self-Fashioning*, who on p. 88 argues that the prominence of conduct manuals in the early sixteenth century "suggests the great 'unmooring' that men were experiencing, their sense that fixed positions had somehow become unstuck, their anxious awareness that the moral landscape was shifting."

19. Jean-Paul Sartre, *Being and Nothingness*, trans. Hazel E. Barnes (New York: Pocket Books, 1966), passim; also Trilling, *Sincerity and Authenticity*, who places in this era a critical transition from simpler antique notions of being "true to oneself," to the modern self-consciousness that subverted those notions. The double-bind of identity is comparable to the classic Oedipal double-bind described by psychoanalysts, in which the father gives the boy two contradictory commands for the formation of his identity. One is, "Be like me"—emulate me, respect me, resemble me, and obey my morality; the other is, "Don't be like me"—do not sleep with my wife, do not take the prize that was the original source of your emulation of me. See, for example, Green, *Tragic Effect*, p. 27.

20. Hiram Haydn, *The Counter-Renaissance* (New York: Grove Press, 1950), makes one of the sharpest and most informative attacks on this notion. Colin Morris, *The Discovery of the Individual 1050–1200* (Great Britain: Camelot, 1972), as his title suggests, strongly challenges the traditional dating of this change. Because of these and many other recent attacks, I prefer to echo the demur of Joan Webber, *The Eloquent "I"* (Milwaukee: University of Wisconsin Press, 1968), p. vii: "In this study . . . it has not been a part of my intention to explain why such a phenomenon occurred in seventeenth-century England . . . The art of the period has already been overexplained, in works which find 'the seventeenth-century mind' created out of all sorts of revolutionary occurrences that make the seventeenth century a watershed between the Middle Ages and the modern world . . . And instead of talking about cause and effect . . . it is probably better to speak of significant parallels."

21. Greenblatt, *Renaissance Self-Fashioning*, p. 256 and passim, discusses this ambiguity. There are interesting parallels between the ways Greenblatt's historical figures combat their limitations and the ways Shakespeare's dramatic figures undertake the same task. The emphasis in both cases is often on replacing the determinism of family with the voluntarism of basic life-choices. The early Protestant Antony Dalaber argues that one's religion determines and provides one's family, rather than vice versa (p. 83); similarly, in Thomas More's Utopia, the usual system whereby the son takes up the father's trade gives way to a system whereby one's choice of career selects one's family (p. 43). But these assertions have an air of desperation about them, and the possibility of nullifying the self in attempting to reshape it is always present to Greenblatt's self-fashioners, as it is to Shakespeare's. The early Protestants compulsively "undid" their deeds and martyred themselves (pp. 83–84), and "More's act of self-fashioning is precisely an act of self-cancellation" (p. 57).

22. Anthony Esler, *The Aspiring Mind of the Elizabethan Younger Generation* (Durham, N.C.: Duke University Press, 1966), finds in the period's literature of moral instruction a "particular insistence" on "the evils of overreaching ambition" as a sin against God, the state, and the cosmic order (p. 25). These tracts, like Shakespeare's plays, seem to denounce "ambition *per se*" rather than the more tangible violations that it might provoke; and they denounce it "in vivid poetic language and imagery" (p. 23). Shakespeare himself would have been included in Esler's generalized "Elizabethan younger generation," who entertained "personal ambitions . . . large enough to bring them into conflict with the very structure of their world. They were driven by vaulting aspiration into repeated collision with the limitations imposed upon the men of their time by their social and physical environments" (pp. 197–198). Eventually, Esler maintains, these men reverted "to the melancholy classical commonplaces their fathers had drilled into them . . . now they knew in the depths of their embittered souls that high aspiration was indeed a futile passion in a delusive world" (p. 241).

Adaptations of the Prodigal Son story, which were popular among the Elizabethans, may have suggested to Shakespeare the idea that these moral precepts could be built into an effective fictional structure by capitalizing on an equation of personal aspiration with Oedipal rebellion. Richard Helgerson, *The Elizabethan Prodigals* (Berkeley: University of California Press, 1976), remarks that "in the prodigal son plays, paternal admonition serves as a guide to the ideal self . . . Remember your father and his precepts, and remember who you are. The idea of the self is given *to* the young men . . . When they rely on themselves, they go wrong" (p. 37). Usually they are led astray by women, who "appear in prodigal son plays only as vicious harlots, shrewish wives, or criminally indulgent mothers" (p. 35)—three typically sinister faces of the Jocasta figure, according to psychoanalytic theory. These plays, like Shakespeare's, warn that it is dangerous "to abandon one's true identity for what Whetstone calls a 'vizard of self-conceit' " (p. 39). One consequence of such implicitly Oedipal defiance, as in Shakespeare and in Freudian theory, is nullification: "To be, they suggest, means to emulate your father and to obey his counsel. Not to be means to stand in your own conceit, to follow the bent of your own disposition" (p. 38). This pattern led a young man to believe, as Shakespeare's ambitious figures are led to believe, "that in disobeying his father he was disobeying the governing powers of the universe and of his own being" (p. 40).

I. Kinship and Kingship

1. W. A. Armstrong, "The Elizabethan Conception of the Tyrant," *Review of English Studies* 22 (1946), 175–177, describes a common pattern of talionic vengeance against usurpers. Cesare Ripa, *Iconologie*, ed. and trans. J. Baudoin (Paris, 1644), I, 168, remarks that the figure of Rebellion

can never remove his armor and rest, because he may be surprised at any moment by another usurping rebel.

2. Michael Neill, "Shakespeare's Halle of Mirrors: Play, Politics, and Psychology in *Richard III*," *Shakespeare Studies* 8 (1975), 99–129; see also Waldo F. McNeir, "The Masks of Richard the Third," *English Literature Studies* 11 (1971), 167–186. James Winny, *The Player King* (London: Chatto and Windus, 1968), describes the theatrical metaphor that implies "a disparity between his ideal of majesty and his personal ability to fill the role assigned to him" in several of Shakespeare's faulty or illegitimate monarchs (p. 46).

3. René Girard, *Violence and the Sacred*, trans. Patrick Gregory (Baltimore: Johns Hopkins, 1977), pp. 266–268. E. M. W. Tillyard, *Shakespeare's History Plays* (London: Chatto and Windus, 1951), p. 208, remarks that Richard becomes "the instrument of God's ends. Whereas the sins of other men had merely bred more sins, Richard's arc so vast that they are absorptive, not contagious." John F. Danby, *Shakespeare's Doctrine of Nature* (London: Faber and Faber, 1949), p. 61, notes that all the murders before those Richard commits appear as "the outcome of debated primogeniture," but "it is now a question of Richard's personal ambition."

4. David Riggs, *Shakespeare's Heroical Histories* (Cambridge: Harvard University Press, 1971), p. 109, comments on this paradox. Tillyard, *Shakespeare's History Plays*, p. 159, touches on the emblematic nature of these scenes. Coppélia Kahn, *Man's Estate: Masculine Identity in Shakespeare* (Berkeley: University of California Press, 1981), pp. 59–61 and 75, explores the implications of these scenes in the overall patriarchal scheme. Ricardo J. Quinones, " 'Lineal Honour' and Augmentative Time in Shakespeare's Treatment of the Bolingbroke Line," *Topic* 7 (1964), 12–32, suggests that the crimes against lineality necessarily lead to a loss of progeny or a conflict between fathers and sons.

5. See Kahn, *Man's Estate*, p. 64; also Neill, in *Shakespeare Studies* 8:106, and Winny, *Player King*, p. 34.

6. See note 6 of my Introduction.

7. For a more detailed look at this phenomenon, see the early pages of my section on the Henry IV plays below. The birth of the warrior-goddess Athena may be related to this motif, a motif whose importance in Shakespeare's works has long been suggested but never adequately explored. M. Karl Simrock, *On the Plots of Shakespeare's Plays*, ed. J. O. Halliwell (London: Shakespeare Society, 1850), p. 129, asserts that Caesarean birth in myth "always indicates power and heroic strength." Ludwig Jekels, "The Riddle of Shakespeare's *Macbeth*," in *The Design Within*, ed. M. D. Faber (New York: Science House, 1970), p. 238, points back to Simrock's suggestion that Macduff is analogous "to mythical characters like Rogdai, Rustem, Woelsung, and others, men or demi-gods, who have supposedly been 'ripped' from their mothers' wombs, in token of their strength and power."

8. Tillyard, *Shakespeare's History Plays*, p. 196.

9. For a good sampling of such work, see *Representing Shakespeare,* ed. Murray M. Schwartz and Coppélia Kahn (Baltimore: Johns Hopkins University Press, 1980), passim.

10. Edmund Plowden, *Commentaries or Reports,* pp. 238, 213a; quoted by Ernst Kantorowicz, *The King's Two Bodies* (Princeton: Princeton University Press, 1957), pp. 9–11, and by Maynard Mack, Jr., *Killing the King,* Yale Studies in English, vol. 180 (New Haven: Yale University Press, 1973), pp. 4–5.

11. J. Leeds Barroll, *Artificial Persons* (Columbia: University of South Carolina Press, 1974), p. 83.

12. Neill, in *Shakespeare Studies* 8:120.

13. Sigmund Freud, *A General Introduction to Psychoanalysis,* trans. Joan Riviere (New York: Permabooks, 1953), p. 160; see also André Green, *The Tragic Effect,* trans. Alan Sheridan (New York: Cambridge University Press, 1979), pp. 203–204; and note 6 of my Introduction.

14. See the note to this phrase in the Riverside Shakespeare.

15. Kahn, *Man's Estate,* p. 193, remarks that "Even the most pathologically solitary hero, Richard III, defines himself by systematically exterminating his family and violating its bonds in novel ways . . . an intense ambivalence toward the family runs through Shakespeare's works, taking the familiar shape of a conflict between inheritance and individuality, and between autonomy and relatedness." My point is that these novel violations of the family bonds point toward the creation of a new family in which Richard fathers himself through a noble mother, thus acquiring both inheritance *and* individuality, both autonomy *and* relatedness. Grace Mary Garry, "Unworthy Sons: Richard II, Phaethon, and the Disturbance of Temporal Order," *Modern Language Studies* 9 (1978–79), 15, describes Richard as a disobedient and even patricidal son to surrogate fathers such as Gloucester, Lancaster, and York, leading to a talionic vengeance against his own surrogate-paternal role as king.

16. Murray Krieger, "The Dark Generations of *Richard III,*" in Faber, *Design Within,* p. 352.

17. The intriguing paradox here is that the Duchess of York describes Richard as himself "a false glass" who reflects his father distortedly (2.2.53). He thus becomes a "proper man" in the mirror Anne provides by a sort of double-refraction system, and might therefore hope to become his father's authentic son again, in lineaments as well as lineage. But mirror propagation in Shakespeare's plays proves to be a dangerous delusion; the new self it creates may resemble the former self or even correct its flaws, but it is incapable of independent life. The process of Richard's rebirth proves as barren as Queen Margaret's "repetition" of the husband and son that Richard has "marr'd" (1.3.163–64). Like Queen Elizabeth, she must replace her natural offspring with plaintive echoes of their loss.

18. *The Tragedy of Locrine,* Malone Society Reprints (Oxford: Oxford University Press, 1908), lines 1090–91; see also lines 1675–79. Sir Thomas

Smith is quoted by Ernest W. Talbert, *The Problem of Order* (Chapel Hill: University of North Carolina Press, 1962), p. 25. For more examples of this Renaissance notion of inadvertent self-eradication, see the second part of chapter 2 below and its notes 76–83.

19. See note 61 to chapter 3 below.

20. Caroline Spurgeon, *Shakespeare's Imagery* (1935; rpt. Boston: Beacon Hill, 1958), pp. 218–220, cites this and a few of my other examples to show the predominance of the family-tree motif in *Richard III*.

21. The Chorus of Samuel Daniel's *Philotas* warns against "Restlesse ambition," since "it doth cost farre more ado to hold / The height attain'd, than was to get so hie, / Where stand thou canst not, but with carefull toile, / Nor loose thy hold without thy utter spoile" (lines 729, 740–743; see lines 766–767); in *The Complete Works in Verse and Prose of Samuel Daniel*, ed. Alexander B. Grosart (London, 1885) III, 131–132.

22. Danby, *Doctrine of Nature*, p. 81, remarks that in the first tetralogy, unlike the second, "an intellectual thesis . . . actively controls [Shakespeare's] material."

23. J. M. R. Margeson, *The Origins of English Tragedy* (Oxford: Clarendon Press, 1967), p. 58; on the royal potential for wisdom, see also Rolf Soellner, *Shakespeare's Patterns of Self-Knowledge* (Columbus, Ohio: Ohio State University Press, 1972), p. 114, citing Huarte's *Examen de Ingenios* (trans. 1594).

24. Roland M. Frye, "Shakespeare's Mirror Image of Failure: *Richard II* and *Coriolanus*," *Forum* (Houston) 11 (1973–74), ii–iii, 13, observes that "Richard seems chronically unable to be himself," and is "thus given to an almost incessant play-acting."

25. Spurgeon, *Shakespeare's Imagery*, pp. 238–241, discusses this conversation, and a few lesser examples, as evidence that "the ideas of birth and generation, also of inheritance from father to son, are a good deal in Shakespeare's mind in this play," increasing the dramatic "effect of Nemesis." She also (pp. 220–223) discusses the images of ruined vegetation.

26. Shakespeare misrepresents the queen's maturity—she would have been ten years old at the time of this scene—perhaps to permit this figurative treatment of pregnancy as well as to permit her moving farewell to her husband (5.1). In this regard, Shakespeare's imprecision resembles his imprecision about Lady Macbeth's children, as my next chapter will argue. In both cases he is willing to neglect consistency to explore and emphasize the talionic price that a man's defiance of lineality exacts from his own procreative powers.

27. Alvin Kernan, "This Goodly Frame, The Stage," *Shakespeare Quarterly* 25 (1974), 4. For the theatricalism of Richard's identity, see Georges A. Bonnard, "The Actor in Richard II," *Shakespeare Jahrbuch* 87/88 (1952), 99–100; for the same phenomenon throughout the tetralogy, see Daniel Seltzer, "Prince Hal and Tragic Style," *Shakespeare Survey* 30 (1977), 13–27; James L. Calderwood, *Metadrama in Shakespeare's Henriad* (Berkeley:

University of California Press, 1979); and Anne Righter, *Shakespeare and the Idea of the Play* (London: Chatto and Windus, 1962), pp. 113–138.

28. See Anthony Wilden, commentary in Jacques Lacan, *The Language of the Self* (Baltimore: Johns Hopkins University Press, 1968), pp. 159–177 and passim, on the connections between mirrors and the child's formation of identity; also D. W. Winnicott, "Mirror-Role of Mother and Family in Child Development," in his *Playing and Reality* (New York: Basic Books, 1971), pp. 111–118; cited by Kahn, *Man's Estate*, p. 5. Joel Fineman, "Fratricide and Cuckoldry: Shakespeare's Doubles," in Schwartz and Kahn, *Representing Shakespeare*, pp. 106–107 n. 16, provides other useful references.

29. Winny, *Player King*, p. 76.

30. The analogy between births such as Glendower's and Tamburlaine's, and eruptions of trapped air, recalls Lucan's description of Julius Caesar's martial energies: "As lightning by the wind forc'd from a cloud / Breakes through the wounded aire with thunder loud." James M. Swan, "History, Pastoral, and Desire: A Psychoanalytic Study of English Renaissance Literature and Society" (Ph.D. diss. Stanford University, 1974), pp. 300–302, has interpreted this passage as the source for images of self-induced Caesarean birth in Philemon Holland's *Historie of the World* (translated from Pliny in 1601) and in Marvell's "The Unfortunate Lover"; he also confirms my longstanding suspicion that the much-debated lines 13–24 of Marvell's "Horatian Ode" allude to a similar action, complete with a pun on Caesar's name. See also C. A. Patrides, " 'Till Prepared for Longer Flight,' " in *Approaches to Marvell* (London: Routledge and Kegan Paul, 1978), p. 35.

31. Christopher Marlowe, *Tamburlaine, Part One*, in *The Complete Plays of Christopher Marlowe*, ed. J. B. Steane (Harmondsworth, Middlesex: Penguin, 1969), 1.2.49–51.

32. Edmund Spenser, *The Faerie Queene*, in *Spenser: Poetical Works*, ed. J. C. Smith and E. De Selincourt (New York: Oxford University Press, 1970). For the impregnating power of Jove's lightning, see Plutarch, *Lives of the Noble Grecians and Romans*, trans. Thomas North (1579), ed. W. E. Henley (London, 1895), IV, 299, 330–331; here again such a conception generates a suggestively Oedipal hero.

33. John Milton, *Paradise Lost*, ed. Merritt Y. Hughes (Indianapolis, Ind.: Odyssey-Bobbs Merrill, 1962); subsequent citations are from this edition.

34. Sigmund Freud, *Totem and Taboo*, trans. James Strachey (New York: Norton, 1950), pp. 142–144. In chapter 6 of his *Violence and the Sacred*, Girard examines the Hydra-like threat presented by twins or doubles, which raise the danger of fraternal rivalry over legacies and even identity.

35. Norman Sanders, "The True Prince and the False Thief: Prince Hal and the Shift of Identity," *Shakespeare Survey* 30 (1977), 30, remarks on the propriety of this resemblance.

36. Ronald Berman, "The Nature of Guilt in the Henry IV Plays," *Shake-*

speare Studies 1 (1965), 27, discusses Henry's use of disguise to gain the throne. See also Righter, *Shakespeare and Idea of Play*, pp. 126–127.

37. Ernst Kris, "Prince Hal's Conflict," in Faber, *Design Within*, p. 395.

38. Dreams of saving the father from an assailant, however one wishes to interpret them, are apparently common among young men. Freud, in *Totem and Taboo* (p. 72), speculates about a mechanism whereby "the original *wish* that the loved person may die is replaced by a *fear* that he may die. So that when the neurosis appears to be so tenderly altruistic, it is merely *compensating* for an underlying contrary attitude of brutal egoism."

39. Derek Traversi, *Shakespeare from Richard II to Henry V* (Stanford: Stanford University Press, 1957), p. 125.

40. The parallel is of course imperfect: marrying one's mother does not become appropriate at one's father's death, as inheriting his title might. John W. Blanpied, " 'Unfathered heirs and loathly births of nature': Bringing History to Crisis in *2 Henry IV*," *English Literary Renaissance* 5 (1975), 228–229, discusses the displacement of the parricide into the crown; Freud argues that the Oedipal impulse is often displaced into the mother, who is here equated with the crown.

41. Norman Rabkin, *Shakespeare and the Problem of Meaning* (Chicago: University of Chicago Press, 1981), pp. 33–62, argues eloquently and convincingly that our ambivalence toward Hal is not only permissible, it is essential to understanding Shakespeare's sort of meaning.

42. Warren J. Macisaac, " 'A Commodity of Good Names' in the *Henry IV* Plays," *Shakespeare Quarterly* 29 (1978), 417–419, comments on the meaningful modulations of Hal's name.

43. George Steiner, in a conversation in 1978, reported finding such stories in many mythologies, stories of a hero battling through the night against a Doppelgänger, and receiving a name from him in the morning.

44. Sigmund Freud, *The Ego and the Id*, trans. Joan Riviere, rev. and ed. James Strachey (New York: Norton, 1962), pp. 21–29; in *Totem and Taboo*, this incorporation of the father takes the literal form of a ritual meal in which the patricidal sons consume the father or his totem-surrogate as part of a penitential renunciation of their common deed (p. 142). See similarly Freud's *Civilization and Its Discontents*, trans. James Strachey (New York: Norton, 1961), p. 76. An interesting sidelight here is Jacques Lacan's theory that the Oedipal conflict resides essentially in a boy's relation to the name (*nom*, with a pun on *non*) of the father; see Monique David-Menard, "Lacanians Against Lacan," trans. Brian Massumi, in *Social Text* (Fall 1982), p. 90.

45. Kris, "Prince Hal," in Faber, *Design Within*, p. 399, is an early example; see also Faber, pp. 421–422.

46. Meredith Skura, *The Literary Use of the Psychoanalytic Process* (New Haven: Yale University Press, 1981), p. 16, cites several such objections.

47. Edward Pechter, "Falsifying Men's Hopes: The Ending of 1 *Henry IV*," *Modern Language Quarterly* 41 (1980), 216.

48. Jonas Barish, "The Turning Away of Prince Hal," *Shakespeare Studies* 1 (1965), 15 and 10.

49. Franz Alexander, "A Note on Falstaff," *Psychoanalytic Quarterly* 2 (1933), 592–606; cited by Barish, *Shakespeare Studies* 1:16 n. 5.

50. W. H. Auden, *The Dyer's Hand and Other Essays* (New York: Random House, 1948; rpt. 1962), p. 195.

51. Tillyard, *Shakespeare's History Plays*, pp. 285–291; the quotations are from p. 289. S. C. Sen Gupta, *Shakespeare's History Plays* (London: Oxford University Press, 1964), p. 127, calls Falstaff "a symbol of the unrepressed instincts of humanity, which thirst for fulfillment, rebel against repression"; cited by Sidney Shanker, *Shakespeare and the Uses of Ideology*, Studies in English Literature, vol. 105 (The Hague: Mouton, 1975), p. 65 n. 19. We may add to Tillyard's list the figure of the *picaro*, cited as an element of Falstaff by H. B. Rothschild Jr., "Falstaff and the Picaresque Tradition," *Modern Language Review* 68 (1972), 14–21.

52. J. Dover Wilson, *The Fortunes of Falstaff* (New York: Macmillan, 1944), pp. 18–28; Bernard Spivack, *Shakespeare and the Allegory of Evil* (New York: Columbia University Press, 1958), pp. 87–91.

53. Freud, *Ego and Id*, p. 26, is one of many statements of this theory.

54. Skura, *Literary Use*, p. 36, mentions "the obvious psychomachia in the triple world of *Henry IV, Part Two*, where Hal has to choose between the id (Falstaff) and the superego (the Lord Chief Justice)." Danby, *Doctrine of Nature*, p. 95, asserts that "In the rejection scene Hal and my Lord Chief Justice stand for Authority; Falstaff is Appetite." Traversi, *Richard II to Henry V*, p. 108, sees Hal in 2 *Henry IV* as "engaged in the more arduous and sober pursuit of self-conquest, externally manifested in his submission to the Lord Chief-Justice"; but on p. 158 he doubts that the Justice is "a sufficient counterpart to the 'riot' incarnated in Falstaff."

55. Freud, *Ego and Id*, p. 46.

56. Sigmund Freud, "The Anatomy of the Mental Personality," in *New Introductory Lectures on Psychoanalysis*, trans. W. J. H. Sprott (New York: Norton, 1933), p. 108.

57. Freud, *Civilization*, p. 79. For the sufficiency of a fantasy patricide, see *Totem*, p. 160, and "Moses and Monotheism" in the Standard Edition of Freud's *Works*, trans. James Strachey, XXIII (London: Hogarth, 1964), 87.

58. Freud, *Totem*, p. 145 and p. 143.

59. Freud, *Ego and Id*, p. 28 and p. 38.

60. Freud, *Ego and Id*, pp. 18–21; see also p. 44, and his "Mourning and Melancholia," passim, in *Works*, XIV (London: Hogarth, 1957); see also Hans Loewald, *Papers on Psychoanalysis* (New Haven: Yale University Press, 1980), pp. 270–271.

61. Freud, *Civilization*, p. 42.

62. Ibid., p. 44: "At this point we cannot fail to be struck by the sim-

ilarity between the process of civilization and the libidinal development of the individual," and goes on, pp. 44–45, to suggest "that the development of civilization is a special process, comparable to the normal maturation of the individual." Further, "The analogy between the process of civilization and the path of individual development may be extended . . . The super-ego of an epoch of civilization has an origin similar to that of an individual" (p. 88). However, we must also heed Freud's warning, on p. 91, that "we are only dealing wih analogies and that it is dangerous, not only with men but also with concepts, to tear them from the sphere in which they have originated and been evolved."

63. Freud, "The Group and the Primal Horde," in *Works*, XVIII (London: Hogarth, 1955) 123.

64. J. J. Atkinson, *Primal Law* (London, 1903), p. 228; quoted by Freud, *Totem*, p. 142 n. 1, as the characteristic problem that the totemic law must solve. See also Freud's "Postscript" in *Works*, XVIII, 135, on the necessity of this fraternal pact as a preventative to civil war.

65. For another perspective on these Cain allusions, see Berman, in *Shakespeare Studies* 1:20.

66. Thomas Sackville and Thomas Norton, *Gorboduc or Ferrex and Porrex*, Regents Renaissance Drama Series, ed. Irby B. Cauthen, Jr. (Lincoln: University of Nebraska Press, 1970), 2.1.172–75, 5.2.212–14, and passim, shows this combination of crimes plunging the nation out of civilization and into a welter of bloodshed. Intriguingly, these themes are combined here, as they are in Shakespeare, with occasional suggestions of unnatural birth and the dangers of a usurper's sleep: see 4.1.65–75 and 4.2.181–90. The Homily is quoted by Tillyard, *Shakespeare's History Plays*, p. 70.

67. In *Leviathan*, part I, chapter 13, Hobbes, discusses the difficulty of holding any sort of sovereign privileges in a world where "the weakest has strength enough to kill the strongest, either by secret machination, or by confederacy with others, that are in the same danger with himself." This parallels Freud's observation that the brothers, though individually weaker, manage to overthrow the father and seize his privileges by conspiring together. A few paragraphs later Hobbes points out the same danger that Freud saw arising from such a conspiracy. In the absence of the father, or a just totemic law that takes his place, the brothers will inevitably continue to battle each other to their deaths: "Hereby it is manifest, that during the time men live without a common power to keep them all in awe, they are in that condition which is called war; and such a war, as is of every man, against every man."

68. Edmund Spenser, *The Faerie Queene*, I.i; John Bunyan, *The Pilgrim's Progress*, ed. Roger Sharrock (Harmondsworth, Middlesex: Penguin, 1965), pp. 172–173.

69. Tillyard, *Shakespeare's History Plays*, p. 305, makes note of this deviation from Walsingham and the *Famous Victories of Henry V*.

70. Girard, *Violence and the Sacred*, p. 249; for Freud's notion that the

murdered father is converted into the unifying God, Christian or otherwise, see *Totem*, pp. 144–155.

71. Helkiah Crooke, *A description of the body of man*, 2nd ed. (London, 1631), p. 269, refers to the infant's path of exit as the "out-gate." Shakespeare himself, in *The Winter's Tale*, has the jealous Leontes decide "there's comfort in't / Whiles other men have gates, and those gates open'd, / As mine, against their will" (1.2.196–98). Andrew Marvell urges "His Coy Mistress" to allow him to "tear our pleasures with rough strife / Thorough the Iron gates of Life" (lines 43–44). The metaphor also appears in the military context—the same sort of context it occupies in *Henry V*—in the opening paragraph of Thomas Nashe's *The Unfortunate Traveller* (1594), describing the day "when Turwin lost her maidenhead, and opened her gates to more than Jane Trosse did." The association of the city gates with a sort of civic vagina becomes important in my reading of *Coriolanus*.

72. Henry tells Katherine, "Now beshrew my father's ambition! he was thinking of civil wars when he got me; therefore was I created with a stubborn outside, with an aspect of iron, that when I come to woo ladies, I fright them" (5.2.224–28). He thus turns his father's ambitious legacy into yet another commodity for the acquisition of France, making it an excuse for any roughness in his rapid and pragmatic courtship, making that roughness a verification of his true lineal identity, and making that verification a justification of his own ambitions.

II. The Tragedy of *Macbeth*

1. From *Sermons or Homilies Appointed to be Read in Churches in the Time of Queen Elizabeth of Famous Memory* (London: C & J Rivington, 1825), pp. 114–115.

2. Richard Hooker, *Of the Laws of Ecclesiastical Polity* (1594), Everyman's Library (London: J. M. Dent, 1907), p. 157.

3. Harry Berger, Jr., "The Early Scenes of *Macbeth*," *ELH* 47 (1980), 1–5, detects subversive notes in the play's ostensible endorsement of the natural and political orders, and suggests that repeated insurrections against those orders may be an inevitable product of the social structure.

4. For other explanations of this identification, see Robert B. Heilman, "The Criminal as Tragic Hero: Dramatic Methods," in *Aspects of Macbeth*, ed. Kenneth Muir and Phillip Edwards (Cambridge: Cambridge University Press, 1977), pp. 26–38; Ivor Morris, *Shakespeare's God* (London: George Allen and Unwin, 1972), p. 310; and Muir, "Introduction" to the Arden *Macbeth* (London: Methuen, 1951), pp. l and lvi. For another comparison of Richard III's and Macbeth's talionic punishments, see E. M. W. Tillyard, *Shakespeare's History Plays* (London: Chatto and Windus, 1951), pp. 315–318.

5. Alexander Ross, *Mystagogus Poeticus* (London, 1648), p. 288, made

King Midas a figuration of "the folly and madnesse of some mens wishes, who pray many times for that which proves their destruction."

6. Bruno Bettelheim, *The Uses of Enchantment* (New York: Random House, 1977), p. 72.

7. "An Homily Against Disobedience and Wilful Rebellion" in *Sermons*, pp. 630–631, argues that "he that nameth Rebellion nameth not a singular or only sin, as is theft, robbery, murther, and such like . . . all sins, I say, against God, and all men heaped together nameth he, that nameth Rebellion."

8. *Hamlet*, 2.2.529–30, 3.1.121–23. Compare Aristotle's argument that culpability attaches to intentions only when they are accompanied by acts, with Christ's warning that any man who lusts after a woman in his heart is committing adultery, and that any man who hates his brother is committing murder (Matthew 5:21–28). The potential destructiveness of efficacious thought has been largely the realm of fairy-tale and science-fiction writers: see Jerome Bixby's "It's a Good Life," in which the power belongs to an irresponsible boy, and Ursula LeGuin's *The Lathe of Heaven*, in which the power belongs to dreams that change into nightmares.

9. The doctrine of equivocation depends (like Macbeth's fate) on blurring the distinction between the outwardly expressed and the merely thought. A Jesuit might avoid self-incrimination, without breaking a holy oath to tell the truth, by speaking words acceptable to his inquisitors, but continuing mentally, audibly only to God, with additional words that brought the spoken words into line with his actual heretical beliefs or disloyal intentions. See Lawrence Danson, *Tragic Alphabet* (New Haven: Yale University Press, 1974), pp. 132–135; Muir, "Introduction," pp. xvii–xxi; and Steven Mullaney, "Lying Like Truth," *ELH* 47 (1980), 39–40.

10. Samuel Gardiner, *Portraiture of the Prodigal Sonne* (London, 1599), pp. 33, 111; Nehemiah Rogers, *The True Convert* (London, 1620), p. 77, writes that "God doth often punish sin in it owne kinde"; see also Richard Brathwait, "The Prodigals Glasse," in Patrick Hannay, *A Happy Husband* (London, 1618), sig. I5v; John Newnham, *Newnams Nightcrowe* (London, 1590), p. 5; Thomas Ingeland, *The Disobedient Child*, in *The Dramatic Writings of Richard Wever and Thomas Ingeland*, ed. John Farmer (London: Early English Drama Society, 1905), pp. 68–69; and Shakespeare's *Rape of Lucrece*, line 128.

11. Brathwait, "Prodigals Glasse," sig. I7.

12. Bettelheim, *Enchantment*, p. 70.

13. Wilbur Sanders, *The Dramatist and the Received Idea* (London: Cambridge University Press, 1968), p. 268, remarks on the phallic attributes of Lady Macbeth's fantasy here.

14. Caroline Spurgeon, *Shakespeare's Imagery* (1935; rpt. Boston: Beacon Hill, 1958), pp. 329–331, remarks on night's suppression of daylight, but treats it as an allegory of evil's suppression of good, rather than as a significant violation of cyclical nature. Political rebellion similarly provokes

night to rebel against its obligation to yield to day in Thomas May's 1631 translation of Lucan's *Pharsalia*, book 6, sig. K6v.

15. D. A. Traversi, *An Approach to Shakespeare*, 2nd ed. (New York: Doubleday, 1956), p. 159, observes "the light which radiates from the royal figure of Duncan." See *Richard II*, 3.3.63, 179; *Merchant of Venice*, 5.1.94; and *Henry VIII*, 1.5.56, for examples of this standard metaphor.

16. A similar conflation occurs in the myth of Icarus; see Ross, *Mystagogus*, pp. 87, 361. Charles Masinton, *Christopher Marlowe's Tragic Vision* (Athens, Ohio: Ohio University Press, 1972), p. 130, suggests that Marlowe portrays "the primal sin" of "characters who destroy or disregard their heritage . . . and try instead to become monarchs of realms that do not belong to them. They are jealous of the light, but in trying to usurp the glory of the sun they burn their wings and fall to their deaths." Much the same moral, and the same mythic referents, could be adduced to Macbeth's fall.

17. Michel de Montaigne, "Of the custom of wearing clothes," in *The Complete Essays of Montaigne*, trans. Donald M. Frame (Stanford: Stanford University Press, 1975), p. 167.

18. Sigmund Freud, *A General Introduction to Psychoanalysis*, trans. Joan Riviere (New York: Permabooks, 1953), p. 153.

19. Sir William Cornwallis, *Essayes* (London, 1606), sig. I8r, comments that "sleepe is to me in the nature that Dung is to Ground"; Rogers, *True Convert*, p. 299, describes sleep as the life-giving "dew of nature" for both soul and body.

20. Quoted by Norman Holland, *Psychoanalysis and Shakespeare* (New York: McGraw-Hill, 1964), p. 220.

21. Ibid., p. 221; see also his p. 225.

22. Sigmund Freud, in the Standard Edition of his *Works*, trans. James Strachey, XVIII (London: Hogarth Press, 1955), 136.

23. Holland, *Psychoanalysis and Shakespeare*, p. 219; see also Irving Ribner, "*Macbeth*: The Pattern of Idea and Action," *Shakespeare Quarterly* 10 (1959), 150.

24. See for example Dennis Biggins, "Sexuality, Witchcraft, and Violence in *Macbeth*," *Shakespeare Studies* 8 (1975), 255, 264–266.

25. Coppélia Kahn, *Man's Estate* (Berkeley: University of California Press, 1981), p. 178.

26. Eric Partridge, *Shakespeare's Bawdy* (London: Routledge and Kegan Paul, 1968), mentions some examples in his entries under "act" (p. 56) and "do it" (p. 95).

27. The Oedipal character of the crime is suggested in other, more allusive ways, mostly by the guilty couple themselves. On the night of the regicide (2.2), Lady Macbeth is almost paralyzed by Duncan's resemblance to her father, and by the typical Oedipal fear that "Th'attempt and not the deed / Confounds us"; she then warns her brooding husband as Jocasta warned hers: "Consider it not so deeply" (2.2.9–29). But Macbeth, reading

his sins in his palms, cries out, "What hands are here? Hah! They pluck out mine eyes"; "To know my deed," he adds, " 'twere best not know myself," which is at least as true for Oedipus as it is for Macbeth. The witches also resemble Jocasta in admonishing Macbeth to "Seek to know no more" about the riddling prophecy by which he rose to power, and the ominous prophecy, linked in unspoken ways to the first one, by which he is fated to fall. When he insists on and receives an answer, he finds it "does sear mine eyeballs" (4.1.103–13). Macbeth is thus well-suited to teach Scotland's young men "What 'twere to kill a father" (3.6.3–20).

28. Richard Jonas, *The Byrth of Mankynde* (trans. from Eucharius Roesslin, *De partu hominis*), rev. and ed. Thomas Raynold (London, 1545), I, fol. 9v; cited by Jenijoy La Belle, " 'A Strange Infirmity': Lady Macbeth's Amenorrhea," *Shakespeare Quarterly* 31 (1980), 382.

29. Thomas R. Forbes, *The Midwife and the Witch* (New Haven: Yale University Press, 1966), p. 127 and passim.

30. Lucien Goldmann, *The Hidden God*, trans. Philip Thody (London: Routledge and Kegan Paul, 1964), p. 44.

31. Claude Lévi-Strauss, *The Scope of Anthropology*, trans. Sherry Ortner Paul and Robert A. Paul (London: Jonathan Cape, 1967), pp. 35–39.

32. Willard Farnham, *The Medieval Heritage of Elizabethan Tragedy* (Berkeley: University of California Press, 1936), p. 407; cf. Sanders, p. 282.

33. Edward Forset, *A Comparative Discourse of the Bodies Natural and Politique* (London, 1606), p. 64.

34. La Belle, in *Shakespeare Quarterly* 31: 381–386; as she points out, this disruption of the menstrual flow "is tantamount to murdering infants— albeit unborn," and thus "destroys the lineal flow," making Lady Macbeth analogous to Rosse's Scotland, not the mother of a new generation but instead its grave. The rebirth of Macbeth, then, entails a biological event that reveals how opposed ambitious alterations are to natural fertility.

35. Sigmund Freud, *Collected Papers*, trans. Joan Riviere et al. (London: Hogarth Press, 1934), IV, 330; see also Holland, *Psychoanalysis and Shakespeare*, p. 66, on the ways "other analysts, notably Ludwig Jekels," develop Freud's idea; and Janet Adelman, *The Common Liar* (New Haven: Yale University Press, 1973), p. 7.

36. L. C. Knights, "How Many Children Had Lady Macbeth?" rpt. in *Modern Shakespearean Criticism*, ed. Alvin B. Kernan (New York: Harcourt Brace, 1970), pp. 45–76. Edgar Allan Poe's short piece on "The Characters of Shakespeare" makes an argument similar to Knights's.

37. Sanders, *Dramatist*, p. 263, describes Macduff's responsibility for his own loss of family as unmistakable yet oddly undefined. Holland, *Psychoanalysis and Shakespeare*, p. 222, reports one psychoanalytic reading in which "Macduff proves again, in the logic of the unconscious, that 'the bad son makes a bad father.' "

38. Harvey Graham, *The Story of Surgery* (New York: Doubleday, 1939), p. 375.

39. For a discussion of such sacrificial practices, particularly as they relate to tragedy, see René Girard, *Violence and the Sacred*, trans. Patrick Gregory (Baltimore: Johns Hopkins University Press, 1977), passim. Macduff may also serve as society's pristine agent against the threat of Oedipal rebirth embodied by Macbeth. Victor Calef, "Lady Macbeth and Infanticide," *Journal of the American Psychoanalytic Association* 17 (1969), 537 n. 10, points out that his Caesarean birth leaves Macduff miraculously free from the taint of having entered his mother's genital passages even once. See also Holland, *Psychoanalysis and Shakespeare*, p. 227.

40. Cleanth Brooks, "The Naked Babe and the Cloak of Manliness," rpt. in Kernan, *Modern Shakespearean Criticism*, pp. 385–403, discusses the peculiar strength of these babes. Cf. Philostratus the Elder, *Les Images ou Tableaux de Platte Peinture*, trans. B. de Vigenère (Paris, 1629), p. 480, which captions a drawing of "Hercules Among the Pygmies" with a moral applicable to *Macbeth*: "C'est un mal heur extreme / De s'ignorer soy-mesme, / Un Geant triomphant / Est bravé d'un enfant."

41. Holland, *Psychoanalysis and Shakespeare*, p. 219.

42. Francis M. Cornford, *From Religion to Philosophy* (New York: Longmans, Green and Co., 1912), p. 5. Brathwait's "Prodigals Glasse," sig. I7v, uses the family-tree metaphor to warn about a similar cluster of dangers.

43. John Upton, *Critical Observations on Shakespeare* (London: G. Hawkins, 1746), p. 39 n. 17.

44. This massive deforestation regained momentum when the exhaustion of English forests led the iron smelters to Scotland, where they built their first large furnance at the same time Shakespeare was writing *Macbeth*. See R. N. Millman, *The Making of the Scottish Landscape* (London: B. T. Batsford, 1975), pp. 48–49, 63, 86–87, 101.

45. M. Karl Simrock, *On the Plots of Shakespeare's Plays* (London: Shakespeare Society, 1850), first suggested this identification, and Jekels used it in his "The Riddle of Shakespeare's *Macbeth*" (1943), rpt. in *The Design Within*, ed. M. D. Faber (New York: Science House, 1970), pp. 235–249.

46. Quoted by Charles Trinkaus, *"In Our Image and Likeness"* (London: Constable, 1970), I, 194.

47. Ernst Cassirer, *The Individual and the Cosmos in Renaissance Philosophy*, trans. Mario Domandi (New York: Harper and Row, 1964), pp. 90–91; see similarly Trinkaus, *"In Our Image,"* I, xxii. Joan Webber, *The Eloquent "I"* (Milwaukee: University of Wisconsin Press, 1968), p. 10, sees an analogous principle emerging in Anglican prose: "To turn oneself into art is only to become more fully realized." Even the Puritans, though less sympathetic to art as a moral tool, developed an ethic of perpetual self-recreation; Michael Walzer, *The Revolution of the Saints* (Cambridge: Harvard University Press, 1965), p. 311, observes that "The old order was imagined to be natural and eternal," but that for the Puritan revolutionaries,

virtue and social health must be "the product of art and will, of human doing."

48. Hans Jonas, *The Gnostic Religion* (Boston: Beacon Press, 1963), pp. 250, 328.

49. Trinkaus, *"In Our Image,"* I, 184, describes a similarly divided father-figure in the theology of Philo Judaeus, who "believes man's creation was shared by God with . . . lower creators [who] gave man his lower and potentially sinful portions."

50. Jonas, *Gnostic Religion*, p. 195; on abjuring procreation, see p. 168, also pp. 59, 145; on mistrusting sleep, see pp. 44–45; on the Call away from the mortal self and toward "rebirth" through the Mother-Wisdom, see p. 45. This concept of human alienation from nature was certainly active in Shakespeare's time. Jonas, p. 323, discerns a version of Gnosticism in Descartes' view of man: "As he shares no longer in a meaning of nature, but merely, through his body, in its mechanical determination, so nature no longer shares his inner concerns. Thus that by which man is superior to all nature, his unique distinction, mind, no longer results in a higher integration of his being into the totality of being, but on the contrary marks the unbridgeable gulf between himself and the rest of existence."

In fact, this mental Call away from sleep and away from the hereditary self has revealing analogues in English Romantic thought. Harold Bloom, "The Internalization of Quest-Romance," in *Romanticism and Consciousness*, ed. Bloom (New York: Norton, 1970), p. 6, speaks of "a baffled residue of the self, determined to be compensated for its loss of natural assurance, for having been awakened from the merely given condition that to Shelley, as to Blake, was but the sleep of death-in-life." The point is not that these Romantics were secretly Gnostics, or that Shakespeare was; the point instead is that certain metaphors have repeatedly presented themselves to great fiction-makers over the centuries when they have sought to describe an intuited need for transmundane fulfillment, to articulate that need's moral ambiguities, and to explain the peculiar burdens of self-consciousness it evokes.

51. Richard Brathwait, *The Prodigals Teares* (London, 1614), p. 70.

52. Rogers, *True Convert*, p. 289.

53. John Peter Camus, *Admirable Events*, trans. S. du Verger (London, 1639), p. 223.

54. As the ambiguities about Lady Macbeth's children and Macduff's motives serve Shakespeare's orthodox moral, the slight ambiguity about the propriety of Malcolm's nomination helps sustain the contrary, subversive moral. It leaves unclear, without imputing any wrongdoing to Duncan, whether Macbeth's resistance constitutes an unjustified and suicidal defiance of a unified natural and political order, or a noble assertion of individual rights. For the debate about the proper succession, see Elizabeth Neilsen, *"Macbeth*: The Nemesis of the Post-Shakespearian Actor," *Shakespeare Quarterly* 16 (1965), 193–199; and Michael Echeruo, "Tanistry, the 'Due

of Birth' and Macbeth's Sin," *Shakespeare Quarterly* 23 (1972), 444–450. On the significance of Banquo's "harvest" reference, see Berger, in *ELH* 47:21.

55. Muir, note to 2.3.15 in the Arden *Macbeth* (pp. 61–62).

56. Pelagius, quoted in *The Anti-Pelagian Works*, II, 19, 58, in *The Works of Aurelius Augustine*, vol. XII, ed. Marcus Dods (Edinburgh, 1885): "we have implanted in us by God a possibility for acting in both directions. It resembles, as I may say, a root which is most abundant in its produce of fruit. It yields and produces diversely according to man's will . . . Nothing good, and nothing evil, on account of which we are deemed either laudable or blameworthy, is born with us, but is done by us." Pico, the most prominent advocate of self-perfectibility in philosophy, as Pelagius is in theology, uses the seedling metaphor similarly. His "Oration on the Dignity of Man," trans. Elizabeth Forbes, in *The Renaissance Philosophy of Man*, ed. Cassirer et al. (Chicago: University of Chicago Press, 1948), p. 225, declares, "On man when he came into life the Father conferred the seeds of all kinds and the germs of every way of life. Whatever seeds each man cultivates will grow to maturity and bear in him their own fruit." Sir Walter Raleigh, *The History of the World*, ed. C. A. Patrides (London: Macmillan, 1971), p. 130, writes that "God gave unto man all kinde of seedes and grafts of life . . . whereof which soever he tooke pleasure to plant and cultive, the same should futurely grow in him, and bring forth fruit, agreable to his owne choyce and plantation."

Iago tells Roderigo that " 'tis in ourselves that we are thus or thus. Our bodies are our gardens, to the which our wills are gardeners" (*Othello*, 1.3.319–26). Banquo, in treating even this selectivity as an impious resistance to a divine order, seems closer to Philo's Stoic attitude toward ambitious projects, as Jonas, *Gnostic Religion*, p. 279, describes it: "Rather than modes of self-perfection, they are temptations by the fact that they can be taken as such . . . 'Since it is God who sows and plants the goods in the soul, it is impious of the nous to say, I plant.' Alternatively, the soul may renounce the claim to its own authorship and acknowledge its essential insufficiency—and this . . . general attitude . . . is *itself considered as 'virtue,'* although it is the denial of there being any virtue of the self." Although Shakespeare makes it clear that the seed of Macbeth's ambitious crime lies dormant in Banquo, the decision as to which man will perform it, like the decision "which grain will grow, and which will not," seems more a mystery of divine election than an act of individual will.

57. Ben Jonson, *Discoveries*, in *Ben Jonson*, ed. C. H. Herford and Percy and Evelyn Simpson (Oxford: Clarendon Press, 1947), VIII, 599.

58. Bettelheim, *Enchantment*, pp. 166–183 and passim.

59. Robert N. Watson, "Horsemanship in Shakespeare's Second Tetralogy," *English Literary Renaissance* 13 (1983), 274–300. If, as the article argues, the Renaissance treated skillful horsemanship as a symbol of both self-control and legitimate kingship, Macbeth's fear aptly describes his fate:

the same psychological and political momentum that propelled him up onto the throne throws him painfully off the other side. The moral symbolism is thus conveyed by a piece of slapstick comedy.

60. Sigmund Freud, *Civilization and Its Discontents*, trans. James Strachey (New York: Norton, 1961), p. 13. Leontes performs a similar projection in *The Winter's Tale*, externalizing his sexuality onto Polixenes and therefore refusing to acknowledge that Perdita is his.

61. *Richard III*, 1.4.100–283, shows such an evolving dispute between the satisfied murderer-for-profit and the murderer horrified at his deed and desperate to wash its blood off his hands. William B. Toole, "The Motif of Psychic Division in *Richard III*," *Shakespeare Survey* 27 (1974), 27, argues that these killers reflect Richard's inner divisions.

62. Traversi, *Approach to Shakespeare*, p. 155, argues that this effect is part of the tragic atmosphere, and not a result of a faulty text.

63. Sanders, *Dramatist*, p. 285, comments, "The kingdom of the body has become a prey to faction and division . . . he is not one man. For the rest of the play he seeks to find that singleness again, trying to become 'perfect,' as he puts it."

64. Biggins, in *Shakespeare Studies* 8:277 n. 44.

65. For the moments when Macbeth's outward show falls inadvertently into step with inward reality, see V. Y. Kantak, "An Approach to Shakespearean Tragedy," in *Aspects of Macbeth*, p. 85.

66. *Queen Elizabeth's Englishings*, ed. Caroline Pembroke, E.E.T.S. Publication 113, p. 66.

67. Richard Horwich, "Integrity in *Macbeth*: the Search for the 'Single State of Man,'" *Shakespeare Quarterly* 29 (1978), 369, disputes Traversi's belief that the divided Macbeth's "real wish is . . . to recover an original state of innocence," arguing instead that "Unity of character is not a moral attribute; monsters may possess it as easily as saints." But, as King Claudius and King Leontes demonstrate, neither extreme can remain unified in defiance of human nature. Macbeth might in a sense do well to complete his moral decay, as he might in the same sense do well to complete his bloody task, but he is trapped in a no-man's-land where neither task is perfectible or retractable. The political dilemma thus corresponds to a psychological division with parallels not only in Sartre, but also in Bovillus: "Once the first separation in man has been completed, once he has stepped out of the simplicity of his original state, he can never again return to his unbroken simplicity. He must go through the opposite in order to pass beyond it to find the true unity of his being [which] only becomes really fruitful when it divides itself in two and then reconstitutes its unity through this division" (Cassirer, *Individual and Cosmos*, pp. 89–90). Without a reconciliation such as is granted to Leontes, Macbeth remains a divided creature under a "fruitless crown."

Ben Jonson, in his *Discoveries* (Herford and Simpson, VIII, 597), warns about the analogous problem of forfeiting an original verbal identity: "Nay, wee so insist in imitating others, as wee cannot (when it is necessary) returne to our selves: like Children, that imitate the vices of *Stammerers* so long, till at last they become such; and make the habit to another nature, as it is never forgotten."

68. Thomas Middleton [and William Rowley], *The Changeling*, ed. George W. Williams, Regents Renaissance Drama Series (Lincoln: University of Nebraska Press, 1966), 3.4.135–41.

69. Flavius and Marullus propose a similar system to protect social stability in the opening lines of *Julius Caesar*; but such a system collapses in a world where any man's deeds can make him "Caesar," and Cassius lures Brutus into sharing his thriftless ambition by sophistries about the powers, properties, and ephemerality of hereditary names.

70. An Elizabethan catechism warned that, because the king and the father were essentially the same natural authority, political rebellion is "So outrageous a thing" that it "can in no wise be expressed with fit name." Quoted by Ernest W. Talbert, *The Problem of Order* (Chapel Hill: University of North Carolina Press, 1962), p. 8; see also his pp. 14–15.

71. Spurgeon, *Shakespeare's Imagery*, pp. 324–326, and the elaboration in Brooks, in Kernan, *Modern Shakespearean Criticism*, pp. 392–396, are the classic surveys of the play's garment imagery.

72. Lawrence Stone, *The Crisis of the Aristocracy* (Oxford: Clarendon Press, 1965), pp. 562–566 and passim, suggests that these laws may have arisen from the nobility's uneasy perception of increasing social mobility. Constance Jordan, "The 'Art of Clothing': Role-Playing in Deloney's Fiction," *English Literary Renaissance* 11 (1981), 183–193, argues that while most sixteenth-century authors used fancy but ill-fitting garments to show that upwardly-mobile characters could play only briefly and badly at elevated social roles (cf. *The Winter's Tale*, 4.4.749), Deloney, writing for and about such ambitious middle-class souls, uses clothing to suggest that disguise can foster rather than violate a man's "true" self.

73. The metaphor appears in Ephesians 4:22–24 and Colossians 3:9–10. For Gnostic and existential perspectives on the paradoxes of costumes, see Jonas, *Gnostic Religion* pp. 114–115, and Wylie Sypher, *Loss of the Self in Modern Literature and Art* (New York: Random House, 1962), p. 74, quoting Henri Bergson.

74. "Of the custom of wearing clothes," in Montaigne, pp. 166–169.

75. Brooks, in Kernan, *Modern Shakespearean Criticism*, p. 396.

76. Lionel Trilling, *Sincerity and Authenticity* (Cambridge: Harvard University Press, 1972), p. 75. Brathwait, "Prodigals Glasse," sig. I6r, warns against "Lessening the substance to preferre the rinde" by investing in expensive shows and garments.

77. Knights's argument in Kernan, *Modern Shakespearean Criticism* (p. 58) that we ought to interpret *Macbeth* "as we should read any other poem" evades the fact that Shakespeare wrote his plays for presentation by real people to whom the audience would naturally attribute whole personalities.

But even if the characters were only verbal artifacts in a closet drama, readers would still rightly tend to make the words flesh. Unless we perceive Macbeth as a person with an inner emotional life, we cannot perceive him losing that life; for him to decay into a histrionic shell as a result of his crimes, he must be cognizable as something more than such a shell before committing them. The unexamined assumptions and illegitimate methods of some biographers and psychoanalysts of Shakespearean characters should not discourage us from responding to the aspects of personality that Shakespeare systematically invites us to infer.

78. *Rape of Lucrece*, lines 134–54; Tarquin thus becomes "A captive victor that hath lost in gain" (line 730). As in Sonnet 129, the reward for gratified lust is a debit rather than a credit. L. C. Knights, *Some Shakespearean Themes* (London: Chatto and Windus, 1959), p. 137, remarks on the resemblances between Macbeth's situation and Tarquin's, adding that "lust—a type sin, 'including all foul harms' (1.199)—was defined as the urge to possess something that in the experience inevitably proves mere loss, an over-reaching into insubstantiality and negation." Duncan's murder, from my point of view, is designed to include all foul harms, particularly through the Oedipal overreaching implied in Macbeth's rebirth. Macbeth's resulting nullification may serve to reinforce Shakespeare's metaphor for ambition, by symbolically fulfilling the fear of castration that normally accompanies and represses Oedipal impulses. Having no "thing," as for Viola in *Twelfth Night* (3.4.302), bespeaks an absence of manliness. David Willbern, "Shakespeare's Nothing," in *Representing Shakespeare*, ed. Murray M. Schwartz and Coppélia Kahn (Baltimore: Johns Hopkins University Press, 1980), p. 252, argues that a persistent nothingness "represents an occasion for castration anxiety."

79. Stephen Greenblatt, *Sir Walter Ralegh* (New Haven: Yale University Press, 1973), p. 48, warns that " 'Acting' in the Iago sense leads to a terrible, almost unthinkable annihilation of being," and notes on p. 40 that "Machiavelli does not and cannot offer a picture of the 'real' self beneath the artificial and manipulated one. Beneath the mask there is nothing but a chaos of infinite desire." On the pervasive "nothingness" of *Macbeth*, see also Rosalie Colie, *Paradoxica Epidemica* (Princeton: Princeton University Press, 1966), pp. 233–237; and G. Wilson Knight, *The Imperial Theme* (London: Methuen, 1951), p. 129, which links the "abysmal negation" of Macbeth's experience to his advancement "from deserved honour as a noble thane to a higher kingly honour to which he has no rights." Nullity, in other words, results from an unlineal transformation of identity.

80. *Queen Elizabeth's Englishings*, p. 82.

81. Macbeth says that this vault "falls on th' other—" and he is then cut off by his wife's entrance or else trails off into his own uncertainty. This corresponds to the fact that either his wife's intervention, or his own foreshortened moral vision, provokes a leap of faithlessness into an abyss, an undefined otherness where "nothing is / But what is not" (1.3.141–142).

Brathwait, "Prodigals Glasse," sig. I7r, warns young men against "rising high to give thyself a fall," and his *Teares*, p. 91, speaks similarly of "Ambition, the great mans passion, who builds imaginary kingdomes in the ayre, and climing, for most part, breaks his owne neck." Anthony Esler, *The Aspiring Mind of the Elizabethan Younger Generation* (Durham, N.C.: Duke University Press, 1966), p. 20, argues that Shakespeare's generation heard precisely this moral from their elders: "ambition that aimed too high would surely precipitate even a Wolsey back into the dung again. To grow too fast, to overreach—there was the fatal crime."

82. Rogers, *True Convert*, p. 313.

83. Shakespeare uses the word "content" to pun on the meanings "satisfied" and "that which is contained" in *Love's Labor's Lost*, 5.2.517–18, and in *Richard II*, 5.5.23–41, where the paradox, as in *Macbeth*, is how a man can be "contented" with "nothingness."

84. Lady Macbeth, by Malcolm's report (5.9.35–37) eventually does commit suicide, and Shakespeare may use that fact, as he does other aspects of her degeneration, as an index to the metaphysical changes within her husband. L. C. Knights, *Explorations* 3 (Pittsburgh: University of Pittsburgh Press, 1976), p. 127, observes that "violence towards another is violence towards the self" throughout the play. Kahn, *Man's Estate*, p. 192, accuses Macbeth of "having murdered his deepest self in the attempt to become a man."

85. Brathwait, "Prodigals Glasse," sig. I6v. The same cluster of crimes and punishments recurs in Sands Penuen, *Ambitions scourge* (London, 1611), which resembles *Macbeth* so strikingly in its morals and metaphors that I believe it was written under the direct influence of Shakespeare's play.

86. Quoted by Trinkaus, *"In Our Image,"* I, 203. Cassirer, *Individual and Cosmos*, p. 70, sees a similar human restlessness elsewhere in Renaissance philosophy: "For the will only becomes truly *human* inasmuch as it reaches out beyond all finite goals. All natural existence and life is satisfied to . . . persist in whatever condition it has attained. But to man, everything that is ever attained will seem trivial so long as there is something more to be acquired. For man there is no moment at which to rest, no place to stand still." Desire itself, as described by modern theory, resembles what this book calls ambition: an attribute essential to the experience of human self-consciousness, which is nonetheless strongly taboo, inherently insatiable, and provocative of self-estrangement. For critical elaborations and applications of this theory, see Jacques Lacan, "Desire and the Interpretation of Desire in *Hamlet*," trans. James Hulbert, in *Literature and Psychoanalysis*, ed. Shoshana Felman (Baltimore: Johns Hopkins University Press, 1982), pp. 11–52; Tony Tanner, *Adultery in the Novel* (Baltimore: Johns Hopkins University Press, 1979); and René Girard, *Deceit, Desire, and the Novel*, trans. Yvonne Freccero (Baltimore: Johns Hopkins University Press, 1965).

87. Trilling, *Sincerity and Authenticity*, p. 10.

88. Hans Jonas, *Gnostic Religion*, pp. 333–334, suggests a parallel be-

tween the Gnostics and Heidegger's refusal to subordinate human identity to a predetermining nature.

89. A. C. Bradley, *Shakespearean Tragedy*, 2nd ed., (1905; rpt. London: Macmillan, 1950), pp. 11–39.

90. To create the tragedy of Job, for example, God had to turn part of his power over to Satan. I. A. Richards states that "Tragedy is only possible to a mind which is for the moment agnostic or Manichaean"; quoted by Harry Levin, *The Overreacher* (Cambridge: Harvard University Press, 1952), p. 161.

91. Cornford, *From Religion to Philosophy*, p. 10.

92. Cornford, p. 14; compare Bradley, *Shakespearean Tragedy*, p. 36.

93. J. M. R. Margeson, *The Origins of English Tragedy* (Oxford: Clarendon Press, 1967), pp. x, 180.

94. Ibid., p. 164.

95. Stephen Greenblatt, *Renaissance Self-Fashioning* (Chicago: University of Chicago Press, 1980), p. 210: "Marlowe's protagonists rebel against orthodoxy, but . . . their acts of negation not only conjure up the order they would destroy but seem at times to be themselves conjured up by that very order." Robert G. Hunter, *Shakespeare and the Mystery of God's Judgments* (Athens, Ga.: University of Georgia Press, 1976), p. 45, finds a suggestion that Faustus is the victim of such a conspiracy. Compare Bradley's observation on his p. 38, that in Shakespeare's tragedies the moral order "appears to engender this evil [the hero's tragic flaw] within itself, and in its effort to overcome and expel it it is agonised with pain, and driven to mutilate its own substance." This pattern may reflect the fact that, in both Shakespeare and Marlowe, the heroes are rebelling essentially against the hereditary order that created them; see Masinton, *Marlowe's Tragic Vision*, p. 130, and David Riggs, *Shakespeare's Heroical Histories* (Cambridge: Harvard University Press, 1971), p. 85.

96. See Toole, in *Shakespeare Survey* 27:31 n. 2; and Kahn, *Man's Estate*, p. 192.

97. Rolf Soellner, *Shakespeare's Patterns of Self-Knowledge* (Columbus: Ohio St. University Press, 1972), pp. xvi–xvii, with reference to Wilhelm Dilthey, and to Jacob Burckhardt's classic *The Civilization of the Renaissance in Italy* (1860).

98. Stone, *Crisis*; Michel Foucault, *The Order of Things* (New York: Pantheon, 1970).

99. Alvin Kernan, "The Henriad," in Kernan, *Modern Shakespearean Criticism*, p. 246.

100. Laurence J. Lafleur, intro. and trans. of René Descartes, *Discourse on Method* and *Meditations*, Library of the Liberal Arts (New York: Bobbs-Merrill, 1960), p. x.

101. Greenblatt, *Ralegh*, p. 94.

102. Greenblatt, *Self-Fashioning*, p. 257.

103. Hans Loewald, *Papers on Psychoanalysis* (New Haven: Yale University Press, 1980), pp. 393–394.

104. The film's Duncan-figure himself gained the throne by regicide. In the aftermath of the Macbeth-figure's crime, his wife gives birth to a still-born child, an emblem of their exclusion from regeneration and of her futilely reborn husband. The heroic Macbeth-figure is finally pinned to his castle's wall by arrows from his own troops as well as his enemies, suggesting his fatal entrapment between two warring identities, and allowing him to serve as a scapegoat for the associative guilt of his soldiers, who hope to escape punishment by killing him themselves.

105. Sigmund Freud, *Totem and Taboo*, trans. James Strachey (New York: Norton, 1950), pp. 134–136; on the relationship between these rituals and Greek tragedy, see his pp. 155–156. Girard, from a different viewpoint, also argues that unanimity in the deed and the subsequent feast is necessary to forestall the violent cycle. Freud, p. 137, speculates that after a sacrificial killing, "it was agreed that the responsibility for the murder should be placed upon the knife; and this was accordingly cast into the sea." This bears suggestive resemblances to what I have described as the mismanaged fertility-sacrifice of Duncan by Macbeth and his wife, who try to project their guilt onto the floating dagger or the "keen knife" (1.5.52), then try to disperse that guilt into "great Neptune's ocean," "The multitudinous seas," or merely "A little water" (2.2.56–64).

106. Margeson, *Origins*, pp. ix–x.

III. *Coriolanus*

1. André Green, *The Tragic Effect*, trans. Alan Sheridan (New York: Cambridge University Press, 1979), p. 196; see also Otto Rank, *The Myth of the Birth of the Hero*, trans. F. Robbins and Smith Ely Jelliffe (New York: Robert Brunner, 1952), pp. 65, 91. Avi Erlich, *Hamlet's Absent Father* (Princeton: Princeton University Press, 1977), pp. 262–264, discusses the conflicts generated in Shakespeare's plays by lost or ambiguous father-figures.

2. B. A. Brockman, intro. of his *Coriolanus*, Casebook Series (London: Macmillan, 1977), p. 12.

3. Some major documents in this dispute are: W. Gordon Zeeveld, "*Coriolanus* and Jacobean Politics," *Modern Language Review* 57 (1960), 321–334; Clifford Huffman, *Coriolanus in Context* (Cranbury, N.J.: Associated University Presses, 1971), passim; Sidney Shanker, *Shakespeare and the Uses of Ideology*, Studies in English Literature, vol. 105 (The Hague: Mouton, 1975), pp. 178–194. Bertolt Brecht's version of the story is the most famous reinterpretation of its politics, pushing them rather far to the left.

4. Brockman, *Coriolanus*, p. 33. David G. Hale, "*Coriolanus*: The Death of a Political Metaphor," *Shakespeare Quarterly* 22 (1971), 202, remarks

that "Shakespeare chooses to shift the play's concern from pointing a political moral to dramatizing the conflict within Coriolanus." Opposed to
this view is L. C. Knights's comment, in " 'Integration' in *The Winter's
Tale*," *Sewanee Review* 84 (1976), 599, that *Coriolanus* "is not in any sense
a myth or parable of the inner life."

5. A. C. Bradley, *Shakespearean Tragedy*, 2nd ed., (1905; rpt. London:
Macmillan, 1950), p. 18.

6. Michael Walzer, *The Revolution of the Saints: A Study in the
Origins of Radical Politics* (Cambridge: Harvard University Press, 1965),
p. 225.

7. Gordon Ross Smith, "Authoritarian Patterns in Shakespeare's *Coriolanus*," in *The Design Within*, ed. M. D. Faber (New York: Science House,
1970), p. 314.

8. Delmore Schwartz, "Coriolanus and His Mother," in his *Summer
Knowledge* (New York: Doubleday, 1959), p. 83. Schwartz's poem seems to
me to focus perceptively on many of the problems and conflicts this chapter
discusses. Lines quoted by permission; © 1958.

9. Stephen Greenblatt, *Renaissance Self-Fashioning* (Chicago: University of Chicago Press, 1980), p. 9.

10. C. F. Keppler, *The Literature of the Second Self* (Tucson: University
of Arizona Press, 1972), p. 11. When the citizens threaten Coriolanus with
"precipitation / From off the rock Tarpeian" (3.3.102–03), then settle on a
banishment that endangers them and ultimately destroys him, their actions
resemble those of the Doppelgänger as Keppler describes them (p. 28): "a
pushing forward of the first self, whether by a gradual crowding or a headlong
driving, toward the precipice of catastrophe. Often the first self goes over,
but this is not necessarily to say that the second self is left to enjoy his
triumph any more than the first self is 'saved' when, overeager or miscal-
culating, the second self goes over in his victim's place. . . . the relationship
between the selves is too sensitively intimate a one to be brought to an end
by their physical separation."

11. Vincenzo Cartari, *The Fountaine of Ancient Fiction*, trans. Richard
Linche (London: 1599), sig, V4r.

12. Lawrence Danson, *Tragic Alphabet* (New Haven: Yale University
Press, 1974), p. 146. In *Don Quixote*, the hero is similarly driven to me-
tonymy as a desperate device against a world too degraded to provide his
knightly identity with the conflict it needs to survive. See Michel Foucault,
The Order of Things (New York: Pantheon Press, 1970), p. 47; Georg Lukács,
The Theory of the Novel, trans. Anna Bostock (1920; rpt. Cambridge, Mass.:
M.I.T. Press, 1971), pp. 98–105. In this analogy, Sancho serves as the te-
nacious and degradingly corporal Doppelgänger.

13. Lucien Goldmann, *The Hidden God*, trans. Philip Thody (London:
Routledge and Kegan Paul, 1964), p. 59; quoting Georg Lukács, *Die Seele
und die Formen* (Berlin: E. Fleischel, 1911), p. 344.

14. Plutarch, *Lives of the Noble Grecians and Romans*, trans.

Thomas North (1579); quoted in Geoffrey Bullough, *Narrative and Dramatic Sources of Shakespeare* (London: Routledge and Kegan Paul, 1964), V, 506.

15. G. Wilson Knight, *The Imperial Theme* (London: Methuen, 1951), pp. 154–158; Maurice Charney, *Shakespeare's Roman Plays* (Cambridge: Harvard University Press, 1961), p. 179; Danson, *Tragic Alphabet*, p. 149, remarks that "only when Coriolanus *is* his sword is Coriolanus wholly manifested."

16. D. J. Enright, "*Coriolanus*: Tragedy or Debate?" *Essays in Criticism* 4 (1954), 7; Roland M. Frye, "Shakespeare's Mirror Image of Failure: *Richard II* and *Coriolanus*," *Forum* (Houston) 11 (1973–74), ii–iii, 13, comments that Coriolanus' "intransigent integrity" makes him "unable to be anything other than himself."

17. Walzer, *Revolution of the Saints*, p. 20. Walzer argues further that "Puritan warfare consisted first of all in . . . the vigilant avoidance of evil company," and that such conflict "was itself an aspect of salvation: a man at ease was a man lost" (p. 279). The Puritans were taught "to think of the struggle with Satan and his allies as an extension and duplicate of their internal spiritual conflicts, and also as a difficult and continuous war, requiring . . . military exercise, and discipline" (p. 290). Like Coriolanus, they battle their society to escape the old bonds of identity which stand between them and their inward ideal of purity: "Calvinist conscience gave to war and to politics . . . a new sense of method and purpose [which] distinguishes the activity of the saints from that of medieval men, caught up in the unchanging world of tradition, fixed in their social place and loyal to their relatives; and also from that of Renaissance men, pursuing a purely personal ambition" (p. 13).

Coriolanus' aspiration resembles this idealism more than it does Renaissance social climbing. He evades Menenius' fable as the Puritans evaded older writers such as John of Salisbury who argued that "political society was . . . a great organism, a body politic . . . as natural as was the family. Men were not properly speaking citizens of this body, but literally *members*, related to the bodily whole in a functional-organic way" (p. 6). Puritans would certainly have been on a playwright's mind at the time *Coriolanus* was written, and these correspondences strike me as potentially significant.

18. Ibid., p. 315; Walzer describes this pattern in ways relevant to both Coriolanus' extremism and Shakespeare's concern with the Renaissance crisis of identity: "All forms of radical politics make their appearance at moments of rapid and decisive change, moments when customary status is in doubt and character (or 'identity') is itself a problem. Before [the 'saints'] attempt the creation of a new order, they must create new men. Repression and collective discipline are the typical methods of this creativity: the disordered world is interpreted as a world at war; enemies are discovered and attacked. The saint is a soldier whose battles are fought out in the self before they are fought out in society. Revolution follows from Puritan saint-

hood . . . also from Jacobin virtue and from the Bolshevik 'steeling' of character; it is the acting out of a new identity, painfully won."

19. Willard Farnham, *The Medieval Heritage of Elizabethan Tragedy* (Berkeley: University of California Press, 1936), p. 424.

20. John Byshop, *Beautifull Blossomes . . . from the best trees of all kyndes* (London, 1577), p. 19.

21. Janet Adelman, " 'Anger's My Meat': Feeding, Dependency and Aggression in *Coriolanus*," in *Shakespeare: Pattern of Excelling Nature*, ed. David Bevington and Jay L. Halio (Cranbury, N.J.: Assoc. University Presses, 1978, pp. 110–111, remarks that "for Coriolanus, as for his mother, nobility consists precisely in *not* eating," and that having been "forced to feed himself on his own anger, Coriolanus refuses to acknowledge any neediness or dependency." See also James M. Swan, "History, Pastoral and Desire" (Ph.D. diss., Stanford University, 1974), pp. 214–215.

22. Plutarch, *Lives of the Noble Grecians and Romans*, trans. Thomas North (1579), ed. W. E. Henley (London, 1895), I, 72. An alternative story of the founding of Rome by a woman named Roma (I, 68) also invites some comparisons with Volumnia's salvation of the city.

23. Marjorie Garber, *Coming of Age in Shakespeare* (London: Methuen, 1981), pp. 75–76, discusses this warning. On the implications of naming in the play as a whole, see Garber, pp. 72–78, and D. J. Gordon, "Name and Fame: Shakespeare's *Coriolanus*," in his *The Renaissance Imagination*, ed. Stephen Orgel (Berkeley: University of California Press, 1975), pp. 203–219.

24. Pierre de La Primaudaye, *The French Academy* (London, 1594), II, 301.

25. René Girard, *Violence and the Sacred*, trans. Patrick Gregory (Baltimore: Johns Hopkins, 1977), p. 289. Cf. Daniel Sabbath and Mendel Hall, *End Product* (New York: Urizen Books, 1977), pp. 96–97, which describes an African tribe, the Chagga, who mark the transformation of a young man into a heroic warrior, not by the usual ritual feigning death and rebirth, but rather by a feigned operation to terminate defecation.

26. Keith Thomas, "The Place of Laughter in Tudor and Stuart England," *Times Literary Supplement*, (21 Jan., 1977), 77–81. Though Coriolanus has his moments as an ironist, he would presumably have needed outlets other than laughter. Stephen Batman, in his *Batman uppon Bartholome*, a collection drawn from Bartholomaeus Anglicus (London, 1582), p. 61, defines "Venter" as the "wombe" that "taketh and seetheth meate and drinke, to feed all the members of the body."

27. Bullough, *Narrative and Dramatic Sources*, V, 516.

28. Thomas á Kempis, *Of the Imitation of Christ*, trans. T. Rogers (London, 1587), sigs. Y2–Y2v; such a fiery purgatory similarly serves to convert the mortal body into an immortal metallic body in Yeats's "Sailing to Byzantium." Fire is associated with Coriolanus' ambitious projects many times during the play; in addition to the examples cited in this chapter, see 2.1.257; 3.1.196; 3.2.23; 4.6.78, 137; 5.1.64; 5.2.6, 46, 71.

29. Cesare Ripa, *Iconologie*, ed. and trans. J. Baudoin (Paris, 1644), II, 93; my translation of "qui ont plus d'ambition pour les vivres que pour les honneurs."

30. Katherine Stockholder, "The Other Coriolanus," *PMLA* 85 (1970), 229.

31. Quoted in Charles Trinkaus, *"In Our Image and Likeness"* (London: Constable, 1970), I, 193.

32. Francis Quarles, *Emblemes* (London, 1635), Book 2, Emb. VII; rpt. in *English Seventeenth-Century Verse*, vol. I, ed. Louis Martz (New York: Norton, 1973), pp. 225–227.

33. G. K. Hunter, "The Last Tragic Heroes," in Brockman, *Coriolanus*, p. 162, is one of the several critics who quote Aristotle's maxim as relevant to this play. Frye, in *Forum*, 11, 20, comments that "As man attempts to become more than human, he actually seems to become strangely less."

34. C. S. Lewis, *English Literature in the Sixteenth Century*, in the Oxford History of English Literature (Oxford: Clarendon Press, 1954), p. 12.

35. Simone de Beauvoir, *The Second Sex*, trans. H. M. Parshley (New York: Bantam, 1970), p. 685. Coppélia Kahn, *Man's Estate* (Berkeley: University of California Press, 1981), p. 163, sees a slightly different sort of "zero-sum game" at work in Coriolanus' dealings with the citizenry: "If they are anything at all, he is nothing"; she cites Alvin Gouldner, *Enter Plato* (New York: Basic Books, 1965), pp. 41–74, who argues that "the Greek contest system" determining glory was essentially a zero-sum game, in which any gain for one man had to arise from an equivalent of loss from another. A version of that system is apparent in Hal's defeat of Hotspur.

36. Charles K. Hofling, "An Interpretation of Shakespeare's *Coriolanus*," in Faber, *Design Within*, p. 297, also remarks on this possible slip.

37. See for example J. C. Maxwell, "Animal Imagery in *Coriolanus*," *Modern Language Review* 42 (1947), 417–421.

38. Danson, *Tragic Alphabet*, pp. 143–146, and Adelman, "Anger," p. 114, comment on Coriolanus' resistance to this degrading multiplicity. See also Wolfgang Clemen, *The Development of Shakespeare's Imagery* (London: Methuen, 1951), p. 155.

39. J. M. Evans, *Paradise Lost and the Genesis Tradition* (Oxford: Clarendon Press, 1968), p. 195.

40. Quoted in L. C. Knights, *Drama and Society in the Age of Jonson* (1937; rpt. London: Chatto and Windus, 1962), p. 146. The Puritans, with whom I have been associating Coriolanus, were gradually changing their idea of the "calling" from an advocacy of stable vocations to an advocacy of unabashed ambitious self-transformations; see Christopher Hill, *The Century of Revolution, 1603-1714* (New York: Norton, 1966), p. 92; and H. M. Robertson, *Aspects of the Rise of Economic Individualism* (Cambridge, England: Cambridge University Press, 1933), pp. 6–14.

41. Thomas Floyd, *The Picture of a perfit Common wealth* (London, 1600), p. 287.

42. Batman, *Batman uppon Bartholome*, pp. 10–11.

43. Evans, *Paradise Lost*, p. 181.

44. Paul Cantor, *Shakespeare's Rome: Republic and Empire* (Ithaca: Cornell University Press, 1976), pp. 47, 205, and passim, suggests some of the connections.

45. Philostratus the Elder, *Les Images ou Tableaux de Platte Peinture*, trans. B. de Vigenère (Paris, 1629 ed.), p. 487; my translation of "hideux serpenteaux à cent testes, qui se coula insensiblement dans les plus secrets cabinets de son estomach & cerveau; là où jouant ses jeux à plaisir, elle le transporta tellement hors de soy, qu'il tua ses propres enfans & sa femme."

46. Arthur Henkel, *Emblemata* (Stuttgart: J. B. Metzlersche Verlagsbuchhandlung, 1967), p. 21; much the same point is made, concerning love, in Donne's "A Lecture upon the Shadow."

47. Janet Adelman, *The Common Liar* (New Haven: Yale University Press, 1973), p. 61.

48. Thomas Churchyard, *A discourse of Rebellion* (London, 1570), stanzas 3 and 10.

49. 1.10.79–92. This is in keeping with the principle annunciated by the Bastard in *King John*: "new-made honor doth forget men's names" (1.1.187). It may also hint at a deadly struggle between father and son, since Coriolanus seems to perform this fatal forgetting as soon as his father-figure Cominius declares he would free the old man "Were he the butcher of my son" (1.9.88).

50. Bullough, *Narrative and Dramatic Sources*, V, 505–506.

51. Rank, *Birth of the Hero*, pp. 61–62.

52. Christopher Marlowe, *Tamburlaine, Part One*, in *The Complete Plays of Christopher Marlowe*, ed. J. B. Steane (Harmondsworth, Middlesex: Penguin, 1969), 2.6.31 and 2.6.1–23.

53. Harry Levin, *The Overreacher* (Cambridge: Harvard University Press, 1952), p. 33.

54. Nehemiah Rogers, *The True Convert* (London, 1620), p. 301.

55. Joseph Weixlman, " '. . . action may / Conveniently the rest convey': Some Key Presentational Images in Shakespeare's *Coriolanus*," *Forum* (Houston) 12 (1974), ii, 9–13.

56. See note 79 to chapter 1; the quotation is from Norman Holland, *Psychoanalysis and Shakespeare* (New York: McGraw-Hill, 1964), p. 229. The analogy between a "gate" and the vagina the fetus must traverse on its way to a Herculean birth appears in George Sandys' version of Ovid's *Metamorphosis* (London, 1626), pp. 181–182.

57. Helkiah Crooke, *A description of the body of man*, 2nd ed., (London, 1631), p. 269.

58. Robert G. Hunter, *Shakespeare and the Mystery of God's Judgments* (Athens, Ga.: University of Georgia Press, 1976), p. 160.

59. Michael Long, *The Unnatural Scene* (London: Methuen, 1976), pp. 65–66; James J. Greene, "*Coriolanus*: The Hero as Eternal Adolescent," in

How To Read Shakespearean Tragedy, ed. Edward Quinn (New York: Harper and Row, 1978), p. 368.

60. Rank, *Birth of the Hero*, p. 83; see also p. 64.

61. For the mythic pattern of death and heroic rebirth, see note 6 of my Introduction. Garber, *Coming of Age*, pp. 7–8, cites discussions of "liminality" and its dangers in Arnold van Gennep, *Les Rites de passage* (1908); Mary Douglas, *Purity and Danger* (London: Routledge and Kegan Paul, 1966); Victor Turner, *The Ritual Process* (Ithaca: Cornell University Press, 1966); and Turner, "Variations of a Theme of Liminality," in *Secular Ritual*, ed. Sally F. Moore and Barbara G. Myerhoff (Amsterdam: Van Gorcum, Assen, 1977).

62. Green, *Tragic Effect*, p. 199.

63. Adelman, "Anger," p. 113. Robert J. Stoller, "Shakespearean Tragedy: *Coriolanus*," in Faber, *Design Within*, p. 330, notes the emphasis on Coriolanus' phallic hardness and views the assault on Corioles' gates as its fitting culmination.

64. Bullough, *Narrative and Dramatic Sources*, V, 503.

65. David B. Barron, "*Coriolanus*: Portrait of the Artist As Infant," *American Imago* 19 (1962), 171–193.

66. Ralph Berry, "Sexual Imagery in *Coriolanus*," *Studies in English Literature* 13 (1973), 301.

67. When Coriolanus appears to propose rape as an incentive for renewing a military attack (1.4.41), critics such as Adelman ("Anger," p. 113) infer actual sexual desire on his part. I think Shakespeare leaves it unclear whether Coriolanus feels lust or merely uses it to rally assistance for his own bloodlust; in fact, Coriolanus might not even understand the distinction.

68. Adelman, "Anger," p. 116.

69. René Descartes, *Discourse on Method* and *Meditations*, trans. Laurence Lafleur, Library of Liberal Arts (New York: Bobbs-Merrill, 1960), p. 104.

70. Samuel Gardiner, *Portraiture of the Prodigal Sonne* (London, 1599), p. 240.

71. Rogers, *True Convert*, p. 294.

72. Seneca, *Oedipus*, trans. Alexander Neville (1581), in *Seneca's Tragedies*, ed. Eric C. Baade (London: Macmillan, 1969), p. 25.

73. See the alphabetized listing of potentially sexual words in Eric Partridge, *Shakespeare's Bawdy* (London: Routledge and Kegan Paul, 1968).

74. David Riggs, *Shakespeare's Heroical Histories* (Cambridge: Harvard University Press, 1971), p. 91.

75. Seneca, *Oedipus*, p. 16.

76. As Freud suggests in *Totem and Taboo*, sacrifice may be the society's exorcism of its collective Oedipal guilt. John Holloway, *The Story of the Night* (London: Routledge and Kegan Paul, 1961), describes the sacrificial

aspects of Coriolanus' death, and of the deaths of Shakespeare's other ambitious figures.

77. Kahn, *Man's Estate*, p. 199, in her discussion of *The Tempest*, mentions this typical function of the Doppelgänger.

78. Sigmund Freud, "Some Psychical Consequences of the Anatomical Distinction Between the Sexes," in the Standard Edition of his *Works*, trans. James Strachey, XIX (London: Hogarth, 1961), 248–258; and "The Sexual Theories of Children," IX (London: Hogarth, 1959), 217–218.

79. Batman, *Batman uppon Bartholome*, p. 61. Schwartz's Coriolanus feels himself "fucked / By every craven knight vicarious there" at this point in the story (p. 97).

80. David Willbern, "Shakespeare's Nothing," in *Representing Shakespeare*, ed. Murray M. Schwartz and Coppélia Kahn (Baltimore: Johns Hopkins University Press, 1980), p. 252.

81. John Donne, "A nocturnall upon S. Lucies day," lines 17–18, in *The Complete Poetry of John Donne*, ed. John T. Shawcross (New York: Anchor Press, 1967).

82. Shakespeare himself, as early as 1 *Henry VI* (3.1.12), uses the verb to suggest forgery in our modern, criminal sense. Willbern, "Shakespeare's Nothing," p. 249, comments on the "forgery" of Coriolanus' unlineal name.

83. Expressions such as "like himself" derive from a conventional Latin phrase, *par sibi*, which generally meant "worthy of himself"; see Reuben Brower, *Hero and Saint* (New York: Oxford, 1971), p. 366 n. 3. This would not necessarily have prevented Shakespeare, however, from using the odd implications of the English phrase to reinforce our sense of Coriolanus' self-alienation and self-simulation.

84. Lionel Trilling, *Sincerity and Authenticity* (Cambridge: Harvard University Press, 1972), p. 66.

85. Stephen Greenblatt, *Renaissance Self-Fashioning*, p. 200. Similarly, Ernst Cassirer, *The Individual and the Cosmos in Renaissance Philosophy*, trans. Mario Domandi (New York: Harper and Row, 1964), p. 84, remarks that the free choice that characterizes humanity for Pico della Mirandola "is not a process that takes place once and that closes when certain results are achieved, but rather one which must be completed over and over again."

86. Rogers, *True Convert*, p. 284.

87. Patricia K. Meszaros, " 'There is a world elsewhere': Tragedy and History in *Coriolanus*," *Studies in English Literature* 16 (1976), 281.

88. *Sermons or Homilies Appointed to be Read in Churches in the Time of Queen Elizabeth of Famous Memory* (London: C. & J. Rivington, 1825), p. 50.

89. Abraham Fraunce, *The Third Part of the Countesse of Pembrokes Yuychurch: Entituled, Amintas Dale* (London: 1592), M.L.A.A. Photo Facsimiles 75, p. 2. When Coriolanus is indirectly compared to "those mysteries

which heaven / Will not have earth to know" (4.2.35–36), the comparison between his fire and that of Prometheus gains credibility.

90. Crooke, *Description of the body of man*, p. 309.

91. Kahn, *Man's Estate*, p. 10, citing Nancy Chodorow, *The Reproduction of Mothering* (Berkeley and Los Angeles: University of California Press, 1979).

92. Hans Loewald, *Papers on Psychoanalysis* (New Haven: Yale University Press, 1980), pp. 14–16.

93. Kahn, *Man's Estate*, p. 11; citing Ralph Greenson, "Dis-Identifying from Mother: Its Special Importance for the Boy," *International Journal of Psycho-analysis* 49 (1968), 370–374.

94. Holland, *Psychoanalysis and Shakespeare*, p. 229, describes a psychoanalytic claim that "Macbeth and Lady Macbeth represent a child and a mother, each imperfectly differentiated from the other. Out of this blurred relation of self and object the oedipal conflict springs: Macbeth tries to achieve an identity by hostile action against his environment; Lady Macbeth turns that hostility from herself toward Duncan." The fact that one could penetratingly describe the hidden Oedipal conflict in *Coriolanus* by substituting the names of Coriolanus and Volumnia in this passage, with Duncan corresponding to the Roman citizenry, may support my thesis that Shakespeare consistently describes the tasks of ambition by a deep comparison to the tasks of birth, or rebirth.

95. Rank, *Birth of the Hero*, p. 66.

96. Quoted by Swan, "History, Pastoral and Desire," p. 302.

97. Harold Bloom, *A Map of Misreading* (New York: Oxford, 1975), p. 38.

98. Long, *Unnatural Scene*, p. 60.

99. Bullough, *Narrative and Dramatic Sources*, V, 506. The passage goes on to remark that the Romans called this valor "*Virtus*, by the name of vertue selfe, as including in that generall name, all other speciall vertues besides." Coriolanus' martial qualities would therefore have been an appropriate focal point for a study of the problems of pursuing extraordinary virtue in general, a study of the hazards of ambition.

100. Greene, "*Coriolanus*," p. 375; see also p. 367; Cantor, *Shakespeare's Rome*, p. 60; and W. I. Carr, " 'Gracious Silence'—A Selective Reading of *Coriolanus*," *English Studies* 46 (1965), 223–224.

101. Brower, *Hero and Saint*, pp. 358–360, argues that Coriolanus is described in clear echoes of Homeric and Virgilian heroism, and that such phrases as "it is held" and "if it be" indicate the abstract and derivative quality of the honorable principles that shape him.

102. Walzer, *Revolution of the Saints*, pp. 144–147, discusses the Puritans' developing distrust of elaborate rhetoric.

103. Charney, *Shakespeare's Roman Plays*, pp. 171–174, and Anne Righter, *Shakespeare and the Idea of the Play* (London: Chatto and Windus,

1968), pp. 189–191, comment on this defensive use of the theatrical metaphor.

104. Bullough, *Narrative and Dramatic Sources*, V, 508.

105. Trilling, *Sincerity and Authenticity*, p. 64; see also his p. 75.

106. Quoted in Trinkaus, "In Our Image," I, 120.

107. Green, *The Tragic Effect*, p. 196.

108. Byshop, *Beautifull Blossomes*, p. 53.

109. See n. 24 above.

110. Francis Bacon, "Of Nature in Men," in *Bacon's Essays*, ed. Guy Montgomery (New York: Macmillan, 1930), p. 99.

111. Robert J. Stoller, "Facts and Fancies: An Examination of Freud's Concept of Bisexuality," in *Women and Analysis*, ed. Jean Strouse (New York: Grossman, 1978), p. 358; quoted by Kahn, *Man's Estate*, pp. 10–11.

112. La Primaudaye, *French Academy*, II, 398. Bradley, *Shakespearean Tragedy*, pp. 29–30, suggests that Shakespeare "does not appear to have taken much interest in heredity, or to have attached much importance to it," but the force that reclaims and consumes Coriolanus in this scene is essentially genetic; see Danson, *Tragic Alphabet*, p. 155; Adelman, "Anger," p. 118; and Derek Traversi, *Shakespeare: The Roman Plays* (Stanford: Stanford University Press, 1963), p. 272. Hermann Heuer, "From Plutarch to Shakespeare: A Study of *Coriolanus*," *Shakespeare Survey* 10 (1957), 52, demonstrates that North's translation of this scene shifts Plutarch's emphasis so that "It is now a question of the acknowledgment or denial of the natural." Shakespeare then alters North's version to stress this "element of unnaturalness" even further by adding Virgilia and young Martius to the scene, surrounding Coriolanus with his genetic context (p. 54). But Heuer declares himself mystified how "Coriolanus should have been prompted to trespass against the sacred laws of nature and his own treasured convictions" (p. 57). From my perspective, his treasured convictions were precisely what necessitated a war on nature, even though he did not at first realize that Rome and Volumnia were part of that limiting force.

113. Robert M. Adams, ed., *Ben Jonson's Plays and Masques* (New York: Norton, 1979), p. 42 n. 2, remarks that "A man without a recognized father was known to the Romans as a *filius terrae*, 'son of earth.' " Since Coriolanus is often associated with Hercules, it is interesting to connect this fact with Hercules' struggle against a mob of pygmies who according to Philostratus the Elder were known as "the children of the earth, those who are entirely given over to the bodily passions" (*Les Images*, p. 484; see also p. 482). These pygmies assault Hercules in his sleep, as a sort of aftershock to his battle with Antaeus, the son of Gaia (the earth), as representations of his own bodily vulnerabilities. Eugene Waith, *The Herculean Hero* (London: Chatto and Windus, 1962), p. 18, states that "Both in classical times and later, these stories were sometimes interpreted allegorically as triumphs of man's higher nature over bestiality and evil." Fraunce, *The Third Part*,

p. 46, moralizes Hercules' struggle with Antaeus along these lines: "so the spirit still striveth with the body, but never can overcome it, till he lift it up so high from the ground, that with his feete, to weete his affections, he receave no new assistance from his mother the earth." This is the same ambitious endeavor that leads Coriolanus to disdain the shadow he treads on at noon (1.1.259–61), in an effort to raise his human nature out of its earthly roots, its bodily aspects, and hence out of what he understands as evil.

114. Danson, *Tragic Alphabet*, p. 151; see similarly Brian Vickers, *Shakespeare: "Coriolanus,"* Studies in English Literature, vol. 58 (London: Edward Arnold, 1971), p. 11.

115. Walzer, *Revolution of the Saints*, pp. 176, 149, 57.

116. Volumnia's warnings echo those of Elizabethan antirevolutionary tracts. The mother in Thomas Fenne's *Fennes Frutes* (London, 1590), p. 11, tells her son, "needes woudst thou be recounted among the Gods immortall . . . but now . . . thou art so far from being heavenly, that thou art most vile." John Christoferson, *An exhortation to all menne to take hede and beware of rebellion* (London, 1554), sig. A5v, warns that ambitious men turn to rebellion and "by meanes therof, undo theyr wives and children, & disfame all their posteritie."

117. Bacon, "Of Nature in Men," p. 98; see Horace, *Epistles*, bk. I, ep. x, line 24. Philip Brockbank, intro. and ed., *Coriolanus*, Arden ed., p. 60, argues that "All that is 'soft, mild, pitiful and flexible' has been shut out in *Coriolanus* and flows back into the stage silence," as a fulfillment of earlier "intimacies, recognitions of kinship, and touches of nature." This may be a representation of the more extreme regression that Swan, "History, Pastoral and Desire," p. 333, sees depicted in Marvell: "He exists, that is, prior to language, just as he existed originally and, at some level, still exists in the silence, literally the *infancy*, the wordlessness, of his symbiotic relationship with his mother." In any case, silence is the natural enemy, and marks the natural death, of the new self that only rhetorical bluster could keep alive in peacetime. We may compare this destruction of Coriolanus' fantastic self with the psychoanalyst's calculated silence, by which the subject "ends up by recognizing that this [verbally fabricated] being has never been anything more than his construct in the Imaginary"; see Jacques Lacan, *The Language of the Self*, intro. and trans. Anthony Wilden (Baltimore: Johns Hopkins University Press, 1968), p. 11.

118. The parallel between Shakespeare, the poet who creates the hero out of words, and Coriolanus, the man that poet describes who creates the hero out of his own deeds, is reinforced by the fact that the silence that must eventually fall will mark the death of both the poet's project and the hero's. As I suggested in my discussion of *Macbeth*, the poet is sympathetically implicated in the ambitious quest, however much he may express disapproval of it, because without it there would be no heroism and therefore no play. He struggles as much as his hero does to maintain, through fig-

uration and simulation, a higher if artificial version of life. Girard, *Violence and the Sacred*, p. 293, notes in figures from Sophocles to modern intellectuals "an ambiguous attitude toward those beings whom the stricken city has driven from its precincts in an effort to regain its lost unity. Even when he is not actually espousing suspect causes, the poet retells ancient, time-honored legends in a new way, giving them a slightly impious and seditious ring." Therefore "the poet too must become a *pharmakos*." One great playwright's ambivalence about the exile and destruction of Oedipus reappears some two thousand years later in another great playwright's ambivalence about the exile and destruction of Coriolanus, who is also banished to allow his city to regain its lost unity. The harsh irony by which Coriolanus' loud stuggle to create a heroic identity is revealed as futile by a single silent gesture, like the harsh irony by which the masque-like portents in *Macbeth* become devastatingly literal, visual, even simple-minded, finally strikes as severe a blow against the playwright's grand creative ambitions as it does against the hero's. The mocking laughter Coriolanus hears from the Olympian heavens threatens to descend also from the "heavens" of the Globe theater.

119. Trinkaus, *"In Our Image,"* I, 119.

120. For the suggestion of demonic conspiracy in *Doctor Faustus*, see the opening Chorus, line 22, and Hunter, *Shakespeare and the Mystery*, p. 45. Lukács, *Theory*, p. 100, comments that the natural world in the novel, "reveals itself 'as it really is' only as an opposition to every one of the hero's actions. Nevertheless this outside reality is no more than a sluggish, formless, meaningless mass entirely lacking any capacity for planned and consistent counter-action."

121. Lukács, *Die Seele*, p. 327; quoted in Goldmann, *Hidden God*, p. 37.

122. Hans Martensen, *Jacob Boehme (1575–1624)*, trans. T. Rhys Evans, new rev. ed. (London: Loxley Bros., 1949), p. 132.

123. In Bullough, *Narrative and Dramatic Sources*, V, 536–537, Coriolanus' ambitions are roused by a divine force like the ones in Homer, then defeated when a Roman lady "sodainely fell into suche a fansie, as we have rehearsed before, and had (by some god, as I thinke) taken holde of a noble devise"—the generational panorama that reclaims Coriolanus for mortal nature.

124. Peter Blos, *On Adolescence* (New York: Free Press, 1962), pp. 4–5; cited by Kahn, *Man's Estate*, p. 196; see also her p. 200 n. 15, on the use of mirror-figures to salvage a threatened selfhood and to encompass an ambivalence toward envelopment by the mother.

125. Meredith Skura, *The Literary Use of the Psychoanalytic Process* (New Haven: Yale University Press, 1981), p. 182.

126. Joan Webber, *The Eloquent "I"* (Milwaukee: University of Wisconsin Press, 1968), p. 11.

127. Theodore Ziolkowski, *Disenchanted Images* (Princeton: Princeton University Press, 1977), pp. 18–226 passim, mentions these dangers in his

discussion of iconological implications of mirror involvements; see also Garber, *Coming of Age*, pp. 180–193; and notes 17 and 28 to chapter 1 above.

128. Una Ellis-Fermor, *Shakespeare the Dramatist and Other Papers*, ed. Kenneth Muir (London: Methuen, 1961), p. 73. Cantor, *Shakespeare's Rome*, p. 205, associates efforts to find "a world elsewhere" in the Roman plays with an "urge to transcend the conventional limits of humanity."

129. Adelman, "Anger," p. 123 n. 23, comments that "the Aufidius invented by Coriolanus seems designed to reassure Coriolanus of the reality of his own male grandeur by giving him the image of himself; [which] helps to account for his tragic blindness to his rival's true nature as opportunist and schemer."

130. Anthony Wilden, commentary in Lacan, *Language of the Self*, p. 160.

131. Greenblatt, *Renaissance Self-Fashioning*, p. 213.

132. Skura, *Literary Use*, p. 21, comments on the fact that the psychoanalytic concept of "incorporation" refers both to a fantasy of devouring another person and to the fantasy that, in doing so, one can absorb that person's identity and qualities.

133. The term is used by Lionel Ovesey, and is cited by Swan, "History, Pastoral and Desire," p. 228. See also Holland, *Psychoanalysis and Shakespeare*, pp. 328–329; Brockbank's Arden introduction, p. 49; and Berry, in *Studies in English Literature* 13:301. The dream Aufidius describes (or invents) here resembles the dream Iago attributes to Cassio (3.3.413–26). That narration, too, has been treated as evidence of the speaker's homosexual impulses, but on another level the desire is again a desire to absorb an ideal identity; see Shelley Orgel, "Iago," *American Imago* 25 (1968), 266.

134. Skura, *Literary Use*, p. 211.

135. See for example Matthew Besdine, "The Jocasta Complex, Mothering and Genius," *Psychoanalytic Review* 55 (1968–69), 269–270; and Loewald, *Paper on Psychoanalysis*, p. 16 n. 11.

136. Charney, *Roman Plays*, 167–168, and Danson, *Tragic Alphabet*, 154, note the coincidence of these various butterfly references.

137. Rogers, *True Convert*, p. 79.

138. Adelman, "Anger," p. 118, points out that "Coriolanus does not acknowledge the child as his and his wife's: he first imagines himself in his mother's womb, and then imagines his child as an extension of his mother."

139. Bradley, *Shakespearean Tragedy*, p. 29; similar points are made in his "Character and the Imaginative Appeal of Tragedy in *Coriolanus*" (1912), rpt. in Brockman, p. 61; in Irving Ribner, *Jacobean Tragedy* (London: Methuen, 1962), p. 3; and in Waith, *Herculean Hero*, p. 133.

140. Goldmann, *Hidden God*, p. 62.

141. Lukács, *Die Seele*, p. 339, quoted in Goldmann, p. 38.

142. Coriolanus' political entrapment resembles that of Marlowe's Barabas, whose character and situation lead him to betray both sides in a long-

standing war; the politicians on both sides then conspire to destroy him with what they have in common. Coriolanus' spiritual entrapment, analogous to the political, recalls that of Marlowe's Faustus, who is diabolically trapped and torn between Promethean and Christian notions of virtue. Faustus, like Coriolanus, can neither transcend mundane limitations nor retreat to a meek acceptance of paternal Grace; the shredding of each man's body becomes an objective correlative to the ambitious man's loss of unified identity. Charles Masinton, *Christopher Marlowe's Tragic Vision* (Athens, Ohio: Ohio University Press, 1972), p. 123, describes Marlowe's protagonists in terms that suggest their deep affinity with Shakespearean overreachers such as Coriolanus and Leontes: "Ironically, their misled attempts to break through the limitations of their original conditions of being bring only an increased awareness of limitation," despite a "furious drive to replace what they sense to be man's lost perfection."

143. Quoted by Trilling, *Sincerity and Authenticity*, p. 160. Volumnia, using her formidable rhetorical skill at turning situations inside-out, accuses Coriolanus of imposing on his family the schizophrenia she actually imposes on him (5.3.103–18). In doing so, she echoes Octavia in *Antony and Cleopatra*, and Zenocrate in *Tamburlaine, Part One*, who is also opposing an assault, necessitated by the hero's transcendent ambitions, on her family and her homeland.

IV. *The Winter's Tale*

1. Michel de Montaigne, "Of experience" and "Of physiognomy," in *The Complete Essays of Montaigne*, trans. Donald M. Frame (Stanford: Stanford University Press, 1975), pp. 816 and 811.

2. Robert G. Hunter, *Shakespeare and the Mystery of God's Judgments* (Athens, Ga.: University of Georgia Press, 1976), discusses the Elizabethans' reliance on this semi-Pelagian doctrine. Paul Oskar Kristeller, in *The Renaissance Philosophy of Man*, ed. Ernst Cassirer et al. (Chicago: University of Chicago Press, 1948), p. 218, describes a similar assumption about human duty in the Florentine philosophers, particularly Pico della Mirandola.

3. G. K. Hunter, *John Lyly: The Humanist as Courtier* (Cambridge: Harvard University Press, 1962), pp. 5–10.

4. Wilbur Sanders, *The Dramatist and the Received Idea* (London: Cambridge University Press, 1968), p. 265, remarks that "the dominant characteristic of Duncan . . . is not Grace *above* nature, a quality ultimately superhuman in origin and not answerable to the phenomenal world, but a grace-*in*-nature, an immanent principle of health . . . transparently grounded in the true nature of things." Much the same statement could be made about the "graceful" Polixenes (5.1.171).

5. Henri Rondet, *Original Sin: The Patristic and Theological Back-*

ground, trans. Cajetan Finegan (Shannon, Ireland: Ecclesia Press, 1972), p. 120.

6. Northrop Frye, *Anatomy of Criticism* (New York: Atheneum, 1965), p. 209.

7. Sidney Shanker, *Shakespeare and the Uses of Ideology*, Studies in English Literature, vol. 105 (The Hague: Mouton, 1975), p. 27 n. 4, observes this equation in Ralegh's *History of the World*.

8. Sigmund Freud, "Moses and Monotheism," in the Stadard Edition of his *Works*, trans. James Strachey, XXIII (London: Hogarth Press, 1964), 86.

9. Rondet, *Original Sin*, p. 120. Sharon MacIsaac, *Freud and Original Sin* (New York: Paulist Press, 1974), p. 2, similarly describes a "failure of integration which results in the painful sense of self-alienation" as "the most characteristic aspect of *peccatum originale originatum*."

10. Edward Forset, *A Comparative Discourse of the Bodies Natural and Politique* (London, 1606), pp. 7–8.

11. "A Sermon of the Misery of Mankind," in *Sermons or Homilies Appointed to be Read in Churches in the Time of Queen Elizabeth of Famous Memory* (London, 1825), p. 13; on royal transcendence, see chapter 1 n. 23, above.

12. "A Sermon of Good Works annexed unto Faith" in *Sermons*, p. 55.

13. Rondet, *Original Sin*, p. 175.

14. Niccolò Machiavelli, *The Prince and The Discourses*, Modern Library ed. (New York: Random House, 1950), p. 56.

15. Sigmund Freud, *Civilization and Its Discontents*, trans. James Strachey (New York: Norton, 1961), p. 90, warns that even in healthy individuals or cultures, "the id cannot be controlled beyond certain limits. If more is demanded of a man, a revolt will be produced in him or a neurosis, or he will be made unhappy. The commandment, 'Love thy neighbor as thyself,' is . . . an excellent example of the unpsychological proceedings of the cultural super-ego"; this passage is highly suggestive of Leontes' foolish ambition and its deranging consequences.

16. Wilfrid Holme, "The fall and evill successe of Rebellion from time to time" (London, 1573), sig. E3v.

17. Charles Trinkaus, *"In Our Image and Likeness"* (London: Constable, 1970), I, 148–149.

18. Peter Lindenbaum, "Time, Sexual Love, and the Uses of Pastoral in *The Winter's Tale*," *Modern Language Quarterly* 33 (1972), 7–8 n. 6.

19. Roy Battenhouse, "Theme and Structure in *The Winter's Tale*," *Shakespeare Survey* 33 (1980), 129, defends the doctrinal soundness of Hermoine's exclamation in a slightly different way, but its relevance remains the same. He also notes that Christian theorists identified original sin as a neglect of Grace; I am suggesting that Leontes renews original sin by newly neglecting the importance of Grace.

20. We tend to use the term "original sin" loosely, to cover several

different concepts. Theologians distinguish between *peccatum originans*, Adam's actual crime, and *peccatum originatum*, the condition of sinfulness all his children inherit. They also distinguish between the mysterious state of sin into which we are born, which most describe as a privation of blessedness prior to baptism, and the flawed nature of fallen man which baptism cannot alter, which Kant called "radical evil" and churchmen call concupiscence; see Rondet, *Original Sin*, p. 7. The guilt transmitted to the child conceived of baptized parents may therefore resemble the illness of Leontes, as Camillo enigmatically describes it to Polixenes: "a sickness / Which puts some of us in distemper, but / I cannot name the disease, and it is caught / Of you that yet are well" (1.2.384–87).

21. John Anthony Williams, *The Natural Work of Art* (Cambridge: Harvard University Press, 1967), p. 9.

22. In "Twicknam Garden," quoted at the end of this section, John Donne similarly conflates the poison of the spider with the venom of the serpent that a concupiscent man brings into his Paradise of Love.

23. Murray M. Schwartz, "Leontes' Jealousy in *The Winter's Tale*," *American Imago* 30 (1973), 250–273, links that jealousy to traumatic distortions in some early oral phase, now manifest in Leontes' references to food. But the determination to deny one's appetites and mortal dependency may be, as I suggested in disputing Janet Adelman's analysis of Coriolanus, the cause rather than the effect of distorted attitudes toward nourishment and the maternal breast. As Coriolanus seeks to expel digestively his inherited mortal aspects, Leontes imagines vomiting his knowledge of Hermione's sexuality, and is pleased that Mamillius was not fed Hermione's corrupted milk; his revulsion is toward hereditary sinfulness, as Coriolanus' was toward cowardly commonness.

24. See for example Charles K. Hofling, "Notes on Shakespeare's *The Winter's Tale*," *Psychoanalytic Review* 58 (1971), 90–110; also John Ellis, "Rooted Affection: The Genesis of Jealousy in *The Winter's Tale*," *College English* 25 (1964), 545–547. Closer to my point of view are Lindenbaum, in *Modern Language Quarterly* 33:11; and L. C. Knights, " 'Integration' in *The Winter's Tale*," *Sewanee Review* 84 (1976), 602, who "can find no support in the play for J. I. M. Stewart's suggestion that Leontes is projecting on to Hermione his own repressed homosexual feelings," and concludes instead that Leontes' "jealousy is rooted in a revulsion against his own sexuality and therefore against sexuality in general." Stephen Reid, "*The Winter's Tale*," *American Imago* 27 (1970), 273–274, concludes from the same evidence that "Only by accepting—not denying—one's feminine impulses is one free to employ one's masculine impulses." This suggests a psychoanalytic resonance to what I perceive as the play's broader warning: that one is free to exercise virtue only by acknowledging, not denying, one's propensity to sin.

25. See Augustine, *C. Julian op. imperf.* 2.45. PL 45:1161, and *Nupt. et concup.* 1.24.27, PL 44:429; see also Aquinas, *Summa Theologica* 3a 27.2

ad 2. For an elaboration of this doctrine in Augustine, see the *Dictionnaire de Théologie Catholique* (Paris: Librairie Letouzey et Ané, 1933), vol. XII, bk. 1, p. 395; for Aquinas, see p. 478; for a similar point in the writings of St. Bonaventure, see p. 467. MacIsaac, *Freud and Original Sin*, p. 72, discusses this doctrine's development.

26. F. C. Tinkler, "The Winter's Tale," *Scrutiny* 5 (1937), 348–349, comments that Bohemia represented "a sufficiently remote locality to serve as the generalized setting for Shakespeare's shepherd community. Sicilia, on the other hand, was well known to have been the centre of one of the most brilliant cultures of Europe."

27. Eric Partridge, *Shakespeare's Bawdy* (London: Routledge and Kegan Paul, 1968), pp. 73–74.

28. E. K. Chambers, *Shakespeare: A Survey* (London: Sidgwick and Jackson, 1925), p. 297.

29. Aurelian Townshend, "Pure Simple Love," in *English Seventeenth Century Verse*, vol. II, ed. Richard S. Sylvester (New York: Norton, 1974), p. 252. *The Oxford English Dictionary* cites Renaissance usages of "cipher" meaning a "character (o) of no value by itself, but which increases or decreases the value of other figures according to its position," or "A person who fills a place, but is . . . a nonentity, a 'mere nothing.' "

30. David Riggs, *Shakespeare's Heroical Histories* (Cambridge: Harvard University Press, 1971), p. 141.

31. Fitzroy Pyle, *"The Winter's Tale": A Commentary on the Structure* (London: Routledge and Kegan Paul, 1969), p. 10.

32. Lindenbaum, in *Modern Language Quarterly* 33:12, sees a reference to phallic immaturity in the reference to boyhood's muzzled dagger. If so, then Leontes' nostalgia for his own boyhood at the crucial moment becomes all the more clearly an evasion of sexuality as well as of time.

33. Morris Croll, *Style, Rhetoric, and Rhythm*, ed. J. Max Patrick et al. (Princeton: Princeton University Press, 1966), passim; see also Herschel Baker, *The Wars of Truth* (Cambridge: Harvard University Press, 1952), p. 341.

34. The sexual implications of "standing" are explicit in *Macbeth* (2.3.34) and implicit in *Coriolanus* (1.4.41). See also Partridge, *Shakespeare's Bawdy*, p. 190.

35. Mark Van Doren, *Shakespeare* (New York: Henry Holt and Co., 1939), p. 314.

36. Hunter, *Shakespeare*, p. 145.

37. Quoted in Lucien Goldmann, *The Hidden God*, trans. Philip Thody (London: Routledge and Kegan Paul, 1964), p. 71.

38. Rondet, *Original Sin*, p. 166.

39. "A Sermon of the Salvation of Mankind," in *Sermons*, pp. 29–30.

40. J. H. P. Pafford, ed., *The Winter's Tale*, 4th ed., The Arden Shakespeare (London: Methuen, 1963), p. 58.

41. Rondet, *Original Sin*, p. 125.

42. "A Sermon of the Salvation of Mankind," in *Sermons*, p. 23, sets up an analogy between original sin and a prison. In a much more recent and striking parallel, an attorney sued the state of Illinois on behalf of a five-month fetus, demanding that the woman carrying it be freed from prison, because "My client has committed no crime, outside, perhaps, of original sin" (UPI, May 30, 1981). The need for such a qualification would presumably have been even clearer to Shakespeare's audience, to whom orthodoxy was an everyday, and at times life-and-death, concern.

43. Geffrey Whitney, *A Choice of Emblemes* (London, 1586), p. 13.

44. Plutarch, *Lives of the Noble Grecians and Romans*, trans. Thomas North (1579), ed. W. E. Henley (London: David Nutt, 1895), IV, 323. Philostratus the Elder, *Les Images ou Tableaux de Platte Peinture*, trans. B. de Vigenère (Paris, 1629), pp. 480–484, suggests that the pygmies who attack Hercules in his sleep represent the degrading demons who inhabit mortal flesh and rise to the surface during sleep.

45. Alexander Ross, *Mystagogus Poeticus* (London, 1648), p. 224.

46. Quoted by Rondet, *Original Sin*, p. 171.

47. A similar comparison is made by Ernest Schanzer, "The Structural Pattern," in *"The Winter's Tale,"* ed. Kenneth Muir (Glasgow: Macmillan, 1968), p. 89.

48. *The Complete Poetry of John Donne*, ed. John T. Shawcross (New York: Anchor, 1967), pp. 115–116; Schwartz refers to the poem in studying Leontes' attitudes toward feeding.

49. Rondet, *Original Sin*, p. 115, cites *De Genesi contra Manichaeos*, I, 29; PL col. 187.

50. Schanzer, "The Structural Pattern," p. 95.

51. C. L. Barber, *Shakespeare's Festive Comedy* (Princeton: Princeton University Press, 1959), discusses a similar dialectical pattern in the earlier comedies.

52. Philip M. Weinstein, "An Interpretation of Pastoral in *The Winter's Tale*," *Shakespeare Quarterly* 22 (1971), 97–101, discusses Bohemia as a flawed but corrective counterpart to Sicilia.

53. David Kaula, "Autolycus' Trumpery," *Studies in English Literature* 16 (1976), 287–303.

54. The words are from Clerimont's song in *Epicoene*, 1.1.91–102. John Byshop, *Beautifull Blossomes . . . from the best trees of all kyndes* (London, 1577), pp. 21–24, warns against the delusive appeal of elaborate clothing and cosmetics. Arthur O. Lovejoy, *Essays in the History of Ideas* (Baltimore: Johns Hopkins University Press, 1948), p. 330, notes Tertullian's warning against betraying God as the "Author of nature" by coloring one's garments. See also Erasmus on *Fucus* in the *Praise of Folly*.

55. See Burgundy's rejection of the newly disowned Cordelia, *King Lear*, 1.1.206. Thomas F. Van Laan, *Role-Playing in Shakespeare* (Toronto: University of Toronto Press, 1978), pp. 37 and 170, observes that the paternal interventions blocking marriage in *Midsummer Night's Dream* and *Romeo*

and Juliet bring familial identity dangerously into conflict with personal identity. Near the end of Sidney's *Arcadia*, Euarchus resembles Polixenes in denying his disguised son and nephew any special rights as princes, and instead condemning them for allowing sexual passions to displace them from their royal roles into false, degrading identities and circumstances.

56. Roland M. Frye, *Shakespeare and Christian Doctrine* (Princeton: Princeton University Press, 1963), p. 243, points out that Cleomines is guilty of claiming, on behalf of his king, "sufficient contrition," a claim Luther characterized as inherently "presumptuous."

57. Janet Adelman, *The Common Liar* (New Haven: Yale University Press, 1973), p. 167.

58. Northrop Frye, "Recognition in *The Winter's Tale*," in Muir, p. 197.

59. Van Laan, *Role-Playing*, p. 114, suggests that the redemptive power in the romances usually rests in someone who has remained strictly faithful to her "true identity" as a human being, "and this suggests that the magic depends in part on some sort of collaboration . . . that, perhaps, the fidelity in some way 'earns' the divine intervention." By accepting her own mortal identity and humanity's mortal limitations, Paulina can succeed in the sort of semi-Pelagian project Leontes mishandled, and repair the damage caused by his denials.

60. D. P. Walker, *Spiritual and Demonic Magic from Ficino to Campanella* (London: Warburg Institute, 1958), p. 32 and passim.

61. C. S. Lewis, *English Literature in the Sixteenth Century*, in the Oxford History of English Literature (Oxford: Clarendon Press, 1954), pp. 4–13.

62. Robert Egan, "This Rough Magic: Perspectives of Art and Morality in *The Tempest*," *Shakespeare Quarterly* 23 (1972), 175.

63. Charles Masinton, *Christopher Marlowe's Tragic Vision* (Athens, Ohio: Ohio University Press, 1972), p. 114.

64. Theodore Ziolkowski, *Disenchanted Images* (Princeton: Princeton University Press, 1977), pp. 20–24. See also Abraham Fraunce, *The Third Part of the Countesse of Pembrokes Yuychurch: Entituled, Amintas Dale* (London, 1592), M.L.A.A. Photo Facsimiles 75, pp. 2–10. Ernst Cassirer, *The Individual and the Cosmos in Renaissance Philosophy*, trans. Mario Domandi (New York: Harper and Row, 1964), pp. 96–97, discusses the Renaissance tendency to interpret the Prometheus story as the artful man's surpassing of the natural man.

65. Cassirer, *Individual and Cosmos*, p. 43.

66. Nehemiah Rogers, *The True Convert* (London, 1620), p. 303. Cesare Ripa, *Iconologie*, ed. and trans. J. Baudoin (Paris, 1644), I, 20–23, attributes the same sort of corrective value to the figures of Art and Artifice. See also Cassirer, *Individual and Cosmos*, p. 96; and Edward Tayler, *Nature and Art in Renaissance Literature* (New York: Columbia University Press, 1964), p. 29.

67. S. L. Bethell, *"The Winter's Tale": A Study* (London: Staples Press,

n.d.), passim; J. Bryant, Jr., "Shakespeare's Allegory: *The Winter's Tale*," *Sewanee Review* 63 (1955), 202–222.

68. Inga-Stina Ewbank, "The Triumph of Time," in Muir, pp. 113–114.

69. Freud, "Moses," pp. 86–87.

70. Rolf Soellner, *Shakespeare's Patterns of Self-Knowledge* (Columbus: Ohio State University Press, 1972), p. 95, writes that "The central theme of *Love's Labor's Lost* is the quest for the self, a quest in which man, with the best of intentions, can go astray. Every man is born with his passions [and] cannot simply rule them out; nature will take its revenge." See also his p. 359.

71. Van Laan, *Role-Playing*, p. 225, finds in Shakespeare's early comedies (but not in his later plays) the implication "that for every character there exists an ideal role . . . which he is capable of fulfilling successfully."

72. Samuel Gardiner, *Portraiture of the Prodigal Sonne* (London, 1599), pp. 229–234, 254.

Index

Footnotes are indexed only where there is a substantial treatment of new material

Index

Index

Index

75, 79, 81; in *Macbeth*, 130–131; in
Coriolanus, 179–181, 184, 188–191,
198, 201, 204; in *The Winter's Tale*,
224, 261, 262–263
Thomas, Keith, 154
Thomas à Kempis, 155
"Throne of Blood," 140
Tillyard, E. M. W., 20, 65, 286nn3, 4
Time, 52, 93, 111; in *The Winter's
Tale*, 225, 230, 234, 244, 253–254,
256, 266–267
Tourneur, Cyril, 115
Townshend, Aurelian, 238
Tragedy, 11, 224, 278; and *Macbeth*,
85–86, 101–102, 108, 136–141;
and *Coriolanus*, 142, 143, 145–146,
147, 176, 184–185, 197, 204, 219–
220
Traversi, D. A., 120, 238
Trilling, Lionel, 131, 135, 179, 283n17
Trinkaus, Charles, 228

Troilus and Cressida, 193
True Convert, The, 112, 173–174, 216
Tudor myth, 34
Twelfth Night, 204

Upton, John, 107

Valla, Lorenzo, 195, 204, 228
Van Doren, Mark, 240
Vegetation, *see* Seasonal life

Walzer, Michael, 146
Williams, John Anthony, 231
Wilson, J. D., 65
Winter's Tale, The, 13, 222–279; com-
pared to other plays, 35, 95, 111, 157,
163, 199, 203
Witchcraft, 101, 111, 190, 205, 248,
272–274

Zeus, 5, 111, 152, 182